EXPANDING LIBERTIES

Also by Milton R. Konvitz

Fundamental Liberties of a Free People

Civil Rights in Immigration

The Constitution and Civil Rights

The Alien and the Asiatic in American Law

On the Nature of Value: The Philosophy of Samuel Alexander

A Century of Civil Rights (*with Theodore Leskes*)

First Amendment Freedoms

Bill of Rights Reader

EXPANDING LIBERTIES

LIBERTIES

Freedom's Gains in Postwar America

Milton R. Konvitz

New York · The Viking Press

135613

To Mary and Josef,

who have helped me learn

how freely to receive

and how freely to give,

I give this book

which they gave me

A position that is not a constant point of departure soon becomes meaningless and therefore dead. . . . The power of expansion and the strength of resistance found one another and created new forms of existence.

—LEO BAECK

Contents

Preface

About a century ago Sir Henry Maine thought that the degree to which the personal and property rights of women were recognized was a fair test of a society's civilization. The essence of civilization, wrote Maine, is found in self-control; "every one of those conquests, the sum of which we call civilization," he said, "is the result of curbing some of the strongest, because the primary, impulses of human nature."

Also trying to discover a reliable index to a society's civilization, Hermann Cohen, the Neo-Kantian philosopher, found it in the treatment accorded the stranger, the alien; for when a society shields the alien from oppression and wrong, it does this not because the man is a member of one's family, clan, religious community, or people, but simply because he is a human being. "In the alien, therefore," wrote Cohen, "man discovered the idea of humanity."

Each scholar wrote from his own angle of vision; one was an English historian who lectured at Oxford and Cambridge, the other was a Jewish philosopher in Marburg, Germany. Had either of them been a Negro, very likely he would have formulated the test of civilization in terms of how a racial minority is treated.

But Maine and Cohen—and our hypothetical Negro—would have agreed that whether one tests civilization by the position of women, or of the alien, or of a racial minority is a matter decided by historical forces. The essential and broad question always is the degree in which a society has curbed its impulses to dominate the weaker members, to oppress, exploit, and humiliate those who could be subjected to *force majeure*—the degree in which certain people are excluded from the idea of humanity and the protection of humane laws and other institutions that afford human dignity and membership in a common fellowship.

But not only historical forces point the way to test the degree of civilization. In his forties, Sir Henry Maine was for seven years legal member of the viceroy's council in India, where he worked on the codification of Indian law. Surely he saw the misery and oppression to which the Hindu caste system sentenced millions of human beings from birth to death. Yet as a scholar, when it came to the formulation of broad generalizations for a philosophy of history, he could see and write as an Englishman who only England knew. We may be sure that he thought he was looking at humanity and the broad sweep of human history, though he in fact saw only the course of English history, which in 1875 had left women out of account. John Stuart Mill's *Subjection of Women* had been published only six years before, and John Bright had presented his bill for woman suffrage in the House of Commons in 1870. Thus, when Maine wrote his *Early History of Institutions* (1875), England was agitated over the question of the status and rights of women—a question that stirred the nation until 1928, when the voting rights of men and women were at last equalized. Perhaps Maine would have looked for a test of civilization in the legal, social, and economic status of the working class but for the fact that Parliament in 1871 had enacted liberal labor laws.

I could not help thinking of Sir Henry Maine as I gave thought to a study of the new freedoms that have emerged in the United States since World War II—roughly a quarter-century after 1939. Could one avoid the pitfalls of subjectivity in selecting the freedoms on which one is to focus attention? "History is all party pamphlets," Emerson wrote in his *Journal;* thus, Maine's *Early History of Institutions* was in part, and unconsciously, a pamphlet on behalf of women's rights. More recently Croce emphasized that all history—even the "early" history of institutions—is in fact contemporary history, for its writing reflects the experience, circumstance, and attitudes of the historians. But the insurmountable difficulties are compounded when the subject of study is a period of time through which the author has himself lived, and events from which he was not intellectually, emotionally, or morally detached.

Yet we all feel a great need to interpret the events that we observe or live through. We cannot provide them lodging in our minds unless they are subdued to some order. We are all, I think, Kantians in assuming that the mind has categories that seem to impose themselves on the raw facts of experience. In our time sociologists, historians, political analysts, novelists, and poets try to transmute facts into events, days and years into eras and milieus, darkness into illumination, and chaos into order. If there can be no definitive history of the past, there certainly can be no definitive contemporary history. "A different Caesar crosses the Rubicon not only with each author but with each generation," wrote George Herbert Mead. "That is, as we look over the past, it is a different past. . . . It is not simply the future which is novel, then; the past also is novel. . . . The world is continually blossoming out into a new universe." It was, therefore, insensibility that compelled the author of Ecclesiastes to cry out that "there is nothing new under the sun." Even the past is ever new, or at least renewed; if anything, one could say with more truth that there is nothing old under the sun.

But the historian of contemporary events faces a grave difficulty that the historian of past events is spared; for the former is concerned with events in duration rather than in time—to use Bergson's distinction. Events that happen before our eyes interact. Just as one cannot deal with the separate notes of a melody, taking each one by itself, so, too, with historical events—it is their interaction that gives them meaning and value. Emerson put this truth in his own way in the essay on "Experience": "The years teach much which the days never know." An experience is not fully experienced while it is happening. In its fullness, an experience has pulled forward the past and has occupied the future; the future, no less than the past, is part of a present that has meaning and value.

Yet the intellect is compelled to conceptualize, to separate—to deal with events as motion in space rather than as experiences in duration, and to see events abstracted from their futures, to see things mechanically rather than as an evolutionary stream. Thus the attempt to write responsibly of events which happened in one's own day involves metaphysical, psychological, and ethical problems that are impossible to solve satisfactorily. To take them at their full value, however, would mean a paralysis of the mind and will. The human need to impose—or to "find"—an order for experiences and events cannot be frustrated but at the cost of sanity, or, at least, at the cost of intellectuality. The mind must take a leap over the problems and obstacles that form a seemingly impassable abyss. A leap is always a calculated risk, but to stand still is not a way to avoid risks.

Well, all this is said to make known to the reader that the author knew well enough what he was getting into. But the problems of human liberty—and especially the problems of constitutional liberty under the Bill of Rights of the United States Constitution—have been his special concern for at least the quarter-century under study in this book. These problems were the hound, the bay horse, and the turtle-dove which he had lost and from whose trail, like Thoreau, he could not free himself. He talked of them in his teaching, and when he sat in his house, and when he walked by the way. This book was written simply because the facts, the essential details, of the problems had to be traced and set down in some comprehensible order, and the principles and values that they triggered in the mind had to be stated, defined and re-defined, and set in an analytical and historical provenience that would give the feel of knowledge and understanding. I do not, however, mean to suggest that work on the book resulted in the building up of a store of certainties. Nothing could be further from the truth. I began with questions and ended with a few answers, but with perhaps more questions than I had at the start.)

A great deal has happened since World War II touching the civil liberties and the civil rights of Americans. This period was a time of war; it was a time that saw McCarthyism and its end; it was a time of the Korean War and the Cold War; it was a time of the Warren Court, as the Supreme Court has come to be called since 1954; it was a time of civil rights demonstrations, of "Freedom Now!" It was a time of fear, and a time of comfort and relaxation; a time of defeats for the spirit of liberty, and also of victories and gains, of vindication and reconciliation. No one man could begin to tell the whole story. Goethe taught us a long time ago that in self-limitation is the beginning of wisdom. I have selected, therefore, only certain of the problems that beckoned; but these I have examined in some depth and breadth, and concentrated on the freedoms that emerged in this period for the first time or came up for a new lease of life. Even with this principle of selection in mind, there had to be omissions if the book was not to be a mere catalogue or an encyclopedia.

My choice of topics and an indeterminate part of the presentation have, then, been determined by my own perspective and my own commitment. This has made objectivity more difficult but not, I trust, impossible. "Man's capacity to rise above his social and historical situation," E. H. Carr has written, "seems to be conditioned by the sensitivity with which he recognizes the extent of his involvement in it." History, he added, is "a continuous process of interaction between the historian and his facts, an unending dialogue. . . . It is not merely the events that are in flux. The historian himself is in flux." Professor H. Stuart Hughes has put the truth even more bluntly and pointedly: "A conservative [historian] cannot help writing as a conservative, and a radical as a radical," he said, "and they should not feel obliged to apologize for so doing."

If an optimist is a man who says the bottle is half full, and a pessimist is a man who says the bottle is half empty, when it comes to civil liberties and civil rights I tend to see the bottle half empty. To my mind, deprivations of rights and liberties must be fully explained and justified, and I tend to throw the heavy burden of proof on the government—whether it acts through the legislature, executive, or judiciary. I take the liquid in the bottle for granted but tend to see the empty part. But this, I assume, is precisely what puts me in the civil liberties camp.

But I am by no means unaware of what is *in* the bottle. This is precisely why I have chosen to concentrate, in this study, on the new freedoms rather than on the deprivations. As recently as 1956 Bertrand Russell cried that "there is, on the whole, much less liberty in the world now than there was a hundred years ago." I do not see that at all. And certainly in the United States, which Russell often has in mind when he lets loose his poisoned barbs, there has been a progressive development of human potentialities and values. We often hear the complaint that our problems have been aggravated because our moral development has not kept pace with scientific development. Speaking at the Thirteenth International Congress of Philosophy, in 1963, Gabriel Marcel said, "Man today is becoming more and more accustomed to suffering and to death." It is one thing to see the half-empty bottle, and another to see nothing but emptiness, not even to see the bottle. In the United States, in the last twenty-five years, progress in civil liberties and civil rights has been made at an unprecedented pace. On numerous fronts—including the rights of even men and women in our prisons and in our mental institutions, migrant laborers, Indians on reservations—those who are "the least" among us—the government and the nation have taken steps to implement or broaden the reach of the Bill of Rights, and even to go beyond the plain compulsions of the Constitution to new ideals of freedom. Everywhere provincials are being molded into citizens of one free nation. We are told by Plutarch that Zeno of Citium "wrote an exemplary *Republic,* based on the principle that men ought not to be separated into cities and nations each of which has its own laws, inasmuch as all men are fellow-citizens with but one life and but one order of things [cosmos], but ought instead to constitute one group and be ruled by a common law." It is only in our own day that we have seen a clear commitment to the development of this ideal in the United States; and in the United Nations and the Council of Europe we see evidence that this ideal of the Stoics and of Alexander the Great is making headway toward universal acceptance. The test of civilization will be not the degree in which women or aliens or any other group are accorded equality and liberty, but the degree in which any group, no matter how small or weak, is excluded from full participation in the life, society, work, and ideals of a common humanity.

In writing this book I found myself, then, constantly at a point of tension. As a constitutional historian, I found myself celebrating the intensified concern with freedom and the significant ground gained despite the toil and troubles of wars and the alarms of wars, and, like a sundial, I wanted to record only the sunny hours. But as a civil libertarian I naturally tended to be critical even of the gains and advances, since these seldom came in full measure or gallantly. They often were let in by a back door and sometimes came disguised—for example, civil rights in places of public accommodation as federal regulation of interstate commerce, as if the subject-matter were cattle or cat-food sent from one state to another. As a constitutional lawyer, I know, of course, the problems involved in such matters; and if I were sitting as a judge I might feel compelled to throw my mind into the common stock of an undifferentiated constitutionalism and make no distinction between men and cattle, or between men eating in a lunchroom and men buying food for cats. But my station in life is not that of a judge but of a critic, and so my duties are quite different—and so are my liberties. I must affirm the Constitution, but no less do I feel compelled to affirm liberty, knowing all the time that both are, at any one time, imperfect, changeable, and in a process of change, and that both are compelled somehow to participate in a common life and to sustain each other. Our system is one imposed by imperfect men on imperfect men, and the critic is himself an imperfect man, and even an imperfect critic; but he has his station in life, and the station has its own duties and liberties. There should be no confusion of functions. I am not writing court opinions or acts of Congress but *about* them.

While I undertook the study as an occasion to bring facts and judgments into some manageable, comprehensible order, the decision to prepare it was impelled by the teacher's impulse to bring into the public consciousness an understanding of some new problems and some new possibilities in the developments of constitutional liberty. No one knows what the future may bring. No one could have foretold the work of Newton or of Einstein, of Marx or of Freud—or of Earl Warren, Republican candidate for Vice President on the ticket with Thomas E. Dewey five years before President Eisenhower appointed him Chief Justice to succeed Fred M. Vinson—or that Harry S. Truman or that Lyndon B. Johnson would be President of the United States, or that Dr. Martin Luther King, Jr., would become leader of a civil rights movement inspired by the teachings of Gandhi, a man of India who, while in South Africa, had been inspired by an essay written by an obscure backwoodsman in Concord, Massachusetts. History and religion do not instruct us to be optimists; but neither do they instruct us to be pessimists. We live in tension and are compelled to throw our weight one way or another, knowing that the world is larger than our vision or our thoughts or our hopes, and that there are always new risks in new situations, and that there are no guaranties, and that everything is held precariously. Problems are never totally and ultimately solved; but they may be, I trust, illumined.

Josiah Royce spoke of "ideals that long for realization." There are more naturalistic ways of describing the emergence or flowering of human values; but there are times when one feels as if ideals have a life of their own, and that legislators, judges, and men without emoluments of title—for example, Tolstoi, Gandhi—are used as voices to speak words that come from somewhere else. The last twenty-five years have seemed eminently to be such a time, in which millions of men everywhere seemed to be moved by a spirit greater than themselves—men who demanded more liberty, more and better education, a bigger share of the fruits of nature and of their own labor, more responsibility for the direction of their lives and destinies.

Among American institutions it has been the Supreme Court—more than other governmental agencies, or the churches, or the schools and universities—through which the enlarged demands were often made; and so it is natural that much which is contained in this book should emanate from the opinions of the Court.

Let me say something about those opinions. The Justices are often criticized for writing opinions that are too long, or for writing too many concurring or dissenting opinions. The Sunday-law cases of 1961, for example, contain opinions by five Justices, in 235 pages. But much of the criticism is unjustified. For the Court does not, like a jury, merely decide for the plaintiff or the defendant. It is compelled to expose the process by which it seeks a decision, which comes to us in a context of critical thinking. The Court approaches problems not abstractly but pragmatically and experimentally, and its answers cannot be abstracted from the facts in the case; and the severest intellectual and moral test for the Court often is to decide what facts to consider significant and what facts to ignore. This process not only takes place in the minds of the Justices, but is also one that must be fully played out on the stage that the opinions present. It is possible for a student studying for an examination to read somewhere a "digest" of *War and Peace* or of *Hamlet;* but somewhere on the library shelves there must be a novel and a drama with these titles. The Court opinions are not the "digests" but the novel and the drama.

If the Court decisions can be summarized as "points," the "points" can be understood only against and within the detailed facts and issues out of which they arose. This means that the reader who seeks understanding must not spare himself the trouble to cope with the questions in the way in which they came up in the litigation. This effort takes time and patience, and a cultivated taste for facts, facts, and more facts. He who runs may *not* read constitutional law. Yet this law and the pedestrian process by which it evolves have come to play a key role in a civilization attuned to jet-engine speed. Getting there—wherever ,and whatever there is—is no longer half the fun. Yet the Court's process revolves around the getting there. The quest for the decision is at least as important as the decision itself.

This is of vital importance, for only in this way is it possible for the Constitution to remain a living moral, social, and intellectual force. The Court's decisions cannot take a dogmatic, canonical, final form. Its work is never done, and never can be; for almost every day it must face new historical tasks. Yet it is, paradoxically, by this process that constitutional principles and ideals are kept unified and coordinated at the very time that they undergo development and even transformation. The day of conceptual or mechanical jurisprudence in the area of constitutional law is over. There are those who shed tears over our "vanishing" Constitution; but ironically they do this precisely at a time when the Constitution means and signifies more to the American people than ever before in our history.

In analyzing the Court's decisions and opinions, I have tried to be faithful to this constitutional process, and not to falsify it by oversimplification or abstraction. Some parts of the discussion may, therefore, seem complex to the non-expert—for example, some of the discussion relating to the Communist Party cases. But the only way to meet the difficulties these cases present is to go through the difficulties. To pretend that they are not there or to treat them with bravado would be to pretend that there are simple solutions for complex problems—problems often so complex that sometimes one is forced to think that only an omniscient God can adequately comprehend them. But it will do no good to despair; the problems are of such transcendent importance that, in face of them, we can do nothing but work on them with whatever intelligence and aptitude for patience we possess, and hope that in the end the grace of a luminous view will be won.

If there are times when the author seems to forget his own counsel and presumptuously seems to mete out harsh judgment on the work of a legislator or a judge, he pleads, with Dr. Johnson, that those who dare not censure have not earned the right to praise; and one who writes a study of the new freedoms means very much to have the right to praise.

My friend Professor Sidney Hook read most of the chapters in manuscript and gave me the benefit of his critical mind. There were many disagreements; but even when I decided to have my way I learned from his observations and suggestions, for which I was and will ever remain grateful. I am also indebted to Aaron Asher, of The Viking Press, who helped me with his questions, his great editorial sense, and his lively interest in the book and the problems with which it is concerned.

My desire to write the book would have remained unfulfilled had not the Center for Advanced Study in the Behavioral Sciences, at Stanford, California, offered me a fellowship for the academic year 1964–1965. I find it impossible to express adequately my sense of gratitude to Dr. Ralph Tyler, Director, the members of his staff, and the Board of Directors, for making it possible for me to be able to claim that I, too, in Arcadia have lived.

M. R. K.

Cornell University
Ithaca, New York
January 1966

One
First Amendment
Freedoms

I

Religious Liberty

Nothing so clearly distinguishes the United States Supreme Court of the last twenty-five years from the Court of the past as its engagement in litigation involving religious liberty. The Court has, of course, played a dramatic part in the civil rights drama, but this was a drama in which other agencies and individuals also had significant roles. But when it comes to the sticky, complex, and often explosive questions of religious liberty, the Court has had to occupy, alone, not only the center but almost the whole of the stage. Of course other institutions—local school boards, state legislatures—created the problems which the Court was called upon to deal with and, insofar as it could, untangle; but it alone seemed to act as the hero or the villain.

And nothing so clearly distinguishes the United States among democracies as does the degree to which Americans enjoy religious liberty and the degree to which church and state are, in theory and in fact, separate. There has been interaction between the American people and the Supreme Court, almost like that between an actor on the stage and his audience, each provoking and affecting the other. Though at times the hissing seemed to drown out the applause, in the end public opinion has tended to approve the Court's performance; for the people on the whole share the Court's conviction that—to paraphrase the words of Jefferson—the state knows no more of the way to heaven than each man does, and is less concerned to direct him right than he is to go right.

1. The Evolving Doctrines

During its first five decades the Court was not once asked to decide a case involving religious liberty. The first arose in 1845. New Orleans had enacted an ordinance that gave to one chapel a monopoly on all funerals, forbade the exposing of corpses in Roman Catholic churches

3

other than the chapel specified in the law, and imposed a fine on priests who officiated at funerals conducted at any other chapel. A priest was fined for violating the ordinance. He took his case to the Supreme Court,[1] contending that New Orleans had curtailed the free exercise of his religion, guaranteed by the United States Constitution.

The Court denied the appeal, on the ground that the First Amendment was a limitation only on the federal government; an infringement of religious liberty by a state or its agency (such as a city) was a matter for the state itself, under the state constitution or laws.

Twenty-seven years later, in 1872, the Court had its second case involving religious liberty, a case that, unlike the first one, is still followed as an important precedent. *Watson* v. *Jones*[2] was a dispute between the pro-slavery and the anti-slavery factions in a Presbyterian church in Louisville. Each claimed to control the church and to be "the true Walnut Street Presbyterian Church."

The Supreme Court held that it had no power to decide independently which of two factions represented the "true" church and which the schismatics—or heretics. The Court held that it was bound by the decision of the appropriate ecclesiastical authority. Thus, among truly independent congregations, the appropriate authority would be the majority of the congregation's members if the church's principle of government has been majority rule, or the officers if the church vested in them final authority. The dissenters might withdraw, but they must relinquish the church property. Where, however, the local church is part of a larger organization with which it is connected by ecclesiastical government (which was the case of the Presbyterian church in Louisville), then the questions of faith, discipline, church rule, or law are left to the hierarchy of church judicatories, whose decisions will be binding on the courts.

In a frequently quoted passage,[3] Justice Samuel Freeman Miller said for the Court that in this country

the full and free right to entertain any religious belief, to practice any religious principle, and to teach any religious doctrine which does not violate the laws of morality and property, and which does not infringe personal rights, is conceded to all. The law knows no heresy, and is committed to the support of no dogma, the establishment of no sect. The right to organize voluntary religious associations to assist in the expression and dissemination of any religious doctrine, and to create tribunals for the decision of controverted questions of faith within the association, and for the ecclesiastical government of all the individual members, congregations and officers within the general association, is unquestioned. All who unite themselves to such a body do so with an implied consent to this [internal church] government, and are bound to submit to it. But it would be a vain consent and would lead to the total subversion of such religious bodies, if any one aggrieved by one of their decisions could appeal to the secular courts and have them reversed.

Few decisions of the Supreme Court have been as important as *Watson* v. *Jones,* especially since it was the first case in which the Court based its decision on principles of religious liberty. A wrong decision at that time could have generated—as *Plessy* v. *Ferguson*[4] did in the area of race relations—a line of cases that could have brought us great grief. The Supreme Court, in *Watson* v. *Jones,* could not have begun with a more auspicious precedent.

In a case decided in 1952, in which the decision was based on *Watson* v. *Jones,* the Supreme Court characterized Justice Miller's opinion as one radiating

a spirit of freedom for religious organizations, an independence from secular control or manipulation, in short [giving them] power to decide for themselves, free from state interference, matters of church government as well as those of faith and doctrine.[5]

It should be noted, however, that the Court in *Watson* v. *Jones* based its decision not on constitutional principles but on what it referred to as a "rule of action . . . founded in a broad and sound view of the relations of church and state under our system of laws." At that time, in 1872, it had not yet been settled that the Fourteenth Amendment, ratified only four years before, guarantees religious liberty against infringement by the *states.* In looking for a precedent for its decision, the Court turned to the "general law" that deprived civil courts of authority to review "questions of faith, religious doctrine and ecclesiastical government."[6]

It should be remembered that the division in the church in Louisville over slavery brought the feuding parties into the civil courts on the question of control of the church as property, real estate—which certainly pertains to the realm of Caesar; but this question of property in turn depended on how the particular congregation viewed its own constitution respecting questions of faith, doctrine, and church government—which certainly pertain to the realm of God. Implicit, therefore, in the disposition of the case by the Supreme Court was the principle of separation of church and state.

Six years later, the Court for the first time had a case in which the decision was based on the Court's interpretation of the First Amendment's guarantee of religious liberty. This was almost a century after the adoption of the Bill of Rights.

Reynolds v. *United States*[7] was one of three cases involving Mormons decided by the Court between 1878 and 1890.[8] The Mormons were the first of our indigenous religious sects to be openly and systematically persecuted and subjected to violence. When they settled in Missouri in the 1830s, their leaders were jailed, and in 1838–1839 their expulsion was officially ordered. In 1844 Joseph Smith and his brother were arrested on charges of treason in Illinois and were murdered in jail by a mob. Again the Mormons had to wander, and under Brigham Young they settled in Utah, which became a territory in 1850. Two years later Young formally announced the doctrine of plural marriages, based on a vision of Joseph Smith's a year before his murder. Polygamy at once became a lurid subject for the newspapers. Congress passed laws against polygamy in its territories, and these laws prepared the ground for the Reynolds case, which has remained one of the most frequently cited cases on religious liberty and church-state relations.

Reynolds was charged with violating the federal law against polygamy in the territories. His defense was that, as a member of the Mormon Church, he was required by its religious doctrines to enter into plural marriages, and that the law of Congress violated his religious freedom as guaranteed by the First Amendment.

In *Watson* v. *Jones* the Supreme Court had held that it is not the business of a civil court to examine matters of religious faith or church doctrine. Did this mean that, if a church made plural marriages a matter of *religious* duty, this put the matter beyond the reach of the civil law? Not at all, said the Court, in affirming Reynolds' conviction. The Court made a distinction between religious *belief* and *behavior*. The First Amendment put all questions of religious belief beyond the reach of the federal government, but it did not forbid Congress to enact laws directed at *actions* which are considered by the legislature to be violative of social duties or good order. Suppose, the Court asked rhetorically, a person's religious belief required him to offer human sacrifices? The government had the right to preserve monogamy in the territories by prohibiting polygamy there. To make religious belief the test of valid law would mean to permit each citizen to write his own code of laws. "Government could exist only in name under such circumstances."

In tracing the history of the First Amendment to its sources, Chief Justice Morrison Waite referred to an action of James Madison when he was a member of the Virginia legislature. In 1779 the Anglican Church was formally disestablished in Virginia. Then a movement got under way—supported by Patrick Henry and George Washington—to make all Christian churches in effect the established church of the state, on an equal standing, to be equally supported by taxation. Against this proposal Madison published his famous "Memorial and Remonstrance" in 1784—a state paper to which the Supreme Court was to give close attention in the late 1940s. In this document, said Chief Justice Waite, Madison had "demonstrated" "that religion, or the duty we owe the Creator," "was not within the cognizance of civil government."

The proposed bill for the establishment of all Christian churches was defeated; not only that, but the legislature then went on to enact a bill "for establishing religious freedom," which Thomas Jefferson had drafted in 1777, and which he had submitted to the legislature when he was Governor of Virginia in 1779, but which was then too radical for the lawmakers. Madison, George Mason, and others were, however, able to push this bill through the legislature in 1786. This, the Virginia Statute of Religious Liberty, is perhaps the most famous of all American documents on religious freedom. Chief Justice Waite quoted the following from the statute:

That to suffer the civil magistrate to intrude his powers into the field of opinion, and to restrain the profession or propagation of principles on supposition of their ill tendency, is a dangerous fallacy which at once destroys all religious liberty, . . .

and this famous sentence:

That it is time enough for the rightful purposes of civil government, for its officers to interfere when principles break out into overt acts against peace and good order. . . .

"In these two sentences," said the Court, "is found the true distinction between what properly belongs to the Church and what to the State."

This history of the First Amendment's religious freedom clauses, and their meaning, was, of course, germane to the Reynolds decision and is basic for an understanding of some of the more recent cases, as we shall see. But then the Court went on to point to a doctrine of church-state separation, which became the basis for the Supreme Court's no-establishment decisions some seventy-five years later. This part of the Reynolds opinion is, therefore, pregnant with meaning for generations that followed.

The Court's opinion related that, a little more than a year after Jefferson's bill was adopted by Virginia, the Constitutional Convention met. Jefferson was then in France as Minister of the new government under the Articles of Confederation. When he saw the draft of the new Constitution, he wrote to Madison expressing his disappointment at the absence of "a bill of rights, providing clearly . . . for freedom of religion" and certain other guarantees.[9] Accordingly, Madison, at the first session of the first Congress, proposed the First Amendment and other provisions, which, when adopted and ratified, became the Bill of Rights. Then Chief Justice Waite referred to the famous letter by Jefferson, dated January 1, 1802, when he was President, to the Danbury Baptist Association, and quoted the following "wall of separation" passage:

Believing with you that religion is a matter which lies solely between man and his God; that he owes account to none other for his faith or his worship; that the Legislative powers of the Government reach actions only, and not opinions, I contemplate with sovereign reverence that act of the whole American people which declared that their Legislature should "make no law respecting an establishment of religion or prohibiting the free exercise thereof," thus building a wall of separation between Church and State.

This statement was relevant in *Reynolds* v. *United States* insofar as it makes again the distinction between belief and acts, and limits the powers of government to the latter exclusively. But, as we shall see, in 1947 and 1948 the importance of the passage was shifted to the "wall of separation" principle. Next to the First Amendment itself, the opinion in *Reynolds* v. *United States,* and the state papers on which it relied and from which it quoted, remain the basic, original sources of the most important constitutional principles of religious liberty in its various aspects.

Commenting on this quotation from Jefferson's letter, written eleven years after the Bill of Rights was ratified, Chief Justice Waite wrote:

Coming as this does from an acknowledged leader of the advocates of the measure [the First Amendment], it may be accepted almost as an authoritative declaration of the scope and effect of the amendment thus secured.

These two cases, *Watson* v. *Jones* and *Reynolds* v. *United States,* formulated principles and doctrines that are still very much alive. But they were followed by two cases, decided in the 1890s, that have generated "countervailing" principles and doctrines. The clash of constitutional doctrines has divided the Court in the last quarter of our century. We shall briefly examine the two cases, for they show how deeply rooted are the constitutional contradictions.

In *Church of the Holy Trinity* v. *United States* (1892),[10] the Court was called on to consider an act of Congress which prohibited the importation of foreigners under contract "to perform labor in the United States." Did this law prohibit a church from making an agreement with a clergyman in England to have him migrate to New York and act as its minister? The Court held that Congress had not intended to have the act applied to contracts made with professional persons on an individual basis; the evil that Congress had in mind was the influx of cheap unskilled laborers, who would pay off the costs of their passage by working at substandard wages.

This part of the decision does not, of course, bear on church-state problems. But the Court went on to argue specifically regarding the importation of clergymen under contract with churches in the United States, as distinguished from professional men generally, and said that it would not construe the act in such a way as to show that Congress intended to behave in an unfriendly way toward religion. An antireligious intention should not be imputed to legislation, for Americans are a religious people; more than that, "this is a Christian nation." The Court cited phrases from the Declaration of Independence and other documents to show that there was always the intent to have friendly and cooperating relations between church and state. American laws, business, customs, and society, said the Court, all manifest this spirit. It mentioned specifically the oath taken in court, which concludes with an appeal to God; the opening of sessions of "all deliberative bodies and most conventions" with prayers; last wills and testaments that start with the phrase "In the name of God, amen"; "all laws respecting the observance of the Sabbath," when all courts, legislatures, and other public bodies are closed. These, said the Court,

and many others which might be noticed, add a volume of unofficial declarations to the mass of organic utterances that this is a Christian nation. In the face of all these, shall it be believed that a Congress of the United States intended to make it a misdemeanor for a church of this country to contract for the services of a Christian minister residing in another nation?

As we shall see, this list of official religious acts was only the beginning; it grew in later cases as the Court split over the question how high and how strong the "wall of separation" is.

In the last religious liberty case of the nineteenth century—there were seven in all, three of which involved Mormons and polygamy, and two the Roman Catholic Church—the Court had before it an 1897 act of Congress which included an appropriation for the construction of an addition to a hospital, chartered by members of a Roman Catholic sisterhood and operated by the Roman Catholic Church, located in the District of Columbia. The District commissioners entered into a contract with the hospital corporation to construct the building and to pay for each patient they would send.

In a taxpayer's suit to declare the contract contrary to the Constitution, the Court, in *Bradfield* v. *Roberts* (1899),[11] upheld the contract. Providence Hospital, said the Court, was owned and operated by a chartered corporation; *as a corporation,* it was a secular entity. This character was not affected by the fact that the corporation was composed of persons who happened to be Catholic nuns. The law of incorporation was indifferent to the religious affiliations of incorporators; their religious beliefs could not be inquired into.

But the hospital was conducted under the auspices of the Roman Catholic Church. Well, what if it is? asked the Court. Whoever operates the hospital must do so in accordance with its official charter, i.e., it must act as a secular corporation, organized for the purpose of healing and caring for the sick, without regard to the religious faith of the patients. In brief: it is a matter of no constitutional concern to Congress that the funds it appropriated went to a corporation all of whose members belonged to one religious denomination, which operated an institution, though under religious auspices, for a public purpose, and used the public funds to fulfill a civic duty.

It can readily be seen how this decision could be used to give to the separation doctrine a restricted meaning. Moreover, it is easy to see how the reasoning that was applied to the Roman Catholic hospital could lend itself to the case of a Roman Catholic school, which, with respect to the teaching of secular subjects, is operated for a public purpose, for the pupils who attend the school comply, by such attendance, with the state's compulsory-school-attendance laws, and thus, if such a school were given public funds, they would be used to fulfill a *civic duty*.

I am not suggesting that this reasoning should be accepted as valid, but only that the later debate over federal aid to parochial schools cannot be understood without realization that the lines of the argument go back essentially to the Supreme Court's first cases on religious liberty. Each side in the controversy can find in these precedents pretty much what it is looking for; the "logic" of the argument is determined by the conclusion that is desired. These nineteenth-century cases, though few in number, are necessary as the introduction to the church-state controversy of the recent past.

2. The Contribution of the Jehovah's Witnesses

Between 1900 and 1938, the Court decided seven cases involving religious liberty.

Two cases in effect upheld the constitutional right of parochial and private schools to exist, and to teach religious subjects and foreign languages. These may be freely taught over and above the secular subjects which the state may require if the pupils are to satisfy the compulsory-school-attendance laws; and of course the schools must meet the state's inspection and supervision requirements.[12]

Three cases[13] dealt with the claims of pacifists, in which, in effect, the Court held that there is no constitutional right to be relieved of military duty by reason of religious conviction; but Congress may grant, and at any time withdraw, the privilege of exemption for conscientious objection.

In one of the latter cases, *United States* v. *Macintosh,* decided in 1931, Justice George Sutherland, for the Court, said, "We are a Christian people," and so must assume that the laws of the land were made for war as well as for peace, and that, as such, they "are not inconsistent with the will of God." This was the last time that the statement that "we are a Christian people" was made in a Supreme Court opinion.

A case[14] that involved the use of funds belonging to the Indians (but of which the government was trustee) for their education in religious schools involved no broad principle and need not detain us. But the seventh case, *Cochran* v. *Louisiana State Board of Education,*[15] decided in 1930, is still important in the controversy over the use of government funds for supplies to pupils attending parochial schools. A Louisiana statute provided for the purchase of secular textbooks for use by children in public and in private and parochial schools. The statute was attacked as unconstitutional under the Fourteenth Amendment for depriving taxpayers of their property without due process of law by granting property, purchased with tax money, to private persons. (It was not argued that the expenditure was a violation of the separation doctrine, for it had not yet been held that the guarantees of the First Amendment applied also to the states, under the Fourteenth Amendment.)

The Court upheld the statute. Writing for a unanimous Court, Chief

Justice Charles Evans Hughes adopted the state court's interpretation of the statute, that the appropriation was for the *benefit of the child* rather than the school, and was used for the purchase of secular, not religious, books, to be used by children regardless of the school attended. The public funds, the Court said, were used for a public purpose.

This "child-benefit theory" has been used to sustain federal expenditures on behalf of children in all types of schools, without distinction, for school lunches,[16] school health services, and the like, and the reach of the principle, abstractly considered, is without visible limit.

Starting in 1938, the Court began to get cases involving the Jehovah's Witnesses. From 1938 to 1946 the Court decided fifteen cases dealing with this sect—more than the total of all cases on religious liberty decided by the Court in its first 150 years.

This litigation regarding the sect stands to the credit of its counsel, Haydn C. Covington, whose office became a kind of N. A. A. C. P. for Jehovah's Witnesses. Covington built up a remarkable record of success in his cases before the Supreme Court, and those he won contributed significantly to the strengthening of constitutional liberties. The record, which would be impressive in any case, is especially notable in view of the belief of Jehovah's Witnesses that governments are the work of Satan, and that Jehovah's Witnesses should not, under any circumstances, participate in their affairs. Four of the cases were decided on broad free-speech and related First Amendment guarantees; eleven cases (and two additional ones involving members of the sect, in 1951 and 1953)[17] were decided on religious-freedom grounds.[18]

These cases settled the principle that freedom of religion, which is protected against *federal* action by the First Amendment, is also protected against infringement by *state* action, through the provision of the Fourteenth Amendment that declares that no state shall deprive any person of "liberty" without due process of law.

In 1925 the Supreme Court for the first time said that it assumed that freedom of speech and of the press were among the "fundamental personal rights and liberties" protected by the Due Process Clause of the Fourteenth Amendment against abridgment by any state.[19] In 1940, in one of the first cases involving Jehovah's Witnesses, *Cantwell* v. *Connecticut*,[20] the Court extended the principle of its 1925 decision to religious liberty. This, obviously, was a development of tremendous proportions, for, as the Jehovah's Witnesses cases alone show, infringements of religious liberty are much more likely to come from state than from federal action. Especially is this true in the area of education, which historically has been mainly a state and local responsibility.

These cases have firmly established the Constitution as a fortress of protection against persecution of, or discrimination against, unpopular sects or cults. Their ministers may preach and their missionaries may disseminate their beliefs without interference from the state; more than that, the state must protect them, in the enjoyment of their religious liberty, against people who would shut them up or keep them out of their city or town.

Jehovah's Witnesses have no official ministers, because each member considers himself a minister and teacher of the gospel, and each has a duty to engage in house-to-house canvassing and other forms of missionary work, to prepare repentant sinners for the battle of Armageddon and salvation, and to engage in this work zealously. They thus proved to be agents ideally suited—like the civil rights demonstrators two decades later—to test the capacity of the Bill of Rights. Their obstinacy in presenting test cases made the Court into a constitutional laboratory in which one after another experiment was tried. Never before did the Court have so many and such nice questions of civil liberties; but from this time on the pattern was set, and it carried over, as we know, from religious liberty cases to a great variety of cases involving many of the constitutional guarantees that never before were tested. These Jehovah's Witnesses cases conditioned not only the Supreme Court, but also many and large elements of the American people, to think in terms of their *constitutional* rights and liberties, to dare to assert them in the face of unfriendly forces, to seek their vindication in the courts, and to look to the Supreme Court as their ultimate sanctuary.

Justice Felix Frankfurter at times tried to divert some of this passionate attachment to the judicial process and to the Court that these cases of Jehovah's Witnesses stimulated, and to direct it toward the process of legislation. The "liberal spirit," he argued, cannot "be enforced by judicial invalidation of illiberal legislation." Our preoccupation with the question of constitutionality created, he said, a false value.[21] But the forces—social, institutional, and political—continued along the line of action projected by the Jehovah's Witnesses and their constitutional victories in the Supreme Court; and one can see nothing that is likely to change this course of development in the foreseeable future.

These Jehovah's Witnesses' cases, by giving the Supreme Court repeated opportunities to vindicate the constitutional rights and liberties of a small, weak, and unpopular minority, established important precedents, placed the Court at the center of the American system of government as the protector of fundamental freedoms, and prepared the ground for the later civil rights movement to develop along the line of nonviolent resistance.

For the civil rights movement would have had no chance if the Negro had lacked a basic respect for and trust in the American constitutional order. The cases won by the Jehovah's Witnesses (and those won also, over the years, by the N.A.A.C.P.) could not but generate a pervasive feeling of trust and hope that human rights can be secured without resort to force or violence. Even though little could be expected from petitioning legislative bodies, including the Congress, the door of hope remained open as long as the Supreme Court would sit and hear cases, and therefore one could trust such leaders as Martin Luther King, Jr., and follow the path of peace. Who can tell what America might have suffered had the Negro leaders and masses had good reason to put no more trust in the Court than they could have put in the Congress before 1964?

The point in this context is that a large share of that trust in the Court was built up by the Court under Chief Justice Harlan F. Stone and Chief Justice Frederick M. Vinson by decisions in case after case brought by Jehovah's Witnesses. In American history this will be reckoned as no mean contribution made to the Republic, paradoxically by a sect that is, on religious grounds, opposed to all states, governments, and laws.

This development also emphasizes the centrality of religious freedom in the complex of constitutional liberties and in American society. Religious freedom, enjoyed as it is to its maximum, conditions all our expectations and provides a setting and an atmosphere which predispose us to want, to expect, and to insist on the enjoyment of all other fundamental liberties and human rights. Men who cultivate a spirit of religious independence and who learn to respect the right to be different in religious beliefs and loyalties will expect respect when they differ in the color of their skin, which should by no means be as important as a difference in religion—something that reaches into a man's mind, heart, and soul—or when they differ in political affiliation, or in intellectual or cultural matters. Religious liberty thus transcends in importance and influence all other liberties. It was not, therefore, accidental that it was in a case involving Jehovah's Witnesses that the Supreme Court, in 1943, said that the nation's unity may be fostered only by persuasion and example, and never by compulsion; and that there must be no fear that diversity will disintegrate our social organization; that our right to be different means a right to be different with respect to things that matter greatly, even "as to things that touch the heart of the existing order," for

if there is any fixed star in our constitutional configuration, it is that no official, high or petty, can prescribe what shall be orthodox in politics, nationalism, religion, or other matters of opinion or force citizens to confess by word or act their faith therein.[22]

Two decades before the civil rights movement got under way, Jehovah's Witnesses went on our city streets and into our public parks to preach and to distribute their literature. They tested the laws, passed or interpreted to thwart their efforts, by peacefully, yet intentionally, doing the acts they were prohibited from doing. In fact, they practiced nonviolent resistance in the 1930s and 1940s in scores of American cities and towns, though they lacked an express Gandhian ideology, and, like the Negroes who followed them on the streets and in other public places, they went to the courts for the vindication of their constitutional liberties.

The most essential right that the Jehovah's Witnesses won was the right to seek converts to their faith, the right to try to reach the minds or hearts of other men by peaceful persuasion; and this was, of course, precisely what the later civil rights demonstrations also attempted to do. Neither Jehovah's Witnesses nor the Negroes enjoyed the friendly regard of the larger communities, or the respect of the "establishment," or the financial resources to resort to the costly mass media; and so they took to the streets, which became their newspaper and radio and television facilities. And as the rights and liberties of the Jehovah's Witnesses were vindicated by the Supreme Court, unintentionally their cases became the foundation stones on which the Negroes were later to build.

The closeness, in the constitutional context, of Jehovah's Witnesses and Negroes in their struggle for civil rights is truly amazing. The former have no churches; they meet in a building that they call Kingdom Hall; and their faith compels them to look beyond themselves to the nonbelievers. Their "congregations" are the men and women who do *not* come to the Kingdom Hall; *they* are the ones who must be addressed. So, too, the civil rights movement: it faced outward, to the white community. The Negroes met in their churches only to find there the strength to go outside to face and address the unconverted.

Uniquely, these two groups—worlds apart in all other ways—had the same needs and tried to meet them in similar ways; and when they clashed with the authorities they both looked to the Supreme Court for vindication.

And the Court, in the cases brought by Jehovah's Witnesses, gave the fullest measure of protection to their unpopular cause. These cases settled the law that, with respect to peaceful outdoor assemblies, a city's permit system may not go beyond the barest necessities of traffic regulation of the streets and parks; that there may not be a total ban on such outdoor assemblies; that outdoor assemblies are guaranteed by the First and Fourteenth Amendments; that a licensing system will be upheld only if it is reasonable, only if it permits and regulates outdoor meetings but imposes no unnecessary restrictions, and only if the system is administered fairly and without discrimination against any weak or unpopular group or cause.

When he addressed the Congress[23] on March 15, 1965, on the voting rights of Negroes, President Johnson told the Congress and the American people that the Negroes in Alabama had the constitutional right to march and to demonstrate, subject to reasonable regulation of the streets and highways. In fact, in these statements President Johnson "incorporated by reference" the Supreme Court decisions in the Jehovah's Witnesses cases.

3. Separation of Church and State

The Reynolds case, as we have seen, implied that the First Amendment reflected a philosophy of church-state separation; but it was not until about seventy years later, in 1947, that the Supreme Court for the first time specifically articulated and accepted the separation principle. This was done in *Everson* v. *Board of Education*.[24] The Court now unanimously adopted Jefferson's phrase, "wall of separation," as authoritative. Now for the first time the Court expressly interpreted the first of the two religion clauses of the First Amendment: "Congress shall make no law respecting an establishment of religion"; and from this time forth it was this clause that presented the most challenging and difficult questions to the Court.

The Jehovah's Witnesses cases never touched on this clause but only on the second one: "[Congress shall make no law . . .] prohibiting the free exercise [of religion]." To this clause, as included in the concept of "liberty" of the Fourteenth Amendment, the Court gave the broadest possible interpretation and application.

Now in the Everson decision, Justice Hugo L. Black for the Court said: "In the words of Jefferson, the clause against establishment of religion by law was intended to erect 'a wall of separation between Church and State.' *Reynolds* v. *United States*."

What does separation involve? Justice Black said:

The "establishment of religion" clause of the First Amendment means at least this: Neither a state nor the Federal Government can set up a church. Neither can pass laws which aid one religion, aid all religions, or prefer one religion over another. Neither can force nor influence a person to go to or to remain away from church against his will or force him to profess a belief or disbelief in any religion. No person can be punished for entertaining or professing religious beliefs or disbeliefs, for church attendance or non-attendance. No tax, in any amount, large or small, can be levied to support any religious activities or institutions, whatever they may be called, or whatever form they may adopt to teach or practice religion. Neither a state nor the Federal Government can, openly or secretly, participate in the affairs of any religious organizations or groups and vice versa.

While the Court unanimously accepted the separation principle as the meaning and intent of the Establishment Clause, it split 5 to 4 on its application to the facts in the case. A school board in New Jersey, acting under the terms of a statute, provided for the free bus transportation of pupils attending both public and Roman Catholic schools. The majority of the Court, in an opinion by Justice Black, upheld the constitutionality of the statute and the action of the local school board as not violative of the separation principle.

The dissenting Justices argued that while the majority avowed the principle of separation, their decision in fact violated it; for here money raised by taxation was used to support a transgression of the principle. Justice Robert H. Jackson argued that parochial schools were the foundation on which the Roman Catholic Church was built, so that rendering "tax aid" to the church school was indistinguishable from rendering aid to the church itself; and Justice Wiley B. Rutledge asked: "Does New Jersey's action furnish support for religion by use of the taxing power?" His answer was: "Certainly it does. . . ."

The majority reasoned that the parochial schools met the state's compulsory-school-attendance laws, so that a child attending such a school met the secular education requirements. The bus-fare law did no more than "provide a general program to help parents get their children, regardless of their religion, safely and expeditiously to and from accredited schools." By providing this service, the state was trying to shield children from street and traffic hazards, thus doing what it deemed "best for the school children's welfare." And Justice Black, in an early part of his long opinion, cited with approval the Cochran case. Thus the majority decision upholding the bus fares for parochial school pupils seemed to be based on the child-benefit theory: the bus service was for the benefit not of the religious school but of the child, regardless of the school he attended.

Justice Rutledge's dissenting opinion (in which he was joined by Justices Frankfurter, Jackson, and Harold H. Burton) brought out all the ambivalences, ambiguities, and contradictions that are inherent in the decision when it is put up against the principle of separation. Like the majority in the Everson case, Americans avow belief in the principle of church-state separation; and, like the majority, Americans at the same time want things which the dissenting Justices had no trouble in labeling contradictions of the separation principle. Logical consistency will probably never be fully achieved. As we saw, the contradictions were inherent in the very first cases involving religious liberty decided by the Court.

Justice Rutledge contended that the arguments in favor of the bus fares for parochial school pupils can be used with equal force to justify payment for textbooks, school lunches, athletic equipment, writing and other materials, and "indeed [for] all other items composing the total burden," including even teachers' salaries, buildings, and equipment; for today transportation is no less essential to the school than are the other items. If the parochial school, by satisfying the state's compulsory-school laws, promotes the general welfare, and if payment of public money for aid to its pupils is in fact payment for a public function—as the Court held in the Cochran case and as the majority held in the Everson case—then, said Justice Rutledge, "I can see no possible basis . . . for the state's refusal to make full appropriation for support of private, religious schools, just as is done for public instruction." And many Americans have continued to make these same points, in the courts, at hearings on federal aid bills, and in other forums. They say with the dissenting Justices:

Of course paying the cost of transportation promotes the general cause of education and the welfare of the individual. So does paying all other items of educational expense. . . . To say that New Jersey's appropriation and her use of the power of taxation for raising the funds appropriated are not for public purposes but are for private ends [the benefit of the child], is to say that they are for the support of religion and religious teaching [the purpose of the child's travel]. Conversely, to say that they are for public purposes [*Cochran*] is to say that they are not for religious ones [majority in *Everson*].

And if they are not for religious ones, then all the other expenses of the parochial school are not for religious purposes. "I do not understand," said Justice Rutledge, "why the state cannot go further. . . ."

Is this an instance of the "slippery slope" fallacy or a legitimate argument against the logic of the Cochran and Everson decisions? The Court has not yet found an answer to this question that has satisfied all Justices or reconciled public opinion, and I doubt that it ever will. The paradoxes, ambivalences, and contradictions are built into the problems, and the best that the Court can do is to decide the cases on the basis of their facts—the way it decides that a book is or is not "obscene," or the way a jury decides that a defendant was or was not "negligent." The decision comes not out of a void or an emptiness, nor out of a realm of pure conceptions or "neutral principles," but out of a complex situation in which conceptions and specific facts are inextricably mixed.

A year after the Everson decision, the Court had before it a released-time arrangement whereby religious instruction classes were conducted during regular school time *within* a public school building by denominational teachers. In *McCollum* v. *Board of Education*,[25] eight Justices held that this practice violated the First and Fourteenth Amendments. They reaffirmed the broad principles of the Everson case, only this time eight, and not four, Justices found that the separation principle had been breached. Justice Stanley Reed dissented—not, however, with respect to the principle involved, but only with respect to its application; he thought that the released-time arrangement did not violate the principle of separation, just as the bus fares in the Everson case had not violated this principle.

But Justice Reed's dissenting opinion has a historic and forensic significance, for it was the first opinion in the Supreme Court in the twentieth century to argue for a "soft line" on church-state separation, and it became the pattern for the forces in American society that favor measures of cooperation between church and state.

Like the Court in *Church of the Holy Trinity* v. *United States,* 1892, Justice Reed listed various official practices to show that "separation" does not necessarily mean an absolute prohibition on all forms of "aid." Thus, he pointed to the fact that all churches "receive 'aid' from government in the form of freedom from taxation"; that in the

Everson decision the Court upheld bus fares for parochial school pupils "for safety reasons"; that in the Cochran case the Court held that Louisiana may give free textbooks to pupils in religious schools "on the ground that the books were for the education of the children, not to aid religious schools." He cited the National School Lunch Act; *Bradfield* v. *Roberts,* 1899; chaplains in Congress; chaplains in the armed forces; the Servicemen's Readjustment Act of 1944, under which veterans may, at government expense, study for the ministry in denominational schools; Bible-reading and recitation of the Lord's Prayer in the schools of the District of Columbia; chaplains at the United States Naval Academy and Military Academy, and compulsory attendance at religious services at the chapels at both institutions. In the light of these "precedents, customs, and practices," Justice Reed concluded:

The prohibition of enactments respecting the establishment of religion do[es] not bar every friendly gesture between church and state. It is not an absolute prohibition against every conceivable situation where the two may work together. . . . The Constitution should not be stretched to forbid national customs. . . . Devotion to the great principle of religious liberty should not lead us into a rigid interpretation of the constitutional guarantee that conflicts with accepted habits of our people.

Reviewing the historical record regarding Jefferson, Justice Reed concluded that "a rule of law should not be drawn from a figure of speech ['wall of separation between church and state']."

Since then, little has been added to the opposing lines of argument in the opinions of the Court. The Court continues to avow adherence to the principle of separation but to divide on its application. The picture was made especially bewildering because Justice Black, who stood for the "absolutist" position, found that the bus fares were *not* a breach of the wall of separation, while Justice Frankfurter, who spoke for a philosophy of "balancing," dissented in the Everson case.

Four years after the McCollum case, the Court had to consider the released-time program of New York City, which called for the religious classes to be given *outside* the public school buildings. In *Zorach* v. *Clauson,*[26] six Justices, in an opinion by Justice William O. Douglas, found this system sufficiently different from that presented in the McCollum case to conclude that it did not violate the principle of separation. Justices Black and Jackson dissented, maintaining that there was no essential difference from the McCollum case; and Justice Frankfurter dissented on the ground that the plaintiffs should have been permitted to show that the program involved coercion of pupils, and thus restricted the free exercise of religion. But again all Justices avowed belief in the principle of separation; the three dissenters, however, argued that the principle was in this case honored in the breach rather than in the observance. Now Justice Black was with Justices Jackson and Frankfurter, who had made the identical charge against him in the Everson case.

Justice Douglas's opinion in the Zorach case—in order to justify the decision upholding the released-time program—took a line regarding separation that was closer to Justice Reed's dissenting opinion in the McCollum case than to Justice Black's in Everson. "There cannot be," he said,

the slightest doubt that the First Amendment reflects the philosophy that Church and State should be separated. . . . The First Amendment within the scope of its coverage permits no exception; the prohibition is absolute.

That's to enter like a lion. But then he went on in the very next sentences to say:

The First Amendment, however, does not say that in every and all respects there shall be a separation of Church and State. Rather, it studiously defines the manner, the specific ways, in which there shall be no concert or union or dependency one on the other. That is the common sense of the matter. Otherwise, the state and religion would be aliens to each other— hostile, suspicious, and even unfriendly. . . .

We are a religious people whose institutions presuppose a Supreme Being. . . . When the state encourages religious instruction or cooperates with religious authorities by adjusting the schedule of public events to sectarian needs, it follows the best of our traditions. For it then respects the religious nature of our people and accommodates the public service to their spiritual needs. To hold that it may not would be to find in the Constitution a requirement that the government show a callous indifference to religious groups. That would be preferring those who believe in no religion over those who do believe. . . .

And, like Justice Reed in the McCollum case, now Justice Douglas for the majority listed the "precedents, customs, and practices" that show that "separation" is, well, not quite "separation": tax exemption for churches and other practices already mentioned, and some others now listed for the first time:

The appeals to the Almighty in the messages of the Chief Executive; the proclamations making Thanksgiving Day a holiday; "so help me God" in our courtroom oaths—these and all other references to the Almighty that run through our laws, our public rituals, our ceremonies . . . the supplication with which the Court opens each session: "God save the United States and the Honorable Court."

The multiple, and confusing, opinions in the Everson, McCollum, and Zorach cases hardly prepared the nation for the Court's momentous decisions that were to come in the early 1960s, involving the delicate and explosive issues of prayers and Bible-reading in the public schools. And that the Court itself would have trouble with, and from, these cases can be seen when, with the advantage of hindsight, we now reread parts of Justice Frankfurter's dissenting opinion in the second flag-salute case, *West Virginia State Board of Education* v. *Barnette*.[27]

The majority of the Court in the Barnette case held the flag-salute as a compulsory school exercise to be a violation of the First Amendment. Justice Frankfurter, dissenting, asked argumentatively whether the Court will now be called upon to determine what claims of conscience should be recognized and what claims rejected as satisfying the "religion" which the Constitution protects. As his first example, Justice Frankfurter referred to Bible-reading in public schools. The educational policies of the states are, he said, in great conflict over this.

Is this Court to overthrow such variant state educational policies by denying states the right to entertain such convictions in regard to their school systems, because of a belief that the King James version is in fact a sectarian text to which parents of the Catholic and Jewish faiths and of some Protestant persuasions may rightly object to having their children exposed? On the other hand the religious consciences of some parents may rebel at the absence of any Bible-reading in the schools.

Justice Frankfurter saw other troubles for the Court once it allowed itself to interfere with the administration of the public schools. He said that parents of children who attend parochial schools feel that they carry a double educational burden, for they pay for two systems. They see that children attending public schools enjoy

derivative advantages such as free textbooks, free lunch, and free transportation. . . . What of the claims for equality of treatment of those parents who, because of religious scruples, cannot send their children to public schools? What of the claim that if the right to send children to privately maintained schools is partly an exercise of religious conviction, to render effective this right it should be accompanied by equality of treatment by the state in supplying free textbooks, free lunch, and free transportation to children who go to private schools? What of the claim that such grants are offensive to the cardinal constitutional doctrine of separation of church and state?

While he said that of course the Court did not, in the Barnette case, have before it for decision these situations, still the Court must decide the flag-salute issue with regard "for what may come after." If a state may not require the flag-salute of all children because it may offend the conscience of some, may it "compel all children [who] attend public school to listen to the King James version although it may offend the consciences of their parents?" It presents, he said, "awful possibilities to try to encase the solution of these problems within the rigid prohibitions of unconstitutionality. . . . We are dealing with matters as to which legislators and voters have conflicting views. Are we as judges to impose our strong convictions on where wisdom lies?"

This was said in 1943. Four years later Justice Frankfurter was among the dissenters in the Everson case who contended that bus fares for parochial school pupils was a violation of the separation principle; and in the Zorach case he was one of three dissenters from the decision which upheld the released-time system of New York City. These facts underscore the difficulties one encounters if one tries to rationalize the votes of the Justices in the establishment-of-religion cases in the light of what they individually and collectively have said that the separation principle means.

Justice Frankfurter's prescience with regard to the types of cases to which the Court opened the door by its decision in the Barnette case, however, was validated in the early 1960s. First came the attack on prayer in the public schools, in *Engel* v. *Vitale*,[28] in 1962. The case aroused a great deal of interest throughout the nation. A brief supporting the prayer requirement was filed by the attorneys general of twenty-two states, while no state filed a brief in opposition.

In 1951, the New York State Board of Regents had issued a "policy statement" which asserted that the American people have always been religious, and that a program of religious inspiration in the public schools would assure that pupils would acquire "respect for lawful authority and obedience of law [and that] each of them will be properly prepared to follow the faith of his or her father, as he or she received the same at mother's knee or father's side and as such faith is expounded and strengthened by his or her religious leaders." The statement then said that the Regents believed that, at the commencement of each school day, "the act of allegiance to the flag might well be joined with this act of reverence to God: 'Almighty God, we acknowledge our dependence upon Thee, and we beg Thy blessings upon us, our parents, our teachers and our country.' "

There was no universal acclaim of this action by the Board of Regents, and only a small minority of school boards in the state acted to require the Regents' Prayer, as it came to be called, in the local public schools. Certainly many people felt that the prayer was a product of the McCarthy atmosphere, in which some persons tended to attach politics to religion in order to prove their anti-Communism.

The school board of New Hyde Park was, however, one of those that accepted the Regents' recommendation; but the board's order to the schools contained provisions to insure that no pupil need take part or be present during the "act of reverence." A group of parents of children in New Hyde Park public schools brought suit in the state courts to declare the practice unconstitutional. The American Civil Liberties Union assisted the parents in the litigation. In 1961 the New York Court of Appeals, with two judges dissenting, upheld the constitutionality of the prayer exercise. The parents appealed to the Supreme Court.

In the Supreme Court, briefs supporting the parents who attacked the prayer requirement were filed by the American Ethical Union, the American Jewish Committee, the American Jewish Congress, the Synagogue Council of America, and related Jewish groups.

By 6 to 1, with Justices Frankfurter and Byron R. White not participating, the Supreme Court held that the practice violated the constitutional prohibition respecting an establishment of religion.

In his opinion for the majority, Justice Black said that there could be no doubt that the Regents' Prayer was a religious activity—"a solemn avowal of divine faith and supplication for the blessings of the Almighty." The Establishment Clause, he said,

must at least mean that in this country it is no part of the business of government to compose official prayers for any group of the American people to recite as part of a religious program carried on by the government.

The Court held that it made no difference that the prayer was "denominationally neutral," or that the recitation was not coerced. The important fact was that the Establishment Clause was violated by the school board's order that established "an official religion." It is, said the Court,

neither sacrilegious nor antireligious to say that each separate government in this country should stay out of the business of writing or sanctioning official prayers and leave that purely religious function to the people themselves and to those the people chose to look to for religious guidance.

The case may be said to have decided that: (1) The First and Fourteenth Amendments bar governmental assistance not only to any one denomination, but also to religion in general. (2) It makes no difference whether the assistance is substantial or consists only of a "neutral" twenty-two-word prayer. (3) The fact that pupils are not compelled to participate does not save such a practice from violating at least the Establishment Clause. (4) It makes no difference how "inoffensive" the religious act is as long as it is intended by the officials as an act of religious reverence, worship, or devotion.

Justice Douglas's concurring opinion has a special interest because he stated that in retrospect the Everson case was "out of line with the First Amendment," strongly implying that he would now hold that bus fares for parochial school pupils are unconstitutional; and he also implied that the practices cited by Justice Reed in the McCollum case —to which Justice Douglas added others—were also unconstitutional. In this list he included the pledge of allegiance, which Congress in 1954 amended to include the italicized phrase: "one Nation *under God,* indivisible, with liberty and justice for all";[29] and he character-ized the formula which announced the convening of the Court—"God save the United States and this Honorable Court"—as "a supplication, a prayer."

Justice Potter Stewart was the sole dissenter. He too cited many customs and practices, including the act of Congress in 1952 that calls upon the President each year to proclaim a National Day of Prayer,[30] and "The Star-Spangled Banner," made the national anthem by an act of Congress, which contains the verse: "And this be our motto, 'In God is our trust.' "[31] All these instances show, said Justice Stewart, that, as Justice Douglas wrote for the Court in the Zorach decision, "We are a religious people whose institutions presuppose a Supreme Being." To Justice Stewart, the customs, laws, and practices cited were apparently all constitutional, and just as they did not "establish" reli-gion, so, too, the Regents' Prayer did not "establish" an "official religion."

In the following year, 1963, two cases that challenged the practice of Bible-reading in public schools reached the Supreme Court. A case from Pennsylvania involved a statute that required that at the opening of each school day there be read at least ten verses from the Bible, without comment. In the school in question, the Bible was read in the school's radio and television workshop, and the exercises were broadcast into each room through an intercommunications system. This was followed by a recitation of the Lord's Prayer, also over the intercommunications system, and also by the students in their classrooms, who stood and joined in repeating the prayer in unison. The exercises were closed with the flag salute. A case from Baltimore involved a schoolboard rule, based on a statute, that provided for a reading of a chapter of the Bible "and/or the use of the Lord's Prayer." The Pennsylvania law was challenged by parents of schoolchildren who were Unitarians, and the Maryland law by avowed atheists. In each instance children were excused from the exercises on the request of parents. These cases, *School District of Abington* v. *Schempp* and *Murray* v. *Curlett*,³² were consolidated in the Supreme Court.

The Supreme Court, by 8 to 1, held that the school exercises violated the Establishment Clause. Justice Stewart again was the sole dissenter.

In his opinion for the Court, Justice Thomas C. Clark said that while "we are a religious people whose institutions presuppose a Supreme Being," we also are a people whose history and government show that religious freedom is "strongly imbedded in our public and private life."

Thus in 1963 there was the same ambivalence, the same view regarding the two sources of our national values—religious institutions *and* the revolt against them in the secularistic enlightenment—that we found in the Court's cases in the nineteenth century. There was, however, one important difference: then the contrast or conflict was found in different cases, separated by years—there were twenty-one years between *Reynolds* v. *United States,* 1878, and *Bradfield* v. *Roberts,* 1899; now it was found in the same case, in the same opinions, and in the clash between majority and dissenting opinions. The Court directly faced a choice, but it was not between right and wrong, between good and evil; it was a choice between right and right, between competing values of almost equal dignity. This made the decision much more difficult and contributed greatly to the public view that the Court was imposing on the country an arbitrary interpretation of the Constitution.

In the Bible-reading cases, Justice Clark quoted with approval from Justice Black's opinion in the Everson case that "[n]either a state nor the Federal Government can set up a church. Neither can pass laws which aid one religion, aid all religions, or prefer one religion over another." He also quoted from Justice Rutledge's opinion in that case that the purpose of the First Amendment was not to strike merely at the official establishment of a single sect, creed or religion, outlawing only a formal relation. . . . Necessarily it was to uproot all such relationships. But the object was broader than separating church and state in this narrow sense. It was to create a complete and permanent separation of the spheres of religious activity and civil authority by comprehensively forbidding every form of public aid or support for religion.

In the Regents' Prayer case and the Bible-reading cases the Court said that while the Establishment Clause and the Free Exercise Clause may in some instances overlap, they forbid "two quite different kinds of governmental encroachment upon religious freedom." The former clause, unlike the latter,

does not depend upon any showing of direct governmental compulsion and is violated by the enactment of laws which establish an official religion whether those laws operate directly to coerce non-observing individuals or not. This is not to say, of course, that laws officially prescribing a particular form of religious worship do not involve coercion of such individuals. When the power, prestige and financial support of government is placed behind a particular religious belief, the indirect coercive pressure upon religious minorities to conform to the prevailing officially approved religion is plain. . . . The first and most immediate purpose [of the Establishment Clause] rested on the belief that a union of government and religion tends to destroy government and to degrade religion.[33]

The Court in both cases said that when government "allies itself with one particular form of religion," the "inevitable result" is that it incurs "the hatred, disrespect and even contempt of those who held contrary beliefs."

It is not clear that the Court in these two cases put the rationale of the Establishment Clause as it should be put. The Court said that, when the government lends support to a religious belief, (1) the action exerts pressure upon dissenters to conform to the officially aided religion, (2) the action tends to degrade religion, and (3) the action will cause dissenters to feel hostile toward the government. Reasons (2) and (3) are not, I think, persuasive; for "public opinion" may well feel that government aid "honors" rather than degrades religion; and as to dissenters feeling hostility toward the government, this feeling may be engendered in a minority whenever its members do not approve a governmental action, whatever it may be; but is a government to be paralyzed because some citizens will not like what the government does, for example, in relation to housing, or conservation, or foreign economic aid?

The first reason does support the Establishment Clause but it tends to assimilate that clause to the Free Exercise Clause and to make them both a prohibition upon all kinds of "governmental encroachment upon religious freedom."

The heart of the Establishment Clause is to be found, I think, in the preamble to the Virginia Bill for Religious Liberty, drafted by Jefferson and shepherded through the Virginia legislature by Madison —and quoted by the Court in the Everson case, as follows:

Almighty God hath created the mind free; that all attempts to influence it . . . are a departure from the plan of the Holy author of our religion, who being Lord both of body and mind, yet chose not to propagate it by coercion on either . . .; that to compel a man to furnish contributions of money for the propagation of opinions which he disbelieves, is sinful and tyrannical; that even the forcing him to support this or that teacher of his own religious persuasion, is depriving him of the comfortable liberty of giving his contributions to the particular pastor, whose morals he would make his pattern. . . .

That no man shall be compelled to frequent or support any religious worship, place, or ministry whatsoever. . . .

The essential meaning is clear: I am not to be compelled to support *even my own religion.* For God created me a free man; my mind must remain free. For if I perform a religious act which the state requires of me, how can I be sure that its performance is a sacrifice or an act of my heart? When the act is compelled by Caesar, it becomes an act that is rendered *unto Caesar,* even when Caesar compels it as ostensibly an act to be rendered unto God. In any case, I am no longer absolutely free; my mind has been invaded by Caesar; and though I might freely render the act, had Caesar not pushed me to it, his pushing me removes my freedom, or at least renders my act ambiguous, and thus partly idolatrous insofar as it may look toward Caesar, or insofar as Caesar's shadow falls upon it, or upon me as I perform the act.

This situation is analogous to the second series of sit-in cases, decided also in 1963.[34] The manager of the store in Greenville, South Carolina, asked the Negro demonstrators to leave, and when they refused they were arrested. But the city had at the time a segregation ordinance that was, of course, unconstitutional, unenforceable. The state contended that the store acted voluntarily and independently of the ordinance; that the store had a segregation policy, which it would have maintained even if there had been no ordinance. But the Supreme

Court unanimously held that "The State will not be heard to make this contention" "even assuming . . . that the manager would have acted as he did independently of the existence of the ordinance." For, as the Court said,

When the State has commanded a particular result, it has saved to itself the power to determine that result and thereby "to a significant extent" has "become involved" in it, and, in fact, has removed that decision from the sphere of private choice.

Thus, even though I might want to pray, or read from the Bible, once the state directs me to perform this act, it has removed my act "from the sphere of private choice."

Every parent who wants his child to participate in religious activities at home, or in church or synagogue, knows how dangerous it is to command or order the child—dangerous to the interests the parent wishes to serve. The child might want to perform the act freely; but once he suspects that he is being coerced or pressured, his resentment may drive him to an obstinate refusal or to seek some excuse for abstaining. The parent learns that perhaps he cannot do more than teach by example, by his own actions, and leave the rest unsaid and to chance. For the child's instinct is a healthy one, and it must be respected: he wants to be *absolutely free* in a matter that touches his spirit, his soul—a realm in which the slightest taint of coercion can cause resentment, anger, or rebellion. For as the prophet Jeremiah said (17:9): "The heart is of all things most crafty, and desperately sick. Who understands it?"

The Free Exercise Clause protects one against coercion to do what one does not believe or approve; the Establishment Clause protects one against coercion to do *even what one would want to do voluntarily* and what one would approve *if it were done freely*. Taken together, their purpose is not to degrade or weaken religion in any respect whatsoever, but, on the contrary, as with the other guarantees of the First Amendment, to recognize and to implement the belief that "Almighty God hath created the mind free"; and that man is not man unless his mind remains free; and that God is not served except by a mind that is free. Had God wanted a coerced worship, He would have created not man but an unfree agent; and what God did not choose to do, the government, *a fortiori*, may not do.

Now it is something of a paradox that the most important state paper on religious freedom in American history claims this freedom for man in the name of God, and for the sake of the purity of man's worship of God. But the paradox is only apparent and not real; for the disestablishment of religion was for the sake of religion; to save religion from its "friends," who can hurt religion at least as much as can its enemies. One could, then, suggest a rephrasing of Justice Douglas's statement, and say: "We are a religious people whose institutions" of freedom "presuppose a Supreme Being" who "created the mind free," and the First Amendment was put into the Constitution to make certain that the mind shall forever remain free.

This is not to "establish" secularism. The First Amendment enshrines no *ism* at all; but this only means that the Constitution leaves room for many *isms*, freely adopted or rejected. This is, in the phrase of Tennyson, to "embrace the purpose of God" for man; to make a covenant with God, and not a conspiracy against Him. The First Amendment, with the Establishment and Free Exercise Clauses, belongs not only in the Constitution, but also in the sacred scriptures of everyone who has heard the voice of his conscience say: "This is the way, walk ye in it"—walk as a *free* man.

And so even if *all Americans* were members of the same religious denomination, the Establishment Clause would have the identical role that it now has, when we are a nation of minorities. It is not only the nonbeliever, but also the believer, who must plead to be excused from the Regents' Prayer or from any other *state-conducted* religious exercise, each for the sake of his own conscience; and the latter so that he may be sure that his prayers will lift his soul to heaven and not to Caesar; for the roots of religion are in the hidden recesses of a man's conscience and not in the power of princes or in "earthly dignities." No other provision in the Constitution so firmly guarantees the *essential* freedom of man as does the Establishment Clause, for it alone is addressed directly to *man's condition as man*.

In a long and scholarly opinion, Justice William J. Brennan said that while the school exercises in the Bible-reading cases clearly violated the Establishment Clause, he did not consider every involvement of religion in public life unconstitutional.

Reviewing the history of religious exercises in schools, Justice Brennan pointed out that as the free public schools supplanted the private academies and sectarian schools in the first half of the nineteenth century, morning devotions were retained, but in time religious exercises tended to become nonsectarian.

But at the turn of the century only Massachusetts had a statute that made prayer or Bible-reading mandatory; elsewhere the statutes either permitted such exercises or left the matter to local option. After

1910, however, eleven more states joined Massachusetts in making the exercises compulsory. In no state was there a constitutional or statutory ban on such practices, though in a number of states such practices were prohibited by court or administrative decision.[35] Contrary, then, to general opinion, religious exercises in schools were made compulsory by the statutes of only a few states, and the ban on such practices had been imposed by state courts before this was done by the Supreme Court.

Attorneys for the states contended that daily prayer and Bible-reading served educational purposes to such an extent that their religious character might be overlooked. Thus, it was argued, the morning devotional exercises fostered better discipline and elevated the school day to a spiritual level. The superintendent of the Baltimore schools argued that

the acknowledgment of the existence of God as symbolized in the opening exercises establishes a discipline tone which tends to cause each individual pupil to constrain his overt acts and to consequently conform to accepted standards of behavior during his attendance at school.

Justice Brennan rightly observed that whatever secular purposes the religious exercises may be said to serve could be attained by non-religious materials. It has not been shown, he said,

that readings from the speeches and messages of great Americans, for example, or from the documents of our heritage of liberty, daily recitation of the Pledge of Allegiance, or even the observance of a moment of reverent silence at the opening of class, may not adequately serve the solely secular purposes of the devotional activities. . . .

This is, of course, a relevant and forcefully true comment; but one can also contend that the attempt to achieve such secular ends through religion can only degrade and debase religion. For religion is not a substitute for a tranquilizer or a monitor. This episode alone almost justifies the Establishment Clause as necessary for the integrity and purity of religion itself.

On a related point Justice Brennan quoted from an article in *Christian Century*:

An observance of this sort is likely to deteriorate quickly into an empty formality with little, if any, spiritual significance. Prescribed forms of this sort, as many colleges have concluded after years of compulsory chapel attendance, can actually work against the inculcation of vital religion.[36]

But outlawing the practices in these cases, said Justice Brennan, should not be taken to mean that every involvement of religion in public life violates the Establishment Clause. Only those involvements of religion with secular institutions are unconstitutional which

(a) serve the essentially religious activities of religious institutions; (b) employ the organs of government for essentially religious purposes; or (c) use essentially religious means to serve governmental ends, where secular means would suffice.

There are practices which seem to violate the Establishment Clause, the striking down of which would, however, seriously interfere with religious liberties; and Justice Brennan cited the following practices as falling within this class: the employment of chaplains in the armed forces and in prisons; draft exemptions for ministers and divinity students; excusing children from school on their religious holidays; allowing the temporary use of public buildings by religious organizations when their own churches have become unavailable because of a disaster or an emergency.

There are practices which cannot be effectively attacked in the courts, and Justice Brennan cited the use of legislative chaplains and invocational prayers. He also pointed out that the Court's decisions do not bar teaching in the schools *about* religion or *about* the Bible.

Regarding tax exemption, Justice Brennan argued that it should not be held violative of the Establishment Clause if it is made "incidentally available to religious institutions." If religious institutions are allowed to share benefits which government makes available generally to "educational, charitable, and eleemosynary groups," it does not mean that the taxing authorities "have used such benefits in any way to subsidize worship or foster belief in God." But the benefit must be available to all such organizations, those "which reject as well as those which accept belief in God."[37]

In the operation of a general and nondiscriminatory welfare program, it is, said Justice Brennan, no violation of the Establishment Clause for a state to allow unemployment compensation to a person who is unemployed by reason of his religious beliefs or practices.[38]

Then there are activities which, though religious in origin, have ceased to have religious meaning. This was the basis for the Court's holding that Sunday laws do not violate the Establishment Clause. Such laws today—though this concededly was not true of their original purpose—are accepted as serving a predominantly secular end.[39]

Justice Brennan seemed to think that similar reasoning might sustain the use of the motto "In God We Trust," on currency, documents, and public buildings. Though its original inspiration was certainly religious, by now it is so firmly fixed as our motto that it is simply just that. "The truth is," observed Justice Brennan,

that we have simply interwoven the motto so deeply into the fabric of our civil policy that its present use may well not present that type of involvement which the First Amendment prohibits.

Similarly, patriotic exercises in public schools and elsewhere, whatever their origins, no longer have a religious purpose or meaning. Thus,

The reference to divinity in the revised pledge of allegiance . . . may merely recognize the historical fact that our Nation was believed to have been founded "under God." Thus reciting the pledge may be no more of a religious exercise than the reading aloud of Lincoln's Gettysburg Address, which contains an allusion to the same historical fact.

With respect to the pledge of allegiance, a case was brought in a New York court in 1956 by Joseph L. Lewis and another person on behalf of the Freethinkers of America, who objected to the phrase "under God" as a violation of the separation principle. In 1957 a justice of the New York Supreme Court dismissed the petition. In 1960 the Appellate Division upheld this decision; and in June 1964 the Court of Appeals, without an opinion, unanimously sustained these decisions. On November 23, 1964, the United States Supreme Court denied a writ of certiorari to review the judgment of the Court of Appeals,[40] and there was no indication, as there sometimes is, that some Justices dissented from this action. It should be noted that the lower courts in New York stated that a schoolchild could not, however, be compelled to repeat the pledge, and that the child could leave out the phrase "under God" without any penalty.

One may be sure that the decisions of the New York courts and of the Supreme Court do not mean that they approved of the 1954 amendment of the pledge of allegiance by Congress.[41] Many of the judges must have felt that the action by Congress honored neither God nor the Constitution. The amendment accomplished for religion and for the nation as much as was accomplished by the 1952 act of Congress that calls upon the President to set aside and proclaim each year a suitable day, other than Sunday, as a National Day of Prayer, "on which the people of the United States," so the statute provides, "may turn to God in prayer and meditation at churches, in groups, and as individuals";[42] or as much as the act of 1956 that authorized a special Post Office canceling stamp with the legend: "Pray for

Peace";[43] or the act of 1955, which provided that when the Secretary of the Treasury ordered new dies for dollar bills, they should bear the inscription: "In God We Trust."[44]

In 1953 Senator Ralph Flanders of Vermont introduced the following Joint Resolution to amend the Constitution:

Section 1. This Nation devoutly recognizes the authority and law of Jesus Christ, Saviour and Ruler of Nations through whom are bestowed the blessings of Almighty God.

Section 2. This amendment shall not be interpreted so as to result in the establishment of any particular ecclesiastical organization, or in the abridgment of the rights of religious freedom, or freedom of speech and press, or of peaceful assemblage.

Section 3. Congress shall have power, in such cases as it may deem proper, to provide a suitable oath or affirmation for citizens whose religious scruples prevent them from giving unqualified allegiance to the Constitution as herein amended.[45]

This resolution was taken with sufficient seriousness to call for public hearings by the Senate Committee on the Judiciary in May 1954. Fortunately the resolution was not reported out of the committee. The complexity of motivations behind the resolution is in part shown by the fact that Senator Flanders was the sponsor, in December 1954, of the motion of censure against Senator Joseph R. McCarthy.

Actions such as these cannot but damage and degrade religion by giving it supports that are artificial, that can never ring true. But unlike prayers and Bible-reading in schools, these statutes create only non-acts or shadows of acts and facts. A child's life is altered, is affected, in some way, by the prayers or other distinctively religious ceremonies in school. They have the impact on him—howsoever slight—of realities, actual events. But this is not true of the pledge of allegiance, except for the few whose consciences are touched by all such ceremonies, and certainly not true of the other examples cited. Yet if the Supreme Court had reversed the New York Court of Appeals and had held the reference to God in the pledge of allegiance a violation of the Establishment Clause, millions of Americans would have reacted with shock and anger. The Court surely has enough to do to limit its calendar to cases that are not made up of only make-believe events and happenings.

But there is an aspect of the tax-exemption problem that is likely to make trouble for the courts and for the churches if Congress should continue to exempt churches from the tax on "unrelated business income."[46]

When it became known that a leading university claimed exemption on profits it earned from a spaghetti factory, Congress in 1950 rewrote the law to restrict exemptions for most organizations to businesses that are "related" to the functions of the organizations; but the revision specifically excluded churches and allowed them, by this action, to go into "unrelated" businesses and to claim exemption from taxes on the profits earned by such businesses.

This special exemption of the church-owned "unrelated" businesses puts the matter outside Justice Brennan's classification of *"uniform* tax exemptions *incidentally* available to religious institutions," and affords the churches a *special* privilege, in violation of the Establishment Clause.

"The legal right of a taxpayer to decrease the amount of what otherwise would be his taxes," Justice Sutherland said, "or altogether avoid them, by means which the law permits, cannot be doubted."[47] But this right does not exist if the exemption allowed by Congress is in violation of the Establishment Clause—as I think the exemption of church-operated "unrelated" businesses is.

Some examples of the abuses of which some churches and church organizations are guilty have been publicly reported.[48] The Knights of Columbus, for instance, in 1953 bought the land under Yankee Stadium in a transaction that involved a lease back; and the organization also has department stores, warehouses, and a steel-tube mill among its assets of $200,000,000. Three Protestant churches of Bloomington, Illinois, in 1952 bought from Hilton a hotel in Dayton, Ohio, and leased the hotel back to Hilton; in 1963 title was transferred back to the original owners; the churches made a profit of almost a half-million dollars. A Baptist church in Los Angeles owns an office building and the Philharmonic Auditorium.

The case of the Christian Brothers has attracted some attention. The religious order operates a winery in Napa Valley, California, that sells over a million cases of wines and brandies annually. Taking advantage of the fact that the business is operated under the name De LaSalle Institute and not under the name of the Roman Catholic Church, the federal authorities in 1961 collected $4,000,000 in back taxes. The levy was, it may be noted, vigorously opposed.

Two exceptions to these abusive practices are the Mormons, whose church owns many profitable businesses, on which it pays full federal, state, and local taxes, though it could claim exemption; and the Seventh Day Adventists, who have paid income taxes since 1951 on a large furniture and lumber company in Oregon (but they do not pay taxes on profits from their vegetarian food business, which sells products that Seventh Day Adventists buy for religious reasons, though this business competes with companies which pay the 52-per-cent corporate-income-tax rate to the federal government).

There are clear voices among churchmen, however, that protest strongly against the gross abuses that tend to bring religion into disrepute. In May 1963 the General Assembly of the United Presbyterian Church in the United States adopted a report of its Special Committee on Relations Between Church and State that contained the following significant provisions on tax exemptions:

The church has no theological ground for laying any claim upon the state for special favors. The church must regard special status or favored position as a hindrance to the fulfilling of its mission. . . . The church should know that it renders its witness ambiguous by its continued acceptance of special privileges from the state in the form of tax exemptions. . . .

In view of these considerations, the Special Committee on Church and State *recommends* that:

a. United Presbyterians study the nature of our Church's involvement in economic activity and seek ways by which it can begin the process of extricating itself from the position of being obligated, or seeming to be obligated to the state by virtue of special tax privileges extended to it.

b. The United Presbyterian Church carefully examine its national and local related business enterprises to assure itself that under present tax laws these enterprises are not unfairly competitive with secular business operating in the same fields. . . .

c. The United Presbyterian Church continue efforts to obtain repeal of the section of the Internal Revenue Code that allows "churches and church organizations" exemption from the corporate income tax on profits from businesses unrelated to the purpose of activity of the church or church organization.

d. Congregations be encouraged to take the initiative in making contributions to local communities in lieu of taxes, in recognition of police, fire, and other services provided by local government. This consideration commends itself especially to well-established and financially stable churches and particularly to those communities where tax problems are developing due, in part, to the increase in exempted properties for all purposes— educational, governmental, charitable, and religious. . . .[49]

This action of the United Presbyterian Church, which has over nine thousand churches, including 75 per cent of all Presbyterians,[50] may well prefigure new and amazing developments in church-state attitudes and practices on the part of churchmen of all denominations. After the dust raised by the Supreme Court decisions in the Regents' Prayer case and Bible-reading cases has settled, it may be that the spirit of discomfiture and chagrin will be replaced by a "sweet reasonableness" such as that found in the General Assembly of the United Presbyterian Church and in some other church groups.

The United Presbyterian Church was willing, in 1963, to question other church-state relations which Justice Brennan—and perhaps most of us, too—assumed as fixed and unalterable. For example, on the matter of the legal exemption from military service of ministers and divinity students, the report stated:

The right of the state to call citizens to, or defer them from, military duty for the good and freedom of the whole society is not here questioned. No class of citizens, as such, has an inherent right to claim exemption from this duty. The fact that a man serves God, or aspires to serve him, in a church vocation does not in itself excuse him from the responsibility shared by all citizens for the defense and security of the state. Ministers and candidates for the ministry, as citizens, have no ground for claiming any special status from the state that differs from that of scientists, physicians, policemen, farmers, machinists, etc. . . .[51]

The report also expressly recognized that state pay for military chaplains "raises serious questions and represents an unsolved problem in the relations between church and state," and therefore called for a conference to consider "whether a way may be found out of this impasse. . . ."[52]

The *religious*—apart from the constitutional—justification of the Supreme Court's decisions regarding prayers and Bible-reading in schools appears clearly from these recommendations in the United Presbyterian report: That

United Presbyterians actively strive to recapture from popular custom the observance of religious holidays in order to restore their deepest religious meaning.

Since the association of seasonal activities with religious holidays in the public schools tends to pervert their religious significance, such association be discouraged as foreign to the purpose of the public school.

Religious holidays be acknowledged and explained, but never celebrated religiously, by public schools or their administrators when acting in an official capacity.

Whenever possible, students of various religious faiths should be allowed sufficient time to permit the celebration of their religious observances away from public school property. However, organized religious groups should avoid jeopardizing the integrity of the public educational process by unreasonable demands for time away from public school for any reason.

Religious observances never be held in a public school or introduced into the public school as part of its program. Bible reading in connection with courses in the American heritage, world history, literature, the social sciences, and other academic subjects is completely appropriate to public school instruction. Bible reading and prayers as devotional acts tend toward indoctrination or meaningless ritual and should be omitted for both reasons. . . .[53]

Since these history-making actions of the United Presbyterian Church, other important voices have also been heard to support the spirit and principles of the Supreme Court decisions and to extend them—as the Presbyterians have done—into areas in which the Court has not acted.

In February 1964, a National Study Conference on Church and State, held at Columbus, Ohio, was convened by the National Council of the Churches of Christ in the United States (which coordinates the activities of thirty-one denominations, with a total membership of forty million). The Columbus conference was attended by over three hundred delegates.

Relating specifically to the Court decisions regarding prayers and Bible-reading, the conference report stated that "Christians should welcome the decisions," which are "far from being anti-religious." For

Christians do not believe that the question of authentic religion can ever be decided by formal rites and words alone. . . . In addition, the decisions are consistent with our concern for the religious liberty of all men. . . .[54]

The report forthrightly stated that

Distinctly religious observances (e.g., nativity pageants and baccalaureate services) are properly functions of the Church and are not to be included among the proper functions of the public school. . . . Even in homogeneous communities where traditional observances are still carried on, churches need to consider whether such activities strengthen or weaken the distinctive witness of the church. . . .[55]

Regarding tax exemption, the report stated that the theories that can be used to justify it do *not*, however, justify either of the following:

(1) The exemption from taxation of religious institutions to the extent of their cost to their government.
(2) The preferential treatment of any or all religious institutions over other institutions which primarily function charitably or in the cultivation and transmission of ideas and values.

The report recommended that employment-tax laws be made fully applicable to churches and that church exemptions from excise taxes be eliminated, and expressed disapproval of the exemption of churches from income taxes on unrelated businesses.[56]

There can be little doubt, I think, that the Supreme Court opinions, starting with the Everson case in 1947, have played a *teaching* role, the importance of which can hardly be overstated. It was not, however, until 1963 and 1964, after the decisions in the Engel and Schempp and Murray cases, that organized Protestant church bodies showed, by forthright and courageous pronouncements, that they stood with the Court on the principle of separation and that they were willing themselves to apply the principle to untested issues. When the Engel and Bible-reading cases went before the Court, it was only the Jewish, Ethical Culture, and Humanist groups that filed briefs supporting the principle of separation, and these groups—especially the Jewish organizations—stood exposed to intemperate and wild charges from churchmen of various denominations, and were in danger of economic and social reprisals.[57] This experience only proved once more that it is action by minority groups that leads to vindication of constitutional liberties which are for the enjoyment of all Americans. In recent decades it was the work of the Jehovah's Witnesses, of the Jewish organizations, and of the N.A.A.C.P. that contributed so heavily to the emergence, clarification, or implementation of fundamental rights and liberties. But the teaching aspect of the work of these groups—and especially of the Supreme Court—is what, in the long run, counts; for unless the decisions of the Court permeate the thoughts and feelings of the mass of American citizens, the decisions can be wounds to the body politic, forces that divide the people into opposing, distrusting, and even hating camps. The "wall of separation" decisions could have become a wall of separation dividing neighbor from neighbor, denomination from denomination. This has not happened; on the contrary, the churches have learned to read the Supreme Court opinions as important lessons on the spirit, duties, and opportunities of churches. Just as the decision in the school-segregation case inspired the churches and brought them to the realization of their duties and opportunities as *religious* witnesses to fundamental truths, so too, though less spectacularly, have the decisions on the Establishment Clause contributed to new vitality of thought in the life of the churches. In the history of religion in American life, the work of the Supreme Court decisions will need to be reckoned among the great liberating works of the spirit—perhaps they will rank in importance with the work of Pope John XXIII in their spiritual effects on the churches of all denominations.

Perhaps the history of the Sunday-law cases bears out this point even more clearly.

In a case decided in 1902, Justice Oliver Wendell Holmes cynically observed that "Sunday laws, no doubt, would be sustained by a bench of judges, even if every one of them thought it superstitious to make any day holy."[58] Sixty years later the Supreme Court obligingly fulfilled his prophecy.

In the United States, Sunday-closing laws can easily be traced back to the colonial "Lord's Day" laws. Their religious origin is too clear to be denied. Yet no one objected to them except Jews and Seventh Day Adventists, whose economic life was seriously affected. As far back as 1908 Louis Marshall pleaded in vain with the New York legislature to adopt the following principle:

No person who observes the seventh day of the week as the Sabbath, and actually refrains from secular business and labor on that day, shall be liable to prosecution for carrying on secular business or performing labor on Sunday, provided public worship is not thereby disturbed.[59]

Until recently, the seventh-day observers had no substantial outside support, but in the last few years unwelcome and embarrassing support came from certain commercial interests. The exodus to the suburbs gave rise to the highway discount houses and shopping centers, which found Sunday especially attractive for retail sales and shopping. Their activities brought the Sunday laws to the front pages. It was not a matter now of religious observance, but rather competition with city merchants, whose shops were closed on Sunday. It was estimated that in 1962 discount houses took in $800,000,000 in Sunday sales. City merchants brought pressure on state and city officials to enforce vigorously dormant "blue laws" or to enact tougher legislation. Some legislatures responded sympathetically. Aiding these city merchants were some labor unions—and some church groups, especially from churches associated with the Lord's Day Alliance.

In time four cases developed for Supreme Court consideration, in which these mixed values of commerce and religion had to be faced, separated, and evaluated. The cases, which were consolidated in the Supreme Court, involved attacks on the Pennsylvania and Maryland statutes by a highway discount house, and attacks on the Pennsylvania and Massachusetts statutes by Jewish merchants who kept their places of business closed on Saturday for religious reasons.[60] The Justices wrote eight opinions, in about fifty thousand words, reflecting the complexity of the issues. In the cases brought by the Orthodox Jewish merchants, briefs were filed by the Synagogue Council of America and other leading Jewish groups, the General Conference of Seventh Day Adventists, and the American Civil Liberties Union.

The Court upheld the constitutionality of the closing laws. In the two cases involving the discount house and its employees, the vote was 8 to 1, with Justice Douglas dissenting. In the other two cases—those involving the Orthodox Jewish storekeepers—the vote was 6 to 3, with Justices Douglas, Brennan, and Stewart dissenting. Chief Justice Earl Warren wrote the majority opinion in each of the four cases. Justice Frankfurter wrote a long concurring opinion. One of the odd facts is that Justice Black, who generally takes an "absolutist" position in cases involving First Amendment freedoms, voted with the majority to uphold laws which three Associate Justices found to be infringements of religious liberty.

The majority held that, even though it was clear that originally the Sunday laws were intended to aid the Christian religion, "as presently written and administered, most of them, at least, are of a secular rather than a religious character." Their purpose is to provide a uniform day of rest. The fact that the day chosen by the legislature is a day that has special significance for the dominant Christian denominations "does not bar the State from achieving . . . [the law's] secular goals." The statutes do not, therefore, "establish" Sunday as a religious institution, but are, rather, an expression of the states' interest in the "health, safety, recreation and general well-being of our citizens."

As to the claims of the Jewish merchants, the majority observed that the statutes do not "make unlawful any [of their] religious practices," for they may close their shops in accordance with their religious beliefs. The six Justices recognized the economic burden involved in a compulsory two-day closing, but this is an indirect effect of a law that regulates a secular activity—this is not the purpose of the law. This indirect effect makes the practice of Orthodox Judaism more expensive, but is not, for this reason, a prohibition on the free exercise of religion.

Opponents of the laws showed that thirteen of the fifty states have no Sunday laws prohibiting work or sales; that thirty-one states restrict work or labor on Sunday, but twenty-one of these states grant exemptions to persons who observe another day as their Sabbath, as far as work or labor is concerned; that thirty-seven states restrict sales or commerce on Sunday, only few of which make provision for the seventh-day Sabbatarian. The contention was made that the *secular* ends of the Sunday laws in the thirty-seven states could be achieved even if they were to exempt the seventh-day observers.

The majority of the Court rejected this argument, saying that, while such an exemption may well be "the wiser solution to the problem," the Court's concern was not with the wisdom of the legislation but only with its constitutionality.

In his dissenting opinion Justice Brennan said that the laws, as they affected the Jewish merchants in their two cases, were in fact a "clog upon the exercise of religion" and a "state-imposed burden on Orthodox Judaism," making that religion "economically disadvantageous"; and Justice Stewart added that these laws compel an Orthodox Jew "to choose between his religious faith and his economic survival. That is a cruel choice"—one which no state may constitutionally demand. Justice Douglas shared this view that the laws violated the constitutional prohibition upon interference with the free exercise of religion, and argued that by them the states compelled minorities "to observe a second Sabbath, not their own," and thus preferred one religion over another, "contrary to the command of the Constitution." But he went further and said that the laws were also an establishment of religion by putting behind the practice of one religious group the sanction of the law. "No matter how much is written, no matter what is said," Justice Douglas wrote, "the parentage of these laws is the Fourth Commandment; and they serve and satisfy the religious dispositions of our Christian communities."

The majority left the door open for the possibility of another attack on the laws by saying: "We do not hold that Sunday legislation may not be a violation of the 'Establishment' Clause if it can be demonstrated that its purpose—evidenced either on the face of the legislation, in conjunction with its legislative history, or in its operative effect—is to use the State's coercive power to aid religion." But the briefs in these cases probably went as far as was possible to meet these conditions, yet failed to convince anyone on the Court but Justice Douglas, and so it may be gravely doubted if the Court will disestablish Sunday.

Eight of the Justices were in agreement that a state has the power to set one day of the week apart from the others "as a day of rest, repose, recreation and tranquillity—a day when the hectic tempo of everyday existence ceases and a more pleasant atmosphere is created, a day which all members of the family and community have the opportunity to spend and enjoy together, a day in which people may visit friends and relatives who are not available during working days, a day when the weekly laborer may best regenerate himself." These words of Chief Justice Warren say nothing about religion or religious acts. They state the case for a day of rest, whether that day be Sunday in the United States, Saturday in Israel, or Friday in Syria—a uniform day of rest as a *civil* institution. Justice Frankfurter, in his concurring opinion, referred to the interest of the International Labor Organization in a uniform day of rest—laws that ensure that "the weekly rest is taken at the same time by all workers on the day established by tradition or custom . . . to enable the workers to take part in the life of the community and in the special forms of recreation which are available on certain days." Justice Frankfurter pointed out that to require persons to rest one day a week, but to leave it to each person to choose which day it should be—any one of seven days—would provide a periodic physical rest, but "not that atmosphere of entire community repose which Sunday has traditionally brought and which, a legislature might reasonably believe, is necessary to the welfare of those who for many generations have been accustomed to its recuperative effects."

As if intended as a rebuke to the Supreme Court for not deciding that laws that compel closing only on Sunday are still, as they were in their origin, an establishment of religion and a violation of both the Establishment and the Free Exercise Clauses, the United Presbyterian Church in 1963 affirmed

its conviction that the church itself bears sole and vital responsibility for securing from its members a voluntary observance of the Lord's Day. The church should not seek, or even appear to seek, the coercive power of the state in order to facilitate Christians' observance of the Lord's Day.

The church is also concerned about persons who suffer economic injustice because of the inner constraint of religious conscience and the external coercion of the law. The church is aware that many who press for the seven-day commercial week . . . appear to be motivated primarily by economic self-interest. . . . However, any efforts by the church to strengthen existing Sunday closing laws would almost certainly be widely construed as the church's seeking its own interest.

Its Special Committee on Church and State recommended that:

United Presbyterians not try to make existing laws more stringent in their prohibitions of Sunday activities, nor seek to pass such laws where they do not exist. . . .

United Presbyterians carefully investigate the effect of existing Sunday closing laws on persons who, because of their faith, voluntarily cease economic activity on a day other than Sunday, and are required by law to cease their economic activity on Sunday as well. United Presbyterians should seek amendments exempting such persons from Sunday laws as a part of an authentic concern about their fellow men.[61]

The report of the National Study Conference, conducted by the National Council of Churches, went even further when it reached the following conclusions regarding Sunday laws:

We speak . . .

c. *to our government*

1) We disclaim any desire to seek legislation, or to support continuance of existing law, wherever its effect is to provide special protection or privilege for ourselves or for any other segment of our society on the basis of religious preferment or tradition. . . .

2) Because we are convinced of the necessity of one day's rest in seven for all people, we urge legislation requiring that all businesses and industries regularly be closed for a previously and publicly self-announced day each week. . . .

3) In view of the generally accepted principle of a five-day work week we recommend that the law provide that one of the days free from labor for each employed person be selected at the discretion of such employee as his day of rest or worship.

4) We recommend that wherever the principle of a common day of rest remains established in the law, thus tending to create an inequitable situation for those who keep another day of rest, such law be so rewritten or construed as to seek to remove such inequity.[62]

There can be no doubt that the churchmen who wrote and accepted these reports were not impressed with the opinions of the Justices who made up the majority in the Sunday-law cases but were persuaded by the dissenting opinions of Justices Douglas, Brennan, and Stewart.

Yet one cannot help wondering why it was that, before these cases were decided in 1961, and before the dissenting opinions were made a part of the public record, their voices were not heard on the side of reason, justice, and the principle of separation. These events—like those respecting the Regents' Prayer case and the Bible-reading cases —are evidence of the effectiveness of the Supreme Court as a liberating intellectual and spiritual force. Even when churchmen disapproved of the decision, they felt themselves compelled to think deeply and speak honestly, in consonance with their religious convictions and American ideals.

Admittedly, the first reactions after the Court announced its decision outlawing the Regents' Prayer were abusive of the Court. Billy Graham cried out, "God pity our country when we can no longer appeal to God for help!" And James A. Pike, Protestant Episcopal Bishop of California, lamented that the Court had "deconsecrated the nation." Former Presidents Hoover and Eisenhower spoke out against the decision; and, at the annual Governors' Conference, only Governor Rockefeller refused to vote for a resolution attacking the decision and calling for a constitutional amendment to overrule it. Cardinal Spellman said that he was "shocked and frightened" and that the decision struck "at the very heart of the Godly tradition in which America's children have for so long been raised." And Bishop Fulton J. Sheen observed that "Our schools are now officially put on the same level as the Communist schools. In neither may one pray. . . ."[63]

By the spring of 1964, 147 resolutions had been introduced in the House of Representatives calling for a constitutional amendment to overrule the Supreme Court's decision in the Engel and Schempp and Murray cases. The House Judiciary Committee held hearings during seven weeks in 1964; but, contrary to the expectations of the sponsors, the great weight of the testimony was in opposition to the resolutions. Spokesmen of the National Council of Churches, the United Presbyterian Church, the American Baptist Convention, the American Lutheran Church and the Lutheran Church–Missouri Synod, the Protestant Episcopal Church, the Disciples of Christ, Jewish, and other religious groups opposed the resolutions. The Roman Catholic Church took no stand; but after the hearings the Legal Department of the National Catholic Welfare Conference made known its position against amendment; and the Catholic Press Association, at its convention in April 1964, adopted a resolution against tampering with the First Amendment. The House Judiciary Committee refused to report out any of the resolutions.[64] Thus the initial reaction against the decisions had undergone a radical change, and the spirit and the reach of the religious freedom clauses were more widely and deeply understood and respected than ever before.

"The first word," Paul Tillich has written, "to be spoken by religion to the people of our time must be a word spoken against religion."[65] The experience with the Sunday-closing laws, and with prayers and Bible-reading in the schools and other intrusions by Caesar into the realm of God, has shown that the real enemies of the authentic, living human spirit are those who would misuse, exploit, and subject God to their own petty purposes—men who, frequently taking God's name in vain, serve idols of their own creation. As in the days of Elijah and

Jeremiah, the true prophets must expose and struggle against the false prophets; and so religion must speak against religion, against those who confuse religion with patriotism, Caesar with God.

In this struggle, paradoxically, authentic religion has found its strongest ally in one of the branches of Caesar's realm, the United States Supreme Court. Like an artist, the Court has taken parts of reality and experience which we hardly or seldom had noticed, and has given them shape and form. Many people, seeing the representations, were at first shocked; the Court, they thought, should perform only a single task—to copy, to repeat, to repeat; but what they saw looked to their eyes avant-gardist. But only haters of life insist on life as mere repetition. Forces of life live by creating, by using the old to create the new, by interfusing the old and the new. The Court, in the church-state cases, even when its work showed obvious imperfections and failures, dealt with reality and experience in such ways that its work compelled men to think, rethink, feel, and reorder their own sense of reality and experience. Its work has had similar effect in other fields too—civil rights and the administration of criminal justice come readily to mind—but the impact of its work on religion and religious institutions is likely to be the most notable and enduring, for there it spoke directly to what is most vital and valuable to and in the spirit of man.

The old Roman phrase that sometimes guided both state and church was *coge intrare*—"force them to enter." Under the double protection of the First Amendment's Free Exercise and Establishment Clauses, the world has, for the first time, seen how religions can flourish and the state exist and thrive when church and state each tends to its own business and fulfills its own mission.

Perhaps no single event in American history so dramatically articulated this aspect of American life as did the election of John Fitzgerald Kennedy as President of the United States.

Roman Catholics have been governors of states and members of Congress and of cabinets, and as far back as 1836 President Jackson was not kept from appointing Roger B. Taney as Chief Justice of the Supreme Court, to succeed John Marshall, though he knew that Taney was a devout Catholic. But it was not until 1928 that a political party ventured to nominate a Roman Catholic for President of the United States. Alfred E. Smith was a devout Catholic, and this fact played a prominent, and perhaps decisive, part in the campaign and in his defeat.

In the course of the campaign, Smith felt compelled to meet the religious issue by a statement[66] in which he showed that during his eight years as governor of New York the public school appropriations had gone up from $9,000,000 to $82,000,000; that he had taken leadership in pressing for legislation on behalf of women and children, though at that time such legislation aroused considerable controversy within the Catholic Church and among Catholics; and that he had defended the constitutional liberties of unpopular men who were under attack in the period of war-hysteria and the Red scare.

It had been suggested that, as President, Smith might face conflicts between his religious principles and public duty. If there were such a conflict, how, asked Smith, would a Protestant resolve it? "Obviously," he answered, "by the dictates of his conscience." Well, said Smith, "that is exactly what a Catholic would do."

More than thirty years later Kennedy met the same questions, challenges, and prejudices, and his position was essentially the same as Smith's. In an address before the Greater Ministerial Association in Houston, Texas, a state in which his candidacy had been under strong Protestant attack, Kennedy took up the challenge. He said:

Whatever issue may come before me as President—on birth control, divorce, censorship, gambling or any other subject—I will make my decision in accordance with what my conscience tells me to be the national interest, and without regard to outside religious pressures or dictates.[67]

He concluded his address by saying that if he should lose the election on "the real issues," he would return to his place in the Senate, but, he added,

If this is decided on the basis that 40,000,000 Americans lost their chance of being President on the day they were baptized, it is the whole nation that will be the loser in the eyes of Catholics and non-Catholics around the world, in the eyes of history, and in the eyes of our people.

The precise role of religion in the election of 1960 is difficult to assess.[68] But it is hardly subject to dispute that Kennedy's election was the clearest implementation and vindication of Article VI of the Constitution, which provides that "no religious test shall ever be required as a qualification to any office or public trust under the United States," and of the religious-liberty provisions of the First Amendment.

It would be no exaggeration to claim, however, that the spirit of religious liberty which was confirmed by the election of President Kennedy had been formed and strengthened, to no small degree, by the Supreme Court of the United States.

II

Freedom of Association

1. A Nation of Joiners

There is no doubt that Americans are "a nation of joiners."[1] To dissuade potential suicide victims, there is the National Save-a-Life League. To look after the interests of airplane passengers, there is the Airways Club. To win public acceptance of homosexuals as a legitimate minority group, there is the Mattachine Society. To stop telephone companies from substituting numbers for names of exchanges, there is the Anti Digit Dialing League. There are numerous clubs of walkers and hikers. There is the American Society of Hoboes; and there is the exclusive club of nonconformists known as The Dissenters. Thus even professed nonjoiners form themselves into associations of nonjoiners.

The American proclivity to form and join organizations has been noted with wonder by almost every student of the American character. Tocqueville, who visited the United States for nine months in 1831–1832, observed that in no country in the world "has the principle of association been more successfully used or applied to a greater multitude of objects than in America." Societies, he said, "are formed to resist evils that are exclusively of a moral nature, as to diminish the vice of intemperance."[2] (At that time, when the population of the United States was about 13,000,000, the American Temperance Society had a membership of 1,200,000, organized in 8000 local affiliates.)[3] In the United States, Tocqueville went on.

associations are established to promote the public safety, commerce, industry, morality, and religion. There is no end which the human will despairs of attaining through the combined power of individuals united into a society.[4]

Besides political associations and commercial and manufacturing companies, Tocqueville noted

48

associations of a thousand other kinds, religious, moral, serious, futile, general or restricted, enormous or diminutive. The Americans make associations to give entertainments, to found seminaries, to build inns, to construct churches, to diffuse books, to send missionaries to the antipodes. . . . If it is proposed to inculcate some truth or to foster some feeling by the encouragement of a great example, they form a society. Whenever at the head of some new undertaking you see the government in France, or a man of rank in England, in the United States you will be sure to find an association.[5]

The first time, he said, that he heard that a hundred thousand Americans "had bound themselves publicly" to abstain from liquor, it appeared to him "more like a joke than a serious engagement," for he did not see why "these temperate citizens could not content themselves with drinking water by their own firesides"; for had these men lived in France, each of them singly would have written to his government "to watch the public houses all over the kingdom"; but he learned that as soon as several Americans

have taken up an opinion or a feeling which they wish to promote in the world, they look for mutual assistance; and as soon as they have found one another out, they combine. From that moment they are no longer isolated men, but a power seen from afar, whose actions serve for an example and whose language is listened to.[6]

Some fifty years later Lord Bryce[7] largely confirmed Tocqueville's observations. Associations, Bryce noted, were

created, extended, and worked in the United States more quickly and effectively than in any other country. In nothing does the executive talent of the people better shine than in the promptitude wherewith the idea of an organization for a common object is taken up. . . .[8]

In 1906, two years after his visit in the United States, Max Weber refuted the German view of Americans as a nation of "atomized individuals." "In the past and up to the very present," he wrote, "it has been a characteristic precisely of the specifically American democracy that it did *not* constitute a formless sand heap of individuals, but rather a buzzing complex of strictly exclusive, yet voluntary associations."[9]

The picture in the middle of the twentieth century was not, in essentials, different. If individualism, in some significant sense, characterizes American life, it is of a special kind that has been described as "group individualism."[10] If anything, the role of the large formal organization "has enormously increased during the last fifty years."[11] In his comprehensive review of American life and society at mid-century, Max Lerner concluded that

The associative impulse is strong in American life: no other civilization can show as many secret fraternal orders, businessmen's "service clubs," trade and occupational associations, social clubs, garden clubs, women's clubs, church clubs, theater groups, political and reform associations, veterans' groups, ethnic societies, and other clusterings of trivial or substantial importance.[12]

While it is probably still true, as it was when Tocqueville wrote, that no nation compares with the United States as "a nation of joiners," there is some evidence that this aspect of American civilization—like more tangible features—is being duplicated in the experience of other nations, at least insofar as concerns the use of pressure groups;[13] but association remains a distinguishable and significant characteristic of American society.[14]

2. This Perilous Liberty[15]

Despite this proclivity of Americans to form or join associations, it was not until 1958, in *National Association for the Advancement of Colored People* v. *Alabama*,[16] that the United States Supreme Court, for the first time, directly recognized freedom of association as a liberty guaranteed by the First Amendment.[17] Fully to appreciate the significance of this holding will require, as background, an understanding of some historical and theoretical conditions.

Nowhere in the Bill of Rights of the Constitution is association mentioned; and the omission was not due to bungling or an oversight. No draft of the Bill of Rights submitted by James Madison, nor any amendment proposed by any other member of Congress, which debated the Bill of Rights in 1789, mentioned association.[18] Indeed, Madison's best-known contribution to *The Federalist* is an attack on voluntary associations, political or economic, which he called "factions."[19] Madison was well aware of the "propensity to this dangerous vice," which he defined as a number of citizens, whether a majority or a minority, "who are united and actuated by some common impulse of passion, or of interest, adverse to the rights of other citizens, or to the permanent and aggregate interests of the community"; and he complained that "a factious spirit" had already "tainted our public administrations." Factions, Madison argued, thrive on liberty: "Liberty is to faction what air is to fire." A society can therefore prevent factions by denying liberty. This was not, of course, what the Constitution proposed to do. Nor did the constitutional scheme propose to prevent factions by "giving to every citizen the same opinions, the same passions, and the same interests"—through *Gleichschaltung*. No, to proceed in these ways was to truncate the very "nature of man," in which are to be found the causes of faction. The cure for "the mischiefs of faction" was to control its effects.

Just how the Constitution was going to accomplish this happy result is not a question that is relevant to our discussion, which intends only to show that Madison, thinking of associations as the effects of a dangerous, and even vicious—albeit natural—human propensity, was not one to urge a constitutional guarantee of freedom of association.

Washington, in his Farewell Address[20]—one of the most influential of public papers—reiterated Madison's point and warned the American people "in the most solemn manner against the baneful effects of the spirit of party generally." This spirit, he said, "unfortunately, is inseparable from our nature . . ." but it is "a spirit not to be encouraged," for there is "constant danger of excess." This spirit

agitates the community with ill-founded jealousies and false alarms; kindles the animosity of one part against another; ferments occasionally riot and insurrection. . . . A fire not to be quenched, it demands a uniform vigilance to prevent its bursting into flame, lest, instead of warming, it should consume.

As we know that Washington submitted a draft of the Address to Madison and received suggestions from him,[21] the emphasis and spirit of these statements are not surprising.

Nor is it surprising that the Founding Fathers felt hostile toward the idea of voluntary associations. The roots of this hostility were deeply embedded in the history of political theory.

Hobbes in the *Leviathan* warned against "the things that weaken or tend to the dissolution of a commonwealth," and against "the great number of corporations which are as it were many lesser commonwealths in the body of a greater, like worms in the entrails of a natural man."[22] He conceded the legitimacy of the municipal corporation and the company of merchants, but only because they enjoyed the Crown's letters patent and so were creatures of the state. In addition, there are, said Hobbes, lawful private associations, which are lawful because not expressly prohibited; but the only example of this species cited is the family. All other associations are unlawful; his condemnation is sweeping:

Factions for government of religion, as of Papists, Protestants, etc. or of state, as patricians, and plebeians, of old Rome, and of aristocalls and democraticalls of old time in Greece, are unjust, as being contrary to the peace and safety of the people, and a taking of the sword out of the hand of the Sovereign.[23]

The central conception of Hobbes, to which almost everything else in his theory was consequential, was his stark individualism, an application of materialism and atomism to human beings and society. "The absolute power of the sovereign," as Professor George H. Sabine noted,

was really the necessary complement of his own individualism. . . . There is no middle ground between humanity as a sand-heap of separate organisms and the state as an outside power holding them precariously together by the sanctions with which it supplements individual motives. All the rich variety of associations disappears, or is admitted suspiciously and grudgingly as carrying a threat to the power of the state. It is a theory natural to an age which saw the wreck of so many of the traditional associations and institutions of economic and religious life. . . .[24]

Locke's views, which influenced greatly the writing of the Declaration of Independence, the Constitution, and the Bill of Rights, also tended to disparage associations, but for a reason opposite to that of Hobbes. As Hobbes made the sovereign the monopolist of all rights and liberties, Locke placed all rights and liberties in the individual. The individuals, by free consent, made the community, and then they made the government; but community and government were limited by the inherent and inalienable rights, which were vested innately and indefeasibly by God.

Men, according to Locke, have two kinds of concerns: secular or civil, and sacred or other-worldly. They form a civil society only "for the procuring, preserving, and advancing" of their civil interests—life, liberty, and property. In the same way, by consent and compact, they may form a church, which, Locke said, is "a voluntary society of men, joining themselves together of their own accord" in order to worship God in such manner as they see fit and in order to achieve "the salvation of their souls." The church—since, by definition, it had no civil or secular or this-worldly concerns—"is a thing absolutely separate and distinct from the commonwealth."[25] Churches were, therefore, voluntary associations, which men had an inherent and inalienable right to form.

But, it should be noted, Locke's individualism left no room for rights vested in these or any associations. The rights and liberties were —and remained—in the individuals. (As we shall see, this point became important in American constitutional development.)

Locke was not interested in developing a general theory of associations beyond establishing the principle of separation of church and state, and the principle that churches are voluntary associations beyond the reach of government (though it would be more correct to say that men as churchmen were beyond the reach of government). Was the state competent to ban or control all other associations that could be classified as falling within the (civil) interests of men as citizens? Or did Locke think that "the individual has a natural and inalienable right to associate"?[26] It is not possible to say. Locke left a literary and philosophical heritage of rich complexities, ambiguities, and paradoxes, which later made some vexing constitutional issues that are by no means altogether resolved.

Rousseau, perhaps more clearly than Hobbes or Locke, denigrated association. Every association, Rousseau argued, creates a "general will" for its members; but in relation to the state or other associations, it creates only "a particular will"; and if men vote to express the "general will" of their associations, rather than each man his "particular will," "it may then be said that there are no longer as many votes as there are men, but only as many as there are associations." What, then, is best for society? Rousseau's answer was clear enough: "It is therefore essential, if the general will is to be able to express itself, that there should be no partial society [i.e., voluntary associations] within the state, and that each citizen should think only his own thoughts."[27]

In his *Sur l'économie politique*, written four years before the *Contrat social*, Rousseau stated the argument forcefully:

Every political society is composed of other smaller societies of various kinds, each of which has its interest and rules of conduct. . . . All individuals who are united by a common interest compose as many others, either temporary or permanent, whose influence is none the less real because it is less apparent. . . . The influence of all these tacit or formal associations causes by the influence of their will as many modifications of the public will. The will of these particular societies has always two relations; for the members of the association, it is a general will; for the great society,[28] it is a particular will; and it is often right with regard to the first object and wrong as to the second. An individual may be a devout priest, a brave soldier, or a zealous senator, and yet a bad citizen. A particular resolution my be advantageous to the smaller community, but pernicious to the greater. It is true that particular societies being always subordinate to the general society in preference to others, the duty of a citizen takes precedence of that of a senator, and a man's duty of that of a citizen; but unhappily personal interest is always found in inverse ratio to duty, and increases in proportion as the association grows narrower, and the engagement less sacred; which irrefragably proves that the most general will is always the most just also, and that the voice of the people is in fact the voice of God.[29]

Where members of an assembly are seduced by private interests, said Rousseau, an examination will disclose "a secret division, a tacit confederacy," so that the assembly is in fact divided into other bodies, the members of which act justly and honorably in respect of their respective associations, but their will is "unjust and bad with regard to the whole, from which each is thus dismembered."[30]

Translated into words much more familiar to Americans today, Rousseau in effect was saying that if associations or "factions" are permitted to be formed and to grow in self-esteem and power, it is inevitable that a partisan will rationalize his self-interest and will act on the principle that "What is good for General Motors [or whatever the 'faction'] is good for the country." It is best, then, that there be no "factions," and that "each citizen should think only his own thoughts."

But Rousseau was not sure that the best would in fact be obtained, and so he stated that if in fact there are to be associations, "it is best to have as many as possible and to prevent them from being unequal."[31]

As we saw, Madison essentially agreed with Rousseau in wishing that the American people would be free from the evil of factions; but he was a Lockean in his thoughts concerning religion and churches; and with respect to churches he placed great stress on what Rousseau added only as an afterthought with regard to all associations: If there are to be churches, and the American people are none the less to enjoy freedom of religion, then this happy result can be brought about only by a "multiplicity of sects . . . which is the best and only security for religious liberty in any society."[32] As a Lockean, Madison met no problem in putting the religion clauses into the First Amendment; but with respect to associations in general, he was a follower of Hobbes and Rousseau—whether or not he had read their works—as were apparently also the other members of the Congress that passed the Bill of Rights, to none of whom did it occur that it would be in the public interest to guarantee freedom of association—freedom of "factions."

3. The Locus of American Freedoms

In the light of this background of political theory, it is no wonder that, until very recently, it was by no means settled that associations, whether incorporated or unincorporated, could claim constitutional protection of their "life" or "liberty." The Fourteenth Amendment provides: "Nor shall any State deprive any *person* of life, liberty or property without due process of law" (italics supplied). Does "person" mean only a natural person? In 1907 the Supreme Court stated that "the liberty guaranteed by the Fourteenth Amendment against deprivation without due process of law is the liberty of natural, not artificial persons."[33] The Court, however, held corporations to be "persons" when it was a question of protection of property.[34]

The Court's difficulties in relation to this problem may be illustrated by the important case *Pierce* v. *Society of Sisters of the Holy Names*.[35] A 1922 Oregon statute prohibited parochial and private schools for children between eight and sixteen years of age. The Supreme Court held the act to be unconstitutional for depriving the Society of Sisters and the Hill Military Academy, each an Oregon corporation, of their property without due process of law. For a unanimous Court, Justice James C. McReynolds said:

Appellees are corporations, and therefore, it is said, they cannot claim for themselves the *liberty* which the Fourteenth Amendment guarantees. Accepted in the proper sense, this is true. . . . But they have *business and property* for which they claim protection. These are threatened with destruction. . . . This court has gone very far to protect against loss threatened by such action. . . .[36]

Thus, when this case was decided in 1925, the Supreme Court had in fact construed and applied the Due Process Clause of the Fourteenth Amendment to read as follows:

Nor shall any State deprive any *human being* of life, liberty or property without due process of law; nor shall any State deprive any corporation [or association] of property without due process of law.[37]

In 1937 Justice Black protested against this constitutional development, but the principle of his protest was not to put corporations under the protection of the Due Process Clause insofar as concerned their *liberty*, but rather to exclude their *property* from protection even as their liberty had been excluded. "Neither the history nor the language of the Fourteenth Amendment," he wrote, "justifies the belief that corporations are included within its protection."[38]

As recently as 1949 Justice Douglas, with the concurrence of Justice Black, argued that there was "no history, logic, or reason" that supported the view that corporations are protected by any clause—Privileges or Immunities, Due Process, or Equal Protection—of the Fourteenth Amendment, and that the cases that extended constitutional protection to corporate property should be overruled.[39]

While all the other Justices disregarded this argument of Justices Black and Douglas insofar as it related to constitutional protection of corporate property, it was problably taken into consideration when the question was whether an association could claim freedom of speech or assembly. In *Hague* v. *C.I.O.*,[40] an unincorporated labor organization and its officers (and the American Civil Liberties Union) sought to enjoin enforcement of the ordinance of Jersey City that prohibited public assembly on the streets or in the public buildings or parks without a permit. The authorities denied permits to hold public assemblies called for the purpose of organizing workers into unions, or to distribute pamphlets, or to rent a hall for a public meeting. The police stopped persons (including Roger Baldwin and Norman Thomas) as they entered the city, seized literature in their possession, and arrested or "deported" them. The Supreme Court, in a 5-to-2 decision, held the ordinance unconstitutional. But—and this is our main concern here—the Supreme Court dismissed the C.I.O. and the A.C.L.U. as parties, two of the Justices holding that these associations were not "citizens" under the Privileges or Immunities Clause of the Fourteenth Amendment, and two others holding that the associations had no right of free speech under the Due Process Clause. The Court permitted only the officers of the organizations, as natural persons, to maintain the action. Had the *property* rights of these associations been involved, they would have had the capacity to sue, for a corporation or an unincorporated association is a "person" with standing to sue to vindicate its property rights against a denial of due process.[41]

The only rationale for these decisions is that only individuals—natural persons—are vested with the inherent and inalienable rights that were in the minds of John Locke, Thomas Jefferson, James Madison, and all others who contributed to the framing and enactment of the

Bill of Rights, and especially the First Amendment, and of those responsible for the Fourteenth Amendment.

But the Court (not including Justices Black and Douglas) made an exception in favor of the property rights of corporations. The Court has never offered a rationale for the distinction between life and liberty, on the one hand, and property, on the other, in the face of the clear language of the Due Process Clause, which speaks of "life, liberty, or property."[42]

In giving these values equal dignity, the Fourteenth Amendment followed Locke, who spoke of "life, . . . liberty, or possessions,"[43] or of "lives, liberties and estates."[44] Sometimes Locke used the term "property" to mean "that property which men have in their persons as well as goods"[45]—a conception that may have influenced Madison to think that men have a property in their rights just as they have rights in their property.[46]

But gradually the Supreme Court moved toward the proposition that corporations—associations, incorporated or unincorporated—deserved as much constitutional protection of their "liberty" as of their "property." Justices Black and Douglas have been at least partly vindicated: the inequality in protection as between liberty and property was gradually eliminated; and in 1958 the Court took the final step of recognizing freedom of association as a First Amendment freedom, and thus broke away from the views of Madison and the other Founding Fathers, which had stood in the way of this constitutional development.

The first important step was taken in 1936. Louisiana imposed a special tax on the big-circulation newspapers. The nine affected publishers brought suit to enjoin enforcement of the act. The Supreme Court unanimously held the statute unconstitutional as an infringement of freedom of the press. Publishers are protected from the imposition of prejudicial "taxes on knowledge."[47]

The important thing to note here is that the newspapers were published by corporations, not by individuals, yet the Court simply assumed that corporations are entitled to the guarantee of liberty in the Due Process Clause, and made no mention of the earlier precedents to the contrary.

Again, in 1941 the Court had before it a case involving freedom of the press in which one of the parties was the corporate publisher of a newspaper, and the Court held that this freedom had been unconstitutionally infringed by the state.[48] Justice Frankfurter, who came on the bench in 1938, dissented and argued, among other things, that corporations cannot claim liberty under the Fourteenth Amendment, and observed that the majority was "strangely silent" on this issue.

Indeed, the Court has remained silent on this issue. It has simply acted. The rationale of the decisions can only be inferred or conjectured. But this is not difficult to do. In view of the fact that newspapers are largely owned and published by corporations,[49] the constitutional guarantee of freedom of the press would be a nullity if corporations were not recognized as "persons" entitled to "liberty."

Now one can push this line of argument another step and say that the "liberty" of newspaper publishers would be a nullity if their property were not also constitutionally protected, for without such protection a state's "taxes on knowledge" could well be confiscatory. At least in the case of corporations engaged in the communications industry it may be said that liberty and property are inextricably intertwined, so that one cannot be guaranteed without the other.[50]

In the light of these considerations, it is indeed strange that it was Justices Black and Douglas—the most consistent "liberals" and "activists" on the bench—who argued most strongly against the recognition of corporations as "persons" entitled to the guarantees of "life, liberty, or property" of the Fourteenth Amendment. Had the Supreme Court in the nineteenth century failed to protect the *property* of corporations, it is very doubtful if in the twentieth century it would have found a way to protect their *liberty;* and it is not possible to estimate how impoverished our civil liberties would be without these developments. For even our churches are not natural persons, and the title to church-owned property is not ordinarily in the name of an individual. Freedom of religion is dependent upon such tangible properties as church buildings, altars, cemeteries, which are physical possessions as well as religious symbols;[51] and freedom of the press is dependent upon buildings, printing presses, trucks, which are physical possessions without which freedom of the press could no more exist than can mind without body.

It is, of course, true that not every corporation or association needs the liberties guaranteed by the First and Fourteenth Amendments; their needs and interests are often entirely secular or financial. But cannot the same judgment be made of individuals? Are all natural persons really concerned to enjoy freedom of speech, press, and assembly? Yet what is guaranteed for the university professor must also be guaranteed for every John Doe. At this point the Equal Protection Clause cuts into the other guarantees, so that there are no have-nots when it comes to constitutional liberties and civil rights.[52] If a corporation owning a newspaper is entitled to property, so is General Motors or General Mills; and if the corporation—or association—is entitled to property, the same Constitution protects its liberty.

In 1952 the Supreme Court for the first time held that "the basic principles of freedom of speech and press applied to motion pictures."[53] It paid no attention to the fact that the claimant of this freedom, the movie producer, was a corporation. Had the Court placed motion pictures under the umbrella of the First and Fourteenth Amendments but limited the constitutional guarantees to natural persons, the two points of the decision would have canceled each other.

The locus of our basic freedoms is no longer only the isolated individual. They may be claimed, too, by associations, incorporated or unincorporated. This marks one of the most important—though largely unnoted—gains for civil liberties and civil rights in constitutional history.[54]

It should be noted, however, that what we have said is true of associations—incorporated or unincorporated—only with regard to the liberties and property rights protected by the Fourteenth Amendment. The Supreme Court has taken a contrary position in Fifth Amendment cases. A corporation or voluntary association is not a "person" within the meaning of the privilege against self-incrimination, and so may not invoke the guarantee of the Fifth Amendment. Officers of corporations or associations cannot refuse to produce corporate books or documents in their custody on the ground that these might incriminate the officers or the corporation.[55] There is nothing in the language of the Fifth Amendment that compels this result, for the Amendment provides that "No person . . . shall be compelled in any criminal case to be a witness against himself. . . ." The Court could have held that the term "person" here has as comprehensive a meaning as the same term has in the Fourteenth Amendment. But the complex problems involved in the Fifth Amendment privilege cannot be explored here.

4. A New First Amendment Freedom

The cases that we have discussed involved, almost without exception, corporations engaged in industry or commerce. Because members of an unincorporated association are personally liable for debts incurred by the association, it was in the interest of business to permit businessmen to form a corporation under a law that would limit the personal liability of the investors and would also facilitate the conduct of business. In time, associations organized for religious or charitable purposes followed the example of business. As we have seen, the A.C.L.U. is an incorporated association, and, as we shall soon see, this is true also of the N.A.A.C.P. The courts had no trouble in accommodating the business corporation and giving it full constitutional protection for its property and enterprise. We have seen that when a corporation's business was dependent upon its enjoyment of freedom of the press, the Supreme Court extended to it the "liberty" guaranteed by the First and Fourteenth Amendments. The benefits to civil liberties were merely by-products of the needs of the business corporation that the legal order tried to satisfy.

Let us look for another moment at the case of *Pierce* v. *Society of the Sisters of the Holy Names,*[56] decided by the Court in 1925. The real issue in the case was, of course, the right of parents to establish and conduct a parochial or private school and to send their children there instead of to a public school. But note the language of the unanimous opinion of the Supreme Court:

Appellee the Society of Sisters is an Oregon *corporation,* organized in 1880, with *power* to . . . establish and maintain academies or schools, and acquire necessary *real and personal property.* It has long devoted its *property* and effort to the secular and religious education and care of children, and has acquired the *valuable good will* of many parents and guardians. . . . It owns *valuable buildings.* . . . The *business is remunerative,*—the annual *income* from primary schools exceeds $300,000—and the *successful conduct* of this requires long-time *contracts* with teachers and parents. The . . . Act of 1922 has already caused the withdrawal from its schools of children who would otherwise continue, and their *income* has steadily declined. . . .

The non-pecuniary religious dedication of the Society of Sisters of the Holy Names had to be translated into a purely business, profit-making effort—as if the society were in the business of making shoes—in order to secure constitutional status and protection. The First Amendment freedoms had to be sneaked in through a back door while the constitutional watchdogs were not looking—or were looking only at the "property" and the "business." What beautiful use Karl Marx could have made of this and similar cases to prove his charge that democratic liberties were only elements of an ideology that was bourgeois root and branch, and that they were tolerated only as they were consistent with a social order dominated by commercial and industrial interests.

Perhaps the most important constitutional development since 1937, which has become clear only since Earl Warren became Chief Justice in 1953, is the freeing of fundamental liberties from dependence on property and business principles of law and constitutionalism. American civil liberties and civil rights now generally have independent status. It was considered necessary by Congress,[57] in enacting the Civil Rights Act of 1964, to base the public-accommodations section on the constitutional power of Congress to regulate commerce among the several states, rather than on the broad, basic rights provisions of the Fourteenth Amendment—as if Congress were doing nothing really different from regulating the movement of cattle or freight from state to state. But the 1964 act is a special case and requires separate consideration as an exception to the new dignity and sanction that have been won for basic human rights.

And perhaps no case can better serve as a symbol of this development than *N.A.A.C.P.* v. *Alabama*,[58] decided in 1958, for a consideration of which we have prepared ourselves by our discussion up to this point.

The N.A.A.C.P. was chartered by the State of New York in 1909 as a nonprofit membership corporation. In 1962 it had nearly 400,000 members in fifty states and the District of Columbia. These were organized in approximately 1600 local units. (Since the charge has often been made by Southern leaders that the Association is a Northern organization that "invades" the South to "agitate" the Southern Negro, it may be noted that in 1962 the Association had 479 local branches in thirteen Southern and Border states and the District of Columbia, with a membership of 114,227.)[59] Its budget in 1962 was approximately $1,250,000.[60]

The Association opened local branches in Alabama in 1918, and by 1956—the crucial year for the case we are discussing—it had in that state 58 branches and a membership of nearly 15,000. Each local branch is an unincorporated association. In 1951 the Association opened in Birmingham, Alabama, a Southeast Regional Office, with Mrs. Ruby Hurley as Regional Secretary. The Birmingham branch had its own office. In 1955–1956 the Association played an important role in the bus boycott in Montgomery, Alabama, led by Dr. Martin Luther King, Jr., which culminated in a Supreme Court decision that outlawed Jim Crow in intrastate transportation.[61]

The N.A.A.C.P. had, in 1954, won the school-segregation cases in the Supreme Court.[62] Because of the great variety of local conditions, the formulation of decrees was reserved; and in 1955 the Court remanded the cases to the lower federal courts for such orders and decrees "as are necessary and proper to admit [children] to public

schools on a racially nondiscriminatory basis with all deliberate speed.
. . ."⁶³ This meant that the N.A.A.C.P. would need to bring proceedings in the federal district courts to compel local school boards to
comply with the desegregation decisions in the 1954 and 1955 cases
—decisions which were not, and could not have been, self-executing.

At this point it occurred to some Southern politicians that perhaps
the best way to nullify the Supreme Court decisions would be to
cripple the N.A.A.C.P., to incapacitate it so that it could not go on
with civil rights litigation or bring new cases into the courts. In this
way the victory in *Brown* v. *Board of Education* would in fact become
a hollow one. The idea that evolved was a simple one: to keep the
N.A.A.C.P. so busy defending itself, its own life, that it would not
have the time or resources to go on with its civil rights program. Had
Southern officials resorted to actions that would have amounted only
to harassment, they probably would have achieved a large measure of
success in slowing down the N.A.A.C.P., but instead they went into
"an all-out fight" to destroy the Association—at least this became the
objective in Alabama. The attack on the very life of the Association
had, however, this unintended result: it provided a made-to-order test
case of the constitutional right of association. Only a real life-and-
death struggle could provide such a constitutional test. No previous
contest in the Supreme Court had so clearly and imperatively presented the question of the constitutional right of association.

The Alabama case against the N.A.A.C.P., which was started in
1956, is very involved and has many highly technical aspects. The case
was not concluded until 1964, but the facts leading up to the constitutional issue, and its resolution in 1958, can be briefly related.

Alabama requires—as most states do—every corporation organized
in any other state to file with the Alabama secretary of state a certified
copy of its articles of incorporation, and the designation of an authorized agent and a place of business within the state "before engaging in
or transacting any business." The N.A.A.C.P. had operated in Alabama for thirty-eight years without complying with this requirement,
and no one had ever questioned its standing. But this technical violation of the state law became the basis for Alabama's war on the
Association.

The statute provided for a fine on a corporation transacting intrastate business before filing the necessary papers and for criminal prosecution of the officers of such a corporation. Instead of proceeding to
punish the Association and its officers within the provisions of the

statute, the Attorney General of Alabama brought an action to enjoin the Association from conducting further business within the state and to oust it from the state. The theory of this proceeding was that criminal proceedings would provide the state with an inadequate remedy: the state claimed it needed the extraordinary remedy of an injunction, for the Association—the bill filed by the Attorney General alleged—had given financial and legal assistance to Negroes seeking admission to the state university (when Autherine Lucy had her troubles with the University of Alabama in 1955–1956), and had supported the Negro bus boycott in Montgomery, and thus, without complying with the statute, the Association was "causing irreparable injury to the property and civil rights of the residents and citizens of the State of Alabama for which criminal prosecution and civil actions at law afford no adequate relief. . . ."

The state circuit court issued a temporary restraining order which enjoined the Association from engaging in further activities within the state and forbade it to take any steps to qualify itself to do business in the future. This order was issued *ex parte,* i.e., without affording a hearing to the Association.

The Association moved to dissolve this order, and there was to be a hearing on this motion; but before a date could be set the state moved for the production of the Association's records and papers, including financial records, and the names and addresses of all members and "agents" of the Association within the state. The court ordered the production of these documents before the date set for the hearing.

The Association then filed its answer to the bill and offered to qualify under the statute and submitted with the answer a set of the required forms. But the Association did not comply with the order to produce its records; and for this failure it was adjudged in civil contempt and fined $10,000 (the rationale of civil contempt is that the fine is not to punish but to induce compliance). The court's order provided that if compliance was not shown within five days, the fine would be $100,000. At the end of the five-day period the Association produced substantially all the records called for except its membership list. The refusal to produce this document became the heart of the contest. The Association took the position that disclosure of the names and addresses of its members would lead to economic reprisals against the members.[64] The court then imposed the fine of $100,000. Now, under Alabama law, a party is not entitled to a hearing on the merits of a case until it first purges itself of contempt. The court in effect told the Association: "Put up or shut up!" The Association asked the Supreme Court of Alabama to review the contempt judgment but the court refused. At this juncture the case reached the United States Supreme Court.

In its brief filed with the United States Supreme Court, the Association argued that in the "atmosphere of public and organized private opinion in Alabama," the surrender of its membership lists "would inevitably lead to serious economic pressure, loss of employment, mental harassment, threatened or actual violence."[65] It contended that it has served "as *the collective force* through which Negroes and others interested in fighting racial intolerance have pooled their resources toward bringing about nationwide compliance with the Fourteenth Amendment," and so, as *"an organization* through which Americans collectively act to secure rights guaranteed by the Constitution of the United States," the Association "and its members have a constitutional protection against onerous state sanctions which would restrict said activity and deny rights incident thereto." It asserted the constitutional right of the Association "to exist *as an organization* for the purposes set out in its charter. . . ." It argued that the Association should be assimilated to "newspapers, radio stations, and motion pictures" for the enjoyment of the constitutional protection given to free speech. Since the members individually have this freedom, the Association argued that it has the right to assert it for them, and that in this case it was the only one that was in a position to assert *their* constitutional rights.[66]

In 1958, two years after the proceedings were started in Alabama, the United States Supreme Court unanimously reversed the judgment of the state courts. In his opinion for the Court, Justice John M. Harlan pointed up the fact that the brief of the N.A.A.C.P. took a double stance: it urged *its own* constitutional right to resist inquiry into its membership lists, and it asserted its right to act *for its members* in claiming the right, personal to them, to withhold disclosure of their membership in the Association. "We think," said the Court, "that petitioner [N.A.A.C.P.] argues more appropriately the right of its members, and that its nexus with them is sufficient to permit that it act as their representative before this Court."

In the light of our discussion of the political theories of Hobbes, Rousseau, Locke, and Madison, it seems clear that the Court was saying here that the *locus* of the First Amendment freedoms was the individual and not the organization. Had the Court stopped here, this would have been a dangerous—if not reactionary—decision, for it might mean, for example, that the corporation that publishes a news-paper does not enjoy the constitutional freedom of the press, but that only the individual stockholders have this freedom. But the Court fortunately did not leave this point without important qualifications.

The Court held that the members were constitutionally entitled to withhold information of their connection with the Association; to require them to step forward to claim this right would, obviously, result in nullification of the right at the very moment of its assertion. The Association was, therefore, "the appropriate party to assert these rights, because it and its members are in every practical sense identical."

The Court plainly recognized the fact that freedom of speech and free assembly are closely connected, and that "effective advocacy of both public and private points of view, particularly controversial ones, is undeniably enhanced by group association," and stated: "It is beyond debate that *freedom to engage in association* for the advance-ment of beliefs and ideas is an inseparable aspect of the 'liberty' assured by the Due Process Clause of the Fourteenth Amendment, which embraces freedom of speech."[67]

Thus the Court, 167 years after the Bill of Rights was adopted, for the first time expressly gave association equality of constitutional status with religion, speech, press, assembly, and petition.

In the opinion, Justice Harlan wrote of "the right of petitioner's members to associate freely," "freedom of association," "freedom to associate," "collective effort to foster beliefs," the "constitutionally protected right of association," "the right . . . to associate freely with others," "the free enjoyment of the right to associate," and of "these indispensable liberties, whether of speech, press, or association."

Lest someone think that the purposes of this freedom may be lim-ited only to certain ends, the Court said: "Of course, it is immaterial whether the beliefs sought to be advanced by associations pertain to political, economic, religious or cultural matters." With this sentence the Court in effect revised Locke, who, as we saw, failed to extend his argument for freedom of religious association to associations formed for secular ends. This language of the Court makes freedom of asso-ciation as wide a constitutional net as possible, encompassing all human interests.

The Court, it should be noted, did not give full constitutional recog-nition to the Association as an *entity independent of its members,* in the same way that it recognized a corporation that published a news-paper or produced a motion picture, even though the N.A.A.C.P. is also a corporation (though a membership and not a stock corporation). It came close to doing so but in language that straddles. "The reasonable likelihood," said the Court,

that the Association itself through diminished financial support and membership may be adversely affected if production is compelled is a further factor pointing towards our holding that petitioner has standing to complain of the production order on behalf of its members.

The last phrase—"on behalf of its members"—reads like a last-minute accommodation to meet an objection; and the reference to "diminished financial support" is a faint echo of the case involving the Society of Sisters of the Holy Names. These small impurities in the opinion remain as uncomfortable reminders of the compulsion to disassociate the Constitution from any realm except that which clearly and definitively belongs to Caesar; and what has a better certificate to prove that it belongs to the realm of Caesar than the coin with the proper "likeness and inscription"?[68] Suppose the N.A.A.C.P. were heavily endowed, so that it did not need any additional income, and therefore admitted members without dues? Would that, today, make the slightest difference as to its members? and its own constitutional rights? Many Americans belong to organizations membership in which is not dependent on the payment of dues or making financial contributions; and the Court today could not possibly exclude them from constitutional protection because of the absence of a property or financial nexus. For what the Constitution protects is not the right to pay—or collect—dues, but freedom of association "for the purpose of advancing ideas and airing grievances," or, one may assume, for any other purpose not harmful to any essential public interest: an association to play bridge or tennis, or to conduct a dance once a month, or to taste wines, or to go on hikes, or to watch birds. Freedom of association surely must be conceived of as broadly as freedom of speech and press and must be interpreted and applied in the spirit of the humanist who affirms with Terence: *Homo sum; humani nil a me alienum puto*—"I am a man; I count nothing human indifferent to me."

Two years after the decision in *N.A.A.C.P.* v. *Alabama* the Court affirmed the principle of that case in *Bates* v. *Little Rock*.[69] Two cities in Arkansas levied a license tax on any person or firm engaging in any "trade, business, profession, vocation, or calling." In 1957 the cities amended their ordinances to require organizations to supply certain information, including a list of members and contributors. The ordinances provided that all the information furnished was to be public.

The custodians of the records of the N.A.A.C.P. local branches supplied the municipalities with all the information required except the names of members and contributors. The custodians were convicted of violation of the ordinances. At the trial in one of the cases it was shown that public identification of members of the Association had led to harassment and threats. The state supreme court upheld the convictions.

The United States Supreme Court unanimously reversed the convictions. Justice Stewart, in his opinion for the Court, said:

It is now beyond dispute that freedom of association for the purpose of advancing ideas and airing grievances is protected by the Due Process Clause of the Fourteenth Amendment from invasion by the States. . . . Freedoms such as these are protected not only against heavy-handed frontal attack, but also from being stifled by more subtle governmental interference. . . .

The Court again noted that the protection of freedom of association may entail protection of privacy of association, since compelled disclosure of membership may effectively curtail freedom of association.

But freedom of association may give way, through compelled disclosure of a membership list, when the state has demonstrated an overriding interest in the membership list. A municipality's power to tax is, of course, a fundamental one, and the exercise of this power may sometimes entail an encroachment on individual liberty. But here the Court could find no relevant connection between the power to impose an occupation license tax and the disclosure of the membership list. The Court therefore concluded that the municipalities had failed "to demonstrate a controlling justification for the deterrence of free association which compulsory disclosure of the membership lists would cause."

An opportunity to broaden and deepen freedom of association was presented to the Court in another case brought by the N.A.A.C.P. five years after the decision in the Alabama case, and the Court used the occasion effectively. The facts in this case—*N.A.A.C.P.* v. *Button*[70]—were as follows:

Virginia, like other states, had statutes against the improper solicitation of legal business. In 1956 the legislature amended these statutes to include in the definition of "runner" or "capper"—commonly known as "ambulance chaser," a lawyer's agent who actively incites or solicits the bringing of legal action—an organization which retains a lawyer in connection with an action to which it is not a party and in which it has no pecuniary right or liability. The Virginia courts held that the statutes as amended applied to the N.A.A.C.P.'s activities, which were now under the statute's ban against "the improper solicitation of any legal business."

The Association had 89 branches, with 13,500 members. The branches were organized into the Virginia State Conference of N.A.A.C.P. Branches, which financed only cases in which a litigant retained an N.A.A.C.P. staff lawyer to represent him. The Conference maintained a staff of fifteen lawyers, who were bound by the civil rights policies of the Association. The legal staff made the decision whether a litigant was entitled to Association assistance. The Conference defrayed all expenses of litigation, and usually paid the lawyer on the case a per-diem fee and expenses. The litigant received no money, and the lawyer was not permitted to receive any fees from the litigant. The actual conduct of the litigation was under the control of the attorney, and the client was free at any time to withdraw from an action.

An aggrieved Negro applied directly to the Conference or the legal staff for assistance. The chairman of the legal staff, with the concurrence of the president of the Conference, was authorized to agree to give legal assistance in an appropriate case. In school-segregation situations, however, a local branch would invite a member of the legal staff to explain to a meeting of parents and children the legal steps necessary to achieve desegregation. The staff member would bring to the meeting forms authorizing him, and other Association attorneys of his designation, to represent the signers in legal proceedings to achieve desegregation. After obtaining authorizations, usually the staff lawyer brought into the case other staff members in the area where suit was to be brought, and sometimes lawyers from the national organization. In effect, the prospective litigant retained the "firm" of Association lawyers. The Conference in different ways encouraged the bringing of lawsuits, but the plaintiffs made their own decisions to become such.

Although these activities had been carried on for years in Virginia by the N.A.A.C.P., no attempt was made to proscribe them until the legislation of 1956 was enacted.

In his opinion for the United States Supreme Court, Justice Brennan said that the Association claimed that the act of 1956 infringed

the right of the N.A.A.C.P. and its members and lawyers to associate for the purpose of assisting persons who seek legal redress for infringements of their constitutionally guaranteed and other rights. We think petitioner [the Association] may assert this right *on its own behalf*, because, though a corporation, it is directly engaged in those activities, claimed to be constitutionally protected, which the statute would curtail. Cf. *Grosjean* v. *American Press Co.* . . . We also think petitioner has standing to assert the corresponding rights of its members. See *National Asso. for Advancement of Colored People* v. *Alabama*. . . .[71]

The Court reversed the judgment of the Virginia court and held that the activities of the Association, its affiliates, and legal staff "are modes of expression and association protected by the First and Fourteenth Amendments which Virginia may not prohibit. . . ."

N.A.A.C.P. v. *Alabama* was the first clear decision that American have the constitutional right to associate; *N.A.A.C.P.* v. *Button* was the first clear decision that the associations formed by Americans have the constitutional rights guaranteed by the First and Fourteenth Amendments.

The latter case is significant for another result it achieved. The Court held that civil rights litigation is "a form of political expression," and that, "under the conditions of modern government, [civil rights] litigation may well be the sole practicable avenue open to a minority to petition for redress of grievances."

This statement points up the great debt owed by Americans to associations dedicated to the testing of civil rights and civil liberties claims in the courts. But for their efforts and achievements, Americans would be much poorer in the benefits derived from the Bill of Rights.

In a paper written in 1952, the late Zechariah Chafee, Jr., said of the American Civil Liberties Union what may also be said of the N.A.A.C.P.:

Without such an organization, arrested speakers and writers would have found it very difficult to get efficient lawyers or sometimes any lawyers at all. The constitutional provision entitling the accused "to have the assistance of counsel for his defence" might have remained just empty words on paper. An ordinary lawyer fears the effect of unpopular cases upon his practice. Lawyers who did defend obnoxious persons were threatened with disbarment then [1920–1930] as now, and some were disbarred. Moreover, free speech cases are a specialized branch of the law and call for knowledge and experience which lawyers in general lack. Therefore, it was a great service to the administration of justice in the United States when in many cities a law office, staffed with trained and conscientious men, was able to help courts reach proper decisions in civil liberties cases.[72]

It is important to note, too, that justice is a rather expensive commodity, beyond the financial resources of the poor or even of persons of modest income. The school-segregation cases of 1954 cost the N.A.A.C.P. about $200,000.[73] Can one for a moment think that the individual Negroes involved as the actual litigants in these cases could ever have brought these actions and seen them through the Supreme Court if they had had to retain lawyers and pay all the costs out of their own pockets? Merely the printing in an ordinary civil rights case limited to documents for the Supreme Court costs about $1000. The average civil rights case that has gone through a federal court of appeals costs about $5000.[74]

In the light of these facts, it should not surprise any reader to learn that an examination of 318 civil rights cases in the Supreme Court in the years from 1933 to 1963 showed that in 54 per cent of the cases a civil rights organization had participated; and that in 32 per cent of the cases such an organization had participated by providing financial or legal assistance. But for the leading civil rights cases—those of special importance—the percentages were substantially higher—88 and 52, respectively.[75] "Given the cost of court action," a reliable study of the problem has stated,

the diffuse operation of state invasions of freedom, and the unfortunate unwillingness of the legal profession to provide adequate representation for members of unpopular minorities, individual action seeking to enforce civil rights may be rendered impossible or improbable by the forces of impersonal "market conditions." In these circumstances, the organizational litigator may be the only agency capable of providing the oppressed with an opportunity to assert their rights in court.[76]

Surely the Supreme Court, when it had before it *N.A.A.C.P.* v. *Alabama* and the Button case, knew that the situation in parts of the South was aggravated by certain practices and circumstances that had special importance for civil rights litigation: (1) Imagine trying a segregation case in a courtroom that was itself racially segregated.[77] (2) Imagine trying a civil rights case in a court in which a Negro party or witness was never addressed as Mr., Mrs., or Miss, but by his or her first name.[78] (3) Consider the fact that in 1961 the N.A.A.C.P. found that not a single white lawyer in the state of Mississippi could be induced to undertake a civil rights case, and that in that state there were only two Negro lawyers who would handle such cases, and that these two lawyers were also generally addressed in court by their first names. The Association found only four or five Negro lawyers in

Florida to handle its civil rights work, four in Georgia, five in South Carolina, eight or ten in North Carolina, only seven in Tennessee.[79]

When President Kennedy in 1963 convened a conference of lawyers at the White House, he called on the legal profession to live up to its social responsibility, especially at a time of tense racial unrest. In response to this plea, a special committee of the American Bar Association was appointed as an emergency measure; and this committee, in its report at the annual meeting of the A.B.A. in August 1963, called on lawyers for action to eliminate discrimination within the legal profession itself, and to carry out the duty of the profession with respect to defendants in locally unpopular causes. As a result of the White House conference, there was formed, too, the Lawyers Committee for Civil Rights Under Law, with leading lawyers of New York and Philadelphia as co-chairmen, and in August 1963 this committee sent a lawyer to Mississippi to assist in testing the constitutionality of a sweeping state court injunction against any racial demonstration.[80]

These facts are cited in the context of our discussion of freedom of association to underscore the great significance of the Supreme Court decisions in the cases decided in 1958 and 1963; for more than freedom of association was involved, though only implicitly. What was involved was the future of civil rights and civil liberties developments, and not only in the South but throughout the United States. Had the decision gone against the N.A.A.C.P., the floodgates of attack on the Association would have been opened, and all other civil rights and civil liberties organizations would have found their existence imperiled.

Following the decision in *Brown* v. *Board of Education,* six Southern states—Arkansas, Florida, Georgia, Mississippi, South Carolina, and Tennessee—passed legislation similar to the Virginia statute held unconstitutional in *N.A.A.C.P.* v. *Button.*[81] From the record there can be no doubt that the "action of the [seven state] legislatures was a vigorous political response to the success of these [civil rights and civil liberties] organizations before the courts."[82] Not only was the N.A.A.C.P. attacked as an "ambulance chaser"—under amended laws concerned with champerty and barratry[83]—but in other ways that have been briefly summarized as follows:

Existing laws have been applied in a discriminatory manner, often to deprive the N.A.A.C.P. of meeting halls, sometimes to impose exorbitant taxes upon its operations or to require registration of its membership lists. Financial obstacles have been imposed through enactment of prohibitive excises on dues and membership fees. Harassment by legislative groups has resulted in sequestration and publication of records and membership lists and slanderous exposure of N.A.A.C.P. officials. Members of the Association have been denied or removed from state jobs, either pursuant to specific legislation, or, less openly by administrative discrimination.[84]

Had the attack on the N.A.A.C.P. succeeded—in 1957 the Association had to defend its own life in twenty-five cases[85]—the pattern would have been set for states to destroy any association that is devoted to an unpopular cause. Organizations like a chamber of commerce or a state bar or medical association do not need to have freedom of association vindicated in the Supreme Court; such an organization's policies may be questioned or attacked, but its existence, and its right to exist, will not be challenged. But many of a state's resources may be marshaled to destroy an organization that represents an unpopular, dissenting view.

What should be recorded as the classic example of what may happen when state officials decide to use the state's powers against an association is *N.A.A.C.P.* v. *Alabama.* As we saw, in 1958 the Supreme Court decided in favor of the Association. But Alabama continued with court orders that barred the Association from the state. In 1964 the United States Supreme Court had the case before it for the *fourth* time! In his opinion for a unanimous Court, Justice Harlan noted that the Alabama Supreme Court had applied to the Association procedural rules that it had not applied in other cases, and that not one of the eleven acts charged against the Association could be considered sufficient to justify ouster of the Association from the state. In again reversing and remanding the case, Justice Harlan said: "Should we unhappily be mistaken in our belief that the Supreme Court of Alabama will promptly implement this disposition, leave is given the Association to apply to this Court for further appropriate relief."[86] This was said *eight years* after the state court had first restrained the N.A.A.C.P. from "doing business" in Alabama.

The United States Supreme Court has itself been under attack since 1954, with a virulence perhaps unmatched in American history. Typical of the outcries against the Court was the statement of Senator Barry Goldwater to an audience in Chicago on September 11, 1964: "Of all three branches of government, today's Supreme Court is least faithful to the constitutional tradition of limited government and to the principle of legitimacy in the exercise of power." He accused the Court of exercising "raw and naked power."[87] But there has been no outcry against many of the lower and highest state courts in the South which have flagrantly asserted "raw and naked power" and have shown little or no regard for "the principle of legitimacy in the exercise of power." It is easy enough for a judge to administer equal justice, with full respect for the Rule of Law, when the case before him involves a dispute over title to real estate or the issue of negligence in an automobile accident case—not a great deal of "character" is required from a judge in such cases. But when the case involves principles that run counter to local prejudices or dominant interests, and the judge acts as a partisan, then justice has been corrupted at its spring, and one can no longer think of it as "the synonym of an aspiration, a mood of exaltation, a yearning for what is fine or high."[88] Justice is then debased and is linked with illegality, and even criminality.

It is not only that Alabama has denied the right of association to the N.A.A.C.P.; the state—as Justice Harlan said in the fourth *N.A.A.C.P.* v. *Alabama* case decided by the Court—for eight years denied "the freedom of individuals to associate for the collective advocacy of ideas."[89]

Southern states—especially Mississippi, Louisiana, and Alabama—have resorted also to extra-judicial measures to deny freedom of association. In 1964 the existence of a widespread intelligence network was reported. In Alabama the operation was directed by Governor George C. Wallace. The Alabama files contained approximately 33,000 name cards. Photographs and motion pictures of individuals and crowds at racial disturbances and interracial gatherings have been made. When the funerals of the four girls who were killed in the bombing of a Negro church in Birmingham in September 1963 were held, officials took photographs of virtually every white person who attended. Lawyers from the Department of Justice who came into Alabama were followed by state investigators. After J. A. Hood won admission to the state university under a federal court order, he addressed an audience in a Negro church at Gadsden, Alabama; two state investigators, both with tape recorders, sat in the audience and recorded his talk, in which he asserted that university officials were engaged in a conspiracy to expel him. The tape recordings were turned over to university officials by the governor's office, and Hood was expelled for his talk.[90]

One could go on and on with similar stories of the misuse of law, legal institutions, and official power in Alabama, Virginia, and other Southern states, to show how these states have tried, since 1954, to defeat the constitutional rights of Negroes by denying them and others the constitutional freedom of association. But enough has been said to make clear that winning a case in the United States Supreme Court is a necessary but often an insufficient basis for social change or for the full vindication of a constitutional principle or liberty.

Speaking in the South in September 1964, Senator Goldwater promised, if elected President, to use his power and influence "to see that law-enforcement officers, on the state and local level, get back the power to carry out their job" and to "give back to the states those powers absolutely necessary for fair and efficient administration of criminal law."[91] In light of the record, one may well ask: "fair" to whom? "efficient" for whom? In their attacks on freedom of association, Southern law-enforcement officials have shown that their efficiency has by no means been impaired by Supreme Court decisions, only it has been directed *against* the decisions and to *deny* fairness in the administration of law and in the enjoyment of constitutional guarantees, especially freedom of association.

5. *Freedom of Association, Limited*

The various N.A.A.C.P. cases that we have thus far considered will stand as landmarks in constitutional development; but unfortunately anyone who is interested in freedom of association, while he may begin with those cases, cannot stop there; and once he goes on his perplexities begin.

Let us look at the cases involving Willard Uphaus, decided by the Supreme Court in 1959 and 1960,[92] after the precedent of *N.A.A.C.P.* v. *Alabama* had been established by unanimous decision in 1958.

In 1953 the New Hampshire legislature adopted a resolution which directed the state's Attorney General "to make a full and complete investigation with respect to violations of the [state's] subversive activities act of 1951 and to determine whether subversive persons as defined in said act are presently located within this state." The investigation by the Attorney General as a one-man legislative investigating committee was continued by another resolution adopted in 1955. In the course of his investigation the Attorney General called Dr. Uphaus, who was executive director of World Fellowship, a voluntary corporation organized under the laws of New Hampshire which maintained a summer camp in the state. (He had a doctorate in theology and had been professor of religious education at Yale.) Uphaus testified concerning his own activities but refused to comply with a demand to produce the names of all persons who had attended the camp in the seasons of 1954 and 1955. The state courts held him in contempt for this refusal and ordered him committed to jail until he would comply.

The United States Supreme Court assumed that Uphaus had "standing" to assert any rights his guests may have had in "associational privacy," but decided that the state's interests in obtaining the names of the guests outweighed in "substantiality" the constitutional interests that he asserted.

In the majority opinion by Justice Clark, the Court said that the Attorney General had "valid reason to believe that the speakers and guests at World Fellowship might be subversive within the meaning of the New Hampshire [subversive activities] Act." The Court said that the record revealed that Uphaus "had participated in 'Communist front' activities" and that not less than nineteen speakers invited by Uphaus had either been members of the Communist Party "or had connections or affiliations" with the Party or with organizations cited as subversive or Communist-controlled in the United States Attorney General's list.

The Court said that though "guilt by association remains a thoroughly discredited doctrine," one must bear in mind that this was a legislative investigation and not a criminal prosecution—there was involved here no question of guilt, by association or otherwise.

The legislature had determined, said the Court, that subversive persons—"statutorily defined with a view toward the Communist Party" —"posed a threat to the security of the State." The Attorney General's investigation was, therefore, undertaken "in the interest of self-preservation"; and this governmental interest "outweighs individual rights in an associational privacy. . . ."

The Court took the position that the "privacy" involved here was "tenuous at best" because World Fellowship operated a "public" camp that furnished board and lodging to persons who applied, and a state law required that such camps maintain a register that would be open to inspection by sheriffs and police officers.

Uphaus contended that supplying the list to the Attorney General and, through him, to the legislature, would lead to state officials everywhere copying the names and thus making the guests "suspect" even in their own places of residence. But the Courts brushed aside this objection by saying that "exposure—in the sense of disclosure—is an inescapable incident of an investigation into the presence of subversive persons within the State." The Court concluded:

The governmental interest in self-preservation is sufficiently compelling to subordinate the interest in associational privacy of persons who, at least to the extent of the guest registration statute, made public at the inception the association they now wish to keep private.

Four Justices dissented. Chief Justice Warren and Justices Black and Douglas joined in the dissenting opinion of Justice Brennan. The dissenting opinion argued that in essentials this case was indistinguishable from *N.A.A.C.P.* v. *Alabama*, and so the latter should serve as a guide. In that case Alabama had demonstrated a legitimate purpose in asking for the membership list: it wanted to ascertain whether a foreign corporation was unlawfully conducting activities within the state when it had not qualified to do so. This purpose was specific, and, abstractly considered, a legitimate one. Yet the Court recognized that the disclosure of the membership list would entail a serious curbing of freedom of association; and this fact led the Court to analyze carefully the relationship between the inquiry and the avowed purpose, and concluded that there was no "rational connection," and therefore the inquiry was constitutionally forbidden. In the Uphaus case, said Justice Brennan, there was an even more extreme situation, and the state's interest was not specific but vague. "In effect," said Justice Brennan,

a roving investigation and exposure of past associations and expressions in the political field is upheld because it might lead to some sort of legislation which might be sustained as constitutional, and the entire process is said to become more defensible rather than the less because of the vagueness of the issues. . . . The Attorney General had World Fellowship's speaker list and had already made publication of it. . . . He had considerable other data about World Fellowship, Inc., which he had already published. . . . The relevance of further detail is not demonstrated. But its damaging effect on the persons to be named in the guest list is obvious. And since the only discernible purpose of the investigation on this record is revealed to be investigation and exposure *per se,* and the relevance of the names to that purpose alone is quite apparent, this discloses the constitutional infirmity in the inquiry. . . .

Justice Brennan said that he could see no "serious and substantial relationship" between the disclosure of the guest list and the process of legislation, "and it is the process of legislation, the consideration of the enactment of laws, with which we are ultimately concerned." The inquiry into the names of the guests was only "a vehicle of exposure." The process of compulsory disclosure in the areas of free speech and assembly tends by itself to have a repressing effect on the exercise of these freedoms. If the case involved "a balancing of interests"—governmental against private—then the state must show that its interest is legitimate and substantial if it is to counterbalance "the interest in privacy as it relates to freedom of speech and assembly." The dissenters reminded the majority that the Court, in *N.A.A.C.P.* v. *Alabama,* had said that "state action which may have the effect of curtailing the freedom to associate is subject to the closest scrutiny." The dissenters recognized the fact that if there are to be legislative investigations, most of them would unavoidably involve some kind of exposure. "But it is quite clear," they added, "that exposure was the very core, and deliberately and purposefully so, of the legislative investigation we are concerned with here."

It is important in evaluating the purpose of the one-man legislative investigation in New Hampshire to bear in mind that constitutionally the state's legislative interest could have been only a very narrow one. In 1956, in *Pennsylvania* v. *Nelson,*[93] the Supreme Court, looking at the federal statutes concerned with communism and related matters, held that these laws precluded enforcement of state laws on the same subjects: ". . . Congress has occupied the field to the exclusion of parallel state legislation. . . ."

The importance of this decision for constitutional liberties can hardly be exaggerated, for at the time of the decision forty-two states (as well as Alaska and Hawaii, which had not yet attained statehood) had statutes that prohibited advocacy of the violent overthrow of established government—anti-sedition statutes, criminal anarchy laws, criminal syndicalist laws, and similar statutes; and all of them were primarily directed against overthrow of the United States Government.[94] In reviewing these state statutes, the Court in the Nelson case said: "And our attention has not been called to any case where the prosecution has been successfully directed against an attempt to destroy state or local government." These state laws were a perpetual temptation for official harassment of persons considered to be "agitators," "subversives," persons identified with unpopular causes. Massachusetts, Indiana, Pennsylvania, and Texas outlawed the Communist Party by name and made membership a crime. An ordinance of Birmingham, Alabama, provided a fine of $100 and 180 days in jail for each day that a known Communist remained in the city; and New Rochelle, New York, required registration with the police by any member of "a Communist organization" who "resides in, is employed in, has a regular place of business in, or who regularly enters or travels through any part" of the city. In 1951 some 150 municipalities had ordinances directed at subversive persons or activities; and many municipalities presumed that they had "police power" to deal with the "dangers" and did not need legislation—for example, Detroit closed up newspaper stands that sold the *Daily Worker* on the pretext that the stands were "public nuisances" on public thoroughfares, and Oklahoma City prosecuted persons who sold or distributed Communist publications as "disorderly persons."[95] While many of the legislatures enacted laws simply to show that they were against the sin of subversion, the record[96] of prosecutions and other uses of the laws shows that they had to be considered serious threats to constitutional liberties.

Now, Uphaus contended that the decision in the Nelson case had removed any constitutional base that the New Hampshire statutes might otherwise have had. But the majority of the Court disagreed. The Nelson decision, said Justice Clark, made it impossible for the federal and state prosecutors to race to the courthouse to see who could prosecute first for any crime against *the United States;* but, said Justice Clark, the opinion in the Nelson case "made clear that a State could proceed with prosecutions for sedition against the State itself. . . ." If the state can do this, then, *a fortiori,* "it can legitimately investigate in this area. . . ."

But Justice Clark at this point of his reasoning forgot what Chief Justice Warren had said in the Nelson case: "And our attention has not been called to any case where the prosecution has been successfully directed against an attempt to destroy state or local government."

Assuming that the Nelson decision still left an area for state action, Justice Brennan, in his dissenting opinion in the Uphaus case, argued that New Hampshire chose not to act by way of indictment and trial in court, where the state would encounter "constitutional and evidentiary problems of an obvious and hardly subtle nature." Instead, the state's "choice was to reach the end of exposure through the process of investigation, backed with the contempt power and the making of reports to the Legislature. . . ." The result was that the "sanction of exposure was applied much more widely than anyone could remotely suggest that even traditional judicial sanctions might be applied in this area."

The state's Attorney General had asked the Supreme Court to examine the report he had made to the legislature in 1955. Justice Brennan referred to this report as "a comprehensive volume" that contained "an extensive list of persons, their addresses, and miscellaneous activities and associations attributed to them. . . ." The list was the Attorney General's response to the mandate he had from the legislature to determine whether "subversive persons" as defined in the

1951 act "are presently located within the state." The reports to the legislature were made public. Justice Brennan suggested that the list might fit the definition of a bill of attainder, a *legislative* adjudication of guilt; and Justices Black and Douglas, while joining in Justice Brennan's dissenting opinion, filed a brief opinion in which they condemned the state's legislative program that resulted in Uphaus's imprisonment for contempt as a violation of the constitutional prohibition on bills of attainder.

Following the preceding case, New Hampshire enacted another statute which omitted the provision in the earlier act directing the Attorney General to determine whether subversive persons were presently in the state, and limited his authority to making investigations of violations of law. Uphaus then contended that the new act had removed the base on which the contempt proceedings had rested, but the state supreme court concluded that this was not the effect of the new law. The United States Supreme Court refused to hear an appeal from this judgment on the ground that it was based on a non-federal ground. Justice Brennan, while standing on his dissenting opinion, concurred in the dismissal of the appeal on the asserted ground; but Chief Justice Warren and Justices Black and Douglas dissented.[97]

The dissenting opinion of Justice Douglas argued that the decision in the Uphaus case was inconsistent with *N.A.A.C.P.* v. *Alabama* and *Bates* v. *Little Rock*, the latter decided after the Uphaus decision. He contended that the record was bare of any facts that World Fellowship was at any time engaged in unlawful conduct—it was an organization that promoted the ideas of pacifism. What the Court did in the N.A.A.C.P. cases was not designed, said Justice Douglas, "as a rule for Negroes only." Yet the Court had unanimously allowed Mrs. Bates the constitutional protection that it denied Dr. Uphaus. "The *Bates* case and the *Uphaus* case put into focus for the first time the responsibility of an *individual* to make disclosure of membership lists. We cannot," said Justice Douglas, "administer justice with an even hand if we allow Bates to go free and Uphaus to languish in prison." The Court in the Bates case held that compulsory disclosure of the membership list of the N.A.A.C.P. branch in Little Rock "would work a significant interference with the freedom of association of their members," for the repressive effect on freedom of association would be inevitably felt. "Can there be any doubt," asked Justice Douglas, "that harassment of members of World Fellowship, Inc., in the climate prevailing among New Hampshire's law-enforcement officials will not likewise be severe? Can there be any doubt that its members will be as closely pursued as might be members of N.A.A.C.P. in some communities? If either N.A.A.C.P. or World Fellowship were engaged in criminal activity we would have a different problem. But neither is shown to be."

Dr. Willard Uphaus served a year in prison for his contempt. The Attorney General did not get the guest list of the World Fellowship camp, but he was elected to Congress, and New Hampshire, the "Granite State," which has for its motto "Live free or die," stands firm as ever, unshaken by subversives or pacifists.

Was the Uphaus case so significantly different from the N.A.A.C.P. cases that the membership lists were privileged, while the guest list was not so privileged? Five Justices could see significant differences, while four Justices maintained that the principle of the N.A.A.C.P. decisions was applicable to the facts and issues in the Uphaus case.

But after the Uphaus appeal was disposed of, the Court in 1963 had another N.A.A.C.P. case which had in it elements that brought the Association uncomfortably close to the situation in which World Fellowship had been. This time the Court was not unanimous, as it had been in the N.A.A.C.P. v. Alabama and in the Bates case; the decision was now only 5 to 4 in favor of the N.A.A.C.P., with the majority comprised of the four Justices who had dissented in the Uphaus case, joined now by Justice Arthur J. Goldberg, who had replaced Justice Frankfurter.

The Florida legislature apparently had learned something from New Hampshire: Why not look for subversives in the N.A.A.C.P., just as New Hampshire had looked for them in World Fellowship?

The legislature set up by statute the Legislative Investigation Committee, which conducted inquiries as to Communists, Communist activities, and infiltration of Communists into organizations operating in various fields—race relations came first; then "the coercive reform of social and educational practices and mores by litigation and pressured administrative action"; then labor, education, and "other vital phases of life" in Florida.

The committee called Theodore R. Gibson, president of the Miami branch of the N.A.A.C.P., and he was asked to bring the records showing the members of, and contributors to, the local and state N.A.A.C.P. Gibson testified that the local branch had about a thousand members but refused to produce the membership list, of which he admitted being the custodian. He, however, volunteered to answer some questions on the basis of his personal knowledge. He was shown the photographs of fourteen persons who had previously been identified as Communists, or as members of Communist-front organizations, and Gibson said that he could associate none of them with the N.A.A.C.P. The state courts duly adjudged him in contempt, and a fine and prison sentence were imposed.

Justice Goldberg, in *Gibson* v. *Florida Legislative Committee*,[98] distinguished the case from the Uphaus case as follows:

(1) The record in the Gibson case was insufficient to show "a substantial connection between the Miami branch of the N.A.A.C.P. and Communist *activities*,"[99] which is "an essential prerequisite to demonstrating the immediate, substantial, and subordinating state interest necessary to sustain" the state's right of inquiry into the membership list.

A committee investigator had identified fourteen persons as Communists or members of Communist-"front" or Communist-"affiliated" organizations who had been members of the N.A.A.C.P. in Florida or had participated in its affairs; and he named thirty-eight others about whom inquiry was to be made. But, said Justice Goldberg, "mere presence at a public meeting or bare membership—without more—is not infiltration of the sponsoring organization." Besides, a number of the fourteen named persons were no longer in Florida, and so it was "difficult to see any basis for supposing that they would be current—much less influential—members. . . ."

(2) In the Uphaus case the claim to "associational privacy" was "held to be 'tenuous at best,'" since the summer camp was required by law to maintain a guest register open to public authorities.

(3) "Finally, in *Uphaus,* the State was investigating whether subversive persons were within its boundaries and whether their presence constituted a threat to the State. No such purpose or need is evident here. The Florida Committee is not seeking to identify subversives by questioning the petitioner [Gibson]; apparently it is satisfied that it already knows who they are."

Justice Harlan, in his dissenting opinion, in which he was joined by Justices Clark, Stewart, and White, said that the "Court's reasoning is difficult to grasp." He had a different view of the facts, and noted:

(1) That government evidence in Smith Act prosecutions had shown "that the sensitive area of race relations has long been a prime target of Communist efforts at infiltration."

(2) That at its annual convention in 1951 the N.A.A.C.P. had

adopted an "anti-communism" resolution, which Gibson had himself called to the attention of the investigating committee, and which read in part as follows:

Whereas, certain branches of the National Association for the Advancement of Colored People are being rocked by internal conflicts between groups who follow the Communist line and those who do not, which threaten to destroy the confidence of the public in the Association and which will inevitably result in its eventual disruption; and

Whereas, it is apparent . . . that there is a well-organized, nationwide conspiracy by Communists either to capture or split and wreck the NAACP; therefore be it

Resolved, that this Forty-First Convention . . . go on record as unequivocally condemning attacks by Communists and their fellow-travelers upon the Association and its officials, and . . .

Resolved, that this Convention go on record as directing and instructing the Board of Directors to take the necessary action to eradicate such infiltration, and if necessary to . . . expel any unit, which . . . comes under Communist or other political control and combination.[100]

As we look back upon the association cases that the Court decided in the years 1958–1963, the Uphaus case strikes a discordant note. The four N.A.A.C.P. cases were all won by or on behalf of the Association: *N.A.A.C.P.* v. *Alabama*, 1958, unanimous decision; the Bates case, 1960, unanimous; the Button case, 1963, 6-3; and the Gibson case, 1963, 5-4. A fifth case, *Louisiana ex rel. Gremillion* v. *N.A.A.C.P.*,[101] which we have not discussed because it does not compare in importance to the other cases, was also won by the Association, by unanimous decision in 1961. Only Willard Uphaus and the World Fellowship lost.

Now, any student of legal methodology knows how easy it ordinarily is to distinguish cases on their facts—if one wants to achieve different results—and one can readily admit that there are differences between the facts in the Uphaus case and those in the N.A.A.C.P. cases, But if one keeps before him certain constitutional touchstones, then one can suggest that the Uphaus case was wrongly decided.

In the Button case, and again in the Gibson case, the Court said that free speech and free association are fundamental and "need breathing space to survive." Now, the principle of "breathing space" means that these freedoms cannot be placed in wrappings; that in "exercising" these freedoms men need ample space in which to stretch and move. It means that other values, which otherwise would be respected, must not be allowed to act as encumbrances standing in the way of men "exercising" those freedoms. The principle of "breathing space" means that the freedoms will be protected, not only when the attack touches them, but also when the attack touches only the outer rim of the "breathing space" that the freedoms need.

Now, it is precisely because of such reasoning that the Supreme Court, in protecting freedom of *association*, has held that it must also protect "*associational privacy*."

Not every exercise of freedom of association needs to be secret. If all organizations were secret, society would not be open and free. Still, in an open and free society, there must be protection for "associational privacy," so that, paradoxically, society may be and remain open and free.

One does not care if everyone knows that he is a member of the American Philosophical Association or of the American Studies Association. Indeed, the membership list is published annually. But a member of the Miami or Little Rock branch of the N.A.A.C.P. might greatly care if his membership was publicized; and so, too, one might have cared had he by chance attended the World Fellowship summer camp for one or several days and then had his name *listed in an official report on subversive persons* in the state of New Hampshire. Surely there must be other ways of getting to the identity of subversive persons. Are people who are interested in pacifism less entitled to "breathing space" for their right to associate with one another than are persons interested in civil rights?

It should be emphasized that what was involved in the Uphaus case was not the right of pacifists to belong to World Fellowship. This was not the issue. What was involved was their right to "breathing space" in the exercise of their right to associate. It is difficult to see how they can have this "breathing space" if it is settled that the state may *publish their names in a report that purports to deal with subversives.* We would need to search far and wide for an American who would welcome inclusion of his name in such an "honor roll."

It is a fact that the summer camp of World Fellowship was required by law to keep a guest register. If the state had wanted to publish, in one big directory, the names of the guests of all summer resorts in the state, perhaps no one could constitutionally object. But surely the persons who signed the camp register did not, by that act, mean to authorize the state to publish their names *in a report on subversive persons.*

Who needs protection of their "strong associational interest in maintaining the privacy of membership lists"? It is, obviously, needed by "persons espousing beliefs already unpopular with their neighbors. . . ." An invasion of their "breathing space" surely can have a "deterrent and 'chilling' effect on the free exercise of constitutionally enshrined rights of free speech, expression, and association. . . ."[102]

Florida's interest in uncovering Communists failed as Florida tried to penetrate the "breathing space" of members of the N.A.A.C.P. New Hampshire's interest in uncovering subversives should also have failed as it tried to penetrate the "breathing space" of World Fellowship's summer-camp guests. (Incidentally, a person who becomes a *member* makes a much stronger commitment to an organization than does a person who merely comes as a *guest* to an organization's summer camp. If one can be included in a list that is part of a legislative report on subversives when one is only a *guest*, how much further can a state go when the person is a member?)

In the Button case the Court, through Justice Brennan, said that the freedoms involved are not only "supremely precious in our society" but are also "delicate and vulnerable." This is why, said the Court, they needed "breathing space." When Dr. Uphaus was imprisoned, his confinement symbolized the denial of "breathing space," the confinement of the right of association, in that case, to very narrow space.

But it would be a mistake for us to leave this discussion with the Uphaus case in mind. The emphasis should fall on the N.A.A.C.P. cases, which have fixed the constitutional principles. These decisions are a clear, significant gain. It is obvious that they are a gain for freedom of association, and they mark a considerable advance on the democratic philosophy of John Locke, James Madison, and the other thinkers who contributed to the hopes and fears that went into the framing of the First Amendment.

But, in the context of the civil rights struggle, they are also a gain on that front; for if Alabama or Arkansas or Florida or Louisiana had won in the Court, a way would have opened up for the South to paralyze the N.A.A.C.P. and any other civil rights or civil liberties organization; and since the Bill of Rights is not self-executing, but is dependent upon vindication through litigation, the struggle for freedom and equality would have been effectively arrested.

For a free society needs not only free men, but also free men who freely enter many smaller free societies—"innumerable institutions," as Justice Douglas has said, "through which views and opinions are expressed, opinion is mobilized, and social, economic, religious, educational, and political programs are formulated."[103] These societies have the right not only to express and formulate ideas, but also—

thanks to the Button decision—to litigate, and thereby to vindicate, the constitutional and legal rights of Americans. Without this right of association for civil rights and civil liberties litigation, our Bill of Rights might remain as abstract and insignificant as is the part of the Constitution of the U.S.S.R. that purports to guarantee personal freedoms and rights. There are no civil rights or civil liberties organizations in the U.S.S.R. or in any other totalitarian or one-party state. It took the attacks on the N.A.A.C.P. to demonstrate that, "under the conditions of modern government"—and, we would add, given the conditions of the complexity and high cost of legal actions—"litigation may well be the sole practicable avenue open to a minority to petition for redress of grievances."[104]

One more comment regarding the Uphaus case may be in order. Suppose that all the facts in the case remained the same except that the camp was operated by the N.A.A.C.P. instead of World Fellowship, would there have been a different result? Of course one cannot be sure; but there is the disconcerting fact that the Gibson decision, like the Uphaus, was a 5-to-4 decision; and both cases involved a legislative investigation into subversive activities. Justice White replaced Justice Charles E. Whittaker in April 1962; but this change makes no difference in the context of our discussion, for Justice Whittaker voted to sustain the conviction of Uphaus. Justice Goldberg replaced Justice Frankfurter in August 1962. Justice Frankfurter voted to uphold the conviction of Uphaus, but Justice Goldberg wrote the opinion for the majority that reversed the conviction of Gibson. Although Justice Goldberg's opinion in the Gibson case, "carefully written within the framework" of the Court's decisions,[105] distinguished the Uphaus case, one may venture the thought that, had he been on the Supreme Court in 1959–1960, the decision in that case would have been 5 to 4 in favor of Uphaus.

The crucial difference is, then, in the political theories and jurisprudential philosophies of the Justices, and not only in the nature of the organization before the Court.

III

Academic Freedom

1. Emergence of a New Constitutional Liberty

In a book of lectures published in 1956, Samuel Eliot Morison said that academic freedom is "almost the newest arrival in the freedom ranks." He noted that:

The phrase itself did not enter the English language until the turn of the nineteenth to the twentieth century [in the year 1897]; and President Charles W. Eliot's Phi Beta Kappa address of 1907, "Academic Freedom," is the earliest title one can find in a library on that subject.[1]

As recently as 1937, a survey of the law relating to academic freedom stated: "Academic freedom is not a 'property' right, or a constitutional privilege, or even a legal term defined by a history of judicial usage and separately listed in the digests. . . ."[2]

During the 1950s, however, academic freedom came to the fore in a number of Supreme Court cases, and at last it can be said that academic freedom has emerged as an interest with a strong claim on constitutional protection. In the more important cases the problem of academic freedom arose in the context of freedom of association. Here we shall consider academic freedom only insofar as it may involve, or be involved with, freedom of association.

The first Supreme Court case to mention academic freedom was *Adler* v. *Board of Education*,[3] decided in 1952. A New York statute, adopted in 1939–1940, provided that no person may be employed in a public school or state college if he teaches or advocates, or is knowingly a member of an organization which teaches or advocates, the overthrow of the Government of the United States or of the state by force or violence. In 1949 the Feinberg Law was passed to implement this statute. The new law directed the Board of Regents to adopt rules to keep disqualified teachers out of the public schools. The board was

86

directed to make a listing of subversive organizations, membership in which would be *prima facie* evidence of disqualification. There was a requirement that the listing be on notice and hearing. The board issued regulations which provided for full hearing for the teacher and the right to judicial review.

Two parents of children and four teachers in New York City schools brought an action to enjoin enforcement. The Supreme Court, in an opinion by Justice Sherman Minton, said that the question was whether the state had deprived the teachers "of any right to free speech or assembly." (Note that this was in 1952. It was not until 1958 that the Court, as we have seen, was ready to speak of association as distinguished from assembly.) The Court answered the question by saying bluntly: "We think not." Teachers, said the Court, may be denied "the privilege of working for the school system . . . because first, of their advocacy of the overthrow of the government by force or violence, or secondly, by unexplained membership in an organization found by the school authorities, after notice and hearing, to teach and advocate the overthrow of the government by force or violence, and known by such persons to have such purpose."

Justice Minton's opinion was written wholly from the point of view of the legislature:

A teacher works in a sensitive area in a schoolroom. There he shapes the attitude of young minds towards the society in which they live. In this, the state has a vital concern. . . . That the school authorities have the right and the duty to screen the officials, teachers, and employees as to their fitness to maintain the integrity of the schools as a part of ordered society, cannot be doubted. One's associates, past and present, as well as one's conduct, may properly be considered in determining fitness and loyalty. From time immemorial, one's reputation has been determined in part by the company he keeps. In employment of officials and teachers of the school system, the state may very properly inquire into the company they keep, and we know of no rule, constitutional or otherwise, that prevents the state . . . from considering the organizations and persons with whom they associate.

Justice Minton spoke of the state's exercising its "police power to protect the schools from pollution and thereby to defend its own existence." The Court gave no consideration to the state's interest in freedom of teaching, or the teacher's interest in the right to intellectual freedom.

The decision was 6 to 3. Justice Frankfurter dissented, but on jurisdictional grounds. In his discussion of these grounds, however, Justice

Frankfurter said that he would want to know more than the record showed "of the real bearing of the New York arrangement on the freedom of thought and activity, and especially [the real bearing] on the feeling of such freedom, which are . . . part of the necessary professional equipment of teachers in a free society."

Justice Douglas wrote a dissenting opinion, in which Justice Black concurred, and here for the first time in a Supreme Court opinion we find academic freedom given constitutional dignity. The Constitution, he said,

guarantees freedom of thought and expression to everyone in our society. All are entitled to it; and none needs it more than the teacher.

The public school is in most respects the cradle of our democracy. . . . The impact of this kind of censorship on the public school system illustrates the high purpose of the First Amendment in freeing speech and thought from censorship.

Justice Douglas objected to the New York laws perhaps less for what they technically provided than for their *effect* on the minds of teachers. He pointed out that the teacher is not a party to the proceeding which results in an organization's being found to be "subversive." Then, hanging over her own hearing, is the "inevitable charge that the organization is 'subversive.'" And the "mere fact of membership in the organization raises a *prima facie* case of her guilt." What especially disturbed Justice Douglas was that the "very threat of such a procedure is certain to raise havoc with academic freedom." For Communists tend to infiltrate organizations committed to liberal causes or to sponsoring unpopular programs; and so, even if the organization was not conceived in sin, the presence of Communists will infect the organization. Now, said Justice Douglas,

a teacher caught in that mesh is almost certain to stand condemned. Fearing condemnation, she will tend to shrink from any association that stirs controversy. In that manner freedom of expression will be stifled.

So one effect of the laws will be discouragement of the teacher's freedom of association.

Another effect will be felt in the classroom itself. For a teacher's membership in an organization may be innocent or guilty, and on this vital issue her views as expressed in her classroom teaching may have a strong bearing. If this is so, then

the principals become detectives; the students, the parents, the community become informers. Ears are cocked for tell-tale signs of disloyalty. . . . This is not the usual type of supervision which checks a teacher's competency; it is a system which searches for hidden meanings in a teacher's utterances. . . . A pall is cast over the classrooms. There can be no real academic freedom in that environment. Where suspicion fills the air and holds scholars in line for fear of their jobs, there can be no exercise of the free intellect. . . . A "party line"—as dangerous as the "party line" of the Communists —lays hold. It is the "party line" of the orthodox view, of the conventional thought, of the accepted approach. A problem can no longer be pursued with impunity to its edges. Fear stalks the classroom. The teacher is no longer a stimulant to adventurous thinking; she becomes instead a pipe line for safe and sound information. A deadening dogma takes the place of free inquiry. Instruction tends to become sterile; pursuit of knowledge is discouraged; discussion often leaves off where it should begin.

Justice Douglas argued that the First Amendment was designed to protect the pursuit of truth. Its framers "knew the danger of dogmatism; they also knew the strength that comes when the mind is free, when ideas may be pursued wherever they lead."

In the concluding paragraph of his opinion, Justice Douglas seemed, however, to qualify the absoluteness of the teacher's freedom to teach. "Of course," he said,

the school system of the country need not become cells for Communist activities; and the classrooms need not become forums for propagandizing the Marxist creed. But the guilt of the teacher should turn on overt acts. So long as she is a law abiding citizen, so long as her performance within the public school system meets professional standards, her private life, her political philosophy, her social creed should not be the cause of reprisals against her.

We quoted from Justice Douglas's opinion at length because of its historical importance as the first statement on academic freedom in a Supreme Court case; and also because his opinion forcefully raises issues which will compel our consideration at a later point in our discussion.

The Adler case was decided in March 1952. In December the Court decided *Wieman* v. *Updegraff*,[4] which involved an Oklahoma statute of 1950 that required all state employees to take an oath that they were not, and had not been for the five years immediately preceding, members of any organization listed by the Attorney General of the United States as "subversive" or "Communist-front." Members of one of the state colleges failed to take the oath. The Supreme Court unanimously upheld their claim that the act was unconstitutional. In the opinion by Justice Thomas C. Clark, the ground for the decision was that the statute made no distinction between innocent and knowing membership; membership, standing alone, was sufficient disqualification to take the oath. Said Justice Clark:

At the time of affiliation, a group itself may be innocent, only later coming under the influence of those who would turn it toward illegitimate ends. Conversely, an organization formerly subversive . . . may have subsequently [to listing] freed itself from the influences which originally led to its listing. . . . Yet under the Oklahoma Act, the fact of association alone determines disloyalty and disqualification. . . . To thus inhibit individual freedom of movement is to stifle the flow of democratic expression and controversy at one of its chief sources.

In the context of our discussion, our chief interest is in the concurring opinion of Justice Frankfurter, in which Justice Douglas joined. This opinion remains as the most cogent statement on behalf of academic freedom to have come from the Court. (Perhaps it should be noted that Justices Douglas and Frankfurter had both been professors, the former for nine years, the latter for twenty-five.)

Justice Frankfurter said that to require the oath without distinguishing between innocent and knowing membership in a subversive organization, on pain of losing the position if the teacher refuses to take the oath,

penalizes a teacher for exercising a right of association peculiarly characteristic of our people. . . . Such joining is an exercise of the rights of free speech and free inquiry. By limiting the power of the States to interfere with freedom of speech and freedom of inquiry and freedom of association, the Fourteenth Amendment protects all persons.

This statement, it should be noted, was made six years before *N.A.A.C.P.* v. *Alabama* and undoubtedly helped prepare the Court for full recognition of freedom of association as a liberty guaranteed by the First and Fourteenth Amendments. Then Justice Frankfurter went on to spell out the constitutional principle of *academic freedom*, in part along the lines urged by Justice Douglas in the Adler case. Said Justice Frankfurter:

But, in view of the nature of the teacher's relation to the effective exercise of the rights which are safeguarded by the Bill of Rights and by the Fourteenth Amendment, inhibition of freedom of thought, and of action upon thought, in the case of teachers brings the safeguards of those amendments vividly into operation. Such unwarranted inhibition upon the free spirit of teachers affects not only those who, like the appellants, are immediately before the Court. It has an unmistakable tendency to chill that free play of the spirit which all teachers ought especially to cultivate and practice; it makes for caution and timidity in their associations by potential teachers.

Our democracy, Justice Frankfurter argued, ultimately rests on public opinion. But this public opinion should be disciplined and responsible. It can be that, however, only if "habits of open-mindedness and of critical inquiry are acquired in the formative years of our citizens." Then follows a very significant passage:

To regard teachers—in our entire educational system, from the primary grades to the university—as the priests of our democracy is therefore not to indulge in hyperbole. It is the special task of teachers to foster those habits of open-mindedness and critical inquiry which alone make for responsible citizens, who, in turn, make possible an enlightened and effective public opinion. Teachers must fulfill their functions by precept and practice, by the very atmosphere which they generate; they must be exemplars of open-mindedness and free inquiry. They cannot carry out their noble task if the conditions for the practice of a responsible and critical mind are denied to them. They must have the freedom of responsible inquiry, by thought and action, into the meaning of social and economic dogma. They must be free to sift evanescent doctrine, qualified by time and circumstance, from that restless, enduring process of extending the bounds of understanding and wisdom, to assure which the freedom of thought, of speech, of inquiry, of worship are guaranteed by the Constitution of the United States against infraction by national or State governments.

In the next case to be considered, Sweezy v. New Hampshire,[5] academic freedom moved up in the order of constitutional dignity. In the Adler case it found a place in a dissenting opinion. In Wieman v. Updegraff it was asserted in a concurring opinion. While in the Sweezy case there was no single Court or majority opinion, academic freedom was recognized by six of the eight Justices who sat in the case: in the opinion by Chief Justice Earl Warren (joined by Justices Black, Douglas, and William J. Brennan), and in the concurring opinion by Justice Frankfurter (joined by Justice John M. Harlan).

The case involved the one-man legislative investigation into subversive activities in New Hampshire with which we became acquainted through the Uphaus case.[6] In the course of the investigation, two subjects arose with regard to which Sweezy refused to answer: his lectures at the University of New Hampshire, and his knowledge of the Progressive Party and its adherents. He was held in contempt by the state courts and ordered committed to jail until purged of the contempt. Six Justices voted to reverse the judgment. Four of the Justices rested their holding on the failure of the legislature to specify that it desired to obtain information on these subjects; for it could not give the state Attorney General a roving commission of such scope that his inquiry would, as here, deprive an individual of his constitutional rights and deny him due process of law.

Sweezy's right to lecture and to associate with others, said Chief Justice Warren, were constitutionally protected. "Merely to summon a witness," he said,

and compel him, against his will, to disclose the nature of his past expressions [in classroom lectures] and associations is a measure of governmental interference in these matters. These are rights which are safeguarded by the Bill of Rights and the Fourteenth Amendment. . . .

The essentiality of freedom in the community of American universities is almost self-evident. No one should underestimate the vital role in a democracy that is played by those who guide and train our youth. To impose any strait jacket upon the intellectual leaders in our colleges and universities would imperil the future of our Nation. No field of education is so thoroughly comprehended by man that new discoveries cannot yet be made. Particularly is that true in the social sciences, where few, if any, principles are accepted as absolutes. Scholarship cannot flourish in an atmosphere of suspicion and distrust. Teachers and students must always remain free to inquire, to study and to evaluate, to gain new maturity and understanding; otherwise our civilization will stagnate and die.

Then the Chief Justice turned to freedom of association (this case, like *Wieman* v. *Updegraff*, preceded *N.A.A.C.P.* v. *Alabama*) in these strong terms:

Equally manifest as a fundamental principle of a democratic society is political freedom of the individual. Our form of government is built on the premise that every citizen shall have the right to engage in political expression and association. This right was enshrined in the First Amendment of the Bill of Rights. Exercise of these basic freedoms in America has traditionally been through the media of political associations. Any interference with the freedom of a party is simultaneously an interference with the freedom of its adherents. All political ideas cannot and should not be channeled into the programs of our two major parties. History has amply proved the virtue of political activity by minority, dissident groups, who innumerable times have been in the vanguard of democratic thought and whose programs were ultimately accepted. Mere unorthodoxy or dissent from the prevailing mores is not to be condemned. . . .

We do not conceive of any circumstances wherein a state interest would justify infringement of rights in these fields. . . .

Justice Frankfurter, concurring in the result, stated that the questions put to Sweezy infringed upon his constitutionally protected academic and political freedoms in the absence of a showing by the state that they were justified in the protection of its interests. Of course the state had claimed that the questions were justified; but, said Justice Frankfurter,

when weighed against the grave harm resulting from governmental intrusion into the intellectual life of a university, such justification for compelling a witness to discuss the contents of his lecture appears grossly inadequate. . . .

Justice Frankfurter wrote of "the dependence of a free society on free universities," and explained:

This means the exclusion of governmental intervention in the intellectual life of a university. It matters little whether such intervention occurs avowedly or through action that inevitably tends to check the ardor and fearlessness of scholars, qualities at once so fragile and so indispensable for fruitful academic labor.

Justice Frankfurter quoted with approval from a plea on behalf of free universities in South Africa:

"In a university knowledge is its own end, not merely a means to an end. A university ceases to be true to its own nature if it becomes the tool of Church or State or any sectional interests. . . . Dogma and hypothesis are incompatible, and the concept of an immutable doctrine is repugnant to the spirit of a university. The concern of its scholars is not merely to add and revise facts in relation to an accepted framework, but to be ever examining and modifying the framework itself."

As did Chief Justice Warren, Justice Frankfurter argued that, with respect to the need for freedom, there is no difference among the disciplines; if anything, the social sciences need it even more than do the natural sciences. "Insights into the mysteries of nature are born of hypothesis and speculation. The more so is this true in the pursuit of understanding in the groping endeavors of what are called the social sciences." Work in these disciplines "must be left as unfettered as possible. . . ."

But there is, said Justice Frankfurter, a limit on academic freedom. The state may intrude into "this activity of freedom" only for reasons "that are exigent and obviously compelling."

With respect to inquiry into Sweezy's relations with the Progressive Party, Justice Frankfurter said that while the Court may well take judicial notice—"on the basis of massive proof and in the light of history"—of facts that are a "justification for not regarding the Communist Party as a conventional political party, no such justification has been afforded in regard to the Progressive Party." (The Progressive Party, he noted, was, in 1948, on the ballot in forty-four states, and in 1952 in twenty-six states.) The state had failed to provide justification.

With the decision in the Sweezy case we can say that the Court gave academic freedom full and equal First Amendment status, so that it is on a par, for dignity and sanction, with the freedoms expressly enumerated in the Bill of Rights, and with freedom of association.

Paul Sweezy, at the legislative hearing, denied that he had ever been a member of the Communist Party or that he had ever been in any program to overthrow the government by force or violence, but refused to answer questions concerning his "opinions and beliefs," as well as about his activities in the Progressive Party. But two years later the Court had before it *Barenblatt* v. *United States*,[7] which was distinguished from the Sweezy case in respect of some of the crucial facts.

Louis Barenblatt taught psychology at Vassar College. In 1954 he was called as a witness before a subcommittee of the House Committee on Un-American Activities that was investigating Communist infiltration into the field of education. He was asked if he was then, or ever had been, a member of the Communist Party. He was also asked if he had ever been a member of "the Haldane Club of the Communist Party while at the University of Michigan." He refused to answer these questions and was held in contempt. Following conviction, he was fined and sentenced to six months' imprisonment. By 5 to 4, the Supreme Court affirmed the judgment.

In his opinion for the majority, Justice Harlan held that the subcommittee was legislatively authorized to investigate Communist infiltration into the field of education. But, more important for us, the majority upheld the conviction against the First Amendment claims of Barenblatt.

Congress, said the Court, has wide power to legislate in the field of Communist activity; it, therefore, has the power to conduct investigations into such activity. The tenets of the Communist Party include the ultimate overthrow of the United States Government by force and violence. The Court said that it would not blind itself to world affairs which have determined the whole course of national policy since the end of World War II. The Court has, therefore, "consistently refused to view the Communist Party as an ordinary political party, and has upheld federal legislation aimed at the Communist problem which in a different context would certainly have raised constitutional issues of the gravest character."

Now, should an exception be made because the field of investigation is education? The majority said, No. The Sweezy case was different, they held, in that Sweezy had not been shown ever to have been a member of the Communist Party, and he was asked questions as to the contents of a lecture he had given at the University of New Hampshire, and as to his connections with the Progressive Party—"then on the ballot as a normal political party in some 26 States." That, said the Court, was "a very different thing from inquiring into the extent to which the Communist Party has succeeded in infiltrating into our universities, or elsewhere, persons and groups committed to furthering the objective of overthrow." The investigation was not directed "at controlling what is being taught at our universities" but at "overthrow [of the United States Government]."

The Court also rejected the contention that the purpose of the investigation was purely "exposure." The Court agreed that "there is no congressional power to expose for the sake of exposure"; but here "the primary purposes of the inquiry were in aid of legislative processes," and so "the motives which spurred the exercise" of the legislative power are irrelevant to the constitutional question. "We conclude," said the Court, "that the balance between the individual and the governmental interests here at stake must be struck in favor of the latter, and that therefore the provisions of the First Amendment have not been offended."

Four Justices—Chief Justice Warren, Justices Black, Douglas, and Brennan—dissented, and all agreed on one point: The investigation of Barenblatt had no purpose "except exposure purely for the sake of exposure." His rights under the First Amendment could not be validly subordinated to this purpose.

But three of them went further. Justice Black—with whom Chief Justice Warren and Justice Douglas concurred—argued that the authorizing resolution was too vague and too broad to support the conviction; that even if the "balancing process" was applicable, it was misused by the majority; that, whether the Communist Party was or was not a political party, it could not, "as a group," be outlawed.

Some of these points will claim our interest later; here we are concerned with academic freedom, and especially as it is related to freedom of association, and on this point Justice Black's opinion raised some questions that had implications for colleges and universities throughout the United States.

Assuming for the sake of argument, said Justice Black, that some "balancing" was proper in this case, the majority misconceived the factors or elements that were to be "balanced." It proceeded as if on one side was the government's right to preserve itself, and on the other Barenblatt's right to refrain from revealing Communist affiliations. But these were not the factors. The constitutional interest in Barenblatt's silence was this: "The interest of the people as a whole in being able to join organizations, advocate causes and make political 'mistakes' without later being subjected to governmental penalties for having dared to think for themselves." Why is this an important national interest? "It is this right," Justice Black answered,

the right to err politically which keeps us strong as a Nation. For no number of laws against Communism can have as much effect as the personal conviction which comes from having heard its arguments and rejected them, or from having once accepted its tenets and later recognized their worthlessness. Instead, the obloquy which results from investigations such as this not only stifles "mistakes" but prevents all but the most courageous from hazarding any views which might at some later time become disfavored. This result, whose importance cannot be overestimated, is doubly crucial when it affects the universities, on which we must largely rely for the experimentation and development of new ideas essential to our country's welfare. *It is these interests of society, rather than Barenblatt's own right to silence, which I think the Court should put on the balance against the demands of the Government,* if any balancing process is to be tolerated. Instead they are not mentioned, while on the other side the demands of the Government are vastly overstated and called "self preservation."[8]

This statement by Justice Black is a reinforcement of the argument for academic freedom that was previously made by Justices Douglas and Frankfurter; but here it was made pointedly as the value to be "balanced" against the government's right of self-preservation.

But the argument does not, of course, end here. Justice Black went on to state that the First Amendment means that

the only constitutional way our Government can preserve itself is to leave its people the fullest possible freedom to praise, criticize or discuss, as they see fit, all governmental policies and to suggest, if they desire, that even its most fundamental postulates are bad and should be changed; "Therein lies the security of the Republic, the very foundation of constitutional government."

The Constitution, in other words, does not leave it to Congress, or any other branch of the government, to resolve the balancing process in favor of anything except the freedoms guaranteed by the Constitution itself; for whatever powers the government may have to preserve itself, or to accomplish any other purpose, have been limited by the freedoms that the Constitution itself guarantees. One of these is academic freedom, and, as an important aspect of academic freedom, though not limited to it, freedom of association.

On the balancing issue, students of constitutional law and writers on public affairs are as divided as is the Court itself. We shall have something to say about it at a later point. Here we want to keep our attention on the intertwining of academic and associational freedoms, and so we turn to the last of the important cases that call for our consideration; namely, *Shelton* v. *Tucker*, decided in 1960.[9]

In 1958 Arkansas adopted a law that required every person connected with a public school or any state college or university to file an affidavit listing all organizations to which he at the time belonged or to which he had belonged during the past five years, or to which he had paid dues or contributions. No compensation could be paid to anyone who had failed to file the affidavit; and the filing of a false affidavit was made a criminal offense.

B. T. Shelton, a teacher in the Little Rock public schools for twenty-five years, refused to file an affidavit, and so was notified that he would not be hired for the 1959–1960 school year. He brought an action in the federal courts, and at the trial the evidence showed that he was not a member of the Communist Party or of any organization advocating overthrow of the government, and that he was a member of the N.A.A.C.P.

Two others brought suit in the state court—an associate professor at the University of Arkansas and a high-school teacher of Little Rock. Each refused to file the required affidavit; but the former filed an affirmation in which he listed his membership in professional organizations and denied ever having been a member of a subversive organization; and the latter filed an affidavit in which he stated that he had never belonged to a subversive organization and listed his membership in the American Legion and the Arkansas Education Association; and each stated that he would be willing to answer questions touching upon

his qualifications which his own institutional authorities might constitutionally ask.

The Supreme Court, by 5 to 4, held the statute unconstitutional. In
his opinion for the majority, Justice Stewart pointed out that it was
important to consider the statute against the fact that teachers and
professors in Arkansas did not enjoy tenure; they were hired on a
year-to-year basis—there was no job security beyond the end of each
school year.

The majority held that of course a state has a right to investigate
the competence and fitness of its teachers; and classroom conduct is
not the sole basis for determining fitness to teach. But

to compel a teacher to disclose his every associational tie is to impair that
teacher's right of free association, a right closely allied to freedom of
speech and a right which, like free speech, lies at the foundation of a free
society.

Interference with this right was, said the Court, "conspicuously
accented" when the teachers had no security beyond the current year;
the school authorities could deal with the information in the affidavits
as they saw fit. The information could even be made public, thus
inducing fear: in the state court proceedings a member of a local Citizens Council testified that his group intended to get the information
contained in the affidavits in order to eliminate persons who supported
the A.C.L.U., the American Association of University Professors,
and other organizations disliked by the Citizens Council. But, said the
Court, "even if there were no disclosure to the general public, the
pressure upon a teacher to avoid any ties which might displease those
who control his professional destiny would be constant and heavy."
The possibility of public exposure only aggravated "the impairment of
constitutional liberty."

Justice Stewart put the case for academic freedom in strong terms:
"The vigilant protection of constitutional freedoms is nowhere more
vital than in the community of American schools"; and he quoted
from the Sweezy decision: "Teachers and students must always remain
free to inquire, to study and to evaluate."

The opinion, however, made it clear that the majority did not intend
to ban every inquiry into a teacher's or professor's associational ties.
The Court said:

The question to be decided here is not whether the State of Arkansas can
ask certain of its teachers about all their organizational relationships. It is
not whether the State can ask all of its teachers about certain of their

associational ties. It is not whether teachers can be asked how many organizations they belong to, or how much time they spend in organizational
activity. The question is whether the State can ask every one of its teachers
to disclose every single organization with which he has been associated
over a five-year period. . . . The statute requires a teacher to reveal the
church to which he belongs, . . . his political party, . . . every conceivable
kind of associational tie. . . . Many such relationships could have no possible bearing upon the teacher's occupational competence or fitness. . . .
The statute's comprehensive interference with associational freedom goes
far beyond what might be justified in the exercise of the state's legitimate
inquiry into the fitness and competency of its teachers.

Justices Frankfurter, Harlan, Clark, and Whittaker dissented. In his
dissenting opinion, Justice Frankfurter referred to his own "strong
views against crude intrusions by the state into the atmosphere of creative freedom in which alone the spirit and mind of a teacher can
fruitfully function. . . ." Justice Frankfurter concluded that it was
"reasonable" for the Arkansas legislatures to choose the "form of
regulation" involved "rather than others less restrictive." His line of
reasoning took some surprising turns. He said:

Granted that a given teacher's membership in the First Street Congregation is, standing alone, of little relevance to what may rightly be expected
of a teacher, is that membership equally irrelevant when it is discovered
that the teacher is in fact a member of the First Street Congregation *and*
the Second Street Congregation *and* the Third Street Congregation *and* the
4-H Club *and* the 3-H Club *and* half a dozen other groups? Presumably,
a teacher may have so many divers associations, so many divers commit-
ments, that they consume his time and energy and interest at the expense
of his work or even of his professional dedication. . . . Surely, a school
board is entitled to inquire whether any of its teachers has placed himself,
or is placing himself, in a condition where his work may suffer.

If this is what the test of "reasonableness" may lead to, then Justice
Black's attacks on it are fully justified. Is a school board entitled to
ask teachers how much time they spend with their wives, their children, their mothers-in-law, their friends, their neighbors? What of the
teacher who belongs to only one church but devotes hours every day
to the work of that church, while another teacher belongs to several
churches but attends none? What of the teacher who belongs to no
association but is devoted to bridge-playing? or likes to sleep twelve
hours a day? or spends hours every day reading mystery stories or at
bird-watching or television?
Certainly a local school board, or the board of trustees of a univer-

sity, has an interest in the teacher's performance, his competence or fitness; but then the concern must be with what he does in the classroom. Even if a teacher were to spend all his spare time on preparation for his next class, he might still be incompetent.

If the Arkansas statute could satisfy Justice Frankfurter's test of legislative reasonableness, then the teacher's freedom of association meant nothing.

Justice Frankfurter went to still greater extremes than in the passage quoted above. By way of further justification of his claim that the state's action was reasonable, he said:

A teacher's answers to the questions which Arkansas asks, moreover, may serve the purpose of making known to school authorities persons who come into contact with the teacher in all of the phases of his activity in the community, and who can be questioned, if need be, concerning the teacher's conduct in matters which this Court can certainly not now say are lacking in any pertinence to professional fitness.

Thus, the affidavits may be used to set up a network of espionage, and members of the First Street Congregation may be discreetly asked how a certain teacher conducts himself as a member: Does he teach a class in the Sunday school? How regular is his attendance at church services? Does he come to the Bible-study class? Ostensibly, the inquiry is intended only to find out how much of the teacher's time is given over to "associational" work; but can there be any doubt about the effects of such procedures on the teachers' morale?

At the conclusion of his opinion, Justice Frankfurter stated: "Of course, if the information gathered by the required affidavits is used to further a scheme of terminating the employment of teachers solely because of their membership in unpopular organizations, that use will run afoul of the Fourteenth Amendment." But would the school board need to *state* that a teacher's contract has not been renewed "solely" because of his membership in an "unpopular organization"? But even more seriously: would not the effect of the Arkansas statute be to discourage teachers from joining any but the most respectable—the most innocuous—organizations? And does not this effect undermine academic freedom, and freedom of association as a significant aspect of academic freedom?[10]

While academic freedom has been accorded full constitutional status, the fact that the Arkansas statute would have been upheld as constitutional but for the grace of a single vote makes one terribly uneasy. Everything is settled—and yet nothing is settled. But this can be said with equal force not only of academic freedom but of all the other freedoms. They are always being "balanced"; and in the tug of war between the state's men and the rights men, the constitutional freedoms have a precarious career. "The louder he talked of his honor," Emerson wrote, "the faster we counted our spoons."[11] There are times when we must feel this way about Supreme Court opinions— there are the broad, generous, sparkling generalities, but a decision that takes away almost all that was promised. Yet it would be sinful to be dominated by such gloomy and petty thoughts as one reviews the record. The freedoms have much more than a fighting chance when they are challenged; and it is doubtful if men have a right to ask for more in a world in which certainty is generally only a snare or a delusion.[12]

2. *The Constitution and Educational Ideals*

In reviewing the emergence of academic freedom in Supreme Court cases, there are a number of observations that I would make:

The Court has made it clear that the social sciences need academic freedom no less than do the natural sciences. This needed to be said because there always are those who think that it is asking too much of the public to allow freedom of inquiry and teaching regarding issues over which men may sharply and deeply divide and even fight. But the Court has made it clear that the light of the intelligence must be allowed to penetrate into all areas of social thought and social conflict; and that just as the physicist or chemist may have his laboratory, so may the social scientist have his, and the Constitution will protect both equally.

There have always been those who thought that while teachers and professors in private institutions may, by effort, win a measure of academic freedom, it is too much to expect public authorities to allow their teachers or professors the enjoyment of such a luxury. The Court, however, has done away with this distinction. The cases that we have considered involved public school teachers or professors at state universities, and academic freedom was vindicated for them. A city or state agency may not hire or fire at will, or condition employment on the employee's surrender of his constitutional guarantees. In an opinion written in 1892, when he was a member of the Supreme Judicial Court of Massachusetts, Justice Holmes said: "The petitioner may have a constitutional right to talk politics, but he has no constitutional right to be a policeman."[13] But the academic freedom cases that we have considered make it clear that though a person may have no constitutional right to be a professor at the state university, he cannot be asked to be a professor provided he does not exercise academic freedom.

The Supreme Court cases make no distinction between teachers in the public schools and university professors in the enjoyment of academic freedom. All alike have the same constitutional guarantees. In this respect the Court is probably in advance of public opinion—although in the last few years, thanks to the reports by James B. Conant and to the proclaimed ambition of the U.S.S.R. to overtake and surpass the U.S.A., progress has been made to upgrade the secondary schools and to narrow the gap between them and colleges. The conventional view, however, is that the primary and secondary schools are "the places for the conveying of prevailing tradition," while college is the place for "inquiry" into "the problematic and unfinished aspects of our civilization."[14] From this point of view it would follow that the teachers in the primary and secondary schools do not need freedom; they need only an assigned text and a schedule of lessons—and probably most school boards, principals, superintendents, and parent-teacher associations think just that.

This is a far cry from the picture of the schoolteacher as drawn by Justice Frankfurter in *Wieman* v. *Updegraff:*[15]

To regard teachers—in our entire educational system, from the primary grades to the university—as the priests of our democracy is therefore not to indulge in hyperbole. . . . They must be exemplars of open-mindedness and free inquiry. . . . They must have the freedom of responsible inquiry. . . .

Among the organizations interested in protecting academic freedom, the Academic Freedom Committee of the American Civil Liberties Union is perhaps the only one that includes the public school teachers within the scope of its mandate; the others concentrate exclusively on the college and university professors.[16] Some day, one hopes, this will be changed. Fortunately, the Supreme Court has already prepared the constitutional foundation for the larger view.

In the last few years, the view of academic freedom has been enlarged in one notable respect: it has come to be recognized that the student, too, is entitled to academic freedom. Until recently, he was entirely disregarded. He was the silent, passive recipient of benefits, or the victim of brazen denials or attacks; in either case, he had no status of his own.

But recently the American teen-ager has come into his own, particularly as a consumer worthy of special cultivation. Direct appeals are now made to him—and her. This is in part a by-product of the parents' affluence. Perhaps an awareness of the active political—sometimes even revolutionary—role exercised by students in other countries has also had an effect. Certainly the sit-in demonstrations conducted by Negro students taught students everywhere that they possess a power and unclaimed, unexercised rights. Whatever the reasons, the fact is that in the last few years American students on college and university campuses have asserted *their* right to academic freedom, especially *their* right to hear lectures by guest speakers who are identified with unpopular causes or organizations. Their claims have been recognized by the Academic Freedom Committee of A.C.L.U.[17] The committee statement, it should be noted, does not overlook the high school student's need for academic freedom, though its chief concern is with the college and university students. The American Association of University Professors has also become alert to this aspect of academic freedom.[18]

While the Supreme Court has as yet had no occasion to pass on it, the theoretical basis for the students' claims has already been stated by the Court. Justice Frankfurter, for example, has said that our democracy rests on public opinion; but public opinion must be "disciplined and responsible," and it can be that only if citizens, "in the formative years," acquire "habits of open-mindedness and of critical inquiry."[19] Are such habits fostered if, as students, they are prohibited from hearing speakers of their own choice?

From the standpoint of their elders, there is no doubt that students sometimes make mistakes in providing a respectable forum for persons in the political and intellectual underground; but the young have no monopoly on mistakes; furthermore, it may be argued that, while the old are generally too old to learn from *their* mistakes, we have built our schools and universities on the hope that the young *will* learn from their mistakes; and men—regardless of age—are not free unless they are free to make mistakes. And it can be shown that whenever, in recent years, a university acted to veto the action of students, and prohibited them from hearing a lecture, it was the university rather than the students that made the greater mistake and paid the heavier penalty.

Following a number of incidents in the City and State of New York, the Committee on Civil Rights of the New York County Lawyers Association issued in 1962 a report on campus censorship,[20] in which the forms of such censorship were summarized as follows:

(1) There is the censorship of student organizations and groups which attempt to discuss political *questions*. Some administrations bar these entirely. (2) Refusal to allow student groups to hear political *speakers*. (3) Barring *every* controversial subject from the campus, including writings. (4) Permitting an outside speaker *only* on the authority of an administrative officer.

The committee's conclusion was that all such restrictions defeat academic freedom and all the freedoms guaranteed by the First and Fourteenth Amendments. The committee concluded:

The standard which should be applied in both public and private institutions is this: any written idea or discussion or speaker should be permitted full exposure on the campus, so long as the basic purpose of the exposure is not to violate the law. Anything short of this, we think, is inimical to free society.[21]

The view of public elementary and secondary education expressed by the Supreme Court must raise some questions about the legal claims of parochial schools. In *Wieman* v. *Updegraff*[22]—to cite only one example—Justice Frankfurter spoke of the "free spirit of teachers," "that free play of the spirit which all teachers ought especially to cultivate and practice," "habits of open-mindedness and of critical inquiry [that should be acquired by citizens in their school years]," "the special task of teachers to foster those habits of open-mindedness and critical inquiry which alone make for responsible citizens," "[teachers] must be exemplars of open-mindedness and free inquiry." Thus academic freedom becomes the foundation of American democracy: American government is dependent upon responsible citizenship, which in turn makes possible "an enlightened and effective public opinion"; but men are not likely to be citizens with "habits of open-mindedness and critical inquiry" unless they acquired these habits in their formative years; and so it is that the Constitution rests on the schools as its foundation. But the schools must then be of the character described by the Court if they are to fulfill their task.

But it is doubtful if one could honestly claim that the parochial schools—Roman Catholic, Orthodox Jewish, or Protestant—are committed to the "free play of the spirit," or to foster, in teachers and students, "habits of open-mindedness and critical inquiry." There is, one may assume, a great variety among the schools, from extreme authoritarianism to some degree of permissiveness or latitudinarianism. With respect to the Roman Catholic schools, one could try to score an easy debater's point by referring to the encyclical *Quanta cura*, with its attached famous *Syllabus* in which, in 1864, Pope Pius IX listed eighty of the "principal errors of our times," including liberalism. That encyclical seems very remote from the spirit of Pope John XXIII and his successor Pope Paul VI and the forces let loose by the Twenty-first Ecumenical Council (Vatican II).

In fact, the Roman Catholic schools are today self-critical, as evidenced in part by a three-year study at Notre Dame University under a grant from the Carnegie Corporation.[23] An extensive survey of the schools in the New York City Archdiocese in 1964—with some 222,-000 pupils, taught by 6700 teachers—disclosed considerable ferment and a new spirit of experimentation and liberalization. This survey, conducted by *The New York Times*,[24] showed that fewer church-dominated textbooks were being purchased, that there was a broadened approach to the teaching of religion and religious texts, and a tendency to get away from excessive indoctrination and to present the weaknesses and failures—as well, of course, as the virtues and strengths—of the Roman Catholic Church and religion. More public school textbooks were being used. Catholic voices were being heard even urging the abolition of parochial schools (*Are Parochial Schools the Answer?* by Mary Perkins Ryan carried an Imprimatur). Students are encouraged to engage in free discussions and debates. In brief, one can no longer make categorical judgments about Roman Catholic schools, for they are undergoing (at least many of them) radical changes in methodology, educational and religious philosophy, and attitudes.

On the other side, when one looks at public education in the United States, one finds there, too, great variety; but certain it is that the statements we have quoted from Supreme Court opinions represent an ideal rather than a picture of a factual situation. And just as there are strong forces to make the parochial school less doctrinaire and authoritarian and more liberal, so there are strong forces to do the exact opposite to the public school: witness the attacks on John Dewey's educational philosophy, the movements to introduce some form of religious indoctrination, the attempts at censorship of textbooks, the widespread use of teachers' loyalty oaths, and other attempts to make the public schools less free and more authoritarian and doctrinaire.

Professor Sidney Hook has argued that children have the constitutional right to receive education *in addition* to that provided by public schools;[25] but he has asked whether they have a right "to receive education in private schools from partisan agencies *as a substitute* for public education. . . ." "Only the former," he wrote, "is essential to democratic educational policy; the latter, under certain circumstances, may be an overt threat to democracy."[26]

Logically, Professor Hook is right. If the purpose of public education is the development of intelligence, so that all Americans will be citizens with "habits of open-mindedness and of critical inquiry,"[27] then if any school is found to prepare citizens to have opposite qualities of mind and spirit, it should be banned as a public nuisance and its pupils should be held to violate the state's compulsory-school-attendance law.

But this should be true also of a public school that, for example, inculcates racist attitudes as a matter of dogma that may not be questioned. Taking the nation's schools in their great variety, one would find that many schools—public and private—would not pass by Supreme Court standards.[28]

The most important consideration of all, as Professor Hook says, is that the state should not be permitted to claim a monopoly on education. In *Pierce* v. *Society of Sisters*[29] the Supreme Court said:

The fundamental theory of liberty upon which all governments in this Union repose excludes any general power of the state to standardize its children by forcing them to accept instruction from public teachers only. The child is not the mere creature of the state; those who nurture him and direct his destiny have the right, coupled with the high duty, to recognize and prepare him for additional obligations.

This statement meant to the Court, and has been taken to mean since the decision in 1925, that children have the constitutional right to receive education *in addition* to that received in the public schools[30] and also to attend a private school *as a substitute* for the public school. Both consequences are important for free society. A state monopoly on education could be disastrous, even if the state were to allow after-school teaching as a concession; for such teaching may not be sufficient to countervail the force of the public school. In any case, the principle should be that the child does not belong to the state; that the duty to bring up the child and to educate him belongs to the parents; that the public school is basically, though not exclusively, the agent of the parents, their surrogate; that the parents may select a private school in place of the public school to fulfill *their* duty to *their* child.

The democratic state—as the Supreme Court opinions make clear—also has interests and obligations in this sphere; but since it *is* a democratic state, those interests and obligations must find expression that is consistent with the rights and duties of the parents—and of the child himself as a future citizen.

This principle of the limited rights of the state with respect to the education of children is one that we owe to Jews and Roman Catholics, who placed an overriding emphasis on their duty to provide elaborate religious instruction for their children; while Protestants generally were satisfied with the public school, supplemented by the Sunday school.[31]

In 1958 the hierarchy of the Roman Catholic Church in the United States departed from the position it usually took and claimed that the Church (rather than the parents, let alone the state) has the right to teach—a right given not by state or constitution but by God Himself.[32] This is consistent with the belief that the Church is not a voluntary association (which would generally be the Protestant position) but was instituted by God; it has, therefore, God-given tasks, and God-given rights commensurate with its needs.

This claim demonstrates again how deep and complex the principle of freedom of association may be; and how it touches and weaves into —and out of—freedom of teaching; and how theory and practice interlock to make for an order of legal claims, interests, duties, and rights.

In *The Good Society*[33] Walter Lippmann makes a distinction between what he calls "natural associations" and associations that depend on the state for their existence. The former are held together by "kinship or fellowship"; the latter, "by a framework of legal rights." Examples of natural associations cited by Lippmann are the family, a community, a religious fellowship, a learned society, a club, a trade union, a professional association; the business corporation that enjoys limited liability and a government bureau are cited by him as examples of state-dependent associations—legal creatures in the literal sense. Lippmann states that the associations "into which men group themselves spontaneously, naturally, instinctively, voluntarily" involve the state only to the extent that the state needs to "accommodate the smaller associations to each other and to the social order as a whole"; but the state may not treat them as if they were "government departments" and "under the authority of public officials"—as state-dependent associations are.

Lippmann cautioned against "the error of latter-day liberals who imagined that they had a complete and perfected doctrine." He recognized the fact that his differentiation between the two categories of association leaves room for borderline types, and that we still have no satisfactory theory "as to how the interests of society as a whole can be reconciled with the autonomy of natural associations." There will be need always to achieve reconciliation "through definition, detailed adjudication, and revision of the reciprocal rights and duties of all groups.

Now, if a church—any church—is a natural association, in the sense that it does not owe its existence to the state, it hurts no one, as far as one can see, if it claims to owe its existence to God. Insofar as the claims of the state to a monopoly need to be resisted—and at times such claims are made—it is perhaps well, and sometimes even necessary, to make God the opponent of the state; for men, even when gathered into an association, may feel themselves small and weak when opposed to the Leviathan.

But fortunately, in view of the Supreme Court decisions in the association and academic-freedom cases, it is possible now to lean less on theology and political theory, and more on constitutional principles. Though men may still quarrel and fight when an answer is given in constitutional terms—as we know from the division in the Court itself, and from the fight over the Supreme Court and its decisions—since the Constitution operates in a realm wholly secular, there is more basis for hope that the quarrels and disagreements will be contained within the realm of law, in which intelligence, discourse, and debate are, if not dominant, at least pervasive and persuasive.

IV

The Communist Party
and Freedom of Association

1. The Smith Act Cases

In our discussion of academic freedom as related to freedom of association, we unavoidably touched on the problem of membership in the Communist Party and constitutional guarantees. Here we propose to concentrate on the constitutional status of the Communist Party, perhaps the most complex subject in constitutional law, one that has divided both the Court and the scholars.

Most Americans must be hopelessly confused when they think of the Communist Party. On the one hand, they know that Congress has, over the past twenty-five years at least, passed many acts directed against the Party, its officers and members, and its activities. They recall that Party leaders went to prison for substantial terms. The name of the Party is not seen on ballots, and there are no Communist members of Congress or of any state legislature. On the other hand, Communist Party newspapers are still being published, and once in a while Americans read in respectable newspapers of Communist Party conventions. Party leaders call and attend meetings and issue public statements. It is impossible to give a Yes or No answer even to the question, Has the Communist Party been outlawed?

A State Department Intelligence Report, "World Strength of the Communist Party Organizations,"[1] specified forty-five countries where the Communist Party is said to be illegal. But the term "illegal" is used here in a nontechnical, nonlegal sense, as follows:

a communist party has been listed as illegal whenever it is suppressed in practice, even in the absence of formal, statutory prohibition. Conversely, a party has been listed . . . as legal when it is legally proscribed but operates nonetheless with the tolerance of the government which makes no effort to dissolve the party in accordance with existing statutes.[2]

Using this definition and applying it to the Communist Party of the United States in a rough-and-ready fashion, one could say that the party is *not illegal*. It is, however, doubtful if one would be justified in going further and saying that the party is *legal*.

To give a measure of the complexity we encounter, consider the fact that the *Internal Security Manual,* an official Senate document, containing provisions of federal statutes, executive orders, and congressional resolutions relating to the internal security of the United States, consists of close to five hundred pages;[3] and the *Digest of the Public Record of Communism in the United States,* prepared by a committee of scholars for the Fund for the Republic,[4] consists of about seven hundred pages. The opinions in the Supreme Court cases involving the Party or members or alleged members must total many thousand pages. Where shall one start?

Since our concern with association is, as we have seen, a concern with First Amendment freedoms, we could justifiably start with the Alien Registration Act of 1940, generally referred to by its popular title, the Smith Act.[5] Before passage of this statute there were the Espionage Acts of 1917 and 1918,[6] under which over two thousand persons were prosecuted from 1917 to 1920. The statutes and prosecutions involved freedom of speech. The 1918 act, for example, contained a provision that made it a crime to utter or publish "any disloyal, profane, scurrilous, or abusive language" about the form of American government, or the Constitution, or the flag, or the armed forces. A few of the defendants were Communists, the others were pacifists, Socialists, anarchists, and Wobblies. The acts were applicable only in time of war, and after the Armistice pardons and commutations were granted.[7]

The Smith Act, however, applies in peace as well as in war. It makes it a crime to advocate, advise, or teach "the duty, necessity, desirability, or propriety of overthrowing or destroying the government of the United States or the government of any State . . . by force or violence. . . ." The crime could be committed by a person who "organizes or helps or attempts to organize any society, group, or assembly of persons who teach, advocate, or encourage the overthrow or destruction of any such government by force or violence"; or the crime could be committed by one who "becomes or is a member of, or affiliates with, any such society, group, or assembly of persons, knowing the purposes thereof. . . ." Attempting or conspiring to commit these prohibited acts is also a criminal offense.[8]

Supporters of the legislation in Congress made it clear in their discussions that they knew that Congress could not ban any organization *by name* without violating the constitutional prohibition on bills of attainder; but they wished Congress to go as far as it could constitutionally to outlaw Nazi, Fascist, and Communist organizations.[9]

Although eighteen members of the Socialist Workers Party (Trotskyist) were convicted under the Smith Act during the war,[10] it was eight years after passage of the bill before the first prosecution against Communists. The reasons why there were none before 1948 are speculative. Perhaps the fact that the U.S.S.R. was a war ally had a bearing. In any case, on July 20, 1948, the first indictments against Communists were handed down under the Smith Act. Twelve leaders of the party were named; but one of them, William Z. Foster, was never tried because of ill health. (Foster was the Communist Party's presidential candidate in 1924, 1928, and 1932. In 1930 Earl Browder displaced him as Party head, but when, in 1945, Browder was removed from Party posts, Foster became national chairman, a position he held until 1957. He died in 1961.)

To understand the theory of the case against the Communist Party leaders it is necessary to recall some facts. Communist history went through several stages that are relevant to our discussion:

(1) In 1935 the Comintern (the Communist International), seeing a grave threat in Hitler's rise to power in Germany, abandoned its militant policy against liberal and Socialist groups and urged national Communist groups to form "popular fronts" or coalitions with heretofore despised bourgeois elements. The rallying cry was anti-fascism. American Communists now began to support New Deal measures; penetrated into labor unions, in some of which they gained positions of leadership; and helped organize new unions under the banner of the C.I.O. The "popular front" momentum resulted in the formation of "front organizations," to which were attracted many non-Communists who were anti-Fascists.

(2) Communist Party attacks on Nazi Germany came, however, to an abrupt end as soon as Hitler and Stalin, in August 1939, signed a nonaggression pact. Germany now had no fear of a two-front war, and so Germany invaded Poland on September 1, 1939, and World War II was begun. The Communists denounced France and Great Britain as "imperialists" and carried on a vigorous propaganda campaign to keep the United States from military preparations, and Communist-led unions resorted to strikes.

(3) On June 22, 1941, Germany invaded the U.S.S.R. For Com-

munists the character of the war was suddenly changed. The enemies of Germany (joined by Italy, Romania, Hungary, Slovakia, and Finland) were now engaged in a democratic war against imperialism. The Communist Party, led by Earl Browder—the Party's candidate for President of the United States in 1936 and 1940, convicted of passport fraud and imprisoned in 1940 but freed by President Roosevelt in 1942—now supported fully the war against Germany, and with the Russians demanded the opening of a second front. The Party now was opposed to strikes, and its propaganda pictured capitalism as a "progressive" force. In 1943, as a demonstration of solidarity with its allies, the U.S.S.R. dissolved the Comintern. In 1944 the Communist Party of the United States disbanded as a political party and became the Communist Political Association. The change was intended to be more than nominal; it was intended as further evidence of the solid patriotism of American Communists, and of the American, "democratic" character of communism—ostensibly a movement to achieve the Communist society by peaceful, democratic means.

(4) In June 1944 the Allies landed in northern France, and armored divisions began to race toward the Rhine. On the Eastern Front, the Russian armies, in August and September 1944, forced the capitulation of Finland, Romania, and Bulgaria, and early in 1945 conquered East Germany to the Oder. On April 25, 1945, the Western and Russian armies met in Saxony, and Germany collapsed.

Now, also in April 1945, Jacques Duclos, a French Communist leader, published an article accusing Earl Browder of "right deviationism" and attacking the policy that had culminated in the conversion of a militant, revolutionary party into a tame political association. The article was published in the *Daily Worker* in the following month. In July 1945 the Communist Political Association was disbanded and the Communist Party reconstituted at a national convention. Earl Browder was deposed and removed from all Party posts (and from the Party itself in 1946). Foster became national chairman. These changes coincided with the beginning of the Cold War, and the days of Communist respectability—pretended or real—were over.

We shall soon see how important this historical background is for an understanding of the cases brought under the Smith Act. But certain other facts ought to be recalled if we are to have an insight into the climate of opinion that existed at the time of the first Smith Act trial.

After the Communist Party was reconstituted in July 1945, Communists continued to infiltrate trade unions, and this became a matter of grave national concern. Congress in 1947 included in the Taft-Hartley

Act a provision requiring each officer of a union and its parent body to file annually an affidavit declaring that he was not a member of the Communist Party, and that he did not believe in and was not a member or supporter of an organization that favored the overthrow of the government by force or any illegal means.[11] In 1949 and 1950 the C.I.O. expelled ten Communist-dominated unions. The West Coast maritime workers, led by Harry Bridges, were a constant source of worry because of their capacity to engage in crippling strikes for political rather than economic motives.[12]

In 1947 the Communist Parties of the U.S.S.R., France, Italy, and six other European countries formed the Cominform, ostensibly to aid the Parties in the exchange of experience. In 1948 it expelled the Yugoslav Communist Party because of Tito's defiance of Stalinist supremacy.[13]

In 1947 President Truman issued Executive Order 9835, which prescribed procedures for an employees' loyalty program. It called for a loyalty check on every civilian employee in all executive departments or agencies of the federal government. Loyalty boards were set up. The Civil Service Commission was required to establish a central master index covering all persons on whom loyalty investigations had been made since 1939. The Department of Justice was required to prepare a list—what came to be known as the Attorney General's List—of organizations determined by it, upon investigation, to be "totalitarian, fascist, communist or subversive, or as having adopted a policy of advocating or approving the commission of acts of force or violence to deny others their rights under the Constitution of the United States, or as seeking to alter the form of government of the United States by unconstitutional means." Membership in, affiliation with, or "sympathetic association" with any organization on the Attorney General's List was to be considered in connection with the determination of disloyalty.[14]

In January 1945 the House of Representatives created a standing Committee on Un-American Activities,[15] and later that year the committee conducted six days of hearings dealing with the Communist Party. The chief witnesses were Browder and Foster. The committee was especially interested in the facts behind the reconstitution of the Party following the article by Duclos; but these hearings were ineffectual. In 1946 the committee investigated the Joint Anti-Fascist Refugee Committee, a "front" organization, whose representatives were the first recalcitrant witnesses to appear before the committee.[16] In its investigation of communism in 1946 the committee had the help of

Louis Budenz, who was managing editor of the *Daily Worker* in 1945 when he broke with the Party. His testimony confirmed the suspicion that the American Communist leaders were manipulated by the Communist (or Third) International, which existed in fact though no longer in name.

In 1947 the committee set for itself an eight-point program, which included undertaking "to expose and ferret out the Communists and Communist sympathizers in the Federal Government," to show how Communists had won control over some vital trade unions, and an investigation of Communist influences in Hollywood. It conducted seven sets of hearings. Several of the hearings were devoted to bills, one of which, the Rankin Bill, made it unlawful for a person to run for office as a Communist Party candidate, or "to advocate, or express or convey the impression of sympathy with or approval of, Communism or Communist ideology" in teaching in any school or college, or to send through the mails any publication that does this.

The most sensational committee hearings came in 1948, with the testimony of Elizabeth Bentley and Whittaker Chambers. The former —in testimony first before a Senate committee—asserted that numerous employees of the federal government, whom she named, had worked as Soviet agents during the war. Elizabeth Bentley was an ex-Communist, as was Chambers, and between them they named over fifty persons as their "contacts" whose cooperation they had enjoyed. The most prominent person named by Chambers was Alger Hiss, who had been secretary to Justice Holmes, had held various positions in the Departments of Justice and State, was executive secretary of the Dumbarton Oaks Conference and secretary general of the United Nations Charter Conference, and in 1947 became president of the Carnegie Endowment for International Peace. Chambers, a senior editor of *Time* magazine, and Hiss confronted each other at a committee session on August 17, 1948, and a *cause célèbre* was created. On November 17, 1948, Chambers disclosed what became the celebrated pumpkin papers (copies of documents that, he said, Hiss had stolen from the State Department and given to Chambers as a Soviet courier). Hiss denied the charges. Since, under the statute of limitations, he could not be tried for espionage, a grand jury, on December 15, 1948, indicted him on two counts of perjury. The jury that tried him was unable to reach a verdict in July 1949; at his second trial he was found guilty in January 1950. He served a prison sentence until November 1954.[17]

The importance of the Chambers-Hiss drama in the setting of the committee investigations cannot be exaggerated; for one thing, it convinced many Americans that the danger of Communist espionage and subversion was serious, and that the danger was apparently not being met by the Department of Justice, the Federal Bureau of Investigation, and the other agencies customarily associated with the apprehension of criminals and their prosecution under the criminal laws of the country. Extraordinary dangers called for extraordinary measures to meet them, and many—perhaps most—Americans assented to the objectives and procedures of the House Committee on Un-American Activities which could lead to such spectacular results as the trials and conviction of Alger Hiss.

Thus the committee's work probably had an effect on the Department of Justice, which may have felt that it was, under the surface, being teased, baited, and challenged.

The committee made public the seven pumpkin papers and forty-three other documents, which provided the justification for its tragically true statement: "Communist espionage has broken through the security forces of the United States government and made off with secret information of both military and diplomatic character concerning our national plans, policies, and actions."[18]

The committee in 1948 also conducted hearings on what came to be known as the Mundt-Nixon Bill,[19] which it supported. The purpose of the bill was to require the Communist Party and front organizations to register with the Department of Justice and supply the names of all officers and members, and also to require all publications of such organizations, when sent through the mails, to be labeled: "Published in compliance with the laws of the United States governing the activities of agents of foreign principals." In essentials, the bill reflected the approach of Morris Ernst, prominent civil-liberties lawyer, who argued that the constitutional way to fight communism was to force Communists out into the open. As we shall see, the essence of this idea was later incorporated into legislation enacted by Congress. What is relevant to note at this point is that there were, by the end of the 1940s, many developments that could have been interpreted by the President and the Attorney General as pointing to the imperative need to start enforcing against Communists the laws that already were on the books. Failure to do so could have had, from the administration's point of view, undesirable consequences: (1) the supplanting, by Congress and its committees, of the Executive as the branch of government taking the initiative to defend vigorously the security of the United States; (2) the defeat of Harry S. Truman in the 1948 election—after 1946 the Republican Party controlled the Eightieth Congress and most of the state governorships, and if Truman was to turn the tide in 1948, it was essential that the nation see that the administration was just as eager to expose and destroy the Communist Party as were the Republican leaders of Congress; (3) enactment by Congress of laws that might have repressive, and even oppressive, effects on civil liberties, civil rights, the liberal temper, the New Deal, and the Fair Deal.

Looking back to those years with the advantage, if not wisdom, afforded by hindsight, one can say that, in the light of international and domestic events, it was "natural" that in July 1948 the Smith Act should be used against the leaders of the Communist Party, and "natural" too that courts and juries should be influenced by the events of these years in their interpretation of facts and law.

The leaders of the Communist Party were indicted under the conspiracy provision of the law. The government charged that (1) the defendants conspired in 1945 to disband the Communist Political Association and to form again the Communist Party, as an organization that would teach and advocate the overthrow and destruction of the Government of the United States by force and violence; and (2) the defendants conspired to advocate and teach the duty and necessity of overthrowing and destroying the government by force and violence.

The government's case against Eugene Dennis, Gus Hall, John Gates, and the other eight defendants dealt at length with the circumstances that led to the dissolution of the party in 1944 and its reconstitution in 1945, and relied heavily on Budenz's testimony that a Russian delegate to the United Nations Conference had served as a courier to pass on to the American Communists word that Duclos's article was to be considered authoritative. Much time was taken by testimony that the Party—once one penetrated its Aesopian language—taught and advocated revolution by force and violence. The trial started on March 8, 1949, and ended on October 14, 1949. It took over seven months, and the record filled 16,000 pages. All the defendants were found guilty; one was sentenced to three years' imprisonment and a fine of $10,000, the others to five years and fines of $10,000.

Since the indictments charged the defendants with the crime of conspiracy to *advocate* the overthrow of the government, and conspiracy to organize the Communist Party as an organization of persons who *advocate* the overthrow of the government, there was a serious question of the constitutionality of the Smith Act and the indictments brought under it; for the First Amendment provides that "Congress shall make no law . . . abridging the freedom of speech, or of the press. . . ."

In an opinion for a unanimous Supreme Court in 1919, Justice Holmes formulated for the first time the Clear and Present Danger Doctrine.[20] "We admit," he wrote, that

in many places and in ordinary times the defendants, in saying all that was said in the circular, would have been within their constitutional rights. But the character of every act depends upon the circumstances in which it is done. . . . The most stringent protection of free speech would not protect a man in falsely shouting fire in a theater, and causing a panic. . . . The question in every case is whether the words used are of such a nature as to create a clear and present danger that they will bring about the substantive evils that Congress has a right to prevent. It is a question of proximity and degree. When a nation is at war many things that might be said in time of peace are such a hindrance to its effort that their utterance will not be endured so long as men fight, and that no court could regard them as protected by any constitutional right. . . . If the act (speaking, or circulating a paper), its tendency and the intent with which it is done, are the same, we perceive no ground for saying that success alone warrants making the act a crime.

This Clear and Present Danger Doctrine had had, up to the time of the trial in 1949, a rather checkered career. It will suffice here to say that, with only rare exception, the doctrine was used to support a *denial* of free speech; and no federal statute had ever been invalidated under the test of the doctrine.[21]

In the trial in the federal district court in New York, Judge Harold R. Medina charged the jury that they could convict if they found that the defendants intended to overthrow the government "as speedily as circumstances would permit." The Smith Act, when applied in this way, he held, would satisfy the First Amendment guarantee. He further charged the jury:

If you are satisfied that the evidence establishes beyond a reasonable doubt that the defendants, or any of them, are guilty of a violation of the statute as I have interpreted it to you, I find as a matter of law that there is sufficient danger of a substantive evil that the Congress has a right to prevent to justify the application of the statute under the First Amendment of the Constitution.

This is a matter of law about which you have no concern. . . .

In other words, the court held that the Smith Act was constitutional; that the clear-and-present-danger test was met by advocacy of the overthrow of the government "as speedily as circumstances would permit"; that such advocacy was a clear and present danger as a matter of law (for the judge) and not of fact (for the jury).

The court of appeals affirmed the convictions. Judge Learned Hand, in his opinion for the majority in that court, interpreted the clear-and-present-danger test to mean this: "In each case [courts] must ask whether the gravity of the 'evil,' discounted by its improbability, justifies such invasion of free speech as is necessary to avoid the danger."

The Supreme Court,[22] by 6 to 2, affirmed, and the Court's opinion, by Chief Justice Vinson, approved the meanings given to the clear-and-present-danger test by Judges Medina and Hand and added some interpretive language of its own—e.g., "We must therefore reject the contention that success or probability of success is the criterion"; "certain kinds of speech are so undesirable as to warrant criminal prosecution." The Court spoke of the "impending threat" to the government, in the face of which we dare not "paralyze our Government . . . by encasing it in a semantic strait-jacket"; "Speech is not an absolute . . . all concepts are relative." "If Government is aware that a group aiming at its overthrow is attempting to indoctrinate its members and to commit them to a course whereby they will strike when the leaders feel the circumstances permit, action by the Government is required." "Petitioners intended to overthrow the Government of the United States as speedily as the circumstances would permit." "Their conspiracy to organize the Communist Party and to teach and advocate the overthrow of the Government of the United States by force and violence created a 'clear and present danger' of an attempt to overthrow the Government by force and violence."

Justice Douglas's dissenting opinion made a number of telling points. He correctly contended that the indictments did *not* charge Eugene Dennis and the other defendants with a *conspiracy to overthrow* the government. They were charged with a conspiracy to form *a party* of people who *teach and advocate* the overthrow of government, and with a conspiracy *to advocate and teach* its overthrow. There was no evidence at the trial that the defendants taught techniques of sabotage, assassination, stealing of documents, or other criminal acts. There was no evidence that they taught methods of terror, which would have brought them under statutes punishing seditious conspiracy.[23] Instead, the trial purported to show that the defendants organized a party to teach the Marxist-Leninist doctrine contained in *The Communist Manifesto* (1848), by Marx and Engels, *State and Revolution* (1917), by Lenin, *Foundations of Leninism*

1924), and *History of the Communist Party of the Soviet Union* 1939), by Stalin. The defendants "preached the creed with the hope that some day it would be acted upon."

Now, these books, Justice Douglas pointed out, were not outlawed by the Dennis case convictions. The books could still be read in class-rooms—but only provided that the teacher did not believe the creed. "The crime then depends not on what is taught but on who the teacher is." This means that we must start probing men's minds for their pur-poses and motives, so that men may be innocent or punished, not for what they did, but "for what they thought."

Justice Douglas also stressed that the Court seemed impressed with the fact that the defendants were charged with *conspiracy*. But since no seditious *acts* were charged but only *speech,* "to make a lawful speech unlawful because two men conceive it is to raise the law of conspiracy to appalling proportions."

His most cogent argument was one that went to the heart of the government's case. It is common knowledge, said Justice Douglas, that Communists plot and scheme against the free world. The U.S.S.R. and the Red Army are a threat to world peace. The nature of com-munism as a force in the world is, of course, relevant to the issue of a clear and present danger. But the issue is the clear and present danger of advocacy by the *defendants* within the United States. The issue is *not* whether *Russia* is a clear and present danger to the security of the United States. Well, then, what are defendants' strength and tactical position? "On that there is no evidence in the record." If the Court should look outside the record and take judicial notice of the facts, then it would be compelled to conclude that the defendants *"as a political party"* are "of little consequence." "Communism in the world scene is no bogeyman; but Communists as a political faction or party in this country plainly is. . . . The people know Soviet Commu-nism; the doctrine of Soviet revolution is exposed in all of its ugliness and the American people want none of it."

Now, this was the *political* aspect of communism. There were other questions one could ask about Communists: "Their numbers; their positions in industry and government; the extent to which they have in fact infiltrated the police, the armed services, transportation, stevedor-ing, power plants, munitions works, and other critical places—these facts," Justice Douglas noted, "all bear on the likelihood that their advocacy of the Soviet theory of revolution will endanger the Repub-lic." Unfortunately, however, "the record is silent on these facts."

Can the Court take judicial notice of their existence? Well, if one were to take judicial notice of the facts, he would find it impossible to say that American Communists are potent and are strategically placed to the point where they must be suppressed for their speech. "To believe that petitioners and their following are placed in such critical positions as to endanger the Nation is to believe the incredible." Thanks to the work in recent years of committees of Congress, the Attorney General (under President Truman's Executive Order), of labor unions (in exposing and expelling Communist-dominated unions from the C.I.O.), of state legislatures, and of loyalty boards, the country was hardly on the edge of peril. "It is safe to say," said Justice Douglas,

that the followers of the creed of Soviet Communism are known to the F. B. I.; that in case of war with Russia they will be picked up overnight as were all prospective saboteurs at the commencement of World War II; that the invisible army of petitioners is the best known, the most beset, and the least thriving of any fifth column in history.

After the Supreme Court's decision affirming the convictions, four of the defendants jumped bail, and additional sentences for contempt were imposed; but eventually all the defendants served their Smith Act sentences, and two of the defendants, aliens, were then ordered deported.[24]

The Court's decision was announced on June 4, 1951. By that time the country was in the depths of the McCarthy period, which may be said to have begun, with the peculiar character that it gained from the work of Senator Joseph R. McCarthy, on February 9, 1950, while the Dennis case was on appeal. McCarthy was elected to the Senate in 1946 (and re-elected in 1952). On February 9, 1950, he delivered a speech at Wheeling, West Virginia, which at once won him national attention. In this speech he said:

Ladies and gentlemen, while I cannot take the time to name all the men in the State Department who have been named as *active members of the Communist Party and members of a spy ring,* I have here in my hand a list of 205—a list of *names that were made known to the Secretary of State as being members of the Communist Party and who nevertheless are still working and shaping policy in the State Department.*[25]

This startling "disclosure" was at once carried by the national press and radio, and McCarthyism was introduced into American life and history. Eleven days later, Senator McCarthy delivered a speech on the Senate floor that purported to be his speech as delivered at Wheeling, but in lieu of the paragraph quoted above he substituted the following:

I have in my hand 57 cases of individuals who would appear to be either card-carrying members or certainly loyal to the Communist Party, but who nevertheless are still helping to shape our foreign policy.[26]

After delivery of this speech on the Senate floor, McCarthy presented to the Senate information designed to show the Communist character of eighty-one employees of the State Department identified by numbers.[27] On February 22, 1950, less than two weeks after McCarthy's initial blast, the Senate adopted a resolution calling on its Committee on Foreign Relations (of which Senator Tom Connally was chairman) to conduct a full and complete study. The committee appointed a subcommittee, with Senator Millard E. Tydings as chairman. The subcommittee's report, made July 20, 1950, said:

. . . it should be mentioned that from the very outset the subcommittee was subjected by Senator McCarthy and certain segments of the press and radio to a campaign of vilification unparalleled in the history of congressional investigations. The unwarranted cry of "white wash" was raised, even before the hearings started, and equally unfair and malicious allegations were made throughout the proceedings.[28]

We cannot here pursue the painful story of McCarthyism except to mention that when the Republicans, with the election of Eisenhower as President, assumed control of Congress in 1953, McCarthy became chairman of the Senate's permanent investigations subcommittee, a position from which he wielded great power and from which he terrorized government officials. His charges of corruption or subversion were made against men in high office and in all walks of life, including the Secretary of the Army, whom he accused of concealing evidence of espionage that McCarthy had allegedly uncovered at Fort Monmouth, New Jersey. It was not until December 1954 that the Senate, on a motion to censure McCarthy, voted to condemn him for contempt of a Senate elections subcommittee that had investigated his conduct and financial affairs in 1952, abuse of certain Senators, and insults to the Senate during the censure proceedings. After this action, and with the Democrats' gaining control of Congress in the 1954 elections, McCarthy's power waned and he gradually disappeared from the national scene. (He died in 1957.)[29]

The end of the McCarthy era came at about the same time as the death of Stalin in 1953 and the initiation of the program of de-Stalinization under Khrushchev. The crimes of Stalin were exposed, the Russian citizen was given less cause to fear the secret police, a larger measure of legality of procedure was assured, many of the forced-labor and concentration camps were emptied and closed, a degree of freedom of public discussion was made possible, and the bonds between the Kremlin and the Communist Parties of other countries were somewhat loosened.[30]

We are too close to these events to be able to evaluate them; but we can, I think, state that the history of the McCarthy period was part of the provenience of the decision in *Dennis* v. *United States*—as were also the investigations by the House Committee on Un-American Activities, the Chambers-Hiss drama and the conviction of Alger Hiss, and the tensions of the Cold War. It is difficult to believe that this complex of events had no bearing on how Judge Learned Hand and Chief Justice Vinson resolved the issue of the clear-and-present-danger test.

Justice Douglas's views on the Dennis case are persuasive—especially his argument that the defendants had not been shown to constitute a danger to American security when one concentrated (as did the government's case) on them as "teachers" and "advocates" of revolution by force and violence. As propagandists of revolution, the American Communist Party was perhaps the least successful of all the Communist Parties in the free world; and in recent years its failure has become even more apparent. Membership figures do not, of course, tell the whole story, but with respect to the Communist Party's advocacy function—which was the heart of the indictments—the membership figures are crucially significant.

In 1944 Earl Browder testified before a congressional committee that the Communist Political Association had a membership of about 80,000.[31] At the time of the Dennis case trial in 1949, according to J. Edgar Hoover, Director of the F.B.I., the party membership was 54,174. Mr. Hoover's figures for the several years following were: 1950—52,669; 1951—43,217; 1952—31,608; 1953—24,796.[32] In the last decade the decline has been even more precipitous. In 1962 the newspaper columnist David Lawrence reported that the membership was about 10,000.[33] In 1964 Gus Hall, general secretary of the party, used the same figure.[34] The *Worker's* circulation went down from 100,000 just after World War II to 22,000 in 1964.[35] A former F.B.I. agent has written that in 1962 the F.B.I. had 150 informants in the party, more than one-sixth of its membership. The dues these secret agents paid, he wrote, made the F.B.I. "the largest single contributor to the coffers of the Communist party."[36] (In Great Britain in 1961 the *Daily Worker* had a circulation of over 60,000 copies, and the Party had a membership of between 28,000 and 29,500. The population was about 30 per cent of that of the United States. Even the Netherlands, with a population of under 12,000,000, had in 1961 an estimated 12,000 Communist Party members—several thousand more than the party had in the United States).[37]

It is only when American Communists are viewed *as agents of the U.S.S.R.* that they are potentially dangerous. When viewed in isolation from the U.S.S.R., the Party members are seen only as "candidates for the political psychopathic ward." But when the Party is seen *as a foreign agent* that recruits members for espionage and other unlawful activities—for activities such as those mentioned by Justice Douglas: positions in industry and government, infiltration of the police, of the armed services, of transportation, of stevedoring, of power plants, and of munitions works—then the Communist danger is clear and present. But then the danger is *not speech* but overt *acts* and a conspiracy to recruit members for such *acts*—all on behalf of a foreign power. From this point of view,[38] the number of Party members would be irrelevant to the rationale of the prosecution, for there would be no constitutional question of a clear and present danger—the First Amendment problems would not arise.

Following the government's victory in the Supreme Court in the Dennis case, the Department of Justice proceeded with Smith Act prosecutions for conspiracy against "second-string" Communists. On April 1, 1952, six more Communists were convicted. On January 21, 1953, thirteen Party functionaries—including Elizabeth Gurley Flynn, who died in Moscow in 1964—were convicted and two were acquitted. In all, there were fourteen conspiracy trials, resulting in one hundred and four convictions. There were ten acquittals, and a hung-jury verdict for one. The trial of Elizabeth Gurley Flynn and her twelve co-conspirators lasted nine months; a trial in Honolulu lasted seven months; the trial of William Schneiderman and thirteen co-defendants took six months.[39] Each case had to go over substantially the same ground that was covered in the Dennis prosecution, because each jury separately had to hear and weigh the evidence as to the conspiracy to organize the Party in 1945, the nature of the doctrines taught and advocated; and each defendant's guilt beyond a reasonable doubt had to be established. There was no public interest in the cases after the Dennis case was finished.

Most of the defendants were sentenced to five years' imprisonment; the lightest sentence was for a two-year term. But only twenty-nine of the Communists convicted on conspiracy charges actually served their sentences. To understand what happened between court and prison we must look into another Supreme Court decision, *Yates* v. *United States,* decided in 1957.[40]

On August 5, 1952, fourteen "second-string" Communists—including Oleta Yates and William Schneiderman—were convicted under the conspiracy provisions of the Smith Act. On December 2, 1957, the Supreme Court decided their appeal in the Yates case—five years after the trial. By a 5-to-2 vote the Court reversed the convictions.

The decision was based on two grounds:

(1) The Communist Party was organized in 1945. The defendants were indicted, for conspiracy to organize the Party, in 1951. The Court held that the indictments were three years too late, for prosecution was barred by a three-year statute of limitations. The government contended that "to organize" should be interpreted in a *continuing* sense, so that, until the Party is disbanded, persons who join it may be considered as participants in the continuing process of organizing: this must be the meaning of "organizing" intended by Congress in view of the fact that the Party had first been organized in 1919, and the Smith Act was adopted in 1940, and certainly Congress had no prophetic knowledge of the disbanding of the Party in 1944 and its renewal in 1945.

The Court rejected this interpretation of the act. Congress in 1940, said the Court, had in mind not only the Communist Party but other groups as well, such as syndicalists and anarchists; furthermore, Congress did not write the organizing provision with particular reference to the Communist Party. Against the Party, the main congressional thrust appeared to be the teaching and advocating provision.

In any case, the decision of the Court on this point meant that after 1948 no indictments could be procured charging persons with the crime of organizing the Communist Party.

(2) The defendants had also been prosecuted for conspiracy to teach and advocate. The Court found that the trial judge had departed, in his instructions to the jury, from the Dennis case. The judge had instructed the jury that the defendants violated the Smith Act if they were found to have advocated the necessity and duty of overthrowing the government by force and violence, and that the jury need not find that the defendants had used "language of incitement." The Court held that the judge misunderstood the meaning of the Dennis decision.

There is a distinction between the teaching of abstract doctrine, said the Court, and the teaching of action, and Congress intended in the Smith Act to make this distinction and to prohibit only the latter. "The statute," said Justice Harlan, "was aimed at the advocacy and teaching of concrete action for the forcible overthrow of the Government, and not of principles divorced from action." There must be proof of "advocacy of action, not ideas." The following passage from Justice Harlan's opinion is crucial—I quote from the opinion *in extenso* because I cannot trust myself to paraphrase the untranslatable subtleties:

The essence of the *Dennis* holding was that indoctrination of a group in preparation for future violent action, as well as exhortation to immediate action, by advocacy found to be directed to "action for the accomplishment" of forcible overthrow, to violence "as a rule or principle of action," and employing "language of incitement," . . . is not constitutionally protected when the group is of sufficient size and cohesiveness, is sufficiently oriented towards action, and other circumstances are such as reasonably to justify apprehension that action will occur. This is quite a different thing from the view of the District Court here that mere doctrinal justification of forcible overthrow, if engaged in with the intent to accomplish overthrow, is punishable per se under the Smith Act. That sort of advocacy, even though uttered with the hope that it may ultimately lead to violent revolution, is too remote from concrete action to be regarded as the kind of indoctrination preparatory to action which was condemned in *Dennis*. . . . *Dennis* was thus not concerned with a conspiracy to engage at some future time in seditious advocacy, but rather with a conspiracy to advocate presently the taking of forcible action in the future. It was action, not advocacy, that was postponed until "circumstances" would "permit." . . . The essential distinction is that those to whom the advocacy is addressed must be urged to *do* something, now or in the future, rather than merely to *believe* in something.

After performing these and similar semantic feats the Court said: "We recognize that distinctions between advocacy or teaching of abstract doctrines, with evil intent, and that which is directed at stirring people to action, are often subtle and difficult to grasp, for in a broad sense, as Mr. Justice Holmes said . . .: 'Every idea is an incitement.' But the very subtlety of these distinctions required the most clear and explicit instructions with reference to them, for they concerned an issue which went to the very heart of the charges against these petitioners." The opinion went on with more admonitions about the need for "precise and understandable instructions."

The Court follows the rule that, insofar as possible, statutes are to be construed in such a way that they are constitutional rather than unconstitutional.[41] But at the same time the Constitution requires criminal statutes to give fair notice of what acts the law will punish.[42]

The Court's opinion in the Yates case leaves the advocacy provisions of the Smith Act so vague and indefinite as to render those provisions unconstitutional. It is hard to see how a jury of men and women of ordinary intelligence can determine any defendant's guilt beyond a reasonable doubt by attempting to follow a trial court's instructions that would embody the Court's language quoted above.

One can only conjecture as to why the Court acted as it did in the Yates case. It probably felt that it had done all that was possible in the Dennis case to save the Smith Act and to demonstrate to the nation that there were legal, constitutional ways to meet the Communist threat, even if the nature of that threat was perhaps misconceived. It sent the eleven top Communists to prison. But six years later it saw what might be an endless series of prosecutions of Communists, with hundreds or maybe thousands of them serving prison sentences, as the Party—for many reasons—was becoming even weaker than it was at the time of the Dennis case. The clear and present danger was not the Communist conspiracy against the government, but the Communist conspiracy cases, in their threat to the integrity of the First Amendment. Maybe the Department of Justice should have exercised more judgment and have kept itself from asking for more and more indictments; but the Department is exposed to congressional and other political and partisan pressures. The Court could not, in 1957, overrule the Dennis decision and declare the Smith Act unconstitutional. It was too late for that (except for Justices Black and Douglas); so it acted to leave the statute and its earlier decision ostensibly intact but pulled their teeth. It made indictments under the conspiracy-to-organize provisions impossible by applying the three-year statute of limitations; and it made further convictions under the conspiracy-to-advocate provisions practically impossible by imposing unbearable burdens on the prosecution, the trial judges, and the juries. The result was commendable, but the constitutional spectacle was not exactly an ennobling experience.

After the Yates decision, in one pending case after another, and in cases that had already been seen through the trials, convictions, and sentencing, the government moved the dismissal of indictments. This is why, though 104 Communists were convicted under conspiracy charges, only 29 actually served prison terms.

But the Smith Act also has a so-called membership provision, which makes it a crime to be or become a member of any organization "of persons who teach, advocate or encourage" the overthrow of the government by force or violence, when he knows its purposes. It was not until May 1954 that the government resorted to this provision. At that time it procured the indictment of Claude M. Lightfoot. In the following year he was tried and convicted, and sentenced to five years' imprisonment and a fine of $5000. But two years later his conviction was reversed by the Supreme Court, for reasons not relevant to our discussion, and he was remanded for a new trial.[43] Lightfoot was certainly not known to the American public as a leading Communist; but the leaders of the Party in 1954 were either in prison or otherwise involved in Communist conspiracy cases. How the Department of Justice happened to choose Lightfoot from among some twenty thousand members, we cannot say.[44]

Lightfoot was not retried because two other membership cases, *Scales* v. *United States* and *Noto* v. *United States,* made their way to the Supreme Court, and Lightfoot's retrial was deferred pending their determination. Let us now look at these two cases.

Junius Scales, a member of a North Carolina family that goes back to the Colonial period, became a Party member in 1946 and was for a time Party chairman for North and South Carolina. He was convicted in 1955 and sentenced to six years' imprisonment—a year more than had been imposed on Eugene Dennis, and double the term imposed on Elizabeth Gurley Flynn. In 1957 the conviction was reversed and a new trial granted because of procedural defects.[45] Scales was retried in 1958, convicted, and again given a six-year imprisonment sentence. In 1961 the Supreme Court affirmed the conviction.[46] The decision was 5 to 4, with Chief Justice Warren and Justices Black, Douglas, and Brennan dissenting. The majority, in an opinion by Justice Harlan, upheld the constitutionality of the membership clause of the Smith Act.

Justice Harlan's summary of the trial judge's instructions to the jury was as follows: The jury was told that in order to convict

it must find that within the three-year limitations period [1951-1954] (1) the Communist Party advocated the violent overthrow of the Government, in the sense of present "advocacy of action" to accomplish that end as soon as circumstances were propitious; and (2) petitioner was an "active" member of the Party, and not merely "a nominal, passive, inactive or purely technical" member, with knowledge of the Party's illegal advocacy and a specific intent to bring about violent overthrow "as speedily as circumstances would permit."

The Supreme Court held that these instructions were in accord with the decision in the Yates case.

The Court held that Congress must have intended to punish only "active" members of the Party. The indictment was held not to have been defective for failure to charge "active" membership—the instructions to the jury adequately took care of this matter.

The Court recognized the difficulties in attributing criminality to membership in an organization; a member, as distinguished from a co-conspirator, may, for example, "indicate his approval of a criminal enterprise by the very fact of his membership without thereby necessarily committing himself to further it by any act or course of conduct whatever." But the Court said that all the difficulties are resolved when the statute is held to reach only "active" members "having also a guilty knowledge and intent," which is distinguished from "what otherwise might be regarded as merely an expression of sympathy with the alleged criminal enterprise, unaccompanied by any significant action in its support or any commitment to undertake such action."

On the First Amendment argument, the Court said:

It was settled in *Dennis* that the advocacy with which we are here concerned is not constitutionally protected speech, and it was further established that a combination to promote such advocacy, albeit under the aegis of what purports to be a political party, is not such association as is protected by the First Amendment. We can discern no reason why membership, when it constitutes a purposeful form of complicity in a group engaging in this same forbidden advocacy, should receive any greater degree of protection from the guarantees of the First Amendment.

The Court recognized a distinction between (1) a technical criminal conspiracy, which has only a criminal purpose, and which therefore can claim no protection under the First Amendment, and (2) a quasi-political party, or some other group, which may have both legal and illegal aims. With respect to the latter, the constitutional problem is met by a membership provision in a criminal statute that is construed as was the membership clause of the Smith Act. "Thus," said the Court, "the member [of the Communist Party] for whom the organization is a vehicle for the advancement of legitimate aims and policies does not fall within the bar of the statute: he lacks the requisite specific intent 'to bring about the overthrow of the government as speedily as circumstances would permit.' Such a person may be foolish, deluded, or perhaps merely optimistic, but he is not by this statute made a criminal."

Justice Harlan said that a Smith Act prosecution must meet "strict standards" of proof; accordingly, as in the Yates case, the Court went into the details of the record in the trial of Scales, devoting to them some twenty pages. We must be satisfied with the statement that the Court found the evidence sufficient to support the conviction of Scales.

In the companion Noto case,[47] decided at the same time, the Court unanimously reversed the conviction for membership. In his opinion, Justice Harlan reviewed the trial record and found the evidence insufficient to support the jury's verdict of "present illegal [Communist] Party advocacy"; for *in each case* there must be evidence regarding the Communist Party (in addition to the defendant's own personal criminal knowledge, purpose, and acts) such as would satisfy the "strict standards" formulated in the Dennis and Yates cases. All the Justices were in agreement that the government had failed to accomplish this in the trial of John Noto. (Chief Justice Warren and Justices Black, Douglas, and Brennan offered additional grounds for the reversal.)

Following the decisions in the Scales and Noto cases, the government moved the dismissal of the indictment of Lightfoot and of four others.[48] No further resort has been made to the membership clause, which is as much of a dead letter as are the "advocacy" and "organizing" provisions.

Junius Scales, however, went to prison—the only person to serve a prison sentence for membership in the Communist Party. He had asked the trial judge to reduce the sentence, but this motion was denied, and Scales surrendered to the United States marshal, by order of the trial judge, on October 2, 1961. The extravagance of the situation was aggravated by the fact that while Scales was a Communist at the time of his first trial in 1955, in the following year he was shocked out of his faith by Khrushchev's revelations of Stalin's crimes and also by the brutal Soviet repression of the Hungarian uprising.[49] He publicly left the party in 1957. Later that year the Supreme Court set aside his conviction on technical grounds, as we have observed; but the Department of Justice had him retried in 1958. His trial was for his membership within the three-year period from 1951 to 1954. Technically it was all correct; but if the law supposed that that was enough, Mr. Bumble had warrant for saying that "the law is a ass— a idiot." A petition signed by 550 prominent citizens, led by Norman Thomas, asked President Kennedy to bring the unbecoming spectacle to a merciful end. Among the signers of the petition were Grenville Clark, Robert F. Goheen, Reinhold Niebuhr, two federal judges, and nine of the twelve jurors who had voted for Scales's conviction.[50] The sentence was commuted on the day before Christmas, 1962, after Scales had served about fifteen months of his six-year term.

This completes the history of the Smith Act prosecutions. Technically, the Smith Act remains on the books, magisterially constitutional. But, under the Yates decision, prosecutions for conspiracy to violate the law's prohibitions against "organizing" are firmly barred, except under an unused 1962 amendment, and prosecutions for conspiracy to teach or advocate are, as a practicable matter, impossible; and after the Scales and Noto cases it is hard to see how any Attorney General would hazard another case under the membership clause.

In an imperfect world, perhaps it has all come out about as well as could have been reasonably expected. The Supreme Court's performances as it had before it the various provisions of the Smith Act, however, recall the lines of Pope:

> . . . assent with civil leer,
> And, without sneering, teach the rest to sneer;
> Willing to wound, and yet afraid to strike. . . .[51]

It is not possible to leave the Smith Act cases without touching upon one of their most bizarre aspects: the imprisonment of the attorneys for the defense at the end of the trial in the Dennis case.

As soon as the jury returned the verdict of guilty, the trial judge at once found the five defense attorneys, and Eugene Dennis, who had appeared *pro se,* guilty of criminal contempt and imposed on them various jail terms up to six months. Justice Black summarized the scene in the courtroom as follows: As soon as the trial judge had dismissed the jury, he

asked all the defendants' lawyers [and Dennis] to stand up, then read them a very minor part of a lengthy "contempt certificate" in which they were alleged to have committed many acts of contempt at various times during the protracted trial. Without affording any of them a chance to say a word before he acted, the presiding Judge held all of them guilty of contempt and sentenced each one to prison.

A majority of the court of appeals sustained the convictions. The Supreme Court denied review of the contempt issue but granted leave to review only the question whether the trial judge himself had the right to adjudge and punish, or whether the lawyers had the right to have the contempt charges tried before another federal judge, after notice, hearing, and opportunity to defend. By 5 to 3 the Court sustained the action of the trial judge.[52]

The judge charged thirty-nine occurrences during the trial as items of misconduct; these he did not regard as discrete instances, but rather as manifestations of a conspiracy by the lawyers against him. The court of appeals reversed the convictions on the conspiracy charge and sustained the convictions on thirty-seven specifications. But Justice Frankfurter, dissenting, found that the conspiracy theme was the foundation for all the charges of contempt; for the trial judge believed that the lawyers had entered into a conspiracy to hurt him personally by charging him with racial bias, collusion with the prosecution, headline seeking, and other personal failings. And, Justice Frankfurter noted, he reacted to the lawyers' conduct.

At frequent intervals in the course of the trial his comments plainly reveal personal feeling against the lawyers, however much the course of the trial may have justified such feeling. On numerous occasions he expressed his belief that the lawyers were trying to wear him down, to injure his health, to provoke him into doing something that would show prejudice, or cause a mistrial or reversal on appeal; . . . it is indubitably established that the judge felt deeply involved personally in the conduct for which he punished the defense lawyers. He was not merely a witness to an occurrence, as would be a judge who observed a fist fight in his courtroom or brutal badgering of a witness or an impropriety towards the jury. The judge acted as the prosecuting witness; he thought of himself as such. His self-concern pervades the record; it could not humanly have been excluded from his judgment of contempt.

Justice Frankfurter's comment on the course of the trial in the Dennis case is especially notable when one remembers that he was not one of the dissenting Justices when the case was reviewed by the Supreme Court. "Truth compels the observation," said Justice Frankfurter,

painful as it is to make, that the fifteen volumes of oral testimony . . . record numerous episodes involving the judge and defense counsel that are more suggestive of an undisciplined debating society than of the hush and solemnity of a court of justice. . . . Throughout the proceedings, even after the trial judge had indicated that he thought defense counsel were in conspiracy against him and were seeking thereby to subvert the trial, he failed to exercise the moral authority of a court possessed of a great moral tradition.

Few miscarriages of justice have been condemned in words as stinging as the following from Justice Frankfurter's opinion:

It is a disservice to the law to sanction the imposition of punishment by a judge personally involved and therefore not unreasonably to be deemed to be seeking retribution, however unconsciously, at a time when a hearing before a judge undisturbed by any personal relation is equally convenient. It does not enhance a belief that punishment is a vindication of impersonal law. . . .

One must bear in mind the fact that the lawyers had defended avowed Communists. Lawyers who at any time would take such cases are not easy to find. Professionally, it is often a kiss of death to become known as a civil-liberties lawyer; it is assumed that if a lawyer was *really* competent and "respectable" he would have banks, large corporations, and businessmen as his clients, for that is where the money is. We have already noted this unfortunate deficiency in the legal profession in discussing the role of the N.A.A.C.P. With this fact in mind, we may find a special poignancy in the following passage from Justice Black's dissenting opinion:

Before sentence and conviction these petitioners were accorded no chance at all to defend themselves. They were not even afforded an opportunity to challenge the sufficiency or the accuracy of the charges. Their sentences were read to them but the full charges were not. I cannot reconcile this summary blasting of legal careers with a fair system of justice. Such a procedure constitutes an overhanging menace to the security of every courtroom advocate in America. The menace is most ominous for lawyers who are obscure, unpopular or defenders of unpopular persons or unorthodox causes.

Imprisonment for contempt did not, however, end the lawyers' troubles. Abraham J. Isserman was suspended for two years from practice in the federal district court for the southern district of New York. He was a member of the New Jersey bar, and the Supreme Court of that state issued an order permanently disbarring him.

Now, the United States Supreme Court had a rule that where a member of its bar had been disbarred in any state he would be suspended from practice before the Supreme Court unless he showed good cause to the contrary. Isserman was issued a rule to show cause before the Supreme Court why he should not be disbarred there. Isserman argued that he had already been punished enough for his contempt by the imprisonment and the actions of the federal and New Jersey courts, and that to disbar him from the Supreme Court would be excessive, vindictive punishment. The Court, by 4-to-4 vote, issued an order disbarring him.[53] Justices Black, Frankfurter, and Douglas joined in Justice Jackson's opinion strongly disapproving this action. Justice Jackson said that he did not know of any other case "where a lawyer has been disbarred by any court of the United States or of a state merely because he had been convicted of a contempt." On the other hand, he cited cases where lawyers "have been found guilty of serious contempt without their standing at the bar being brought into question." Justice Jackson's concluding sentence stated: ". . . to permanently and wholly deprive one of his profession at Isserman's time of life, and after he has paid so dearly for his fault, impresses us as a severity which will serve no useful purpose for the bar, the court or the delinquent."[54]

The last link in the chain of judicial miscarriages was the Supreme Court rule by which disbarment was effected by an evenly divided Court. A year later the Court changed the rule to provide that there shall be *no* disbarment except with the *concurrence* of a majority of the participating Justices. A year and a half after the original order of Isserman's disbarment, the Court, by 4-to-3 vote, granted a rehearing and set aside the disbarment.[55]

The Smith Act and the cases which it spawned do not add up to a chapter in American history that can be read with pride. It has a nightmarish effect that evokes the question: Was it all real? Could it possibly be that mature, sophisticated men, in high office, could have thought that America's security and freedom would be strengthened by these actions?

Testifying before the Warren Commission on May 14, 1964, J. Edgar Hoover said that there were limits on the degree of protection that can be given the President, for the Secret Service cannot place thousands of persons under surveillance or house arrest. In New York alone, he said, there may be "three or four thousand such individuals who would be members of subversive organizations"; then there are the members of the "front" organizations, and "Merely because a man belongs to subversive front organizations in my estimation doesn't mean that he is blacklisted and is a menace to the country for life." Later at a press conference Mr. Hoover said that only in a "police state" can thousands of subversives be placed under house arrest in order to protect the President.

Mr. Hoover was, of course, right; but how much more offensive to a free society must be the spectacle of thousands of persons arrested and convicted and sent to prison merely on the evidence that they were members of the Communist Party? It is very doubtful if a substantial number of members of Congress, when they voted for the Smith Act, desired this result; at least one would like to think that most of them would have felt relieved could they have anticipated what came to pass in the Smith Act cases in the Supreme Court. Sometimes things work out *as if* there were a pre-established harmony. For whatever comfort it may be, the Smith Act is constitutional and is part of the United States criminal code; but it is an almost wholly useless relic, and one's interest in it in the future can be only historical and clinical.

2. *The McCarran and the Communist Control Acts*

While the Dennis case was still in the courts, Congress enacted the Internal Security Act of 1950,[56] commonly known as the McCarran Act. With the amendments adopted in 1954, the act is by far the most comprehensive legislation on communism enacted by Congress; by sheer length and complexity, it dwarfs the Smith Act, which, by contrast, looks almost prehistorically primitive.

The McCarran Act is in two parts: Title I, known as the Subversive Activities Control Act of 1950; Title II, known as the Emergency Detention Act of 1950.

The act had its origin in bills considered in 1948 by the House Committee on Un-American Activities and sponsored by Karl E. Mundt and Richard M. Nixon, then both members of the House of Representatives. Added to the bill with this parentage were extensive provisions on immigration, deportation, naturalization, and denaturalization (these provisions two years later also contributed to the Immigration and Nationality Act of 1952, known as the McCarran-Walter Act—not to be confused with the McCarran Act). Then, also, the act picked up a number of bills concerned with espionage. While the McCarran Act, as thus constituted, was under consideration, some of its opponents offered as a substitute a bill to be known as the Emergency Detention Act of 1950. This bill was defeated. After its defeat it was adopted by the sponsors of the McCarran Act and attached as Title II.[57]

The act has many provisions that are not germane to our present concern. We shall concentrate only on what is relevant to our problem.

The act opens with a congressional finding, as a result of evidence before congressional committees, that

(1) There exists a world Communist movement which . . . is a world-wide revolutionary movement whose purpose it is, by treachery, deceit, infiltration into other groups . . ., espionage, sabotage, terrorism, . . . to establish a Communist totalitarian dictatorship in the countries throughout the world through . . . a world-wide Communist organization. . . .

(4) The direction and control of the world Communist movement is vested in and exercised by the Communist dictatorship of a foreign country.

(5) The Communist dictatorship of such foreign country . . . establishes or causes the establishment of, and utilizes, in various countries, action organizations which are . . . sections of a world-wide Communist organization and are controlled, directed, and subject to the discipline of the Communist dictatorship of such foreign country.

(6) The Communist action organizations . . . endeavor to carry out the objectives of the world Communist movement by bringing about the overthrow of existing governments by any available means, including force if necessary. . . . Although such organizations usually designate themselves as political parties, they are in fact constituent elements of the world-wide Communist movement and promote the objectives of such movement by conspiratorial and coercive tactics. . . .

The act then makes a finding that Communist organizations operate to a substantial extent through organizations commonly known as Communist fronts. It also finds that Americans who "knowingly and willfully" participate in the world Communist movement "in effect repudiate their allegiance to the United States, and in effect transfer their allegiance to the foreign country in which is vested the direction and control of the world Communist movement." This section concludes with the following congressional finding, which reads like a judge's instruction to a trial jury:

(15) The Communist movement in the United States is an organization numbering thousands of adherents, rigidly and ruthlessly disciplined. Awaiting and seeking to advance a movement when the United States may be so far extended by foreign engagements, so far divided in counsel, or so far in industrial straits, that overthrow of the Government of the United States by force and violence may seem possible of achievement, it seeks converts far and wide by an extensive system of schooling and indoctrination. . . . The Communist organization in the United States, pursuing its stated objectives, the recent successes of Communist methods in other countries, and the nature and control of the world Communist movement itself, present a clear and present danger to the security of the United States. . . .

A number of things should be noted concerning these findings:

(1) "The Communist organization in the United States" is, of course, the Communist Party of the United States, but the Party could not be named without making the act, at least in this respect, clearly a bill of attainder, and therefore unconstitutional. Congress, therefore, resorted to "Aesopian" language. It resorted to the same device, but for other reasons, when it referred to the "Communist dictatorship of such foreign country," which could only mean the U.S.S.R.

(2) Congress itself found certain facts to constitute a "clear and present danger." This was, I believe, the first time that Congress presumed to have the authority to make such a legislative finding. The McCarran Act, it should be remembered, was enacted in the year after the Dennis trial, in which the judge kept from the jury the question of a clear and present danger and reserved it to himself as a question of law. It follows that if this is a question of law and not of fact, then Congress has at least as much competence to make the finding as has a judge.

Now, Congress did not declare that the Communist Party was a clear and present danger. It was a certain *Gestalt,* or certain configuration or complex, taken conjunctively, that was declared to be the clear and present danger. At least three elements were stated to enter into this configuration: (1) The Communist Party of the United States, "pursuing its stated objectives"; (2) the "recent successes of Communist methods in other countries"; and (3) "the nature and control of the world Communist movement itself." This is important, and is consistent with what Judge Learned Hand and Chief Justice Vinson said in the Dennis case. Neither said that the Party, considered out of context, can be said to be a clear and present danger.

After characterizing the Communist Party, Judge Hand said: "We need not say that even so thoroughly planned and so extensive a confederation would be a 'present danger' at all times and in all circumstances," and then proceeded to describe certain critical aspects of the world and the American position in it at the time of the indictment, and concluded this analysis with the finding that the danger was "clear and present."

So, too, Chief Justice Vinson viewed the American Communist conspiracy together with "the inflammable nature of world conditions, similar uprisings in other countries, and the touch-and-go nature of our relations with countries with whom petitioners were . . . ideologically attuned."

The difficulty with the congressional finding of a clear and present danger is that, while it may have been justified in 1950, the component facts may have changed since then. Suppose there is no evidence of "recent successes" but rather of recent failures "of Communist methods in other countries"? Or suppose that "the nature and control of the world Communist movement" have changed? There is considerable evidence that in fact they have changed. George F. Kennan, in his Elihu Root Lectures in 1963, noted:

Much of the discussion in Western countries today of the problem of relations with world Communism centers around the recent disintegration of that extreme concentration of power in Moscow which characterized the Communist bloc in the immediate aftermath of the Second World War, and the emergence in its place of a plurality of independent or partially independent centers of political authority within the bloc; the growth, in other words, of what has come to be described as "polycentrism." There is widespread recognition that this process represents a fundamental change in the nature of world Communism as a political force on the world scene. . . .[58]

Since 1950, the monolithic nature of world communism has been shaken, though perhaps not broken, by Khrushchev's denunciation of Stalin and the personality cult at the Twentieth All-Union Party Congress in 1956; the murderous quelling of the Hungarian revolt, by Russian troops, later that year; Khrushchev's policy of coexistence; and the Chinese challenge of Russian leadership since 1958—splitting Communists everywhere into ideological factions with different loyalties. But the congressional "finding" leaves no room for flexibility of conception because it anticipates an unchanging world. The problem is aggravated by the circumstance that while the courts have made the question of clear and present danger a question of law, and the "finding" in the McCarran Act is intended to supply a legislative or *legal answer* to this *question of law,* legislative findings are ordinarily *findings of fact,* resulting from legislative hearings and investigations; and the McCarran Act itself states that its findings are the "result of evidence adduced before various committees . . . of Congress."

The so-called "findings" in the McCarran Act are a legislative invasion into political analysis and commentary, where intellectual fluidity cannot be displayed by ideological absolutes without serious damage to national security and interests.

In 1964 the Standing Committee on Education Against Communism of the American Bar Association published a report on *Peaceful Coexistence: a Communist Blueprint for Victory,*[59] consisting of about ninety pages of text and about twenty pages of bibliography, all purporting to support the conclusion that "Communist actions and Communist words prove that Communist goals are unchanged" and that "no genuine change in Communist aims has yet been affected."[60] Reading such statements, one cannot help thinking of the words of Euripides: "Many things the gods achieve beyond our judgment. What we thought is not confirmed. What we thought not, God contrives. So it happens in this story." The Communist world, Secretary of State Dean Rusk observed in 1964, "is no longer a single flock of sheep following blindly behind one leader." He called attention to the fact that the dispute between Moscow and Peking has divided the Communist movement and Communist Parties. (A pro-Peking Communist Party was formed in the United States on April 15, 1965—the Progressive Labor Party was launched at a four-day convention in a New York City hotel attended by 200 delegates representing some 1500 members.) The rulers of the Soviet Union, Mr. Rusk said,

appear to have begun to realize that there is an irresolvable contradiction between the demands to promote world communism by force and the needs and interests of the Soviet state and people.

The smaller Communist countries of Eastern Europe have increasingly . . . asserted their own policies. . . .

Within the Soviet bloc the Stalinist terror has been radically changed. And within the Soviet Union . . . there are signs—small but varied and persistent signs—of yearnings for more individual freedom.[61]

The McCarran Act distinguishes between a "Communist-action" organization and a "Communist-front" organization. The former is one which (1) is substantially directed, dominated, or controlled by "the foreign government or foreign organization controlling the world Communist movement" and (2) operates primarily to advance the objectives of such world Communist movement. The latter is defined as an organization which (1) is substantially directed, dominated, or controlled by a Communist-action organization and (2) is primarily operated to aid and support a Communist-action organization, a Communist foreign government, or the world Communist movement.

Each Communist-action or Communist-front organization was required to register with the Attorney General within thirty days of September 23, 1950. (New organizations must register within thirty days of the time they come into existence.) Registration is to include the names and addresses of the officers, a financial statement, and, in the case of Communist-action organizations, the names and addresses of the members. Substantially the same information is to be submitted in annual reports to the Attorney General. The Attorney General is required to send to each person on the list a notice that his name appears, and if the listed person denies that he is an officer or member the Attorney General shall conduct an investigation to determine the truth or falsity of the denial.

The act established a Subversive Activities Control Board, composed of five members, appointed by the President, with consent of the Senate. When the Attorney General concludes that an organization that is subject to the registration requirements has failed to comply, he is to file with the board a petition requiring it to file. The board is then to hold hearings, at which witnesses may be summoned and the submission of documents required. Parties may be represented by counsel, and there may be examination and cross-examination of witnesses.

The board has authority to determine that an organization is a Communist-action or a Communist-front organization. In determining whether a group is a Communist-action organization, the board is to take into consideration the extent to which its policies are formulated to effectuate the policies of the foreign government or the foreign organization that directs the world Communist movement; the extent to which its views "do not deviate" from those of the foreign government or foreign organization; the extent to which it receives financial aid from such foreign source; the extent to which it fails to disclose information as to its membership; and the extent to which it conducts its meetings in secret.

In determining whether a group is a Communist front, the board is to consider the extent to which the organization is managed by representatives of a Communist-action organization, receives financial support from such an organization, and gives financial support to the promotion of objectives of a Communist-action organization, and "the extent to which the positions taken or advanced by it from time to time on matters of policy do not deviate from those of any Communist-action organization, Communist foreign government, or the world Communist movement."

If the board determines that an organization is within the meaning of the act, it shall make public its written report, which then becomes notice to all members. The party aggrieved by the order may get judicial review in the United States court of appeals, but the fact findings of the board, if supported by preponderance of the evidence, shall be conclusive. The court's order is then subject to review by the Supreme Court upon certiorari.

An organization that fails to comply with a final court order requiring it to register may be fined up to $10,000, and its officers may also be fined and imprisoned for five years. An individual who becomes or remains a member of a Communist-action organization which fails to comply with an order to register must himself register with the Attorney General or be subject to a similar fine and imprisonment.

In order to satisfy the Fifth Amendment guarantee against coerced self-incrimination, the act provides that neither the holding of office nor membership in any affected organization shall "constitute per se a violation . . . of any criminal statute," and the fact of registration as an officer or member "shall not be received in evidence against such person in any prosecution" under any criminal statute.

After the board's order to register becomes final, it becomes unlawful for a member of such a Communist-action or "front" organization to conceal his membership when he seeks government employment, or to hold government employment, or to conceal his membership when he seeks employment in any defense facility. If he is a member of a Communist-action organization, he may not work in any defense facility; and the Secretary of Defense is directed to prepare and publish a list of defense facilities. It is unlawful for a member of a Communist-action or "front" organization to apply for or use a passport.[62] When there is a final order directing an organization to register, it becomes unlawful for it to send any publications through the mails unless the wrapper is marked with the statement that the publication is disseminated by a Communist organization, and the same information is required in connection with any radio or television program that it sponsors. There is also a provision denying federal tax deductions and exemptions to such organizations.

President Truman vetoed the bill, but Congress passed it over his veto. The President's message[63] condemned the measure in the strongest language as being not only "ineffective and unworkable" but representing "a clear and present danger to our institutions." President Truman said that the registration requirements in their application to "front" organizations "can be the greatest danger to freedom of speech, press and assembly, since the alien and sedition laws of 1798." He pointed out that the law would permit the classification of an organization as a "front" organization to be based solely upon "the extent to which the positions taken or advanced by it from time to time on matters of policy do not deviate from those" of the Communist movement. "Thus, an organization which advocates low-cost housing for sincere humanitarian reasons might be classified as a Communist-front organization because the Communists regularly exploit slum conditions as one of their fifth-column techniques. . . . The basic error of these sections is that they move in the direction of suppressing opinion and belief." For, said the President, if the measure were to become law, the part of prudence would be to avoid saying anything that might be construed by someone as not deviating sufficiently from the current Communist-propaganda line. And since no one could be sure in advance what views were safe to express, the inevitable tendency would be to express no views on controversial subjects. . . .

It is claimed that the bill would provide information about the Communist Party and its members. The fact is, the F. B. I. already possesses very complete sources of information concerning the Communist movement in this country. . . .

No considerations of expediency can justify the enactment of such a bill as this, a bill which would so greatly weaken our liberties and give aid and comfort to those who would destroy us.

President Truman in his veto message foresaw what would prove to be the case. To require Communist organizations to come forward with information is, he said, "about as practical as requiring thieves to register with the Sheriff. Obviously, no such organization as the Communist Party is likely to register voluntarily." He pointed out that the act would impose heavy but useless burdens on the Department of Justice, for the hearings to compel registration would take a great deal of time, and "when all this time and effort had been spent, it is still most likely that no organization would actually register." As to the requirement to label publications and broadcasts, the President said that this requirement, "even if constitutional, could be easily and permanently evaded, simply by the continuous creation of new organizations to distribute Communist information."

Seldom has a Presidential message proved to be as prescient. By 1966, fifteen years after the act became effective, not one Communist had registered.[64]

But before we summarize the operations under the law, we must briefly examine the 1954 amendments. On June 25, 1950, the Korean War started. As if in reaction to this conflict between Communist and non-Communist forces, agitation was started to do something really drastic about the Communist Party. Passage of the McCarran Act on September 23, 1950, overriding the President's veto on the previous day, was part of this reaction. But in the next few years, as no results of this long, complex, detailed measure were visible, there were pressures for more and stronger measures. Indiana, Massachusetts, Pennsylvania, and Texas passed laws expressly, explicitly, and by name outlawing the Communist Party. The Indiana statute of 1953 stated that it was the public policy of the state "to exterminate Communism and Communists, and any or all teachings of the same." It declared it to be "unlawful" for anyone to be a member of the Party. The Massachusetts act of 1953 made it a crime to become or remain a member, subject to imprisonment for three years. The same Communist, if he were to be punished under the Pennsylvania act of 1953 or the Texas act of 1954, could go to prison for twenty years.[65]

In 1954 Congress also gave way to the pressures. It enacted the Communist Control Act of 1954.[66] This statute amended the McCarran Act by adding another category of Communist organization—the "Communist-infiltrated" organization[67]—and, as an independent measure, directed certain sanctions against the Communist Party.

This act, avoiding circumlocutions, expressly "finds and declares that the Communist Party of the United States . . . is in fact an instrumentality of a conspiracy to overthrow the Government of the United States." It calls the Party "the agency of a hostile foreign power," and declares the Party's "existence a clear present and continuing danger to the security of the United States." The act expressly states: "Therefore, the Communist Party should be outlawed." The Party, "or any successors of such party regardless of the assumed name," "are not entitled to any of the rights, privileges, and immunities attendant upon legal bodies," and all such "rights, privileges, and immunities . . . are hereby terminated."

The act lists thirteen indicia of Party membership, to be used by juries under instructions by trial courts, including evidence as to whether the accused person has "indicated by word, action, conduct, writing, or in any other way a willingness to carry out in any manner and to any degree the plans, designs, objectives, or purposes of the organization."

Now, the 1954 act does not seem to outlaw the Party. Congress, in Section 2, concludes its "findings" with the statement quoted above: "Therefore, the Communist Party should be outlawed." The phrase "should be" has moral, not legal impact. The Party "should be" but is not outlawed. Its "rights, privileges, and immunities" are "terminated." What does this mean? (It is noteworthy that Congress passed the Communist Control Act on August 24, 1954. The Senate's censure of Senator McCarthy did not come until December 2, 1954. It may be that if the censure resolution had been adopted earlier that year, there would have been less interest in having the Communist Control Act passed.)

The Communist Party did not, of course, come forward, within thirty days of passage of the act, to register, and so the Attorney

General—on November 22, 1950—petitioned the Subversive Activities Control Board for an order to require the Party to register as a Communist-action organization. Hearings began in April 1951 and ended fourteen months later. The stenographic record—exclusive of 507 exhibits—came to 14,413 pages. In April 1953 the board issued its 218-page report concluding that the Party was a Communist-action organization and ordering it to register. Ten ex-Communists and four F. B. I. agents who were in the Party testified for the government. In December 1954 the court of appeals affirmed.

While the case was before the court of appeals, the Communist Party filed a motion for leave to adduce additional evidence, to establish that three of the government's witnesses—Crouch, Johnson, and Harvey Matusow, ex-Communists, professional informers who had been employed by the Department of Justice as witnesses in numerous proceedings—were in fact professional perjurers. The Attorney General did not deny the allegations but argued that the record before the board was sufficient to sustain the board's order apart from the testimony of the three witnesses in question. The court of appeals denied the Party's motion and, as we have said, sustained the board's order.

The Supreme Court, in April 1956, reversed the court of appeals and remanded the case for introduction of additional evidence.[68] The opinion by Justice Frankfurter pointed out that the testimony of the three discredited witnesses covered 668 pages of the record, that the board referred to their testimony 85 times, and that "the fair administration of justice" required remand to the board to make certain that it base its findings "upon untainted evidence."

On remand, the board held additional hearings, expunged the testimony of the three discredited witnesses, issued a 240-page modified report, and reaffirmed its original conclusion.

But concurrently the Party tried to discredit a fourth government witness, and the court of appeals remanded the case to the board to hear the Party's testimony with respect to this witness, Mrs. Markward, and to make available to the Party certain government documents. The board revised its modified report and for the third time concluded that the Party was required to register. Again the court of appeals affirmed; and this decision, at long last, brought the case on the merits before the Supreme Court.

The Court, in June 1961, by 5-to-4 decision,[69] upheld the order of the board. This was almost eleven years after Congress had enacted the McCarran Act and the Attorney General had started the proceedings to compel the Party to register. In that span of years, five different persons had filled the office of Attorney General, and five Justices of the Supreme Court had retired or died and were replaced.

The Supreme Court's report of the case fills 202 printed pages. The majority opinion, by Justice Frankfurter, covers many procedural and constitutional issues. We can touch on only a few of the more significant points.

(1) The Party contended that there was no proof that a foreign government or organization exercised over the American Party "an enforceable, coercive power to exact compliance with its demands." The Court held that the 1950 act did not call for such proof; what Congress had in mind was "a relationship in which one entity so much holds ascendancy over another that it is predictably certain that the latter will comply with the directions expressed by the former solely by virtue of that relationship, and without reference to the nature and content of the directions." Justice Frankfurter quoted with approval from the court of appeals opinion that an "organization or a person may be substantially under the direction or domination of another person or organization by voluntary compliance as well as through compulsion."

(2) The act is a regulatory, not a prohibitory measure, so, even if Congress accepted the definition of Communist objectives as (a) overthrow of existing government by any means necessary, including force and violence, (b) establishment of a Communist totalitarian dictatorship, and (c) establishment of a dictatorship subservient to the Soviet Union, the Party may be found to advance these objectives by "advocacy," and such finding will not violate the First Amendment. The act does not make unlawful the pursuit of these objectives. (If it did, then there would need to be proof of "incitement" as distinguished from "advocacy.")

(3) The government produced evidence that over a period of thirty years there was no substantial difference between the announced positions of the Soviet Union and the Party with respect to some forty-five major international issues. This evidence was considered by the board in determining the extent to which the Party's views "do not deviate from those of the . . . foreign government or foreign organization." The Court held that the evidence was "logically relevant" even though it was not shown that the Soviet view always led and the Party's view always followed.

(4) The act is not a bill of attainder. Congress had before it bills that expressly named the Party, "and it is no doubt also true that the form which the . . . Act finally took was dictated in part by constitutional scruples against outlawing of the Party by 'legislative fiat.' " But the fact remains that the act does not regulate "enumerated organizations but designated activities." The act should not be treated "as merely a ruse by Congress to evade constitutional safeguards." "The Act is not a bill of attainder. It attaches not to specified organizations but to described activities in which an organization may or may not engage . . . Legislatures may act to curb behavior which they regard as harmful to the public welfare, whether that conduct is found to be engaged in by many persons or by one."

(5) The act does not infringe on the First Amendment freedoms of speech and association, because the registration requirement is attached not to the incident of speech "but to the incidents of foreign domination and of operation to advance the objectives of the world Communist movement. . . ."

(6) The Court should not review the legislative "findings." They are the product of "extensive investigations by Committees of Congress over more than a decade and a half." Since Congress found that Communist organizations are not free and independent but are tools of a world Communist movement that is operated by a foreign country, "we must recognize that the power of Congress to regulate Communist organizations of this nature is extensive." This power exists, though limited by the First Amendment. But

the legislative judgment as to how that threat [to security] may best be met consistently with the safeguarding of personal freedom is not to be set aside merely because the judgment of judges would, in the first instance, have chosen other methods. Especially where Congress, in seeking to reconcile competing and urgently demanding values within our social institutions, legislates not to prohibit individuals from organizing for the effectuation of ends found to be menacing to the very existence of those institutions, but only to prescribe the conditions under which such organization is permitted, the legislative determination must be respected.

(7) Regarding the requirement to file the membership list, the Court distinguished the N.A.A.C.P. cases. In passing on the validity of legislation that compels disclosure of membership, the Court should consider as relevant the fact that there is an "angry public," "an ugly public temper"; but the existence of this fact by itself does not incapacitate government from requiring disclosure when the disclosure is "demanded by rational interests high in the scale of national concern." Said Justice Frankfurter:

Where the mask of anonymity which an organization's members wear serves the double purpose of protecting them from popular prejudice and of enabling them to cover over a foreign-directed conspiracy, infiltrate into other groups, and enlist the support of persons who would not, if the truth were revealed, lend their support, . . . it would be a distortion of the First Amendment to hold that it prohibits Congress from removing the mask.

(8) So, too, the requirement that the Party's publications be clearly identified may be regarded by Congress as necessary to the act's objective: "to bring foreign-dominated organizations out into the open where the public can evaluate their activities informedly against the revealed background of their character, nature, and connections. . . . We hold that the obligation to give information identifying [publication] presses, without more and as applied to foreign-dominated organizations, does not fetter constitutionally protected free expression." Justice Frankfurter stressed the fact that the act applies "only to *foreign-dominated* organizations which work primarily to advance the objectives of a world movement controlled by the government of a *foreign* country" (italics in original).

(9) The act provides that where a Communist-action organization fails to register, certain of its officers must register the organization. It was contended that this violated the Fifth Amendment guarantee against self-incrimination. The Court, however, refused to pass on this and a related question, saying that it cannot tell whether the Party's officers may claim the privilege, and if claimed, whether the Attorney General will not honor it. The question was, therefore, raised prematurely.

(10) It was argued that the congressional "findings" that there is a "Communist movement," a Communist "organization," and a "Communist network" deprive the Party of a fair hearing in violation of due process. "Fairly read," said Justice Frankfurter, "these findings neither compel nor suggest the outcome in any particular litigation before the Board. They do not create the impression that there is a single Communist-action organization in the United States, still less that the Communist Party is 'it.' " The Court also rejected the contention that the "findings" in the 1954 act prejudice the Party, for there was no mention of them in the board's opinion or in that of the court of appeals. While the board must have been "aware of them," "we cannot say that their very annunciation by Congress . . . foreclosed or impaired a fair administrative determination."

There were four dissenting opinions, for the dissenters did not agree on all points among themselves. Their positions on constitutional issues were, in brief, as follows:

(1) Chief Justice Warren maintained that the McCarran Act, to be constitutional under the First Amendment, had to be construed as requiring a group to register as a Communist-action organization only if the board finds that "the organization is engaged in advocacy aimed at inciting action." In the instant case the board merely found that the Party engaged in advocating the use of force "if necessary." This, said Chief Justice Warren, "is not the sort of advocacy which incites to action. At most, it is no more than the formulation of an abstract doctrine," which is protected by the free-speech guarantee as understood in the Yates and Dennis cases.

The majority opinion met this argument by saying that what was before the Court was a "regulatory" and not a "prohibitory" statute, and so the case was different from the Yates and Dennis cases. But Chief Justice Warren rejected this differentiation: ". . . it blinks reality to say that this statute is not prohibitory. There can be little doubt that the registration provisions of the statute and the harsh sanctions which are automatically imposed after an order to register has been issued make this Act as prohibitory as any criminal statute."

He also contended that the act, by requiring the Party's officers to submit a registration on behalf of the Party, violated the Fifth Amendment privilege against self-incrimination.

(2) Justice Black said that there could be no objection if the Party had been required to register under an act such as the Foreign Agents Registration Act,[70] which is intended only to label information of foreign origin, so that persons may know that the information does not come from a disinterested source. A person registered under the Foreign Agents Registration Act is "not thereby branded as being engaged in an evil, despicable undertaking bent on destroying this Nation. But that is precisely the effect of the present [McCarran] Act," for the congressional "findings" pronounce "the treasonable nature of those compelled to register." Furthermore, the "plan of the Act is to make it impossible for an organization to continue to function once a registration order is issued against it"; for its members are then denied government employment or work in defense plants; the organization is denied certain tax deductions; and there are other burdens. And so the act is more than a mere registration requirement.

The act, according to Justice Black, is unconstitutional on the following grounds: (a) It is a bill of attainder, for it imposes pains and penalties without a judicial trial. (b) The congressional "findings," together with the fact-findings by the board, an administrative body, leave no room for an individual to challenge alleged facts in a court when he is brought up on charges of failure to register. Thus he is caught in a "legislative-administrative web" which denies him due process. (c) The act outlaws the Party in violation of the First Amendment. It goes further than the Sedition Act of 1798 in suppressing First Amendment freedoms. The nation should be protected "against *actions* of violence and treason" and not "against dangerous ideas." (d) The act is invalid for violation of the self-incrimination provision of the Fifth Amendment.

(3) Justice Douglas found no objection to the requirement that the Party register.

If lobbyists can be required to register, if political parties can be required to make disclosure of the sources of their funds, if the owners of newspapers and periodicals must disclose their affiliates, so may a group operating under the control of a foreign power.

Just as picketing may be "free speech plus," so may an exercise of freedom of association be an exercise of First Amendment freedoms plus—as in the case of the Party—"espionage, business activities, formation of cells for subversion." These additional elements take the organization beyond free speech. Therefore, "the bare requirement that the Communist Party register and disclose the names of its officers and directors is in line with the most exacting adjudications touching First Amendment activities."

But the requirement that officers and directors sign the registration statement and the compulsory disclosure of the membership list violate the self-incrimination provision of the Fifth Amendment. "I do not see how the Government that has branded an organization as criminal through its judiciary, its legislature, and its executive, can demand that it submit the names of all its members. . . ." The Party should have the right to assert the privilege on behalf of its officers, directors, and members, just as in the N.A.A.C.P. cases the organization was allowed to assert for its members their First Amendment rights.

(4) Justice Brennan, whom Chief Justice Warren joined, agreed with the majority and with Justice Douglas that the "order requiring that the Party register and disclose its officers and members is not constitutionally invalid as an invasion of the rights of freedom of advocacy and association guaranteed by the First Amendment to Communists as well as to all others." But he contended that the requirement that the

registration statement be signed and filed by designated officials conflicted with the privilege against self-incrimination guaranteed by the Fifth Amendment.

In summary: The four dissenting Justices agreed on only one ground—that the act is unconstitutional only in that it requires designated officers to sign the registration statement. In this respect the act is in conflict with the Fifth Amendment. Justice Douglas pointed out that this defect could have been cured by Congress's granting immunity for the disclosure.

All the dissenting Justices, except Justice Black, agreed with the majority that requiring the Communist Party to register is not a violation of the First Amendment. On this point, then, the act was upheld as constitutional by 8 to 1.

The reason for this substantial agreement was foreshadowed in Justice Douglas's dissenting opinion in the Dennis case, where, as we have seen, he distinguished the Communist organization as a political party from the organization as possibly a party of communism "in the world scene." In the former aspect, the Party is hardly worthy of notice; in the latter, it may be dangerous; and it is in the latter aspect that its activities—involving espionage, cells for subversion, infiltration of essential services—become "free speech plus."

But while in theory the requirement that the Party register as a Communist-action organization can be justified by convincing facts and arguments, as a practical measure the act makes for a fine study in futility. President Truman's condemnation of the act in his veto message has been amply sustained by the events since 1950.

Following the Court's decision, the Party had until November 21, 1961, to register. The Party and its officers refused. The Attorney General then had to present the case to the grand jury, and on December 1, 1961, the Party was indicted; on March 15, 1962, Gus Hall, general secretary, and Benjamin J. Davis, Jr., national secretary, were also indicted. The latter was indicted for failure to file a registration statement *for the Party,* and the former for failure to register *for the Party* as its "executive officer."[71]

In 1962 a grand jury also investigated the failure of Party officials to register *as individuals.* Philip Bart, the party's organizational secretary, and James E. Jackson, editor of *The Worker,* refused to answer questions put to them and were sentenced to six months in jail for contempt. They had been offered immunity from prosecution if they would answer the questions, but they refused the offer. The contempt convictions were appealed.[72] (The outcome of these convictions was determined by the cases of William Albertson and Roscoe Proctor, decided in 1965 and discussed below.)

The Party went on trial in December 1962, and the jury returned a verdict of guilty on all twelve counts—a separate count for each of the eleven days that it had failed to register up to the date of indictment, and one count for failure to file a registration statement. The court imposed the maximum penalty allowed by the act: a fine of $10,000 on each count, making a total fine of $120,000.

On December 17, 1963, a year later, the federal court of appeals unanimously reversed the judgment of conviction. It held that the government had failed to prove that a person was available who could have acted for the Party without himself running the risk of self-incrimination. No one, the court held, can be forced by a registration proceeding to declare his association with an organization that has been branded criminal. The court, in the opinion by Judge David L. Bazelon, said that "mere association with the party incriminates." Any Party officer could invoke the privilege and refuse to file the registration statement. The court said that the legislation then on the books made the Party "a criminal conspiracy," and so the court would not assume that anyone would care to "volunteer" to "submit data the possession of which implies an intimate knowledge of the party's workings." The scope of this decision was defined by Judge Bazelon as follows:

We do not hold that an organization may claim the privilege against self-incrimination, nor that an individual may claim the privilege on behalf of an organization or its members. We express no opinion concerning the Communist Party's duty to submit the data demanded. We hold only that the availability of someone to sign the forms was an element of the offense; that the officers, who should have signed, were unavailable by reason of their valid claim of the privilege against self-incrimination; that the government had the burden of showing that a volunteer was available; and that its failure to discharge this burden requires reversal of the conviction.

The government petitioned the Supreme Court for a review of the decision, but the Court, on June 8, 1964, denied review, without stating any reasons.[73]

The action of the court of appeals confirmed the argument on which all dissenting Justices of the Supreme Court had agreed in the Communist Party registration case; and so all the efforts of the Department of Justice, of the Subversive Activities Control Board, of the court of appeals, and of the Supreme Court, not to mention the Congress of the United States—involving only heaven knows how many man-hours of work and how many millions of dollars—came exactly to naught at the point of culmination. Every machine has its friction, Justice Holmes said, and so we must not expect a law, or any human invention, to act with perfection; but when friction becomes the machine, then surely it is time to recognize that the experiment was worthless.

The court of appeals left the way open for retrial on the indictment. To safeguard against any infirmity, in February 1965 the government secured a second indictment, which alleged that someone was willing to file the statements on behalf of the Party, and that the Party knew this. In November 1965 the Party went on trial before a federal district court in the District of Columbia; on November 19 the jury brought in a verdict of guilty, and the judge imposed a fine of $10,000 on each of twenty-three counts. Lawyers for the Party filed notice of appeal, claiming that even if a volunteer—a government informant who had infiltrated the Party—was ready and willing to register the Party, registration would require cooperation by the Party's officers, and that would amount to compulsory self-incrimination.

And so, fifteen years after Congress enacted the Internal Security Act of 1950, over the veto of President Truman, the government was still trying to get the Communist Party to register. "That sounds like nonsense, my dear," said Mrs. Bertram in *Guy Mannering*. "Maybe so, my dear," replied Mr. Bertram, "but it may be very good law for all that." President Truman was right: the act is both nonsense and bad law.

On August 22, 1964, Benjamin Davis died. He and Gus Hall had not, by then, been tried under the indictment filed more than two years before.[74] The Department of Justice was waiting for the final decision in the case against the Party for failure to register.

The McCarran Act provides that upon default of an organization and its officers the members of the organization must themselves come forward and register. This duty of Party members came into effect on December 20, 1961. No member has registered.

But no criminal action against an individual member can be brought unless an order is first obtained from the board, after a hearing, determining the individual to be a Party member and requiring him to register. Accordingly, the Attorney General started on May 31, 1962, to file petitions against individuals. By July 1, 1965, such petitions had been filed against forty-four individuals. Hearings were held in Washington, New York, Chicago, and other cities. By mid-1965, orders had been issued against thirty-seven persons. They all filed appeals with the court of appeals. On April 23, 1964, the court upheld the board orders in two test cases involving William Albertson and Roscoe Proctor.[75]

On November 15, 1965, the Supreme Court unanimously held that the act requiring individuals to register as members of the Communist Party was unconstitutional. It held that the orders requiring Albertson and Proctor to register on forms that required them to admit membership in the Party were inconsistent with the constitutional guarantee against self-incrimination. With the decisions in the Dennis and Scales cases on the books, how could the decision have been different?

What *The New York Times* said about the decision on the following day must have been in the minds of many thoughtful citizens:

The world has changed greatly since 1940 and 1950. With all due respect to J. Edgar Hoover, the internal Communist threat in the United States is virtually nonexistent. The real threat of Communism is in its cold-war role, which is external to this country. Even there, the one-time monolithic Communist "bloc" has long since been shattered. So far as European Communism goes, it is not remotely the threat that it was in 1950.

The American Communist party is now on trial in Federal District Court in Washington on charges of failure to register as a representative of the Soviet Government. What about the Communists who "represent" Peking or Havana? What about organizations that most Americans would really consider subversive, such as the Ku Klux Klan or the Black Muslims?

For fifteen years Attorney Generals have been trying to register Communists and they have yet to get one to sign on the dotted line. Surely, the fact that yesterday's adverse decision was unanimous must give the Justice Department and Congress some ground for belief that the way to prevent Communism is not through repression or through whittling away fundamental American rights.

As for the "front" organizations, no such group offered to register voluntarily. On April 22, 1953, the Attorney General brought board proceedings against twelve organizations. Altogether twenty-two such actions have been filed. The most recent one was on January 10, 1963, against an organization known as Advance, An Organization of Progressive Youth,[76] which changed its name to Advance and Burning Issues Organizations. Its career before the board would make a wonderful study in futility. Briefly, this is what happened: The hearings were held in 1963, at which the government presented twenty witnesses and many exhibits in evidence. In September 1964 the hearing examiner issued his findings and conclusions and recommended that the organization be ordered to register as a Communist-front organization. The recommended decision was in 111 pages of findings and 26 pages of appendices. The organization filed 138 exceptions. The board then proceeded to study the evidence. As part of its review, the board—as it stated in its 1965 annual report—was called upon "to make an independent examination of many thousands of non-evidentiary prior reports and statements of eleven of the witnesses who testified for the Attorney General." This review made necessary a special hearing. At this hearing the board learned for the first time that the organization had dissolved! The board then placed the case in the status of "indefinite abeyance."

Eight of the twenty-two organizations had resorted to the same stratagem. Of the remaining thirteen cases, two failed to appeal the order against them; the other eleven appealed to the court of appeals.[77]

The actions of the court of appeals on these eleven cases were as follows:

National Council of American-Soviet Friendship: The board's order was set aside. The court held that participation of Party members in the direction, domination, and control of the organization was insufficient to meet the statute's requirements in the absence of proof that the Party members were active in the management of the Party or were acting as its representatives.

Washington Pension Union: The appeal was dismissed on proof that the group had been legally dissolved.

American Peace Crusade, the *Colorado Committee to Protect Civil Liberties,* and *Labor Youth League:* These cases were placed on inactive status, to be reopened by the board should the groups become reactivated.

Civil Rights Congress[78] and *California Labor School:* Their appeals were dismissed for failure to prosecute them. (The organizations had ceased to function but were nominally still in existence.)

Jefferson School of Social Science,[79] *American Committee for Protection of the Foreign Born, Veterans of the Abraham Lincoln Brigade,* and *United May Day Committee:* The Court affirmed the orders of the board to register.

The Supreme Court granted certiorari to the American Committee for Protection of the Foreign Born and to the Veterans of the Abraham Lincoln Brigade,[80] and on April 26, 1965, vacated the board orders on the ground that the record on which the orders were based was stale.[81] A registration order, said the Court, operates prospectively; it follows that only "reasonably current [Communist] aid and control must be established to justify a registration order." The Court found that the evidence in the case against the American Committee for Protection of the Foreign Born related to events prior to 1959, and in the other case the evidence related to events before 1950. Both cases originated in 1953. Whether they will ever be mercifully terminated remains—after twelve years—to be seen.

The futility of the act is also shown by what has happened under the provision that makes it unlawful for an organization, against which there is a final board order to register, to send through the mails any publication unless it is plainly marked as being disseminated by a Communist organization. *The Worker,* accordingly, describes itself as a publication "which reflects the viewpoint of the Communist Party on the urgent and fundamental issues of the day and on fundamental socialist aims," and *Political Affairs,* a Communist Party magazine, describes itself on its masthead as "A Theoretical Organ of the Communist Party, USA"—as if anyone who had ever read an issue of either publication could have had any doubts about its source or aims.[82]

By 1964 there was only one case against a member of the Party working at a defense facility. A grand jury in Seattle in 1963 indicted Eugene Robel for violation of the McCarran Act by being employed in a defense facility while maintaining membership in the Party. In October 1965 a federal district court judge threw out the indictment, which, he said, had not stated an offense.[83]

And there have been only two cases, under the 1954 amendments, to compel registration as a "Communist-infiltrated" organization. These were both proceedings against the International Union of Mine, Mill, and Smelter Workers. The order directing the union to register, made in 1962, came after 110 days of hearing, at which 150 witnesses testified. Over a thousand documents were received in evidence. The transcript, in 110 volumes, comprised about 10,000 pages. The board's report took 108 printed pages. While the case was pending before the court of appeals, a federal district court judge, at the end of 1965, threw it out as being too stale.[84]

If the purpose of registration is to inform ignorant persons of the true character of an organization, so that they may not be "taken in" by its propaganda, this was eminently achieved twelve years before by a C.I.O. investigation through a committee comprised of Jacob

THE COMMUNIST PARTY AND FREEDOM OF ASSOCIATION | 155

Potofsky, Emil Mazey, and Joseph Curran, as a result of which the union was expelled from the C.I.O. The report by the C.I.O. committee was published in 1951 in an official Senate document.[85] If the purpose is to deprive a union of privileges under the National Labor Relations Act—which is a consequence of a final order to register as an "infiltrated" group—the United Mine Workers, under John L. Lewis, for years demonstrated how a union could get along without qualifying under that act. In any case, when one considers the insignificance of the specimen that the government tried to capture by the use of so much complicated and high-powered machinery, one has distressing questions about the role of intelligence in government.

These cases against a union[86] comprise the total record for a decade under the statute that bears the hopeful title: "Communist Control Act of 1954."

Now compare this record under the acts of 1950 and 1954 with the information contained in the *Guide to Subversive Organizations and Publications,* prepared and released by the House Committee on Un-American Activities—a government publication of over 250 pages.[87] The Introduction states:

This Guide is basically a compilation of organizations and publications which have been declared to be Communist-front or outright Communist enterprises in official statements by Federal legislative and executive authorities, and by various State and Territorial investigating committees. . . .

The Guide lists a total of 663 organizations or projects and 122 publications cited as Communist or Communist front by Federal Agencies; and 155 organizations and 25 publications cited as Communist or Communist front by State or Territorial investigating committees.[88]

The disparity between the number of organizations against which the Attorney General filed petitions with the Subversive Activities Control Board and the number of organizations in the *Guide to Subversive Organizations and Publications* is staggering. Even the original Attorney General's List, made to implement President Truman's Loyalty Order of 1947, contained over 200 names, of which 108 were supposed to be Communist organizations.[89]

One reason for the large number of listings in the *Guide* and by the Attorney General is that these lists carried names of many organizations that were defunct. The latest list of the Attorney General has 283 names of organizations. Only a few are non-Communist, such as the Ku Klux Klan and the German-American Bund—George Lincoln Rockwell's American Nazi Party is not listed. The list is largely obsolete. It is estimated that perhaps only eleven of the Communist-front organizations listed are still active. The practice of continuing to list dead organizations makes about as much sense as would a statement by the F.B.I. that there are now X number of Communist Party members if the number included all those who had died and all who had left the Party. Could such a figure possibly help the American people understand and evaluate the Communist danger? How does it help us understand that danger by having compilations and lists that make no differentiation between the quick and the dead? Is a disbanded Communist-front organization more of a threat than a dead Communist?

But there is another reason for the disparity in numbers. The Subversive Activities Control Board provides an organization against which the Attorney General has filed a petition full opportunity to be heard, with witnesses, counsel, and the right of examination and cross-examination; moreover, the board's order is subject to judicial review. These safeguards are not provided by the other listing officials. The President's Loyalty Order—Executive Order 9835—provided for listing only "after appropriate investigation and determination." But this can fall far short of what is required in a proceeding before the S.A.C.B.; and even the limited requirement was not always followed, as the Supreme Court found in *Joint Anti-Fascist Refugee Committee* v. *McGrath*.[90] Four Justices in that case—Justices Frankfurter, Jackson, Black, and Douglas—thought that an organization should be entitled to due process—notice and a hearing—as a minimum. "The heart of the matter," wrote Justice Frankfurter in his concurring opinion, "is that democracy implies respect for the elementary rights of men, however suspect or unworthy; a democratic government must therefore practice fairness; and fairness can rarely be obtained by secret, one-sided determination of facts decisive of rights." In drafting the McCarran Act, Congress acted on this principle and provided for fair administrative procedures, subject to judicial review, before requiring groups to register as Communist-action, Communist-front, or Communist-infiltrated organizations.

By implication, Congress in 1950 discredited the blacklisting procedures that fall far short of its own conception of what fairness commands.

The record of cases under the Internal Security Act and the Communist Control Act is depressing to contemplate. The experiment, one might say, has been carried far enough and long enough.

If, however, a registration process is to be continued, the S.A.C.B.

should remain in existence, but the other governmental blacklisting processes should not. If they are to continue, they should reform their procedures to conform with what Justice Frankfurter has referred to as "those essential safeguards for fair judgment. . . ."[91] In matters of this kind, the reverse of Gresham's law should be operative: the superior and genuine should drive from the field the inferior and false. Since Congress has provided for the former, it should bring to an end the latter. The needs of security do not require the coexistence of the unfair procedures alongside the fair.

But if the registration requirements are continued, we should be aware of the fact that they can hardly be justified on purely rational grounds. As one reads the "findings" in the legislation passed by Congress in 1950 and 1954, one would expect Congress to end up by providing that such traitors should be taken out at sunrise and shot. But of course the conclusion is nothing so dramatic or violent—they are merely required to register. They are to step forward and brand themselves, and wear a badge of infamy, like adulterers in Puritan Massachusetts. If what we want is a way *to catch those who have already been caught,* so that the government can *compel* the *known* Party members to register, then these laws are the ones we want. But it hardly seems possible that anything so useless can reasonably be expected to contribute to America's security needs.

3. Conclusion

In October 1956, Attorney General Herbert Brownell, Jr., in a memorandum to President Eisenhower,[92] summarized the official acts that had been taken against the Communist Party and Communists. The more important steps he listed were: (1) the prosecutions under the Smith Act; (2) proceedings under the McCarran Act; (3) convictions for espionage; (4) convictions for perjury and making false statements or affidavits; (5) modernization of the sabotage act; (6) increase in the statute of limitations from three to five years; (7) strengthening of the Atomic Energy Act.

In addition to convictions for conspiracy under the Smith Act, the Attorney General classified some thirty-one other convictions (for perjury, espionage on behalf of the Soviet Union, harboring fugitives from Smith Act prosecutions, and similar crimes).

Compare these figures with the following for the State of California for the five-year period from 1919 to 1924: 164 persons were convicted under the state's criminal syndicalism law, of whom 73 went to prison for 1 to 14 years.[93] That was only one state's record in the days of the Palmer Raids. It has been estimated that in 1919 and 1920 some three hundred persons were sent to prison for violation of state sedition and syndicalist statutes.[94] Even allowing for some exaggeration in this last figure, the number was shockingly large, especially if we note that in 1920 the population of the country was only a little over a hundred million. In contrast, under the federal laws that have been in effect since 1940, only twenty-nine Communists went to prison as co-conspirators to violate the Smith Act, and only one was in prison as a Party member.

The Communist Party has, of course, been harassed. To the facts already mentioned we may add that since 1954 the Commissioner of Internal Revenue has been trying to collect from the Party an income-tax deficiency, which by 1965 had become over $500,000, on the theory that the Party is a political party, and that the Internal Revenue Code does not exempt political parties. This view of the Communist Party contradicts, of course, the view of the Supreme Court in the Dennis and other cases. In 1965 this case, after eleven years, was still before the Tax Court of the United States. In 1956 the government levied on the *Daily Worker* for income-tax deficiencies,[95] and seized the headquarters of the newspaper and the Party.

A great armory of legal weapons has been used against the Party. But an equally great armory of legal weapons has been used in its defense—a fact that explains how it is that the Party still exists and that its existence is not illegal. The Party's leaders are known by name. In September 1964 *The New York Times* published the names of some sixty Party members who were said to constitute the national committee;[96] and its newspaper, though no longer a daily, is still published and readily available.

When one thinks of the United States as the leader of the free world, it does us no harm that we can point to the existence of the Communist Party as one item in a bill of particulars that proves that we ourselves try to practice what we preach to others: no one can be "outlawed" to the point where he will be beyond the protection of the Constitution.

I have already cited the figures for membership in the Communist Parties of Great Britain and the Netherlands. To give some perspective on our own situation, let us look at some other figures.

Americans were surprised in June 1964 when it became known that in a primary election for Los Angeles County Board of Supervisors, an avowed Communist received 31,888 votes, 13 per cent of the total.[97]

This was the only instance of a known Communist's running in any American election, on any level, since 1957, when Elizabeth Gurley Flynn polled 658 votes for Councilman in Manhattan on a People's Rights ticket. The last candidacy under the Communist label was in 1949, when Benjamin Davis was defeated for re-election to the Council in Manhattan with 1212 votes as a Communist and 20,635 as the American Labor Party candidate. Not since 1940 has a Communist run for national office.[98] (On a national level, the only left-wing parties that have run candidates in recent years are the Socialist Labor Party, which is anti-Communist, and the Socialist Workers Party, which is a Trotskyist group opposed to the Communist Party. The former party received 47,522 votes in the national election in 1960 and 42,511 in 1964; the latter received 39,541 votes in 1960 and 28,510 in 1964.)[99]

But in the 1963 Italian elections the Communists polled 25.3 per cent of the popular vote—almost 8,000,000 voted for Communists.[100] There are in Italy between 1,200,000 and 1,500,000 Party members.[101]

The Communist Party of France has an estimated 250,000 members.[102] Belgium, with a population of 9,000,000, has some 11,000 Party members[103]—more than the estimate for the United States, which has a population twenty times the size; and Sweden, with a population about that of New York City, has some 25,000 Communist Party members. [104]

No American in his senses would think that we should envy these European nations their large numbers of Communists. But we can learn from them to be less obsessed with a fear of the Communists that we do have. We can live with them and with the dangers that their existence generates. We have laws under which they can be punished for their *criminal acts*. But do we need mountain-moving machines to move a little heap of dirt? Do we need rigid congressional "findings" in a world that is rapidly changing—a world in which our own hopes, ideals, loyalties, and actions can help bring about changes?

In November 1965 David Lawrence called for the "outlawing" of the Communist Party, to proclaim as "subversive" any organization which is directly or indirectly influenced or financed by a foreign unfriendly government, and for a law that would make it an act of "treason" to be a member of any organization found to be thus subversive. Congress and the Supreme Court are not likely to treat so cavalierly the strict and narrow definition of treason as it appears in Article III of the Constitution. The Constitution has removed from Congress the power to define, let alone to enlarge, the definition of treason. In May 1964 Mr. Lawrence wrote:[105]

The time has come for the Government of the United States to do more to expose the infiltration in civic movements by the Communist Party and its agents, stooges and allies inside this country. . . .

The record reviewed in this chapter shows, I think, that the government has done a great deal to expose communism and Communists —much more than any other nation has done.

When a broad claim is made for Communist "infiltration" in "civic movements," and the critic is not satisfied to limit his charge to Communists, but adds the Communist Party's "agents, stooges and allies," we suspect his use of Aesopian language; for he then attacks not only Communists but also the "civic movements" that are liberal, reform, or civil-libertarian.

The Radical Right tends to blame all our troubles and worries on the Communists and their "agents, stooges, and allies," just as the Nazis blamed the Jews and their "agents, stooges, and allies." The evil in this is that it diverts attention from the real evils and intimidates people who would otherwise devote some of their energies to the real causes of our discontent. If we had never heard of the Communist Party of the United States, would we have today less of a problem of crime, slums, juvenile delinquency, narcotics, poverty, water pollution?

"Unfortunately," wrote Mr. Lawrence in the earlier article,

various court decisions and the complex legal machinery that can be invoked to protect Communist agitators and demonstrators are making it possible for the Communists to achieve results which they perhaps would not attain if a majority of the Justices of the Supreme Court of the United States were to abandon the idea that the Communist Party is just another political party and not a subversive instrument of a foreign government.

What "results" have the Communists achieved? Who benefits—unless the Communists benefit—from exaggerating, beyond all bounds of facts and reason, the "results" of their actions?

And one may ask whether the "complex legal machinery" was created by the courts—or by the Constitution? And in any case, was it created just for the Communists? Is *it* the result of a Communist conspiracy? Is there *simple* legal machinery in cases involving, say, United States Steel, or General Motors, or General Electric? Should we have a different Constitution and special courts for the Communists? And who but our courts can ultimately decide whether a person is in fact a Communist Party member, or an "agent" of the party, or a "stooge," or an "ally"? Should such questions be left to Robert Welch of the John Birch Society, in whose opinion Presidents Truman and Eisenhower, Milton Eisenhower, John Foster Dulles, Allen Dulles, General George C. Marshall, and Chief Justice Warren were all knowing agents of the Communist conspiracy?[106]

Mr. Lawrence has an easy answer to all our problems:

The Communist movement cannot be brushed aside as just an inconsequential effervescence of ideological passion, nor can it be dismissed as only the work of a few irresponsible persons. The damage already done is extensive and will increase unless the Congress of the United States takes effective steps to fight the enemy within our gates.

Certainly no sane person would think of dismissing the Communist movement in face of the fact that one-third of the world's population lives under Communist control. But why claim that "the enemy within our gates" has "already done" "damage" that is "extensive"? And what are the "effective steps" that Congress can take that have not been taken—assuming that Congress respects the Constitution no less than does the Supreme Court?

Congress, in the Communist Control Act of 1954, has said that "the Communist Party should be outlawed." Suppose it were now to go further and say, in a statute, that "the Communist Party is hereby outlawed." And assume that the Constitution is amended to leave out the provision that "No bill of attainder . . . shall be passed." What would be accomplished except to drive Communists deeper underground?

And if membership in the Party may be a criminal offense—as it is under the Scales decision—are Communists to be compelled by law to register and thus confess their criminality while the Fifth Amendment is still part of the Constitution? Or shall we amend the Constitution and leave out of it the privilege against self-incrimination?

And the paradox would yet remain: that the Attorney General would need to proceed to compel Communists to register as such, which he can do only when he already knows that they are Communists. What is gained by a mumbo-jumbo that pretends to uncover secrets already known?

But we have here made assumptions about amendments to the Constitution that are unthinkable. "It takes a great deal of history," Henry James wrote in his biography of Hawthorne, "to produce a little literature." It takes even more to produce a constitutional guarantee such as that against self-incrimination or against bills of attainder. If these and similar human decencies are taken from us, what then will be the difference between Communists and us? And why should the Supreme Court be blamed if it refuses to be the one by whom the offense comes?

The Communist Party is illegal in Jordan, Syria, Iran, Morocco, Egypt, and other countries[107] that are not mentioned in any honor roll of free, democratic states. It is instructive to note that in Europe the only countries in which the Party is outlawed are West Germany, Greece, Turkey, Spain, and Portugal.

West Germany is a special case, for Communists there were viewed simply as an appendage of the East German Communist Party and therefore bound to be subversive and seditious. Despite the fact that the Party has been outlawed since 1956, our State Department estimated that there were in West Germany between 35,000 and 50,000 Party members, with about 5000 Party members active in illegal operations, at the end of 1961. The West German population is 57,000,-000, or less than a third of our own population. Has outlawry killed the Party in West Germany?

Turkey was a one-party state until the new constitution was adopted in July 1961, so we cannot learn from its example. Greece outlawed the party in 1947, yet it has 20,000 Communists in a population of 8,000,000.

We have often been told that Party membership is not the only thing we should consider, for according to the F.B.I. there are at least ten "sympathizers" for every "hard-core" Communist in the United States. If this is so, why should not the same be true for Great Britain, the Netherlands, Switzerland, and other free nations?

It should be noted that the congressional legislation we have examined is, on the whole, a tribute to the moderation and good sense of Congress. The statutes are not an expression of extremism and do not show a flagrant disregard of constitutional principles. If we have Communists despite the laws on the books, we also have narcotics addicts, murderers, rapists, bank robbers, and many other social afflictions, despite all the laws against them. Our federal prison population in 1962 was 23,838; there were 219,030 inmates in our federal and state prisons and reformatories in that year. The F.B.I. reported over two million *serious* offenses *known* to the police in that one year.[108] There is obviously a limit to what a free society can expect to accomplish through legal sanctions. There is good philosophical as well as judicial wisdom in Chief Justice Melville W. Fuller's observation:

Acknowledged evils, however grave and urgent they may appear to be, had better be borne, than the risk be run, in the effort to suppress them, of more serious consequences by resort to expedients of even doubtful constitutionality.[109]

But perhaps we can find some consolation for our frustrations and failures in knowing that autocratic or totalitarian societies do not have an easier life or lighter burden. They too have their grave social problems of criminality, delinquency, poverty, disease, and other acknowledged and unacknowledged evils. Think for a moment of Spain, under the dictatorship of Generalissimo Franco. With a population one-sixth of our own, Spain has 5000 Communist Party members. The following is from the Intelligence Report of our State Department to which I have previously referred:

Since the end of the Civil War in 1939, the Spanish Communist Party [P. C. E.] has been illegal; laws passed in 1939 and 1940 established criminal penalties for membership in the party and participation in Communist-sponsored political activities. However, despite periodic arrests of known and suspected party members and sympathizers, the P. C. E. has maintained an active underground organization that engages in recruitment, the dissemination of propaganda, and occasionally in strikes and demonstrations. . . . Within Spain, communist party members are found in most urban centers and are drawn mainly from classes of manual workers and intellectuals. . . . Communist propaganda reaches Spain clandestinely in the form of leaflets and a number of more or less regular publications, of which *Mundo Obero* (Workers' World), an official monthly, is the most important.[110]

A similar story is told about Portugal, which, with only 5 per cent of our population, has 2000 Communists.[111] All over the world there are dictatorships like those of Franco and Salazar; and yet Communists crop out just as weeds and scrub bushes crop out on mountain crags, deserts, and waste places. Even if we were to destroy all our most precious values and ideals in our effort to destroy "the enemy within our gates," we would still be afflicted with Communists. Why, then, blame the Constitution and the Supreme Court?

It is no more reasonable to blame the Pope and Catholicism for the fact that in the November 1964 elections in Italy—a country where Roman Catholicism is the state religion and where only an insignificant fraction of the population are non-Catholics—26 per cent of over 25,000,000 votes was for Communist Party candidates.[112] To the example of Italy one could add those of France, Argentina, and other countries, which show that religious sanctions may be no more effective in destroying communism than are criminal and administrative sanctions.

There are those who would have a more friendly disposition toward the anti-Communist laws and regulations if they were extended to apply, with equal severity, to organizations on the Radical Right. But this would be to compound the wrong. The John Birchers and other organizations that generate and thrive on fear and hate are as hateful as the Communist Party. They are not as intellectually subtle as the Communists; but, as the success of the Nazi propaganda in Germany demonstrated, their existence is no less a threat to domestic tranquillity than is that of the Communist Party.[113] Such men as Governor Ross Barnett and Governor George C. Wallace are no less subversive of the Constitution than Gus Hall or Claude Lightfoot. If we have no double standard, we can say with impartiality, "A plague o' both your houses!" But we have imposed enough of a strain on the Constitution and all the branches of our government, and especially the courts, by the heavy-handed way we tried to manage the Communist problem. We have learned enough from that experience not to want to extend it to embrace other national problems.

We cannot, as a civilized community, undertake to attack persons, through criminal or quasi-criminal sanctions, not for what they *do* but for what they *are*. It goes against our conscience to give men a status and then treat them differently from all other men merely because we see them as having that status. This is the basic objection, perhaps, to laws that call for different treatment of persons on the basis of their race, color, or religion—treating them for what they are rather than for what they do.

But this feeling is not limited to the unconstitutional classification of people by race or religion. In 1962 the Supreme Court, in *Robinson* v. *California*,[114] had before it a California statute that made it a criminal offense for a person to "be addicted to the use of narcotics." The facts were that two Los Angeles policemen had occasion to examine the arms of the defendant, and they observed scars, scabs, and needle marks, which, on the basis of their experience, the officers interpreted as the results of the injection of hypodermic needles. At the time they saw him, the defendant was not under the influence of narcotics or suffering withdrawal symptoms, but he admitted to them that he had used narcotics in the past. The jury brought in a verdict of guilty under the trial judge's instruction that included the following charge:

That portion of the statute referring to "addicted to the use" of narcotics is based upon a condition or status. . . . To be addicted to the use of narcotics is said to be a status or condition and not an act. It is a continuing offense . . . it continues after it is complete and subjects the offender to arrest at any time before he reforms.

The Supreme Court reversed the conviction. In an opinion by Justice Stewart, the Court said that a state has the power to impose criminal sanctions against the unauthorized possession or use of narcotics, and a state "might establish a program of compulsory treatment for those addicted to narcotics," which "might require periods of involuntary confinement"; but the California statute made the "status" of narcotic addiction a criminal offense. This, said the Court, brought the act within the constitutional prohibition of cruel and unusual punishment. It is, said the Court,

unlikely that any State at this moment in history would attempt to make it a criminal offense for a person to be mentally ill, or a leper, or to be afflicted with a venereal disease. A State might determine that the general health and welfare require that the victims of these and other human afflictions be dealt with by compulsory treatment, involving quarantine, confinement, or sequestration. But, in the light of contemporary human knowledge, a law which made a criminal offense of such a disease would doubtless be universally thought to be an infliction of cruel and unusual punishment in violation of the Eighth and Fourteenth Amendments.

There are, the Court pointed out, "countless fronts on which those evils may be legitimately attacked"; and of course a person who has the "status" of narcotic addiction may be punished when he is found guilty of "any antisocial behavior."

It would, admittedly, be illogical to press the analogy between "being an addict" and being a Communist; but the California act and some of our anti-Communist statutes have this in common: they concentrate, unfortunately, on a person's *being* something or other, rather than *acting* in a particular way; and it is a healthy moral feeling that compels us to question seriously such a legislative approach to a social problem.

The question we touch upon here suggests relations with statutes that make it a criminal offense for a person *to be* a "gangster" or a "vagrant" without regard to conduct otherwise properly denominated criminal. For example, in the Lanzetta case,[115] the Supreme Court had before it a New Jersey statute that provided that any person not engaged in any lawful occupation, known to be a member of any gang consisting of two or more persons, who has been convicted at least three times of being a disorderly person, or who has been convicted of any crime in this or in any other State, is declared to be a gangster. . . .

A person found "to be a gangster" was to be punished by fine up to $10,000 or imprisonment up to twenty years. Lanzetta and two others were found guilty by the New Jersey courts and sentenced to imprisonment at hard labor for from five to ten years. The United States Supreme Court unanimously reversed the judgments and held the act unconstitutional as a violation of the Due Process Clause of the Fourteenth Amendment.

In an earlier case [116] involving this statute, the highest court in New Jersey gave and approved the rationale of the legislation, saying:

Public policy ordains that a combination designed to wage war upon society shall be dispersed and its members rendered incapable of harm. This is the objective of section 4 [the statute quoted above] . . . and it is therefore a valid exercise of the legislative power. . . . The evident aim of this provision was to render penal the association of criminals for the pursuit of criminal enterprise; that is the gist of the legislative expression. . . . The primary function of government . . . is to render security to its subjects. And any mischief menacing that security demands a remedy commensurate with the evil.

This language rationalizing the crime of a person who chooses "to be a gangster" could be used, verbatim, to explain the crime of one who chooses to be a Communist Party member. The constitutional infirmity, however, is, as Justice Pierce Butler said for the Supreme Court in the Lanzetta case, that the "challenged provision condemns no act or omission. . . ."[117]

The distaste that our judges have for using the law to punish men for the crime of *being what they are* rather than for *specific acts* came out dramatically in the mass-conspiracy trial against alleged members of the Mafia who came together at Apalachin, New York. On November 14, 1957, some sixty men came to the home of Joseph Barbara, Sr., at Apalachin. The police were able to identify fifty-nine of the men, of whom twenty-seven became co-defendants charged with conspiracy to commit perjury and obstruct justice by giving false and evasive testimony concerning the gathering which they attended with some thirty-nine others. The federal court of appeals[118] reversed the convictions. The court made it clear that men cannot be sent to prison merely because they are "bad people." The government had no facts on what happened at the meeting in Apalachin; it only drew inferences from the known and supposed character of those who attended the gathering; and because it did not believe the answers the men gave to questions put to them by officials, they were charged with conspiracy to commit perjury and to obstruct justice. The court of appeals said that the Constitution will not support such police action and convictions. "Doubtless many of Barbara's visitors are bad people," said the court, "and it is surely a matter of public concern that more is not known of their activities"; but under our system of constitutional law they could be convicted only of a crime and not on a basis of mere inference from their character.

If this is true in a case involving the Mafia, how much more must it be true in a case that unavoidably involves the First Amendment freedoms of speech, press, assembly, and association?

And so in the end, while one might not adopt all of his reasons, one may share with Justice Black his conviction that "no matter how often or how quickly we repeat the claim that the Communist Party is not a political party, we cannot outlaw it as a group, without endangering the liberty of all of us."[119] And although this was said in a dissenting opinion in 1959, the Supreme Court in 1964 noted,[120] with implied approval, that the government has conceded that "membership, or even leadership, in the Communist Party is not automatically a crime."[121]

V

Censorship of Literature

1. The New Freedom to Read

The social and spiritual effects of the civil rights struggle will be so deep and far-reaching that one will be able to point to it as a revolution; for American society and the American character will be radically changed by that struggle. Simultaneously, the public order and the American's private character have been radically changed by the revolution in attitudes toward sex. In both instances the Constitution has been the battleground for contending forces. "Law is concerned with external behavior," Justice Frankfurter has said, "and not with the inner life of man."[1] Yet the changes in constitutional law with respect to the rights of the Negro and with respect to the right to publish and to read have changed, and will continue to change, the inner life of every American. This is precisely why one may speak of the changes as revolutionary, for they are psychological, moral, and spiritual, and are radically deep.

Perhaps what the law does has its effects on the inner life of man *because* it is concerned with external behavior; for God made man in such a way that the external and the internal reflect each other or react upon each other. At the end of the *Phaedrus*, Socrates prays to Pan that he may grant him the grace that his inner and outer man may be at one. But in a sense they always are at one, or at least in the irresistible process of becoming one. Perhaps this is the reason why the struggles over laws are so often fierce; for while no one can be sure just what the spiritual, inner effects may come to be, everyone is sure that spiritual, inner effects there will be. Laws are, of course, effects or consequences of external forces and actions; but even Engels was forced to admit—for himself, and for Marx posthumously—that laws can and do act as relatively independent forces in society and are causes that have effect even on the economic and social "base."[2]

168

When we think of individual and social attitudes to sex, and of the freedom to publish and to read books in which sexual acts and relations are treated candidly and elaborately, we touch upon some central facts of human nature. But here is the rub: human nature is not anything formed and fixed for all time. Human nature, as Goethe said, is no sooner formed than it is transformed: a man receives his *Gestalt* as the result of *Bildung*; but *Bildung* continues, and his *Gestalt* is changed.

It is today generally admitted that law is a social, cultural, and economic force in history, but it is not always possible to see the interaction between law and society. Much needs to be assumed, merely on the basis of common sense. It would be strange if a generation of young men and women who take for granted the easy availability, in inexpensive paperbound editions attractively on display in drugstores and grocery supermarkets, of *Lolita, Lady Chatterley's Lover, Tropic of Cancer,* and *Fanny Hill,* were not significantly different from their parents in sensibility, attitudes, and moral and aesthetic judgment. But we are disturbingly aware of the fact that common sense is not the most trustworthy guide. Common sense tells us that the sun rises and sets and that the earth is flat. One must look for measurable differences and specific causal relations.

But the difficulties are almost insurmountable when one tries to measure the differences by some yardstick or to pinpoint causal relationships. How can one be sure, for example, that so much is due to reading, or to what one sees and hears in the movies or on television, or reads in advertisements; and that other changes are due to the automobile; or to living away from home on a university campus; or to the decreased role of family life; or to the emergence of teen-agers as an affluent consumer group, with its own purchasing power and its own distinguishing tone and character? A legal change is not dropped into a culture as if society were a test tube. Despite Justice Louis D. Brandeis's inspiring statements about social experimentation through law,[3] society never becomes an austere laboratory in which a legislative or judicial experimenter can observe the effects of a single factor in prophylactic isolation from other causes. The problems are especially aggravated when one is concerned with possible effects on the psyche, which remains substantially immaterial, moral, and spiritual —invisible and immeasurable.

And yet social "experimentation" does not abate. The causal relationships between slums and crime and delinquency still remain to be determined; but our attack on slums does not wait for the scientists' conclusions. And so, too, with our war on poverty—the causes and effects of which are probably too massive and complex ever to be apprehended by one mind.

In its famous footnote 11 in the school-segregation cases of 1954,[4] the Court cited *An American Dilemma* by Gunnar Myrdal and other studies which, said the Court, are "modern authority" that amply support the "finding" that racial segregation, when sanctioned by law, tends to retard the educational and mental development of Negro children. The Court has been attacked and defended for stating this proposition as a "finding" "amply supported by modern authority."[5] But it is rash to think that if the seven articles and monographs listed in footnote 11 were nonexistent or were not called to the Court's attention, the Court in 1954 would have upheld as constitutional racial segregation in the public schools. The absence of the studies would have meant only a failure on the part of psychologists and sociologists to investigate some obvious problems or a failure on the part of the civil rights lawyers to make effective use of the available literature.

But the decision of the Court would have been the same, for what the Court had before it was a constitutional *ideal* and its meaning, implications, and applications. The ideal of constitutional equality is not the result of a social experiment; it is a force that is intended to generate experiments in the faith that they will work toward the enhancement of "life, liberty and the pursuit of happiness." There were no social psychologists or sociologists to advise Jefferson as he worked on the Declaration of Independence, or Madison as he worked on the Bill of Rights, or the Congress as it drafted and passed the Thirteenth and Fourteenth Amendments. The constitutional requirement is that the state must treat its citizens—all men—as equals, *as if* all the weight of scientific authority *in fact* supported the proposition that all men are *in fact* equal, no matter whether such scientific authority in fact exists or not (as it did not exist in 1776, or 1789, or 1865, or 1868, and may or may not have existed in 1954).

This is the case when we deal with social ideals or values. In England at the beginning of the nineteenth century more than two hundred crimes carried the death penalty, and hangings at Newgate and Tyburn were notorious spectacles. The law was changed by sensible jurors and by Parliament, but not because industrious social scientists had conclusively shown the ineffectiveness of capital punishment to retard crimes. The Biblical commandment is to love the poor, to take care of the helpless and needy, to have one law for the native and the sojourner—regardless of the consequences to society or to the beneficiaries of the commandments. For reality was to be molded by the ideals; the social ideals were to be used as forces to change the facts of life, so that the facts might come closer to what the heart desires.

When faced with racial segregation in 1954, the Court did not outlaw the practice in a spirit of philanthropy, to do good to and for the Negro. The Court was moved by the constitutional spirit of equality and liberty. In our world it is no longer possible for men to feel themselves free, equal, and secure in the midst of slaves or inferior castes. The war on poverty may, to a degree, be motivated by a spirit of philanthropy which the Constitution allows but does not compel; but equality of the races is a constitutional requirement, founded on what Matthew Arnold called the spirit of society.

These considerations need to be kept in mind as we discuss the radical changes that have been made in the law regarding the books and magazines that men may publish and sell, may buy and read. The Supreme Court has been severely blamed for the changes—changes which have had effects on the inner life of men and women, though it is impossible to establish definite causal relationships or to describe precisely the changes in the realm of the intangible and invisible. In changing the law with respect to censorship of literature, the Court has not ventured to cite the equivalent of footnote 11 of the Brown case. It has wisely stayed within the realm of constitutional ideals exclusively, and has not made its decisions on grounds that can be disputed among psychologists and social scientists.

I have elsewhere treated elaborately the history of censorship.[6] Here it will suffice to point out only that, contrary to what laymen may believe, censorship of literature in the interest of morality is a relatively recent phenomenon. Ancient societies took measures to protect religion and the gods against blasphemy and heretical beliefs, and to protect the state and its rulers against seditious opinions; but while there were strict laws regarding sexual relations, little thought was given to their representation in literature or art. There was a great deal of license—and licentiousness—in ancient Greek and Roman literature; and sexual actions are reported and treated with candor in the Bible.[7]

It has been suggested that the preoccupation of the censor with sexual morals has "as a rule appeared simultaneously with the rise of the middle class to political dominance," perhaps because

the middle class position can be maintained through generations only by thrift, prudence and self-control—virtues that are believed to be seriously shaken by licentious communications.[8]

This was a plausible explanation in 1930, when it was asserted; but if it were a sufficient explanation, then censorship would be as rigorous in the 1960s as it was a generation ago, in countries like England, Denmark, Sweden, and the United States, where the middle class still maintains its position of political dominance; yet the censorship situation in these countries has undergone extreme changes. We know that there have been radical changes in judicial and public attitudes; we do not know the causal relationships between one and the other. It is, however, safe to point to a number of factors as probably playing an indeterminate role in effecting changes. There are 246 million radio and television sets in the United States;[9] in 1956 motion-picture attendance was about 35 million a week in 14,613 theaters;[10] book publishing has become big business—publishers' total sales were almost 2 billion dollars in 1965;[11] magazines have become big business—for example, the September 1964 issue of *Playboy* sold 2,700,000 copies, and in 1964 this magazine's income from advertising was over 7 million dollars;[12] in 1959 over 100 million men, women, and children read comic books;[13] through 1965, *Peyton Place* and *God's Little Acre* had each sold about 9 million copies in paperback editions.[14] Book clubs have millions of members; in 1964 the annual sale of paperback books was 315 million copies;[15] the spread of literacy; the growth of the advertising business—in 1964 the annual expenditure for advertising was 14 billion dollars;[16] increased support of public libraries; the emancipation of women; ease and frequency of travel—Americans move out of town every three years,[17] in 1964 2,200,000 Americans traveled overseas,[18] and during 1963 Americans were out of town approximately 2 billion nights.[19] Our 24 million teenagers have $15 billion a year to spend.

These and other facts—including two World Wars, in which millions of men were mustered into the armed forces—must have had some bearing on how much censorship, or how much freedom from censorship, people wanted. The sale of millions of inexpensive paperbound books inevitably means that publishers actively compete for the huge market by trying to make their books attractive as merchandise—some even luridly, salaciously attractive; but it also means that many persons will think that "there ought to be a law" to prohibit some of these books. Mobility makes for cosmopolitanism and a relaxation of moral standards; and it also means that books which are banned in one state or city can easily be purchased in another place. All this is of course equally true of other publications and movies.

If ever technology has affected a social problem, this has happened with censorship. With the invention of printing, the Pope instituted the Universal Roman Inquisition or Congregation of the Holy Office, which published the Roman Index; and in England the government resorted to licensing of printing and publishing. These were simple devices to meet the problem of heretical, seditious, or otherwise undesirable publications. In the U.S.S.R. the government has a monopoly on the presses and other mass media of communication. No such solutions are open to Americans; we can do things only the hard way —if at all.

Until very recently censorship was relatively easier than it is now. The case involving *An American Tragedy* by Theodore Dreiser is typical of the old dispensation. In 1927 a Boston bookseller was arrested for selling a copy of the book. The complaint charged that the book contained

certain obscene, indecent and impure language, manifestly tending to corrupt the morals of youth, the same being too lewd and obscene to be more particularly set forth in this complaint.

The complaint, however, was amended before trial to refer to certain pages in the book. At the trial the state offered in evidence passages from the book appearing on the pages referred to in the amended complaint. These passages were read to the jury. The trial judge in the Massachusetts court admitted in evidence the entire chapters in the first volume in which any of the numbered pages appeared.

The defendant offered in evidence both volumes to show the development of the whole story and as bearing upon the question whether the language on the numbered pages was "obscene, indecent and impure." The trial judge excluded this evidence. Then the defendant offered oral evidence of the theme of the story, and this too was excluded. The jury returned a verdict of guilty.

On appeal to the Supreme Judicial Court of Massachusetts, the court in 1930 affirmed the conviction.[20]

On appeal the defendant contended that the entire book should have been admitted in evidence, for the statute was directed only to reach a book which, in the words of the act, "is obscene, indecent or impure, or manifestly tends to corrupt the morals of youth," and this could not be determined without reading the book. The highest court of Massachusetts rejected this argument and said that the state was trying not the book but only the parts of which it complained. And the court said that legally it made no difference what the author's object was in writing the book, "or what its whole tone is." The court said it would have been "impracticable" to try the case had the entire novel been read to the jury, and that

> even assuming great literary excellence, artistic worth and an impelling moral lesson in the story, there is nothing essential to the history of the life of its principal character that would be lost if these passages were omitted. . . . The seller of a book which contains passages offensive to the statute has no right to assume that children to whom the book might come would not read the obnoxious passages or that, if they should read them, they would continue to read on until the evil effects of the obscene passages were weakened or dissipated with the tragic denouement of a tale.

On all counts, as we shall see, the law has been changed since this decision in 1930. But until the important changes were accomplished, step by step, many books, now well known and with credentials to respectability that hardly anyone would now question, were in serious legal trouble. For example, *Strange Fruit* by Lillian Smith was banned in Massachusetts by its court of last resort in 1945;[21] *Memoirs of Hecate County* by Edmund Wilson met a similar fate in the New York Court of Appeals in 1947;[22] Erskine Caldwell's *God's Little Acre* was banned in Denver, Omaha, Jersey City, St. Paul, and other cities in 1946–1949, and censorship of the book in Massachusetts was upheld by the state's highest court in 1950.[23] In 1948 fifty-four bookstores in Philadelphia were raided by the police without warrants for arrests or seizures. Among the books taken were copies of *Studs Lonigan* by James T. Farrell, *Tobacco Road* by Erskine Caldwell, and *Sanctuary* and *The Wild Palms* by William Faulkner.[24]

These bannings and police actions and court decisions did much to discredit the law of censorship.[25] Had the courts and the police acted with more self-restraint and not permitted themselves to become the public arm of private vigilante groups, the revulsion against censorship would not have been as great as it was. But perhaps it is in the nature of censorship to go to inordinate extremes. Until the Supreme Court placed some restraints on the wild and wholesale assassination of books, the "good" citizen seemed to act on the Shavian principle that "the more things a man is ashamed of, the more respectable he is." It has never occurred to him that perhaps he ought to be ashamed of being so often ashamed—of being a censor.

In 1942 Justice Frank Murphy stated for a unanimous Court in *Chaplinsky* v. *New Hampshire*[26] that

There are certain well-defined and narrowly limited classes of speech, the prevention and punishment of which have never been thought to raise any Constitutional problem. These include the lewd and obscene, the profane, the libelous, and the insulting or "fighting" words. . . . It has been well observed that such utterances are no essential part of any exposition of ideas, and are of such slight social value as a step to truth that any benefit that may be derived from them is clearly outweighed by the social interest in order and morality.

These statements seemed to the Court to be self-evident truths, from the critical examination of which it could well be spared. Apparently even Justice Black at that time had no inclination to question the sweep and generality of these propositions, which certainly cut substantially into the "absoluteness" of the First Amendment freedoms by putting certain species of expression beyond the pale of the Constitution.

Indeed it was not until 1957 that the question was squarely presented to the Supreme Court for the first time: whether obscenity is utterance within the area of protected speech and press. This happened in the Roth and Alberts cases,[27] decided in June 1957. But before considering these cases, let us discuss the Butler case,[28] decided in February of that year.

Butler v. *Michigan* involved the sale of a paperbound copy of *The Devil Rides Outside*, by John Howard Griffin. The conviction in Detroit was under a Michigan statute that made it a misdemeanor to sell or distribute any publication

containing obscene, immoral, lewd or lascivious language, or obscene, immoral, lewd or lascivious prints, pictures, figures or descriptions, tending to incite minors to violent or depraved or immoral acts, manifestly tending to the corruption of the morals of youth. . . .

The Supreme Court unanimously reversed the conviction. The brief opinion by Justice Frankfurter pointed up the fact that the book had been sold to an *adult* (in fact, to a police officer), but the statutory test was a book's "potentially deleterious influence upon *youth*." The statute thus called for "quarantining the general reading public against books not too rugged for grown men and women in order to shield juvenile innocence." Surely, said the Court,

this is to burn the house to roast the pig. . . .

We have before us legislation not reasonably restricted to the evil with which it is said to deal. The incidence of this enactment is to reduce the adult population of Michigan to reading only what is fit for children. I thereby arbitrarily curtails one of those liberties of the individual, now enshrined in the Due Process Clause of the Fourteenth Amendment, tha history has attested as the indispensable conditions for the maintenanc and progress of a free society.

The decision was significant on two counts:

(1) The test of obscenity can no longer be what is fit to be read by the young. In the case involving *An American Tragedy*, it will be recalled, the Supreme Judicial Court of Massachusetts upheld the con- viction because, said the court, the bookseller had no right to assume "that children to whom the book might come would not read the ob- noxious passages. . . ." This attitude was a survival from the Victorian days when books were often read aloud to the family sitting near the fire in the parlor, and the test for literature was what was fit for the ears of children. Well, the Supreme Court in 1957 gave a death-blow to this legal anachronism. Horace M. Kallen once said that schools should not prolong infancy. In the Butler case, the Supreme Court in effect said that the obscenity laws must not prolong infancy.

(2) The Court said that an obscenity law may not "arbitrarily" curtail the liberties enshrined in the Due Process Clause—liberties that are necessary "for the maintenance and progress of a free society." Justice Frankfurter's language can hardly be said to be direct and clear. His words do not specifically contradict Justice Murphy's state- ment in the Chaplinsky case, but they do unlock the constitutional door that had been uncritically assumed to be securely locked. At least we now know that the right of *adults* to read is a right "indispensable" to a "free society" and is a right protected as a "liberty" under the Due Process Clause, and that it includes the right to read publications which may be unfit for minors.

Four months later the Court decided the Roth and Alberts cases, which it dealt with in the same opinions. Each case involved the con- stitutionality of a criminal obscenity statute—in the former the federal and in the latter the California statute. Samuel Roth was convicted in a federal court in New York for mailing obscene circulars and adver- tising an obscene book. David Alberts was convicted in a California state court for lewdly keeping for sale obscene and indecent books, and for writing and publishing an obscene advertisement of them.

The Supreme Court affirmed the convictions by 7-to-2 vote. In his opinion for the Court, Justice Brennan observed that this was the first time that the question of obscenity under the First Amendment had been squarely raised. He said that the Court had "always assumed that obscenity is not protected by the freedoms of speech and press."

Justice Brennan argued from history as to the reach of the First Amendment and pointed out that thirteen of the fourteen states in 1792 provided for criminal libel, "and all of those States made either blasphemy or profanity, or both, statutory crimes," and he cited the statutes of five of those states to show that obscenity too was, at the time of the adoption of the First Amendment, considered outside the protection of free speech and press.[29]

Justice Brennan quoted, in italics, the passage from the Chaplinsky decision that we have set forth above, and gave the following rationale for the listed exclusions from the guarantee of the First Amendment:

All ideas having even the slightest redeeming social importance—unortho-dox ideas, controversial ideas, even ideas hateful to the prevailing climate of opinion—have the full protection of the guaranties, unless excludable because they encroach upon the limited area of more important interests. But implicit in the history of the First Amendment is the rejection of obscenity as utterly without redeeming social importance. This rejection for that reason is mirrored in the universal judgment that obscenity should be restrained, reflected in the international agreement of over 50 nations, in the obscenity laws of all of the 48 States, and in the 20 obscenity laws enacted by the Congress from 1842 to 1956. . . .

We hold that obscenity is not within the area of constitutionally protected speech or press.

The Court then proceeded to narrow the range and reach of the decision. It went on to make it clear that its decision was not intended to support a rampant Comstockery.

First of all, said the Court, "sex and obscenity are not synonymous." What is obscene? It is, said Justice Brennan, material "which deals with sex in a manner appealing to prurient interest."

Sex in any form of representation may, of course, appeal to "prurient interest." In a footnote Justice Brennan said that material "appeal-ing to prurient interest" means "material having a tendency to excite lustful thoughts," and he quoted from the definition of "prurient" in *Webster's New International Dictionary* (Unabridged, 2d ed., 1949):

Itching; longing; uneasy with desire or longing; of persons, having itching, morbid, or lascivious longings; of desire, curiosity, or propensity, lewd. . . .

The terms are all suggestive, some more than others, and hardly add up to anything definitely precise. The Court was obviously concerned that the term should not concede too much to the censor. Justice Brennan said:

The portrayal of sex, e.g., in art, literature and scientific works, is not itself sufficient reason to deny material the constitutional protection of freedom of speech and press. Sex, a great and mysterious motive force in human life, has indisputably been a subject of absorbing interest to mankind through the ages; it is one of the vital problems of human interest and public concern. . . . It is therefore vital that the standards for judging obscenity safeguard the protection of freedom of speech and press for material which does not treat sex in a manner appealing to prurient interest.

Then the Court proceeded to spell out three points that considerably liberalized the law relating to obscene publications:

(1) It rejected expressly the so-called *Hicklin*[30] test, which, as in the case involving *An American Tragedy*, permitted conviction on the basis of selected passages. The Court now held that the proper test is whether "the dominant theme of the material taken as a whole appeals to prurient interest." The *entire book* must be read and judged, and not only certain purple passages read to the trial court by the prosecutor or a representative of a Society for the Reformation of Manners, or a Society for the Suppression of Vice, or a Watch and Ward Society.

(2) It rejected expressly the *Hicklin* test which judged obscenity by the effect upon the most susceptible persons into whose hands the publication—or rather the selected passages—might come. The proper test is, said the Court, the effect upon the *normal adult*, rather than upon the young, the immature, or the highly prudish person.

(3) The publication is to be judged by *present-day standards of the community*.

The Court held that when tested against these requirements, the statutes, trials, and judgments in the cases of Roth and Alberts violated no constitutional provision. Although the decision affirmed convictions for criminal obscenity, and although the Court reiterated the proposition from the Chaplinsky decision that obscenity is not within the constitutional guarantee of free speech and press, Justice Brennan's opinion for the Court went far to give protective "breathing space" to the portrayal of sex in literature and art.

It is noteworthy that the Court benefited from six important precedents, all but one cited by Justice Brennan:

(1) The views of Judge Learned Hand have always carried great weight. In a case[31] before him in 1913, involving *Hagar Revelly* by

Daniel Carson Goodman, Judge Hand felt compelled by existing precedents to uphold the indictment, but he wrote an opinion expressing doubts regarding the law of obscenity as it was then understood and as it continued for over forty years thereafter. The *Hicklin* test of obscenity did not, said Judge Hand, seem to answer the understanding and morality of a later day, and he questioned the wisdom of mutilating truth and beauty in the interest of those who are most likely to pervert them to base uses, and of reducing the treatment of sex to the standard of what is fit for a child's library. The law should not, he said, forbid all publications "which might corrupt the most corruptible," and impose upon ourselves a limitation which may perhaps be necessary for the weakest members of society. "To put thought in leash to the average conscience of the time," said Judge Hand, "is perhaps tolerable, but to fetter it by the necessities of the lowest and least capable seems a fatal policy."

(2) Mary W. Dennett, in the late 1920s, pioneered for the freedom of sex information and for a change in law to permit the sending of birth-control literature through the mails. When her own two sons were reaching puberty, she wanted to place in their hands literature on sex that they could understand, but was not able to find such publications; so she wrote a pamphlet with the title "Sex Side of Life," and about 25,000 copies were sold. Then the Post Office Department declared the pamphlet nonmailable; she was tried for mailing obscene matter and found guilty.

The federal court of appeals reversed.[32] In his opinion for the court, Judge Augustus N. Hand said that any article may, under some circumstances, arouse lust; but he denied that the law intended to prohibit everything that might stimulate sex impulses. "We hold," he wrote,

that an accurate exposition of the relevant facts of the sex side of life . . . cannot ordinarily be regarded as obscene. Any incidental tendency to arouse sex impulses which such a pamphlet may have is apart from and subordinate to its main effect. The tendency can only exist in so far as it is inherent in sex instructions, and it would seem to be outweighed by the elimination of ignorance, curiosity, and morbid fear.

(3) Besides the act against using the mails to send "obscene," "filthy," or "indecent" materials,[33] Congress also enacted a statute[34] that prohibited the importation of "obscene" books. The latter act, however, vested discretionary power in the Secretary of the Treasury to admit "the so-called classics or books of recognized and established

literary or scientific merit," but only when they are imported for non-commercial purposes. Before 1930, however, no such discretion had been vested in any official to admit any books as exceptions, and the customs officials banned such classics as Rousseau's *Confessions,* Casanova's *Memoirs, The Golden Ass* of Apuleius, all of Rabelais, Boccaccio's *Decameron*, and many others.

In 1933 an attempt was made to ban a copy of *Ulysses* by James Joyce. In a notable and influential decision[35] in a federal district court, Judge John M. Woolsey ruled that the book was not obscene within meaning of the act, and so was not subject to seizure and confiscation. Although the book was characterized by "unusual frankness," and although it contained many words "usually considered dirty," the book was not, said Judge Woolsey, "dirt for dirt's sake." Joyce, "a real artist," sought to draw "a true picture of the lower middle class in a European city"—"ought it to be impossible," Judge Woolsey asked, "for the American public to see that picture?" Judge Woolsey held that the test is the book's effect "on a person with average sex instincts," for the obscenity law is concerned "only with the normal person."

The government in its case against *Ulysses* singled out certain passages, but Judge Woolsey stated in his opinion that he read the whole book, though he admitted that this was not easy. He insisted, in his opinion, that a book must be read in its entirety if the test of obscenity is to be applied intelligently.

Judge Woolsey also stated that he took into consideration the reputation of the book in the literary world and the judgment of competent critics.

He also considered the intent with which the book was written—whether it was "written for the purpose of exploiting obscenity." He found that *Ulysses* was "a sincere and honest book."

As to the use of certain "dirty" words, Judge Woolsey said:

The words which are criticized as dirty are old Saxon words known to almost all men and, I venture, to many women, and are such words as would be naturally and habitually used, I believe, by the types of folk whose life, physical and mental, Joyce is seeking to describe. In respect of the recurrent emergence of the theme of sex in the minds of his characters, it must always be remembered that his locale was Celtic and his season Spring.

The federal court of appeals affirmed Judge Woolsey's decision, and in his opinion for the court Judge Augustus N. Hand said that the proper test is the book's "dominant effect," and in applying this test,

relevancy of the objectionable parts to the theme, the established reputation of the work in the estimation of approved critics, if the book is modern, and the verdict of the past, if it is ancient, are persuasive pieces of evidence. . . . We think that *Ulysses* is a book of originality and sincerity of treatment and that it has not the effect of promoting lust.

The *Ulysses* decision opened a new era in the legal—and public—understanding of obscenity, though a quarter of a century was to pass before its full impact was to be felt by judges (in Britain as well as in the United States). The great fame of the book and of its author helped, of course, to attract attention to the decision and to keep it from becoming a legal anomaly.

In due course, the law overcame its built-in lag and took over from the *Ulysses* case the following lessons: (a) a book is to be judged as a whole and not by selected passages; (b) the author's reputation is relevant; (c) the opinion of literary critics is relevant; (d) the author's intent in writing the book is relevant; (e) a book is not to be condemned as obscene because it uses "dirty" words if its characters would, in real life, "naturally and habitually" use them in their speech; (f) the test is the book's effect on the average—and not any abnormal—adult.

Given these safeguards—all this "breathing space"—the question whether obscenity is excluded from the guarantee of the First Amendment may not have practical importance.

(4) In 1946, in the *Esquire* case,[36] the Supreme Court made a far-reaching decision on the censorship powers of the Post Office. The second-class mail privilege is a valuable asset to a periodical. Without it, it would need to pay substantially higher postage rates, which would subject it to a serious competitive disadvantage. Broad discretionary powers in awarding or denying the privilege might be used by a postmaster general to destroy disfavored publications, or to impose political, social, or literary orthodoxy on the press. The mail-classification act provided that periodicals, to enjoy the second-class privilege, "must be originated and published for the dissemination of information of a public character, or devoted to literature, the sciences, arts, or some special industry. . . ."

Esquire magazine was granted a second-class permit in 1933. Ten years later the Postmaster General cited the publishers to show cause why the permit should not be suspended or revoked. After a departmental hearing, the Postmaster General did not find that the publication was obscene, and therefore nonmailable; but he did find that the publication did not meet the statutory formula quoted above, and revoked the second-class permit.

What the Postmaster General had in mind was made clear in his opinion, in which he said:

Writings and pictures may be indecent, vulgar, and risqué and still not be obscene in a technical sense. Such writings and pictures may be in that obscure and treacherous borderland zone where the average person hesitates to find them technically obscene, but still may see ample proof that they are morally improper and not for the public welfare and the public good. . . . A publication to enjoy these unique mail privileges . . . is under a positive duty to contribute to the public good and the public welfare.

It is clear enough from these words that if the action of the Postmaster General had been upheld, fright and gloom would have entered every editorial office, for no periodical would have been safe except those whose "respectability" and orthodoxy placed them beyond attack.

The Supreme Court unanimously upheld the injunction against the Postmaster General issued by the federal court of appeals.

The opinion for the Court by Justice Douglas said that Congress did not intend the Postmaster General to have even a "limited type of censorship"; it would have been "startling" if it had wanted to grant such a power, for such a power is "abhorrent to our traditions." The language of the opinion expressed a position that condemned more than was strictly before the Court. There must be, said Justice Douglas,

an accommodation for the widest varieties of tastes and ideas. What is good literature, what has educational value, what is refined public information, what is good art, varies with individuals as it does from one generation to another. There doubtless would be a contrariety of views concerning Cervantes' *Don Quixote,* Shakespeare's *Venus and Adonis,* or Zola's *Nana.*[37] But a requirement that literature or art conform to some norm prescribed by an official smacks of an ideology foreign to our system. The basic values implicit in the requirements [for the second-class permit] . . . can be served only by uncensored distribution of literature. From the multitude of competing offerings the public will pick and choose. . . .

(5) The most serious threats of censorship in the United States have come not from the Post Office or from the Customs Bureau, but from local police action. Following the police raid of fifty-four book-

stores in Philadelphia in 1948—an incident previously mentioned—five booksellers were indicted for unlawful possession, with intent to sell, of indecent and obscene books. The American Book Publishers Council, sensing that a whole category of books was under attack rather than, as in the past, only isolated titles, stepped into the case, and legal costs were shared by the publishers and the booksellers. The action simmered down to nine books, including the *Studs Lonigan* trilogy and *A World I never Made,* by James T. Farrell; two novels by William Faulkner; and *God's Little Acre,* by Erskine Caldwell.[38]

Fortunately the case[39] came before Judge Curtis Bok, an urbane and learned jurist and a member of a distinguished family. He found none of the books obscene. In his opinion Judge Bok made a number of significant points:

(a) In the civil rights controversy there is often the background question, "But would you want your *sister* to marry a Negro?" In the obscenity controversy the ubiquitous background question is. "But would you want your *daughter* to read this book?" Judge Bok dealt with this aspect of the problem:

It will be asked whether one would care to have one's young daughter read the books. I suppose that by the time she is old enough to wish to read them she will have learned the biologic facts of life and the words that go with them. There is something seriously wrong at home if those facts have not been met and faced and sorted by then. . . . I should prefer that my own three daughters meet the facts of life and the literature of the world in my library than behind a neighbor's barn, for I can face the adversary there directly. If the young ladies are appalled by what they read, they can close the book at the bottom of page one; if they read further, they will learn what is in the world and in its people, and no parents who have been discerning with their children need fear the outcome. Nor can they hold it back, for life is a series of little battles and minor issues, and the burden of choice is on us all, every day, young and old. Our daughters must live in the world and decide what sort of women they are to be, and we should be willing to prefer their deliberate and informed choice of decency rather than an innocence that continues to spring from ignorance. If that choice be made in the open sunlight, it is more apt than when made in shadow to fall on the side of honorable behavior.

(b) Judge Bok saw no reason for placing obscenity beyond normal constitutional considerations. Testing in this way, he held that the publication and sale of the books before him were protected by the

First Amendment. Following Judge Woolsey, he said that the vulgarity and obscenity in the characters of the books were inherent in the characters themselves and were not set forth "as erotic allurements or as an excuse for selling the volumes." Nor, he said, do the books have the effect "of inciting to lewdness, or of inciting to any sexual crime. . . ."

(c) Again following Judge Woolsey, Judge Bok distinguished the books before him from publications that are "sexually impure and pornographic, i.e., 'dirt for dirt's sake.' " The latter are publications "whose dominant purpose and effect is erotic allurement—that is to say, a calculated and effective incitement to sexual desire." But the emphasis, he said, must be on the effect rather than on the purpose. Only this approach, he said, will meet the constitutional requirement of the clear-and-present-danger test. He doubted, however, that any book could be shown to fail by this test, for a book, "however sexually impure and pornographic,"

cannot be a present danger unless its reader closes it, lays it aside, and transmutes its erotic allurement into overt action. That such action must inevitably follow as a direct consequence of reading the book does not bear analysis, nor is it borne out by general human experience; too much can intervene and too many diversions take place. . . .

The only clear and present danger to be prevented by section 524 [the Pennsylvania statute] that will satisfy both the Constitution and the current customs of our era is the commission or the imminence of the commission of criminal behavior resulting from the reading of a book. Publication alone can have no such automatic effect.

Judge Bok concluded: (a) The character of the books themselves put them beyond the reach of the obscenity statute; (b) they are not "sexually impure and pornographic" or "dirt for dirt's sake."

Now, as we have seen, the Supreme Court's decision in the Roth case rejected Judge Bok's constitutional approach, for Justice Brennan expressly excluded obscenity from the First Amendment guarantee. The Supreme Court offered two reasons for this conclusion, neither of which seems to be substantial.

The *first ground* was the historical argument that at the time the First Amendment was adopted

obscenity law was not as fully developed as libel law, but there is sufficiently contemporaneous evidence to show that obscenity, too, was outside the protection intended for speech and press.

A number of things need to be said regarding this argument:

(a) The supporting historical evidence for this conclusion is very meager. The earliest court case on obscenity in the United States was probably one reported in 1821.[40] In fact, in England during the eighteenth century pornography circulated freely. A change was initiated by a proclamation of George III in 1787, to "suppress all loose and licentious prints, books, and publications, dispensing poison to the minds of the young and unwary. . . ." It was not until 1802 that the Society for the Suppression of Vice was founded in England. In testimony before the Police Committee of the House of Commons in 1817, the secretary of the society stated that when the society was founded in 1802, prosecutions for such offenses were unknown.[41] The secretary probably underestimated the number of prosecutions, but certainly they were few and far between. Justice Brennan's statement, I am afraid, suggests a mountain where there may have been only a molehill—hardly enough on which to rest a constitutional principle.

(b) In 1964 the Court did not scruple[42] to subject some important aspects of the libel law to the test of the First Amendment, despite the fact that at the time of the adoption of the amendment the libel law was much more fully developed than was the obscenity law. The Court, obviously, does not permit uncritical antiquarianism to take the place of the critical intelligence and a principled constitutionalism.

The reason why the Court used an unwarranted historical argument may be that it seemed to make more palatable the conclusion it desired; namely, that obscenity is not protected by the First Amendment. If it were so protected, the Court would have needed to grapple with obscenity under the clear-and-present-danger test, and this ordeal it wished, understandably, to avoid.

The *second ground* offered by the Court to sustain its conclusion that obscenity is outside the First Amendment was that obscene writings are "utterly without redeeming social importance." This is a strange and dangerous position, for the Court has no right to go into the question of the *value* of publications. To a Roman Catholic the publications of the Jehovah's Witnesses may be "utterly without redeeming social importance," and of course Jehovah's Witnesses feel at least as strongly about Roman Catholic publications. There was a time when almost every solid citizen thought that all works of fiction were totally without value, and that no intelligent person, having the world's work to do, should waste his time on them, and even now there are millions of men who firmly believe that their own "sacred scriptures" are the only books worthy of any man's time.

Note that the Court did not say that obscene books are not protected by the Constitution because they are *dangerous* to private morals or public order. To have said this would have suggested the relevance of the clear-and-present-danger test; and this is precisely what the Court wished to avoid. So we have the anomaly that dangerous writings may be constitutionally protected, while socially useless books are not.

The Supreme Court has often quoted the saying of Justice Holmes: "If there is any principle of the Constitution that more imperatively calls for attachment than any other it is the principle of free thought— not free thought for those who agree with us but freedom for the thought that we hate."[43] The thoughts that we hate are often thoughts that we consider dangerous; there are, said Justice Jackson, evangelists and zealots "whose fanatical conviction is that all thought is divinely classified into two kinds—that which is their own and that which is false and dangerous."[44] But the Constitution hates no thoughts, though it may love some thoughts more than others; and to the Constitution no thoughts are dangerous unless they are shown to create a clear and present danger. Yet the Court says that the Constitution hates, or at least repulses, thoughts that are "utterly without redeeming social importance." Each of us has seen plays and movies and read books and articles that turned out to be a sheer waste of time, that were plainly unimportant and that should never have been offered; but would we say that they should have been banned by law?

Neither the historical nor the social-utility argument is sufficient ground for excluding obscenity from the First Amendment guarantees. But the Court was probably right in seeking a way to avoid entanglement of obscenity with the clear-and-present-danger test.

Apart from Judge Bok, only Justices Douglas and Black and the American Civil Liberties Union have held to the position that the First Amendment extends to obscenity in a way that is in no respect different from the way in which it applies to other kinds of speech or publication.

In his dissenting opinion in the Roth case, Justice Douglas, with the concurrence of Justice Black, contended that the convictions inflicted punishment for "thoughts provoked" by obscene publications and "not for overt acts nor antisocial conduct." He said that

the arousing of sexual thoughts and desires happens every day in normal life in dozens of ways. . . .

If we were certain that impurity of sexual thoughts impelled to action, we would be on less dangerous ground in punishing the distributors of this sex literature. But it is by no means clear that obscene literature . . . is a significant factor in influencing substantial deviations from the community standards.

He argued that those who are susceptible to delinquency seldom read; that a study of delinquents by Sheldon and Eleanor Glueck showed that delinquents read so little, and that what they read had so little effect on their conduct, that their reading was not worth investigating as a possible cause of delinquency; that the Kinsey studies of sexuality showed that literature only to a minor degree served as a sexual stimulant; that many other influences in society stimulate sexual desire so much more frequently and potently that the influence of reading is relatively insignificant;[45] and concluded:

The absence of dependable information on the effect of obscene literature on human conduct should make us wary. It should put us on the side of protecting society's interest in literature, except and unless it can be said that the particular publication has an impact on action that the government can control. . . .

Freedom of expression can be suppressed if, and to the extent that, it is so closely brigaded with illegal action as to be an inseparable part of it. . . . I have the same confidence in the ability of our people to reject noxious literature as I have in their capacity to sort out the true from the false in theology, economics, politics, or any other field.

The A.C.L.U. summarized its position in a public statement in 1962,[46] in which it emphasized the following standard:

Any governmental restriction or punishment of any form of expression on the ground of obscenity must require proof beyond a reasonable doubt that such an expression would directly cause, in a normal adult, behavior which has validly been made criminal by statute.

The statement allows a permissible exception to this test if children are the target group of the material. In that case,

the standard to be applied in judging such material should be whether its effect on children would lead to behavior that would violate a criminal statute.

In any case, the effect on the group must be established "beyond a reasonable doubt."

The effect of subjecting obscenity to the clear-and-present-danger test is, it seems, the same as "absolutizing" the First Amendment; for in our present state of meager knowledge[47] of the effects of obscene publications, it is not possible to prove, "beyond a reasonable doubt," that reading a book will *directly cause* a *normal adult* to commit a *criminal act*. One might just as well say that obscene publications are *absolutely* privileged. One can say, in fact, that this is what Justices Black and Douglas would want to see accepted as a constitutional principle.

The Court in the Roth case (except for Justices Douglas and Black) avoided this result. But it also avoided the other extreme: opening the doors wide to indiscriminate censorship. The result is a compromise, if one is charitably inclined, or a muddle, if one wishes to be harsh. The Constitution, said Justice Brennan, does not protect obscene publications; *but* publications alleged to be obscene are entitled to be judged by certain standards or tests, which the First Amendment demands, but these do not, in this instance, include the clear-and-present-danger test. Obscenity is thus, as it were, something that the Constitution will neither swallow nor spit out.

6) This brings us to a consideration of the last of the precedents that helped prepare the Court for its decision in the Roth case. It is the important case of *Regina* v. *Warburg*, an English case decided in 1954, in which the court redefined the English law without the help of a change in the statute of Parliament, and approached the problem of obscenity in ways that anticipated the Roth case. Justice Brennan cited the case and was probably influenced by it.

The case[48] involved Stanley Kauffmann's novel *The Philanderer,* published by the reputable London firm Secker and Warburg in 1953, and previously published in the United States under the title *The Tightrope*. The book was prosecuted under the act of 1857,[49] and the test of obscenity as laid down by Chief Justice Sir Alexander Cockburn in *Regina* v. *Hicklin* (1868):[50]

The test of obscenity is whether the tendency of the matter charged as obscenity is to deprave and corrupt those whose minds are open to such immoral influences and into whose hands a publication of this sort may fall.

The publisher decided to fight the case at Old Bailey. Justice Sir Wintringham Stable, the trial judge, showed at the outset a special sensitivity and consideration when he asked Mr. Warburg to step down from the dock and be seated near his solicitor, saying that he did not think the dock was a suitable place for the "prisoner" in a trial of this sort. He gave copies of the book to the jurors and asked them to read it, saying:

... would you mind reading it ... from cover to cover. Read it as a book. ... Not picking out bits that you think have, shall we say, a tendency here or there, or picking out bits that you think have a sort of immoral tendency, but read it as a book.

At the completion of the trial, Justice Stable gave a charge to the jury that has since become famous, to which Justice Brennan specifically referred in the Roth case. "Remember," he cautioned the jury,

the charge is ... that the tendency of the book is to corrupt and deprave. The charge is not that the tendency of the book is either to shock or disgust. That is not a criminal offense.

This part of the charge by itself marks a significant departure from precedent; for scores of books had been banned—books by Defoe, Byron, Shelley, ancient and modern classics—because judges and jurors were shocked or disgusted by what they read, or, more often, by what the prosecution chose to read to them, and they uncritically jumped to the conclusion that what shocked or disgusted them must inevitably corrupt and deprave others—never themselves, of course, but others. What others?

Then you say: "Well, corrupt or deprave whom?" and again the test [from the Hicklin case]: those whose minds are open to such immoral influences and into whose hands a publication of this sort may fall. What exactly does this mean? Are we to take our literary standards as being the level of something that is suitable for a fourteen-year-old school girl? ... The answer to that is: Of course not. A mass of literature ... is wholly unsuitable for reading by the adolescent, but that does not mean that the publisher is guilty of a criminal offense for making those works available to the general public.

Justice Stable, in these few sentences, conformed to the *Hicklin* test, but at the same time drew its teeth.

Justice Stable made an especially important contribution when he stressed the significance of fiction as a key to truth and understanding. The jury had before it a novel by an American about Americans. If, said the judge,

we are going to read novels about how things go on in New York, it would not be of much assistance, would it, if, contrary to the fact, we were led to suppose that in New York no unmarried woman of teenage has disabused her mind of the idea that babies are brought by storks. . . ?

You may think that this is a very crude work; but that it is not perhaps altogether an exaggerated picture of the approach that is being made in America towards this great problem of sex. You may think that if this does reflect the approach on that side of the Atlantic towards this great question it is just as well that we should know it. . . .

Novels are important, he said, because they are a source of much information about the lives of people in past centuries, for they attempt to portray the thought and behavior of real people. Novels are important, for they afford us insights into how people in other countries live and think. Is this not important if we are concerned with the direction in which humanity is moving? If the Englishman wants to understand how life is lived in the United States, why, asked Justice Stable, should he not have the freedom to read the novels written by American authors who attempt to portray the lives of people as they are lived in New York, and to portray their speech, turns of phrase, and attitudes? If the facts are unpalatable, should we close our eyes to them for that reason?

Justice Stable, like Judge Woolsey, drew a line between allowable obscenity and obscenity that is pornography or, as Justice Stable put it, "the filthy bawdy muck that is just filth for filth's sake." Dealing candidly, and even crudely, with the realities of sex does not make the writing "sheer filth." It is pornography *when the filth is only for filth's sake*. It is a question, then, of intent, whether the author was

pursuing an honest purpose and an honest thread of thought, or whether that was all just a bit of camouflage to render the crudity, the sex of the book, sufficiently wrapped up to pass the critical standard of the Director of Public Prosecutions.

The jury of nine men and three women brought in a verdict of not guilty, and at once the English press recognized the decision as a milestone in progress toward freedom of the press and the mind. In effect, Justice Stable judicially rewrote the Obscene Publications Act of 1857 and rewrote the obscenity test as it was formulated by Lord Cockburn in the Hicklin case.

Five years after the decision in the Warburg case, Parliament passed a new Obscene Publications Act[51] that in effect confirmed Justice Stable's position. The 1959 statute makes the following important provisions: (1) A book must be judged as a whole. (2) The author and the publisher may enter a case against a bookseller in order to defend the book. (3) Though the tendency of the book may be to deprave and corrupt, yet its publication may be justified as being for the public good on the ground that it is in the interests of science, literature, art, or learning, or other objects of general concern. (4) The opinions of experts as to the book's literary, artistic, scientific, or other merits may be admitted. (5) There is a time limit on prosecutions—within one year for proceedings before magistrates and two years for proceedings before judge and jury. (6) Booksellers may plead "innocent dissemination" (ignorance of the book's contents) as a defense.

Our natural interest in the English law of obscenity is accentuated by the fact that, while for about a century American law leaned heavily on English precedents (notably the *Hicklin* test), in recent years American courts have begun to break new paths, and the English courts have started to learn from them. In the Warburg and Roth cases and the 1959 act of Parliament we see the two systems of law interact.

This cross-fertilization of ideas comes out dramatically in the cases involving D. H. Lawrence's *Lady Chatterley's Lover* in the United States and in England. These cases will stand as the fact and the symbol of "the new morality"[52] in society and in the law of censorship. Because of their social as well as constitutional importance, the developments respecting this book deserve attention in some detail.

2. The Vindication of Lady Chatterley

In 1928 Lawrence wrote the third draft of *Lady Chatterley's Lover*; the unexpurgated version of this draft became the storm center of literary and legal controversy. His publishers, Martin Secker in London and Alfred A. Knopf in New York, would not agree to publish the book without extensive expurgation. Lawrence then had a thousand copies printed in Italy, which he began to mail to friends and subscribers. In England the Home Secretary alerted customs officials and postal clerks.[53] In the United States the Bureau of Customs, which had banned Lawrence's *Women in Love*, published in 1921, lost no time in deciding that *Lady Chatterley's Lover* was—as a customs official wrote—a "gross exposition of obscenity, filth and lewdness."[54] Judged by today's values, the action of the customs (and of the postal authorities too) at that time seems antediluvian. Remarque's *All Quiet on the Western Front,* published in 1929, could be imported only in an expurgated version; Voltaire's *Candide*, Aristophanes' *Lysistrata, The Golden Ass* of Apuleius, Boccaccio's *Decameron*, Burton's seventeen-volume edition of *Arabian Nights*, and even a rare edition of Rabelais, addressed to A. Edward Newton, were banned by customs.

Because he had lived for several years in Taos, New Mexico, Lawrence had friends in that state, and so it was natural that one of them should try to get a copy of *Lady Chatterley's Lover*. When the book was barred by the customs, this citizen of New Mexico wrote to his Senator in Washington, who fortunately happened to be Bronson Cutting, himself interested in literature and intellectual pursuits. Senator Cutting wrote on behalf of his constituent and asked the bureau to justify, if it could, its refusal to permit an adult American to read a book by a recognized genius. The answer came from Andrew Mellon, Secretary of the Treasury, that the bureau would make no exceptions, not even "in favor of so-called classics or the work of leading writers of the day." Senator Cutting was shocked and began to look into the workings of the customs censorship.

In October 1929 Congress took up a consideration of the tariff laws for revision, and after the House had acted on the bill, the Senate, acting as a Committee of the Whole, began to debate the measure item by item. When the provision dealing with obscene matter was reached, Senator Cutting, aided by Senators Millard Tydings and Hugo Black, put the Senate on notice that he was going to attack customs censorship, and he did, with facts, satire, and fervor. Cutting asked for total abolition of the customs censorship power. A petition was sent to the Senate signed by over two hundred university presidents, professors, authors, editors, and jurists, urging the setting up of a commission that would supervise the entry of books for accredited libraries—books "otherwise deemed objectionable." The Senate, acting as a Committee of the Whole, voted to leave out the provision giving the bureau power over books deemed obscene (a power it had had since 1870).

In March 1930 the Senate took up the bill for final action, and Senator Reed Smoot, co-author of the Hawley-Smoot Tariff Act of 1930, would not give up the fight on behalf of censorship. He told his colleagues that he had in his hand books that would disgust them. "I did not believe," he said, "there were such books in the world—books that the Senator from New Mexico referred to and said ought to be in the libraries of the people of the United States. They are lower than beasts!" Among these books was, he said, *Lady Chatterley's Lover,* which, he cried, would come in only over his "dead body." Its author, he said, must have "a soul so black that it would obscure the darkness of hell." Only censorship, using the *Hicklin* test, he said, could protect the family.

I thus conclude. . . . I appeal to the Senate to throw the arm of protection around the army of boys and girls who must constitute the citizenship of our country.[55]

But Smoot was willing to support a compromise: a proviso that "the Secretary of the Treasury may, in his discretion, admit the so-called classics or books of recognized and established literary or scientific merit, but . . . only when imported for non-commercial purposes"; and that all seized books be turned over to the United States Attorney, and claimants could then have a trial before a judge and jury on the question of obscenity.

Senator Cutting, in his reply, teased Smoot about his copy of *Lady Chatterley's Lover*. It must be, he said, his colleague's "favorite work," which he probably had been reading since Christmas; and now, he said, Smoot had succeeded in creating a national curiosity and taste for the forbidden fruit. Could the Senator be induced now, he asked, to read something else by Lawrence, his essay on "Pornography and Obscenity," in which Lawrence himself condemned pornography, as in the following passage:

But even I would censor genuine pornography, rigorously. It would not be very difficult. In the first place, genuine pornography is almost always underworld, it doesn't come into the open. In the second, you can recognize it by the insult it offers invariably, to sex, and to the human spirit.

Pornography is the attempt to insult sex, to do dirt on it. This is unpardonable. Take the very lowest instance, the picture postcard sold underhand, by the underworld, in most cities. What I have seen of them have been of an ugliness to make you cry . . . ugly and degraded they make the sexual act, trivial and cheap and nasty.[56]

The Senate voted 54 to 24 for the Smoot amendment. Senator Black congratulated Cutting, saying that, while he had lost on the vote, he had in fact won a victory. This was true, but Cutting won the greater victory with Judge Woolsey's decision, three years later, that opened the door to Joyce's *Ulysses*. The Senate debate in 1929 and 1930, set off by the customs ban on *Lady Chatterley's Lover*, marked the beginning of the attack on the *Hicklin* test, and of the new spirit toward classical and avant-garde literature and of the interest in the constitutional questions involved in censorship of literature. From this time on there was no longer to be the unquestioned assumption that censorship was merely an undesirable but necessary police action, with which the Constitution had nothing to do.

But while, in a sense, Lawrence helped to legitimate Joyce in 1933, he himself had to wait almost another thirty years for his own vindication.

Lawrence died in 1930. Two years later his agent authorized Secker to publish an expurgated version, and Knopf brought out an American edition of this version, and before long a paperback edition of the same version was published and over the years has sold over two million copies.[57]

In 1955 a French company made a film based, apparently, on this expurgated version and starring Danielle Darrieux. In 1956 an American distributor sought a license to show the picture in New York. The Board of Regents declared the entire picture immoral for presenting adultery "as a desirable, acceptable and proper pattern of behavior." This action of the Regents was upheld by the New York Court of Appeals by 4-to-3 vote.[58]

The United States Supreme Court in 1959 unanimously reversed the Court of Appeals decision. In his opinion for the Court, Justice Stewart said that what New York did was "to prevent the exhibition of a motion picture because that picture advocates an idea—that adultery under certain circumstances may be proper behavior"; but the First Amendment guarantees the freedom "to advocate ideas"—it protects "advocacy of the opinion that adultery may sometimes be proper, no less than advocacy of socialism or the single tax"; and the Constitution protects "expression which is eloquent no less than that which is unconvincing."[59]

After the movie could be seen, it was reported that the story was told "with notable restraint and good taste," and that the film seemed "surprisingly old-fashioned." The real importance of this *Lady Chatterley's Lover*, it was said, "lies in the law books, not in the film itself. The triumph is for freedom, not for art."[60]

The case was a glaring example of the pitfalls that seem inescapable from obscenity censorship; for the statute under which the Regents banned the film was adopted in 1954, and when he approved the bill Governor Thomas Dewey said that its sole purpose was to outlaw "the exploitation of 'filth for the sake of filth.' It does so as accurately as language permits . . . ."[61] The film was obviously a far cry from "filth for the sake of filth"—note its "seal of approval" from three judges of the Court of Appeals, and the unanimous Supreme Court.

In his concurring opinion (in which Justices Frankfurter and Charles E. Whittaker joined), Justice Harlan wrote:

... I cannot regard this film as depicting anything more than a somewhat unusual, and rather pathetic, "love triangle," lacking in anything that could properly be termed obscene or corruptive of the public morals. ...

The Supreme Court announced its decision on June 29, 1959. But the case had been before the public since May 1956, when the film was first refused a license and when it started on its three-year tour of the courts. Perhaps motivated in part to take advantage of the publicity, on March 19, 1959, Grove Press, a reputable publisher of original and experimental writings, announced that on May 4 it would publish the unexpurgated version of the book, in hard covers, to sell at $6.00 a copy.[62] The book was to have a Preface by Archibald MacLeish and an Introduction by Mark Schorer, and was to be a selection of a respected book club. The book could hardly have been published under more honorable auspices.

It is by no means an unimportant fact that *The New York Times Book Review* on Sunday, May 3, 1959, published a full-page advertisement of the Grove Press "first *complete*" edition of the book in the United States.[63] This advertisement was itself an index to a radical change in the climate of opinion; for it is doubtful if a few years earlier *The New York Times* would have accepted an advertisement for this book.

On May 6 post office inspectors seized mailings of the book, and on June 11 Arthur E. Summerfield, Postmaster General, formally barred it from the mails. The twist that he gave to the law as laid down by Judge Woolsey and in the Roth case was interesting. "Any literary merit the book may have," he said, "is far outweighed by the pornographic and smutty passages and words, so that the book, taken as a whole, is an obscene and filthy work."[64] He was required by law to read the whole book; so he did, but he still judged the whole book— by selected words and passages. The post office also seized twenty thousand circulars advertising the book, deposited for mailing by the Readers' Subscription club. These circulars could not themselves be described as in any way obscene, but the post office said that it could ban them because they gave information where obscene material could be obtained.[65] At the hearing Malcolm Cowley and Alfred Kazin appeared as expert witnesses for the publisher.

The publisher and the book club applied to the federal district court for an injunction, and on July 21, 1959, Judge Frederick vanPelt Bryan granted the injunction and wrote a historic opinion.[66] He held that:

1. The court is not required to show special deference to the administrative determination, for in such cases the Postmaster General has no special competence or knowledge that would give his judgment special weight. In this respect he is different from, for example, the Securities and Exchange Commission or the Interstate Commerce Commission. He may ban a book if it is "obscene," but he has no discretion; the determination whether or not a book is "obscene" involves constitutional and legal considerations, and these are peculiarly for the courts.

2. The book is to be judged in terms of its effect on "the average man of normal sensual impulses."

3. The book is not to be judged by excerpts or passages but as a whole.

4. The limits of tolerance are those imposed by "current standards of the community with respect to freedom of expression in matters concerning sex and sex relations."

5. The book should be considered "in the light of its stature as a significant work of a distinguished English novelist."

6. "There is no doubt of its literary merit."

7. There are passages that will shock "the sensitive minded." But these are "relevant to the plot and to the development of the characters and of their lives as Lawrence unfolds them. The language which shocks, except in a rare instance or two, is not inconsistent with character, situation or theme."

8. The critics were unanimous in acceptance of the book.

9. The tests of obscenity

are not whether the book or passages from it are in bad taste or shock or offend the sensibilities of an individual, or even of a substantial segment of the community. Nor are we concerned with whether the community would approve of Constance Chatterley's morals.

10. The book was published and distributed "through normal channels by a reputable publisher." This puts it on a different footing "from hard core pornography furtively sold for the purpose of profiting by the titillation of the dirty-minded."

11. The Constitution protects a work of literature no less than writings dealing with political, economic, or social ideas or criticism.

Judge Bryan relied heavily on the *Ulysses* and the Roth decisions.

Of course, Mr. Summerfield and the government lawyers also professed to have followed these precedents; but in the law, as in life generally, it is the spirit that gives life. There is no substitute for intelligence, sensitivity, common sense, and a strong taste and preference for liberty in all its manifold, and even clashing, manifestations. Judge Bryan's name will be linked, in our legal and social history, with those of Judge Woolsey, Judge Learned Hand, and a few others who make up "a goodly company."

The government appealed the decision and asked the federal court of appeals to permit the post office ban on the book to be continued pending the appeal. The court, on July 27, denied the motion,[67] and so copies of the book and the advertisements began to move through the mails. The book became a best-seller. On August 19, Grove published a paperback edition, priced at fifty cents.

Before the court of appeals, the government's attorney took the following line:

We are not here to argue the obscenity or non-obscenity of *Lady Chatterley's Lover.* We are here to argue the right of the lower court to act as it did in the case. There is no justification in law for the substitution of his [Judge Bryan's] view for that of the Postmaster General.[68]

This was an indefensible argument, for it meant turning the Constitution over to the Postmaster General and letting him become the czar of book publishing and of the press generally. This position could not but discredit the Postmaster General if this was the power that he claimed. Nothing in our system of government could support this position, and especially in the light of the censorship record of the post office, which, in the period from 1946 to 1956 (not to go further back), banned from the mails: Moravia's *The Woman of Rome;* James Jones's *From Here to Eternity;* Wilson's *Memoirs of Hecate County;* Simone de Beauvoir's *The Second Sex;* Hemingway's *For Whom the Bell Tolls;* O'Hara's *Appointment in Samarra;* Caldwell's *God's Little Acre*[69]—hardly a record to invite confidence.

On March 25, 1960, the federal court of appeals unanimously upheld Judge Bryan's decision.[70] In his opinion for the court, Judge Charles E. Clark firmly rejected the Postmaster General's claim for the finality of his decisions and agreed with Judge Bryan's judgment on the merits of the book. Judge Leonard P. Moore, however, did not share his colleagues' respect for the novel but said that the problem was one that only Congress could solve by changing "contemporary judicial standards," and if Congress did not act soon, he said, an author will

produce "Lady Chatterley's Grand-daughter" that will make Lady
Chatterley "seem like a prim and puritanical housewife."

The Postmaster General said that he would take the case to the
Supreme Court.[71] But the Department of Justice showed no enthu-
siasm for this idea, and on June 2, 1960, J. Lee Rankin, Solicitor
General, announced that there would be no appeal.[72] The case cost
Grove Press $75,000.[73]

But before we take leave of the lady and the gamekeeper we must
turn our attention to the book's fortunes in England. Eight days after
Judge Bryan's decision, the Obscene Publications Act of 1959 received
Royal Assent. Then Penguin Books decided that it would mark the
thirtieth anniversary of Lawrence's death by publishing, in 1960, six
of his novels, including an unexpurgated Lady Chatterley's Lover. Sir
Allen Lane, founder of Penguin Books, said that his decision to publish Lady Chatterley's Lover was influenced by the new act of Parliament and by Judge Bryan's decision.[74] The Director of Public
Prosecutions, however, thought that publication of the book would be
a prima facie offense under the new statute. Penguin announced that
the book would be published on August 25, 1960; and since it knew
that the Director of Public Prosecutions had decided on a prosecution,
in order to spare a bookseller from involvement the publisher invited
the police to come to the office and receive copies. An inspector was
sent and was given twelve copies. Now the terrible book was, for the
first time, officially published in the author's homeland, thirty-two
years after its first publication in Italy.

The trial in Old Bailey in October 1960 caused a great sensation.
Thirty-five witnesses testified on behalf of the book, including Dame
Rebecca West, Joan Bennett, and C. V. Wedgwood, among the
women, and Graham Hough, Dr. John A. T. Robinson (Bishop of
Woolwich), E. M. Forster, Sir Stanley Unwin, C. Day Lewis, Stephen
Potter, and Canon T. R. Milford (Master of the Temple). The prosecution was unable to produce a single witness; all it had was the book.
The jury consisted of nine men and three women. Five of the jurors
read with some difficulty, and one of the jurors was an Orthodox Jew
who took his oath wearing a skullcap. Following the precedent in the
trial of The Philanderer, Sir Allen Lane was not made to sit in the
dock but sat at the solicitors' table. There was no book-burning
atmosphere; it was, as an Englishman would say, a "good show." At
the end of the first day each juror was given a copy of the book, and
the jurors were given a special room, with deep leather armchairs,

where they could read in comfort. It took the slowest reader three days to finish the book, and then the trial resumed.

The prosecutor told the jury that thirteen episodes of sexual intercourse are described in the book; that one four-letter word occurs thirty times; another such word, fourteen times; still another six times, and so on. He told the jury what these words were, not realizing, I suppose, that by discussing them publicly he was, in fact, removing their mystery and taking away their sting.

A point was made that Penguin had already printed 200,000 copies of the book, to be sold at 3s. 6d., and they would then be available to "the general public," and that everybody would rush to buy.[75] But whose fault is that? asked the defense. Whenever a book is the subject of a prosecution, it becomes the center of public attention. But the prosecution's bias against "the public" came out in the question the prosecutor put to the jury: "Is it a book that you would even wish your wife or your servants to read?" The defense naturally exploited the class prejudice implicit in this question, and in his closing speech the defense attorney said that the question recalled the observation of a judge in an earlier case: "It would never do to let members of the working class read this," and the attorney added:

I do not want to upset the Prosecution by suggesting that there are a certain number of people nowadays who as a matter of fact don't *have* servants. [Italics in original.] But of course that whole attitude is one which Penguin Books was formed [in 1935] to fight against, . . . the attitude that it is all right to publish a special edition at five or ten guineas so that people who are less well off cannot read what other people read. Isn't everybody, whether earning £10 a week or £20 a week, equally interested in the society in which we live, in the problems of human relationships including sexual relationships? In view of the reference made to wives, aren't women equally interested in human relations, including sexual relationships? . . . If it is right that this book should be read, it should be available to the man who is working in the factory or to the teacher who is working in the school.

In his summing-up to the jury, Justice Sir Laurence Byrne said that it was for the jury to find whether the book was or was not obscene. If they were to find the book obscene, they must then go on to consider a further question:

Have the defendants established the probability that the merits of the book as a novel are so high that they outbalance the obscenity, so that its publication is for the public good.[76]

The jury deliberated three hours and brought in a verdict of not guilty. Later it was disclosed that from the very start nine of the jurors were for an acquittal. On the last day the three dissentient jurors changed their minds when they realized that a book may be published even though it is obscene, provided its publication is "in the interests of . . . literature. . . ."[77]

On conclusion of the case, attorney for the defense applied for costs, which came to £13,000. He said that he appreciated the desire of the Director of Public Prosecutions to test the 1959 act, but why should the publisher be the "vehicle for such a case" at his expense? And then he made this significant argument:

Penguin Books were hopeful that there would not be a prosecution, very largely because, while the form of the law in America is different, all the questions to be considered, such as the standing of the author, the descriptions of intercourse, the four-letter words, the integrity and purpose of the author, the literary merit, were considered in the American case. . . .[78]

Justice Byrne "smiled, a little enigmatically, and pushed his chair back," and said that he would make no order as to costs but would say no more. Thus, clearing Lady Chatterley of her ill repute cost $75,000 plus $36,400; but her vindication was also a vindication of a public right: the right to read. This right might not have been won had the prosecution been directed against a bookseller, who could not have afforded the expense of calling distinguished people as witnesses and the expense of able and respected counsel. The legal troubles of *Lady Chatterley's Lover* again underscore—as do the civil rights cases—the scandalously high costs of justice.

The jury verdict of acquittal came on November 2, 1960. The novel went on sale, and queues formed outside the London bookshops. A special report to *The New York Times* said that purchasers "seemed to be largely respectable, middle-aged persons. There were only a few teen-agers in the lot." This report continued: "Moved perhaps by their admiration for Lawrence, two respectable and responsible newspapers printed the most notorious and universal four-letter words in their columns." In the same week John F. Kennedy was elected President of the United States, but he ran a poor second to Lady Chatterley as the center of interest in London.[79]

Two days after the case was concluded, the *Times Literary Supplement* published a long review of the book, which ended as follows:

As for the passages which have been so much debated, the worst thing to be said about them is that they sometimes make one laugh. It is difficult to see how any young person could get a wrong idea from them, though no doubt it is unwise to scamper around in the rain gathering forget-me-nots. . . . The actual "description of the whole act" is done with great sweetness, with, moreover many of the pitfalls clearly and helpfully indicated. Young persons of either sex are the last out of whose hands anybody should think of keeping this book. The worst it could do to them would be to make them a little over-solemn.[80]

What a different world we live in! In 1929 the London police raided the Warren Galleries and seized the paintings of D. H. Lawrence that were on exhibit, and applied to the magistrate's court for an order to destroy them. The attorneys for the art gallery told the judge that they wished to call Sir William Orpen, Augustus John, Sir William Rothenstein, and several others to testify that the pictures were works of art, and the judge excluded the witnesses, saying: "It is utterly immaterial whether they are works of art. That is a collateral question which I have not to decide. The most splendidly painted picture in the universe might be obscene." The paintings were saved only by the promise that the exhibition would remain closed.[81] But in 1964 the paintings of Lawrence were reproduced and published in London and New York by reputable publishers,[82] and there was not so much as a breath of scandal.

3. Obscenity for Different Audiences

The case of *Lady Chatterley's Lover* is important for many reasons: the fame of the book and of its author; the suppression of the book for over thirty years; the interaction between the laws of the United States and England; its position as a test case in the United States under the Roth decision and in England under the 1959 statute; its symbolic role, as standing for the new freedom from censorship; the availability of the book as an inexpensive paperback, becoming at once a best-seller. A test case involving any other book would not have had the same significance.

By no means the least important aspect was the fact that the emancipation of the book was achieved without directly involving the Supreme Court. Of course, without the Court's decision in the Roth case, Judge Bryan and the federal court of appeals might not have exonerated *Lady Chatterley's Lover;* but the lower courts demonstrated a boldness such as had not been seen in the federal courts since the *Ulysses* case almost thirty years before. It looked as if the federal judiciary had waited for the Supreme Court to free it from the clumsy, heavy hand of the Hicklin case as a binding precedent. The Roth case seemed to have performed this merciful, surgical operation.

Although the Supreme Court in the Roth case, as we have seen, held, in the words of Justice Brennan, that "obscenity is not protected speech," it in fact gave it "breathing space" in an amplitude that only constitutional liberties deserve and enjoy. If the Roth decision itself left anyone in doubt of this, the Court made its position clear a half-year later in two decisions.

In *Sunshine Book Company* v. *Summerfield,*[83] the Court had to decide whether pictures in nudist magazines were obscene. The post office in the early 1950s impounded nudist magazines, holding that, though the text was not obscene, the pictures were. The publishers tried to get judicial relief several times, but with little success.[84] The federal judges presented the rather degrading spectacle of examining and passing on each photograph, seemingly unaware that their published opinions might dishonor the courts. As one reads some of the opinions, one suspects that the pictures cannot be more unpleasant than the voyeuristic judicial opinions that bear out the observation of Steven Marcus that "the investigation of pornography is itself to a remarkable degree an example of the phenomenon being investigated."[85]

In the Sunshine case the Supreme Court granted certiorari and reversed *per curiam*, citing only the Roth decision. This meant that the nudist magazines, domestic and imported, were not obscene and could not be banned as such by postal or customs authorities.

The fact that the Court wrote no opinion is significant. In effect the Court said: "Take our word for it—the magazines are not obscene. Don't expect us to follow the pattern set by some lower courts, for they accomplished nothing by their foolish opinions, which really are more revealing of the judges than of the pictures that they examined microscopically. In the end, all you have is a statement that this picture is obscene and that one is not—why say more?"

At the same time the Court had before it the post office ban on *One—The Homosexual Magazine.*[86] The Court reversed *per curiam* the decision of the court of appeals, and, merely citing the Roth decision, set aside the ban.

Nudism does not generally arouse the violent feelings that homosexuality arouses. Nudism is a cult, and the pictures in the nudist magazines peculiarly make one think that virtue or innocence is in the eye of the beholder. The absolute innocence of Adam and Eve before the Fall has been irretrievably lost, but relative innocence exists, and nudist pictures serve as a partial measure of this virtue; it would be foolish to think that they have a power to corrupt and deprave normal adults; and certainly they are much less alluring than the pictures in *Playboy* and its imitators. The nudist nudes look as if they are trying to believe that they are in the Garden of Eden; the girlie nudes are always in a perfumed garden of illicit love. But the *Esquire* case, as long ago as 1946, ordered the Postmaster General not to waste his time giving trouble to publishers—and readers—of a publication designed to be "The Magazine for Men." There are all kinds of nudes in all kinds of magazines for all kinds of people. In any case, the ample opportunities to see men and women nearly naked in swimming, sports, and entertainment have considerably reduced the occult in sex, and it is inevitable that this should be reflected in advertising literature and art—and in the law.

But homosexuality has for centuries in our culture been an unspeakable sin and thought of as a crime against nature and mankind. There are said to be some two million male and an indeterminate number of female homosexuals in the United States,[87] so that in terms of numbers alone homosexuality is thought of as a major social problem, one that is often mentioned along with narcotics addiction and delinquency. The subject arouses fears, in part because homosexual tendencies may be latent in normal persons. As we know from security cases, homosexuals live in fear of blackmail and exposure, and so normal persons often are subconsciously motivated to attack homosexuality in order to prove their own immunity.

It will suffice to exemplify the harshness of the law to cite the fact that until 1861 the English statute provided capital punishment for the homosexual act for both the active and the passive participants. In recent years, however, a more humane attitude has been manifested; for example, the so-called Wolfenden Report of the Departmental Committee on Homosexual Offences and Prostitution, made to Parliament in September 1957, recommended that homosexual behavior between consenting adults in private life should no longer be a criminal offense.[88] On both sides of the Atlantic the subject is no longer taboo, is no longer hushed up. So, too, the ninth International Congress on Penal Law, meeting at The Hague in August 1964, with jurists from fifty-four nations participating, adopted a resolution to the same effect;[89] and the New York State Temporary Commission on Revision of the Penal Law and Criminal Code in 1964 also recommended that deviate sexual acts "privately and discreetly engaged in between competent and consenting adults" should not be a criminal offense. This is now the law in France, and also, since 1961, in Illinois.

The radical change in attitude can be illustrated with a federal case decided in 1964.[90] A North Carolina court sentenced a man to a prison term of twenty to thirty years for what the state's statute referred to as "the abominable and detestable crime against nature." (Until 1869 the punishment was death; since then it has been limited to sixty years' imprisonment—the state legislature was influenced by the act of Parliament of 1861.) When the state's appellate court denied a petition for review, the defendant petitioned the federal district court for a writ of habeas corpus.

The federal court remarked that the failure of the state legislature to change the law since 1869 was in itself "a shocking example of the unfortunate gulf between criminal law, and medicine and psychiatry," and that imprisoning the defendant for his homosexual conduct "is not unlike putting a person in jail for being addicted to the use of narcotics."

The court set aside the conviction because the defendant had been denied the "effective aid and assistance of counsel." But the judge took the opportunity to observe that imprisonment for homosexuality only contributes to the aggravation of the problem, for prisons will not rehabilitate such persons but will only confirm and intensify their proclivity.

Fortunately, the voice of reason is being heard more and more;[91] the public generally is becoming more enlightened on the subject and in time may be less inclined to act vindictively against those involved. The autobiographical disclosures of André Gide, in his journals (1939), in If It Die (1926), and in other books did not keep him from getting the Nobel Prize for Literature in 1947; and more recently the publication of The Thief's Journal and Our Lady of the Flowers by Jean Genet, and of Naked Lunch by William Burroughs, has made it possible for The New York Times Book Review in 1965 to publish a full-page advertisement of Mr. Madam: Confessions of a Male Madam, by Kenneth Marlowe. This is a far cry from 1929, when the publisher of Radclyffe Hall's The Well of Loneliness was prosecuted for criminal obscenity.[92]

But the per curiam decision of the Supreme Court in 1958 in the case involving the post office ban on homosexual magazines did not settle the legal status of such publications, for two years later the post office questioned the mailability of the magazine *Manual* and several other homosexual periodicals. At the administrative hearing, psychiatric testimony for the government was that the photographs of young men in nude or practically nude poses were attractive to male homosexuals, and that the publications with such photographs would have a malevolent effect upon some adolescent males should they fall into their hands. An expert psychiatrist called by the publishers testified, however, that the average normal person would not be interested in this type of publication, that these publications would not appeal to the prurient interest of the average normal person, and that they would not by themselves make a homosexual out of an ordinary person.

The post office declared the magazines nonmailable on the ground that

the average reader of these magazines is the male homosexual and that each of the issues in evidence here considered fully as a whole in each instance appeals to the prurient interest of the *average reader of such magazines* and that the average male adolescent who might be attracted to each of the issues . . . would be in danger of the possible luring . . . into the abnormal paths of the homosexual.[93]

The post office rejected the contention that, to be nonmailable, the magazines would need to be shown to appeal to the prurient interests of the *average normal person* in the community.

Now this decision posed an interesting and difficult problem. In the Butler case, as we have seen, the Supreme Court in 1957 held a Michigan statute unconstitutional because it provided as a test for obscenity the tendency of a publication to corrupt the morals of youth. In the *Manual* case the post office banned magazines because of their effect on homosexuals.

When this decision came before the Supreme Court in 1962, six of the seven Justices who participated agreed to reverse the judgment, but they could not agree on an opinion; so that the Manual Enterprises cases presents the exceptional situation of a case without a Court opinion.[94] There is an opinion by Justice Harlan, in which Justice Stewart joined; by Justice Brennan, in which Chief Justice Warren and Justice Douglas joined; and a dissenting opinion by Justice Clark. Justice Black concurred in the reversal without an opinion and without joining in either of the two majority opinions. Perhaps he preferred a *per curiam* reversal, as in the 1958 case; this would have been the wiser course for the Court to take.

Justice Harlan's opinion is, I think, important beyond the limits of the case. For a moment, let us go back to the Roth case, in which Justice Harlan concurred in the affirmance of the conviction of David Alberts but dissented from the affirmance of the conviction of Samuel Roth. In his opinion, the consideration of which we have deferred until now, Justice Harlan contended that Roth's conviction could not constitutionally stand, since the trial judge charged that the federal obscenity law made it a crime to sell books which "tend to stir sexual impulses and lead to impure thoughts." Said Justice Harlan:

I cannot agree that any book which tends to stir sexual impulses and lead to sexually impure thoughts necessarily is "utterly without redeeming social importance." Not only did this charge fail to measure up to the standards which I understand the Court to approve, but as far as I can see, much of the great literature of the world could lead to conviction under such a view of the statute. Moreover, in no event do I think that the limited federal interest in this area can extend to mere "thoughts." The Federal Government has no business . . . to bar the sale of books because they might lead to any kind of "thoughts."

Then Justice Harlan went on to make a most important point in a single sentence: "I do not think," he said, "that the federal statute can be constitutionally construed to reach other than what the government has termed as 'hard-core' pornography."

This was, I believe, the first time that a Supreme Court opinion made the point that, at least as far as concerns federal power, obscene publications can be the concern of the government only if they can judicially be found to be *hard-core pornography*. Justice Harlan did not elaborate, but he probably meant the same thing that Judge Woolsey had in mind when he distinguished a book such as *Ulysses* from a publication that is "pornographic—that is, written for the purpose of exploiting obscenity." Judge Bok, too, seemed to have a similar distinction in mind, between protected obscenity and pornography, the latter of which he described as a publication "whose dominant purpose and effect is sexual allurement—that is to say, a calculated and effective incitement to sexual desire." And Judge Clark, in the *Lady Chatterley* case, also referred to "hard-core pornography," which, he said, is "easily recognized" "trash" and is "essentially repulsive."

Now, in the Manual Enterprises case Justice Harlan (with the concurrence of Justice Stewart) said that it was not necessary for the

Court to pass on the question whether obscenity should be tested against the "average person" (as in the Roth and Butler cases) or against the "average homosexual" who would be the recipient of the magazines. For obscenity, to be a violation of the federal act, must have two elements: (1) the publication must be shown to deal with sex in a manner appealing to "prurient interest" (*Roth*); and (2) it must be "so offensive on . . . [its] face as to affront current community standards of decency—a quality that we shall hereafter refer to as 'patent offensiveness' or 'indecency.'" An obscene publication must have a "prurient interest" appeal *and* be "patently offensive." To exclude from consideration the latter, said Justice Harlan,

might well put the American public in jeopardy of being denied access to many worthwhile works in literature. For one would not have to travel far even among the acknowledged masterpieces . . . to find works whose "dominant theme" might, not beyond reason, be claimed to appeal to the "prurient interest" of the reader or observer. We decline to attribute to Congress any such . . . deadening purpose as would bar from the mails all material, not patently offensive, which stimulate impure desires relating to sex. Indeed such a construction of §1461 [regarding nonmailability] would doubtless encounter constitutional barriers.

Turning to the homosexual magazines, Justice Harlan said that the question of their obscenity, "involving factual matters entangled in a constitutional claim, . . . is ultimately for this Court." He therefore examined the magazines and found that, when "fairly taken as a whole," "the most that can be said of them is that they are dismally unpleasant, uncouth, and tawdry." But this did not make them obscene. Said Justice Harlan:

Divorced from their "prurient interest" appeal to the unfortunate persons whose patronage they were aimed at capturing (a separate issue), these portrayals of the male nude cannot fairly be regarded as more objectionable than many portrayals of the female nude that society tolerates.

In other words, even assuming, with the Post Office Department, that the homosexual magazines appealed to the *prurient interest of the average reader of such magazines,* they were, nonetheless, not obscene, for they did "not transcend the prevailing bounds of decency," they were not "beyond the pale of contemporary notions of rudimentary decency," they were not patently offensive.

Justice Harlan's opinion is an acceptable gloss on the Court's opinion in the Roth case and was implied in the Court's *per curiam* decisions in the One, Inc., and Sunshine Book Company cases in 1958—decisions which, like that in the Manual Enterprises case and like the decisions in the *Lady Chatterley* case, could be interpreted as meaning that publications, though obscene, cannot, constitutionally, be banned unless they are found to be patently offensive. The test is, in part, similar to that in the 1959 act of Parliament: a publication, *though admittedly obscene,* may be published—in England, if its publication can be justified as being for the public good on the ground that it is in the interests of science, literature, art, learning, or some other object of general concern; in the United States, if the publication is not patently offensive when judged by contemporary notions of decency. The two tests go together up to a certain point. Beyond this point, the English and American standards move apart. It is hard to see how the homosexual magazines could pass the English test as being "for the public good," for they have no merit from the standpoint of science, literature, art, learning, or any other object of general concern. They could pass the test of the English law only if they are found to be not obscene in the first place, because they are not "such as to tend to deprave and corrupt persons [who already are homosexuals] likely to read" them. If anything, the American standard as expressly interpreted by Justices Harlan and Stewart, and implied by the other Justices, is more permissive.

The Court in the Manual Enterprises case avoided the question of the audience on whom a publication is to be tested—the appeal of the magazines to the "average homosexual" or to the "average person." The reversals were for various reasons: procedural, three Justices; wrong use of the test of obscenity, two Justices; no reasons given, one Justice. The question of the audience teases the mind and invites at least tentative or partial answers. A court cannot say that nudist magazines may be published if they are to be mailed *only* to persons who belong to the nudist cult; or that homosexual magazines may be mailed *only* to persons who are not homosexuals or *only* to persons who already are homosexuals. Despite their silence on the subject, the Justices surely knew that the nudist magazines are seen by fully dressed persons and that homosexual magazines are seen almost entirely by homosexuals, just as magazines that feature female nudes are seen almost entirely by men.[95] The law today permits frank and open appeal to the prurient interest of *different audiences.* Styles of dress—and undress—cosmetic and clothing advertising, the songs we hear, the dances we see—in countless ways sexual interests *of different audiences* are stimulated. A considerable part of the Gross National Product would be lost if our society suddenly, in a moment of insanity, were to stamp out the sexual manifestations of our culture; and the injury would not, of course, be limited to our economic life.

One may reasonably argue that, looking only at the existence of homosexuality,[96] it may be morally and socially desirable that men and women—and especially young people—be sexually stimulated, so that they may have normal, heterosexual desires and interests.

But then Justice Harlan may be right: if society tolerates the female nude, it cannot object to the male nude. Not a legal prohibition, but the rule of *caveat emptor,* must then obtain.

There may, perhaps, be one audience with respect to whose members there may be special legislation. I refer to minors. This was touched on by Justice Frankfurter in his opinion for the Court in the Butler case. It will be recalled that in that case the defendant was convicted under a Michigan act that made it an offense to make available for the general public a book found to have a potentially deleterious influence upon youth. The Supreme Court unanimously reversed, holding that a state may not keep books from the public in order to shield the innocence of the young. But Justice Frankfurter added that Michigan had a statute which made it a crime to sell or give to a minor a book containing obscene language or obscene pictures "tending to the corruption of the morals of youth." Alfred Butler was not, however, convicted under this statute. "We have before us," wrote Justice Frankfurter, "legislation not reasonably restricted to the evil with which it is said to deal." There is in this language just a suggestion that a state may impose restrictions on sales of books to minors which it may not do on sales to adults.

New York in 1955 enacted a statute[97] that prohibited the sale to anyone under eighteen years of age of any book "the cover or content of which exploits, is devoted to, or is principally made up of descriptions of illicit sex or sexual immorality." This statute went beyond the prohibitions in another and more general obscenity statute,[98] by providing that books *that are not obscene* but that are devoted to illicit sex or sexual immorality may not be sold to persons under eighteen years of age.

The New York Court of Appeals in 1964, by 4 to 3, held the act unconstitutional for vagueness and for being in conflict with the First and Fourteenth Amendments.[99] The words of the statute quoted above, said the court,

are either too vague to apprise possible defendants of what they mean, or, if they are to be interpreted as referring exclusively to extramarital sex or sexual perversion, then they would forbid all publications or pictures mainly devoted to those subjects, regardless of the manner in which they are presented, whether by way of fiction, sociological discussion, moralizing, or otherwise. The Oedipus legend in classic Greek drama would be forbidden because it is principally devoted to incest, the Tristan and Isolde legend and Hawthorne's *Scarlet Letter* would be illicit reading for the young because it is principally made up of adultery, Bernard Shaw's *Mrs. Warren's Profession* would be outlawed for obvious reasons. . . . It seems to us that this statute is drawn so broadly as to render criminal sales . . . to the young of pictures and publications of all kinds which are principally devoted to these subjects, in however serious or dignified a manner. . . .

The court questioned, too, what sense it made to permit, as the statute seemed to do, descriptions of the intimate sexual details of married life but to prohibit such presentations if the participants are not married.

The court added that there are other constitutional problems involved, such as the constitutional requirement that the bookseller have knowledge of the contents of the book as violative of the statute; for the Supreme Court, in *Smith* v. *California*,[100] said that if a bookseller is made criminally liable without knowledge of the contents, he will tend to restrict the books he sells to those he has inspected, and he will naturally become timid in the face of absolute liability, and thus his self-censorship will bar non-obscene as well as obscene books. The court of appeals also suggested that there may be a constitutional problem in the question of the effect of the New York statute on restricting sales to adults.

Today books that at one time could not be bought at all are widely read in high schools and colleges, and such books are available in paperback editions at drugstores and supermarkets. The ways to evade age restrictions on the purchase of books are too many to be enumerated. It could only make young people cynical of law in general to see early in life how easy it is to evade or even flout the law. Given the conditions of modern life, a law such as that of New York, by inviting and provoking the habit of lawbreaking, could lead to behavior generally scornful of morality and the social order.[101]

Rhode Island thought that it could remove some of the pitfalls involved in this type of legislation by setting up machinery that would remove the risks from the booksellers, who would not need to guess as to what books would or would not be likely to get them into trouble. In 1953 the legislature created a state commission "to encourage morality in youth." Its nine members were appointed by the governor. The commission was concerned with many problems: for example, what young people did in cars parked at drive-in theaters, and the types of films shown there; juvenile drinking and delinquency. But our concern here is with the duty of the commission "to educate the public concerning any book, picture . . . or other thing containing obscene, indecent or impure language, or manifestly tending to the corruption of the youth . . . and to investigate and recommend the prosecution of all violations."

The commission made up lists of "objectionable" publications, which it sent to the wholesale distributors with a statement that the commission had found the listed titles to be objectionable for display or sale to youths under eighteen years of age, and that thanked the distributor in advance for his cooperation, and that reminded him that the commission had the official duty to recommend prosecution of purveyors of obscenity. On receipt of such notice the distributor sent his field agents to the stores to pick up unsold copies of blacklisted books, which were then returned to the publishers, together with the stock in his possession. A policeman often called on the distributor to see what action he had taken. The system was obviously a kind of "preventive" law enforcement.

Four publishers of paperback books attacked the scheme in the courts, contending that it amounted to governmental censorship in violation of the First and Fourteenth Amendments.

By 8 to 1 the Supreme Court in 1963 declared that the Rhode Island practice was unconstitutional.[102]

The commission argued that it really lacked legal power and merely exhorted and advised booksellers; but the Court said that while this was the form of its actions, its substance was a state imposition of censorship, performed under color of state law. The distributor's compliance was not voluntary, for he could not lightly disregard the thinly veiled official threats to prosecute him for disobedience, and thus books and magazines—including the best-seller *Peyton Place*, by Grace Metalious, *Playboy*, as well as "horror" publications—were effectively blacklisted without a determination of obscenity in a criminal trial hedged with procedural safeguards. This was a form of regulation with hazards to constitutional freedoms "markedly greater than those that attend reliance upon the criminal law."[103] Although, said Justice Brennan, obscenity is not within "the area of constitutionally protected speech or press," it must nonetheless "be ringed about with adequate bulwarks."

The Court gave one other reason for condemning the Rhode Island system:

Although the Commission's concern is limited to youthful readers, the "cooperation" it seeks from the distributors invariably entails the complete suppression of the listed publication; adult readers are equally deprived of the opportunity to purchase the publication in the State.

Thus far, then, no legal blacklisting of books sold to minors but legally approved for adults has been validated by the Supreme Court; and, in view of the many constitutional obstacles, it is doubtful if an acceptable procedure will be devised, if resort will be had to legal sanctions. Today's marketing of books and magazines is such that it may be impossible to impose legal restrictions on their sale to minors without seriously affecting their availability to adults. Shops that specialize in and sell *only* obscene publications can take measures to keep out minors. In San Francisco, for example, there are such shops, from which the owners exclude minors by posted signs and personal vigilance. This device is probably a response to local police pressure in return for a no-raiding promise. But such arrangements can be reached only informally; we have not reached the point where the legislature would legally recognize and sanction such special shops—this would be like licensing prostitution, which also exists under informal police surveillance. Communities tolerate under unwritten laws, but with a measure of police supervision, much that they would not countenance through the validating process of legislation. Law-enforcement officers have certain law-*non*enforcement functions that are expressive of the community's degree of permissiveness or live-and-let-live philosophy. It is in their performance of such functions that the police are often the guardians of a city's youth.

4. Henry Miller and Fanny Hill

In the current struggle against censorship of literature, no book is more important than *Tropic of Cancer* by Henry Miller. It is too soon to measure its liberating effect, but history will, one guesses, find that the book's role has been immense. To say this is not to belittle the role of *Lady Chatterley's Lover*. Without the latter's emancipation, *Tropic of Cancer* would still be smuggled in from Paris and passed from friend to friend with a note of satisfaction in having beaten the customs inspector. The Lawrence book had to be cleared by the courts first, before they could be ready for *Tropic of Cancer*—just as *Ulysses* had to precede *Lady Chatterley's Lover*. But while the influence of Judge Woolsey's opinion can be measured in decades, the effect of the federal courts' action in the case of Lawrence's book can be measured in months—in this area the law's lag behind society and culture has been eliminated; and some might even say that the law has moved too fast, ahead of society and culture. In any case, while clearing Lawrence prepared the courts for clearing Henry Miller, the relation between them is one of sharp moral contrast; for as between them, Lawrence stands for sacred love, Miller for profane; Lawrence stands for redemption, Miller for damnation; Lawrence for wholeness, integrity, and purity, Miller for egoism, fruitlessness, and promiscuity. What *Lady Chatterley's Lover* and *Tropic of Cancer* have in common is seen only on the surface: a concern with sex and the use of certain four-letter words. But to see the books on this level only is like saying that Dostoevski's *Crime and Punishment* resembles a cheap crime novel, for there is violence in both, and both books use conversation. But the irrationality of censorship is exposed precisely by the fact that the censor makes his comparisons on the basis of such exigent and superficial characteristics.

Tropic of Cancer was published in Paris in 1934. Copies of the book were admitted by customs only by special permission from the Secretary of the Treasury under the act of Congress that played a role in the *Ulysses* case. As recently as March 20, 1959, *The New York Times* devoted almost an entire column to the fact that the Customs Bureau had at last granted permission to a leader of a civil liberties group to bring in a copy of the book for his personal literary and scholarly purposes. He had a copy of the book when he arrived from Paris, and the customs at once confiscated it. More than six months later the Treasury Department, to which the traveler's lawyer had made application, issued the order to admit the copy. The reasons for making an exception were that the book had been discussed in many publications and that the person who wanted it was a man of responsibility, who was not bringing in the book for commercial purposes or to satisfy a prurient interest.

In 1953 the federal court of appeals had upheld the customs ban on the book,[104] saying:

The vehicle of description is the unprintable word of the debased and morally bankrupt. Practically everything that the world loosely regards as sin is detailed in the vivid, lurid, salacious language of smut, prostitution and dirt.

On July 21, 1959, Judge Bryan cleared *Lady Chatterley's Lover* for the United States mails, and in March 1960 the court of appeals upheld this decision. A half-year later Grove Press, which had published the Lawrence novel, announced that it had received Miller's permission to publish *Tropic of Cancer* and that the book would soon be issued; though Grove would wait for some time pending an action in the federal court brought by an American traveler (other than the one mentioned above) whose copy of the book was confiscated by customs in October 1960,[105] Grove stated that it would not wait indefinitely. On June 24, 1961, the book was published, with an introduction by Karl Shapiro. It was a hardcover edition, selling at $7.50 a copy.

Grove made use of the critical praise the book had received over the years from T. S. Eliot, Horace Gregory, Wallace Fowlie, George Orwell, Aldous Huxley, Sir Herbert Read, Osbert Sitwell, Lawrence Durrell, John Ciardi, Norman Cousins, and William Carlos Williams —impressive testimony to the book and to the censors in the United States and Great Britain.

When Grove early in June mailed several copies, the Post Office Department seized them. Copies delivered to New York booksellers by truck went on sale. But the Justice Department told the Post Office lawyers that it had no intention of seeking to indict Grove for sending an obscene publication through the mails; thus the onus of censorship would fall entirely on the postal authorities. On June 15, 1961, the Post Office lifted its ban, saying it would let the courts decide on the book's legal status in the case involving the customs ban.[106] Thus the buck was passed from the Justice Department to the Post Office, to the Customs Bureau, to the federal courts—while the book was benefiting from the free publicity. On August 10, 1961, the ban on the importation of the book (as well as of Miller's *Tropic of Capricorn* and *Plexus*) was lifted on the advice of the Justice Department.[107] Thus all federal restraints on the book ended within several months of its publication in the United States but more than a quarter of a century after its first publication in Paris.

Several months later Grove published a paperback edition at ninety-five cents, and by early 1962 some 2,500,000 copies were in print. But the book was in trouble in many communities. Local wholesalers refused to handle it because of extra-legal pressures and fear of legal action. By the end of January 1962 there were more than forty criminal and civil actions all over the country;[108] and by the end of June the publisher was involved in more than sixty cases, at an estimated cost of over $100,000.[109] The result of the cases was hopeless confusion, as between federal law and the states, as between states, and as between trial courts in the same state. For example, a trial in Los Angeles ended in a conviction, while trials in Marin County and San Diego, California, ended in acquittals. The highest state courts in Massachusetts, Wisconsin, and California held the book to be not obscene, but the New York Court of Appeals held that it was obscene.[110] In New Jersey the state's Attorney General said that in his opinion the book was not obscene and he advised the twenty-one county prosecutors that they would be fulfilling their duty by taking no action against distributors of the book; but the prosecutor of Bergen County procured indictments just the same, and a federal judge refused to interfere with the prosecutions.[111]

A typical case was one of the California prosecutions.[112] The jury consisted of seven housewives, a saleswoman, and four men. The prosecutor read selected passages to the court and jury, and the jurors spent fourteen hours in seclusion reading the book. Under the 1961 California statute, the prosecution had to establish that the book was "utterly without redeeming social importance."[113] The prosecutor could not find a single prominent critic or professor to testify that in his opinion the book failed to pass this test; his witnesses included two former district attorneys, two clergymen, one of whom admitted that he had not read any one of ten well-known modern novels, such as *Sons and Lovers* and *Ulysses*; while the defense had, among other witnesses, Mark Schorer and Herbert Gold. The jury was out for six hours and returned a verdict of not guilty. A spokesman for the jury disclosed after the trial that a majority felt that, while the book was in fact obscene, they were sure that there had to be an acquittal. Thus the jury, overlooking subtle differences of nuance, felt about *Tropic of Cancer* under the new California statute the way the jury in Old Bailey felt about *Lady Chatterley's Lover* under the new English law.

The New York Court of Appeals, without the benefit of housewives, on July 10, 1963, decided that the book was obscene under the state's act that punishes publications that are "obscene, lewd, lascivious, filthy, indecent, sadistic, masochistic or disgusting." But the decision was 4 to 3.[114] The majority said that the book is, "in short, 'hard-core pornography,' dirt for dirt's sake . . . and dirt for money's sake . . . [and incompatible] with the current moral standards of our community." On the other hand, the minority, through Judge Marvin R. Dye, found that

Like *Ulysses,* it is a tragic and very powerful commentary on the inner lives of human beings caught in the throes of a hopeless social morass.

Written in Paris in 1934 at a time when Europe was reeling from the aftermath of the devastating moral and material destruction of World War I, the book reflects the debasing experiences and problems known to many in a city such as Paris in the 1930s. In an effort to escape the clutching insistence of an all-engulfing miasma, the author describes his own and his companion's sexual indulgences, tediously repeated, to rediscover that surrender to such demeaning conduct was not the antidote to the underlying human unhappiness caused by the poverty, filth, disease, loneliness and despair in a world in flux.

And Judge Stanley H. Fuld, dissenting, spoke of the book as "a serious expression of views and reactions toward life, however alien they may be to the reader's philosophy or experience . . . ," and he referred to the opinions of Judge Woolsey and Judge Bok.

Only one week before the New York Court of Appeals announced its 4-to-3 decision condemning *Tropic of Cancer* as hard-core pornography, the seven judges of the Supreme Court of California all agreed that the identical book "surely does not constitute hard-core pornography."[115]

On June 22, 1964, the United States Supreme Court ended the confusion of tongues by reversing a Florida ban on the book.[116] The brief *per curiam* indicates, however, a 5-to-4 decision, with the Court divided four ways, as follows: (1) Justices Black and Douglas would reverse for the reasons stated by the former in *Jacobellis* v. *Ohio*,[117] decided the same day; (2) Justices Brennan and Goldberg would reverse for the reasons stated by the former in the Jacobellis case; (3) Justice Stewart would reverse for the reasons stated by him in the Jacobellis case; and (4) Chief Justice Warren and Justices Clark, Harlan, and White were of the opinion that certiorari should have been denied (which would have meant leaving the Florida decision undisturbed).

The effect of the decision of the Supreme Court was that *Tropic of Cancer* was not obscene, and was, therefore, entitled to constitutional protection against federal or state interference. But to understand the Court's rationale we must turn to the Jacobellis case.

This was a 6-to-3 decision involving a French film, *The Lovers*. The manager of a motion-picture theater in Cleveland Heights, Ohio, was convicted in a state court for violating the Ohio obscenity statute by possessing and showing this film. *The Lovers* depicted an unhappy marriage and the wife's falling in love with a young archaeologist, and the film included an explicit but fragmentary and fleeting love scene. The United States Supreme Court reversed the conviction, but the six

Justices who were for reversal could not agree upon one opinion in support of their decision. In all, six opinions were written, four for reversal and two dissenting.

The Lovers had been admitted by the Customs Bureau with an express ruling that the film was not obscene. The film had won a second prize at the Venice International Film Festival of 1958 and was favorably reviewed by film critics in *Saturday Review, The New York Times,* and the *New York Herald Tribune.*[118]

Since the Supreme Court cleared *Tropic of Cancer* on the same grounds on which it cleared *The Lovers,* we must consider with care the opinions in the Jacobellis case.

The Supreme Court in 1915 excluded the movies from the protection of the First Amendment and held that movies were purely business undertakings, offered for profit, and were in no sense part of the country's press.[119] This meant that movies were subject to licensing or censorship by all levels of government. But in 1952, in the *Miracle* case,[120] the Court held that the basic principles of speech and press applied to motion pictures and that New York could not ban the film on the ground that it was "sacrilegious." In the following year the Court held that New York could not ban the French film *La Ronde* on the ground that it was "immoral," and that Ohio could not ban the domestic film *M* as "tending to promote crime."[121] As we saw earlier, in 1959 the Court upset the New York ban on the movie *Lady Chatterley's Lover.*[122]

Now, in the Jacobellis case, six Justices agreed that *The Lovers* was not obscene, and accordingly the judgment of the Ohio courts was reversed.

Justice Brennan wrote an opinion, in which Justice Goldberg concurred. He reiterated that while obscenity is not subject to constitutional guarantees, the Court cannot avoid deciding whether a particular work is obscene, for the question "necessarily implicates an issue of constitutional law." This issue must ultimately be decided by the Supreme Court, though the task is "difficult, recurring, and unpleasant." It must review the facts of each case and make "an independent constitutional judgment on the facts of the case as to whether the material involved is constitutionally protected."

While recognizing that the *Roth* test for obscenity is not perfect, Justice Brennan said that "we . . . adhere to that standard"—that is,

whether to the average person, applying contemporary community standards, the dominant theme of the material taken as a whole appeals to prurient interest.

He also reiterated that obscenity is not constitutionally protected "only because it is 'utterly without redeeming social importance.'" Then Justice Brennan formulated a principle or rationale that is very similar to that provided by the 1959 act of Parliament; he said that

material dealing with sex in a manner that advocates ideas, ... or that has literary or scientific or artistic value or any other form of social importance, may not be branded as obscenity and denied the constitutional protection. Nor may the constitutional status of the material be made to turn on a "weighing" of its social importance against its prurient appeal, for a work cannot be proscribed unless it is "utterly" without social importance." See *Zeitlin* v. *Arneburgh* [the California decision that cleared *Tropic of Cancer*].[123]

Justice Stewart, in a brief opinion, said that in his view a ban constitutionally can apply only to "hard-core pornography"; and then he added:

I shall not today attempt further to define the kinds of material I understand to be embraced within that short-hand description; and perhaps I could never succeed in intelligibly doing so. But I know it when I see it, and the motion picture involved in this case is not that.

The dissenting opinions argue some issues that are of sufficient importance to warrant more than passing mention.

Chief Justice Warren's opinion, in which Justice Clark joined, accepts the *Roth* test, while admitting that it is by no means altogether satisfactory; but it contends that the "community standards" to which that test refers do not mean a national standard. Communities in the United States "are in fact diverse"; the enforcement of the *Roth* test should be left to the state and federal courts, and the role of the Supreme Court should be limited to a review of the record to see whether there is "sufficient evidence" to sustain the finding of obscenity by the trial court. "This is," said Chief Justice Warren, "the only reasonable way I can see to obviate the necessity of this Court's sitting as the Super Censor of all the obscenity purveyed throughout the Nation." Applying the "sufficient evidence" test to the record in the instant case, he said that he would affirm the state court's judgment.

Justice Harlan's dissenting opinion makes a distinction between censorship by a federal agency, such as the Post Office or the Customs Bureau, and censorship by a state. As to the former, he would have a "tight rein" because of the application of the First Amendment to the federal government; but as to the latter, he would apply a test of "rationality," as required by the Fourteenth Amendment. As to states, he said,

I would not prohibit them from banning any material which, taken as a whole, has been reasonably found in state judicial proceedings to treat with sex in a fundamentally offensive manner, under rationally established criteria for judging such material.

On this basis, having viewed the motion picture in question, I think the State acted within permissible limits in condemning the film. . . .

Justice Harlan asks, then, for (1) the First Amendment requirements as to censorship by the *federal government,* and (2) a test of rationality as to censorship by the *states.* The latter would, he said, allow a "greater latitude" in determining what may be banned "on the score of obscenity. . . ."

Chief Justice Warren and Justice Clark ask for *state or local* community standards in *all* cases adjudicated by *federal or state* courts.

There is considerable popular support for the idea that states and local communities should have the right to decide for themselves what books, magazines, and movies they will or will not tolerate. New York clergymen of the three leading faiths accused the Court of trying to "recast moral law" in overthrowing state and local bans on what the communities themselves consider pornography.[124] Senator Eastland of Mississippi sponsored an amendment to the Constitution that would read as follows:

The right of each State to decide on the basis of its own public policy questions of decency and morality, and to enact legislation with respect thereto, shall not be abridged.[125]

Another proposed constitutional amendment that would allow multiple federal and state standards reads as follows:

Freedom of speech and freedom of press shall not extend to the publication, manufacture, sale, dissemination, or distribution of obscene material, and both the Congress and the States may enact legislation with respect to the prohibition thereof. Material is obscene if, applying contemporary community standards, its dominant theme taken as a whole appeals to the prurient interest of the average person.[126]

This argument for states' rights in the area of censorship is met by Justice Brennan in his opinion in the Jacobellis case. He said that he could not see how any "local" definition of the "community" could "properly be employed in delineating the area of expression that is protected by the Federal Constitution." Apart from other considerations, to sustain the suppression of a book or film in one locality, said Justice Brennan,

> would deter its dissemination in other localities where it might be held not obscene, since sellers and exhibitors would be reluctant to risk criminal conviction in testing the variation between the two places. It would be a hardy person who would sell a book or exhibit a film anywhere in the land after this Court had sustained the judgment of one "community" holding it to be outside the constitutional protection. The result would thus be "to restrict the public's access to forms of the printed word which the State could not constitutionally suppress directly. . . ."

We thus reaffirm the position taken in *Roth* to the effect that the constitutional status of an allegedly obscene work must be determined on the basis of a national standard. It is, after all, a national Constitution we are expounding.

Americans are, of course, a diverse people. But they are a diverse people with a common citizenship, knit together by a common Constitution. We know what havoc is brought about by turning over to local communities the question of race relations—involving the right to receive education, to vote, to enjoy public accommodations, and other rights and liberties. Such aspects of diversity we can do without. Should Mississippi have the last word on what should be the test of "decency" and "morality" in the books and magazines its people may read or the films that they may see? In 1959 the Mississippi State Board of Education banned a film on tolerance, *The High Wall*, prepared by the Anti-Defamation League.[127] Films with Negro actors —such as *Edge of the City*, with Sidney Poitier—could not be shown in the South.[128] In many places films dealing with important social problems, such as race relations, narcotics addiction, homosexuality, or alcoholism, would be considered contrary to "community standards"; and we know that these "community standards" would ban not only Henry Miller's books but also books by Hemingway, Faulkner, O'Hara, Steinbeck, and Edmund Wilson, not to mention Gide, Zola, and scores of others. Some of the cases that we have reviewed make this clear enough. The censor's appetite grows on what he eats. He would not stop with homosexual and nudist magazines or with *Tropic of Cancer*.

It is not true that a citizen of Massachusetts need not care if the citizens of Alabama are barred from reading certain books or seeing certain films; for there is a national—federal—interest in the level of education and culture achieved or possible in any part of the country. We are slowly overcoming the idea that equality should be left to "community standards"; should we now open the door to "community standards" as criteria for the meaning of liberty, on the meaning of freedom of speech and freedom of the press? The idea is a frightening one, and it is very strange indeed that three Justices of the Supreme Court, including the Chief Justice, should propose it seriously. It is a capitulation to the states' rights attack on the Court that is the very opposite of creative statesmanship and concern for the integrity of the Constitution.

Justice Harlan first suggested multiple community standards in his opinion in the Roth case, in which he put the idea in the following words:

Different States will have different attitudes toward the same work of literature. The same book which is freely read in one state might be classed as obscene in another. And it seems to me that no overwhelming danger to our freedom to experiment and to gratify our tastes in literature is likely to result from the suppression of a borderline book in one of the States, so long as there is no uniform nation-wide suppression of the book, and so long as other States are free to experiment with the same or bolder books.

Judge Bok in 1949 anticipated the argument that the states should "experiment" on the basis of their own community standards and he answered it convincingly:

It is no longer possible that free speech [or press] be guaranteed Federally and denied locally; under modern methods of instantaneous communication such a discrepancy makes no sense. If speech is to be free anywhere, it must be free everywhere, and a law that can be used as a spigot that allows speech to flow freely or to be checked altogether is a general threat to free opinion and enlightened solution. What is said in Pennsylvania may clarify an issue in California, and what is suppressed in California may leave us the worse in Pennsylvania. Unless a restriction on free speech be of national validity, it can no longer have any local validity whatever. Some danger to us all must appear before any of us can be muzzled.[129]

As we noted, the Court in deciding the *Tropic of Cancer* case adopted by reference the opinions in the Jacobellis case, but there was one exception: Justice White, without opinion, voted to clear *The Lovers* in the Jacobellis case but to uphold the Florida ban on *Tropic of Cancer*.

At the end of two years *Tropic of Cancer* had sold 100,000 copies in cloth and 2,000,000 copies in paperback editions.

England waited, perhaps to see what the American situation would simmer down to. In April 1963 the British government apparently let it be known that it would not interfere with sale of the book,[130] and John Calder published the novel at 25s. The publisher at once had orders for 100,000 copies. Smiths' and Harrods' would not carry the book, and Hatchard's sold but would not display it;[131] a substantial and serious review of the book appeared in the *Times Literary Supplement*,[132] in which it was compared with Céline's *Journey to the End of Night*. In any case, the book was accepted in England, as it was in many parts of the United States, with a feeling of inevitability and with a shrug of the shoulders, as if to say: "It was bound to be—and I couldn't care less"—or, with *Childe Harold*: "A schoolboy's tale, the wonder of an hour!"

But the importance of the book in the history of censorship and in social history is not to be underestimated. First of all, it has greatly reduced the capacity of four-letter words to shock. *Lady Chatterley's Lover* did not accomplish this, for the words are used by the gamekeeper innocently and tenderly. At the trial about *Lady Chatterley's Lover* in Old Bailey, the prosecutor told the jury[133] that one four-letter word appeared thirty times, another fourteen times, and so on— "I have added them up," he said, not realizing how he was demeaning himself and the law by this admission. Instead of suggesting "dirty words," such incidents suggested "dirty minds." The clearing of *Tropic of Cancer* took the punch out of these words altogether, for in this book they are used without innocence and without tenderness, used roughly, violently, scabrously, as if to commit verbal rape on the reader. The emergence of the words marks a tremendous victory over censorship, and over a verbal fetishism that was a constant invitation to censorship.

I do not mean to belittle the force of words. Anyone who writes for publication and spends much of his time in a search for the right or the better word will not underestimate the importance of words, and I certainly do not mean that the four-letter words ought to be used as if they are totally antiseptic. The point is that for generations their offensiveness—*Schrecklichkeit*—was taken as a justification for censorship. We had to move from acceptance of pictorial nudity to acceptance of verbal nudity and nude words in order to shake the foundations of censorship. It can be said that it is a mark of moral progress for the nation when we recognize that the dirty words that are truly shocking, immoral, and intolerable are words that insult people because of their race, religion, or national origin.[134]

In comparison with such words, those of *Tropic of Cancer* are clean and innocent.

I have read a great deal about this book, and I would say that the following brief statement by John Ciardi reflects the judgment of most critics who have commented on it:

> *Tropic of Cancer* must be defended not as an ultimate peak of greatness, but because, whether it succeeds or fails, it is written with power and compassion, and because it is charged in every passage with the author's aesthetic devotion to his form and with his human devotion to the joy of life. To remove such a book from the experience of mature readers on the ground that the prurient may use it abusively is an assault upon the aesthetic experience. It is a denial of freedom on the queasy ground that men are not fit for freedom. It is to say that the least of men shall dictate the diet of the rest.
>
> To base a defense on the claim of greatness is to abuse [a] good cause. What must be defended is the right of the serious artist not to succeed, but to try.[135]

One cannot help thinking that the law shares responsibility for the psychological and moral harm that was done by the heavy concentration, at least when the *Hicklin* test was adopted and for a century thereafter, on the identification of morality—or rather, immorality and criminality—with certain words. To an extent that one cannot, of course, measure, the obscenity laws were breeders of dirty thoughts and degrading sensibilities. When Florence Nightingale observed the deplorable conditions in the hospitals of her day, she said that the least one could expect was that hospitals should not spread disease. So, too, we might say that it is not asking too much of the law that it should not breed criminality—not in the prisons; and not in laws that make words into criminals, which then break into men's minds and there shout: "We are unclean! We are criminals! You are guilty of harboring criminals!" In 1964 the Supreme Court, by reversing the Florida ban on *Tropic of Cancer,* set our minds free from a psychic and moral contamination.*

The last case that calls for our attention is one that involved a book which was the subject of the first reported prosecution for obscene

---

* I do not mean to approve, by implication, the dirty-word actions on the Berkeley campus of the University of California in 1965. No one needs to read *Tropic of Cancer* if he does not want to; but persons walking on a campus are members of a captive audience when they are forced to hear or read words that unnerve or shock them. We give up much privacy when we leave our homes and offices and go outside, but we do not necessarily give a license to be systematically and willfully assaulted by offensive words.

literature in the United States—a book that contains not a single "dirty" word. John Cleland's *Memoirs of a Woman of Pleasure,* commonly known as *Fanny Hill,* was first published in London in 1748–1749. Cleland is reported to have been summoned before the Privy Council, and not the ordinary criminal courts; and twice, at the instigation of bishops, warrants were issued against him; but there is no record of any punishment, and we know that he was given a pension of £100 a year by Lord Granville. The book went through numerous editions—there is a record of twenty editions up to 1845[136]—but it always moved in the underground of literature. In 1821 two itinerant booksellers were punished by a Massachusetts court for peddling *Fanny Hill* among farmers.[137] The book was banned by the Post Office and customs.[138]

Fanny Hill's "Memoirs" were in a way the forerunner of Molly Bloom's soliloquy;[139] and with our advantage of seeing an event after it has happened, we can say that after Judge Woolsey's decision clearing Molly it was "inevitable" that one day the courts would clear Fanny. In any case, once the Post Office lifted its ban on *Tropic of Cancer,* it was reasonable to expect that a reputable publisher would test the law with *Fanny Hill.*

In 1963 G. P. Putnam's Sons—which had published Vladimir Nabokov's *Lolita* in 1957—issued *Fanny Hill* in a hardback edition at $6.00. The corporation counsel of the City of New York and the district attorneys of the five counties comprising the city sought an injunction against Putnam.[140] In dismissing the complaint, the judge[141] called attention to the fact that there is not one obscene word in the book and that it has "high literary quality"; that he was impressed with the testimony on behalf of the book (by J. Donald Adams, Eric Bentley, Louis Untermeyer, and other witnesses); that Henry Miller's book had been cleared by the courts of California, Massachusetts, and Wisconsin; that Mr. Untermeyer had testified that *Fanny Hill* contained

the three great attributes of a good novel: (1) treatment of the subject matter with grace and beauty; (2) skillful and eloquent charm of writing; and (3) characters coming to life. He characterized the book as a "work of art."

The judge observed that Fanny Hill's experiences contained only little more than what the community encountered on the front pages of newspapers as it read of the Profumo and other sensational cases involving sex, and that while

:he saga of Fanny Hill will undoubtedly never replace "Little Red Riding Hood" as a popular bedtime story, it is quite possible that were Fanny :o be transposed from her mid-eighteenth century Georgian surroundings :o our present day society, she might conceivably encounter many things which would cause her to blush.

This decision was reversed, on February 27, 1964, by the Appellate Division by 3-to-2 vote. The majority said that the book was "hard-core pornography"; the minority said that "without question the republication of this book does not involve the kind of hard-core pornography . . . easily recognized. . . ." An injunction was therefore issued; but since it was directed only against the publisher, bookstores sold copies, and the president of Putnam's told the press that the company "sold ten times as many copies as we would have [up to the time of the injunction] if there hadn't been this censorship proceeding."[142]

On July 10, 1964, the Court of Appeals, by 4-to-3 vote, set aside the injunction.[143] This was about two weeks after the Supreme Court had reversed the Florida ban on *Tropic of Cancer,* and the opinion for the majority referred to this action. It also referred to another *per curiam* decision of the Supreme Court in which a Florida ban on *Pleasure Was My Business* had been reversed on the same day that the *Tropic of Cancer* case[144] was decided, and the majority opinion observed that *Pleasure Was My Business* portrayed what supposedly went on in a Florida brothel and perhaps went further than *Fanny Hill.* The eighteenth-century novel, said the court, "does not warrant suppression." It is unlikely, said the court, that the book "can have any adverse effect on the sophisticated values of our century."

Chief Judge Desmond, dissenting, said that the book had been regarded for centuries as obscene, and that since "pornography is the essential element of obscenity," *Fanny Hill* easily met this test. Another dissenting opinion said that the book was "one of the foulest, sexually immoral, debasing, lewd and obscene books ever published, either in this country or abroad."

In London at the end of 1963 Mayflower Books published *Fanny Hill* as a paperback at 3s.6d., and distributed 82,000 copies. A summons was then issued against a London bookseller, whose 171 copies were seized. The publishers tried to persuade the Director of Public Prosecutions to proceed against them under Section 2 of the Obscene Publications Act, 1959, which would have resulted in a case tried with a jury, but the government preferred to proceed, for the

first time since the new enactment, under Section 3, which provides
for a summary proceeding against a bookseller, before a magistrate
instead of a judge, without a jury. But the publishers had a statutory
right to intervene. The magistrate's ruling, however, would not be
binding in any other part of England, and even in London another
magistrate might take a different view of the book in a case against
another bookseller.

The lawyers for the prosecution and the defense were the same
as in the *Lady Chatterley* case three years before. The trial lasted four
days. The prosecution called no expert witnesses, but the defense had
seven witnesses testify on the merits of the book. Peter Quennell, who
wrote the Preface for the American edition; H. Montgomery Hyde,
Member of Parliament for nine years; the literary editor of the *New
Statesman*; Marghanita Laski, the novelist; and the literary critic of
the *Sunday Express,* were among the witnesses.

As in the *Lady Chatterley* case the prosecution made a point of the
fact that the book was being sold at 3s.6d. To this the defense
attorney replied:

If the book is . . . not pornographic, who is to say in the name of the
law that the book should be rationed by price? To say that the price of
a novel was relevant to its obscenity was the voice of the censor and not
of the judge. There had been a complete revolution in the publishing world
and it was absolutely normal to publish a book in paperback form.[145]

At the conclusion of the case the magistrate at once delivered his
verdict that the copies seized by the police should be forfeited. It took
him just one minute to state his verdict, since he gave no reasons.

Since booksellers have returned only 250 of the 82,000 copies
distributed, it is apparent that bookdealers on Charing Cross Road
sell and that Englishmen buy the book. Public reaction to the magistrate's verdict was in part shown by the motion of twenty Members of
Parliament, of all parties, that the Director of Public Prosecutions take
no further action against *Fanny Hill.*[146] In any case, under the 1959
statute, actions before a magistrate must be brought within one year
and by indictment within two years, and so by 1966 *Fanny Hill* will
have won full security against legal molestation.

Following the initiation of the proceedings against the 171 copies,
the *Times Literary Supplement*[147] rebuked the government, saying:

There has . . . been no satisfactory evidence of the corrupting effects of
obscenity, and certainly it is difficult to feel that *Fanny Hill* . . . forms

a worse introduction than the usual alternatives (family doctor, fellow-pupil, headmaster's lecture, and the rest).

Addressing itself to the low price of the paperback edition, the editorial said:

The class barriers—between obscenity for the mass market and obscenity for the gentleman of taste, or between the same work in a well-frequented bookshop and in some hole-and-corner place specializing in already depraved customers—are not only snobbish but unrealistic; if books do corrupt they corrupt anyone irrespective of income.

In the *Fanny Hill* case in the New York Court of Appeals, Chief Judge Desmond concluded his dissenting opinion with a prophecy. "I refuse to believe," he wrote, "that all this can continue to be the law. I predict that the wheel will turn and the pendulum [will] swing back." But this is very doubtful. In the winter of 1960 it was estimated that the total sale of *Lady Chatterley's Lover* was probably over five million copies.[148] In addition, millions of copies of *Tropic of Cancer* and of *Fanny Hill* have been sold. What has been done is irreversible. Going back to the *Hicklin* rule will not restore the *Hicklin* days. The emperor has been seen naked. From now on he can be clad only in "native honour." Unless the Constitution is destroyed, there can be no searching of homes and libraries for books to be burned under supervision of storm troopers. Molly Bloom, Lolita, Lady Chatterley, and Fanny Hill are now citizens of Britain and of the United States, and there is nothing we can do about it. The clock cannot be turned back.[149]

Moreover, the "slippery slope" type of reasoning is hard to control where thinking cannot be rigidly logical and where metaphor, suggestion, and subjectivity have an acknowledged role; and so it is not surprising that Lady Chatterley's granddaughters, who never heard of forget-me-nots, should find themselves altogether legitimate and almost respectable. Thus the story of Candy Christian,[150] which Lawrence would surely have condemned as pornographic—and which was banned by the French government when it was published in Paris —was a best-seller in the United States in 1964. Candy's story at least has the merit of being a spoof on pornography and can be read as good satire.

But what is one to say of the books involved in *People* v. *Birch*,[151] which was before the Supreme Court of New York in 1963? Several booksellers were indicted for selling eight books in violation of the obscenity statute. These books included cheap paperbacks with such titles as *Sex Kitten,* and *The Hottest Party in Town,* and all were written by authors unknown in the literary world. The books contained no four-letter words, but fully 90 per cent of each book was devoted to lurid descriptions of heterosexual and homosexual (male and lesbian) activities. The judge before whom the case came said that "these books are plain unvarnished trash. . . ." . . Then he went on to say: "But novels and stories of no literary merit have a place in our society. There are those who, because of lack of education, the meanness of their social existence, or mental insufficiency, cannot cope with anything better." He said "that free societies are dynamic and that literature and art, *and badly written books too,* are merely the minor reflections of some phase of existing life. . . ." Of the eight books, he said: "Coarse they are, but so is much in our civilization." It may be, he said, that such "vulgar trash" may hurt teen-agers, "but the effect upon and the reactions of children are not legally valid tests to determine what constitutes illegal pornography (*Roth* v. *United States*)." (Italics in original.)

The indictments in this case grew out of raids in April 1963 in which the District Attorney of Queens County had personally led a hundred detectives and investigators who seized thousands of copies.[152] In dismissing the indictments, the court made it clear that the average person would judge such books to be "poor writings, bad in taste, offensive and disgusting," but not "obscene" in the *Roth* sense of the term. If the average reasonable, normal person is the standard, then a publication's special appeal to those who are on a lower level of living and thinking cannot be dispositive.

It is certainly not unreasonable to argue that if freedom of the press protects tabloid newspapers that thrive on lurid sensationalism, no less than responsible and respectable ones, the same freedom protects "badly written books"—"novels and stories of no literary merit"—as well as those praised by literary critics. Who is to say that *Fanny Hill* or a book dealing with the exploits in a Florida brothel have "redeeming social importance," while *Sex Kitten* is "utterly without" such promise of redemption?

It is the same with literature under the free-press guarantee as with religion under the freedom-of-religion provision—the state at one time protected the "true" religion and persecuted or tolerated other religions; but now we know that true religions have no protection if the false ones are not equally protected; and so we have religions which, to the nonbelievers, are not only false but are also socially evil or indoctrinating superstitions and hurtful beliefs about men, society, morality, and politics. Thus the invaluable and the valueless, the noble and the tawdry, the beautiful and the ugly, the true and the false, the good and the evil, are equally protected by the First and the Fourteenth Amendments' guarantees of a free press and religious liberty.

5. Conclusions

We have dealt with the problem of obscenity at length because no one is equipped to pass judgment on it if he has spared himself the hard task of looking at the factual and moral complexity that is inherent in it. Whether one likes to do so or not, one must look at the trees before he can speak responsibly of the forest—and this forest, unfortunately, has in it all sorts of trees, and underbrush, and wild flowers, and rank weeds. The line of obscenity that runs from, say, *Tristram Shandy* to *Tropic of Cancer* is by no means one that can easily be drawn. The problem calls not for pontification but for hard thinking, for lots of light and little heat.

One of our greatest and most serious difficulties, however, is that we are still largely ignorant of the effects of obscene publications on those who read them. This is not to suggest that, if we actually knew that obscenity produces certain evil effects, we would then find easy solutions. We at one time prohibited the manufacture and sale of alcoholic beverages and learned that the cure was in some important ways worse than the disease. There is a respectable body of facts that seems to show a causal relation between cigarette smoking and cancer of the lungs, but we are still far from knowing what society, through governmental action, can do about the sale of cigarettes.

Still, it should be urged that we make the effort to get at the facts concerning the effects of obscenity. The *Times Literary Supplement*[153] has suggested that the Home Secretary

institute a thorough study of the effects which different types of supposedly pernicious literature . . . can have on more or less susceptible readers. For the first essential is that we should all . . . stop simply speculating one way or another on this head. At present the whole discussion is based on guesswork.

We have had hearings before subcommittees of the House of Representatives and of the Senate concerned with juvenile delinquency and with the postal operations, which have produced reports on obscenity, and investigations of comics by state legislative committees, and private studies, but the conclusions that one may draw from them are hardly sufficient to satisfy objective standards of proof. We are still very much in the dark.

Since the obscenity law is an area where American and English courts seem uniquely to interact, perhaps the governments of both nations should join financial, legal, and other resources for a common study of this problem. No one should underestimate the difficulties such a study would involve, or the length of time it would require, but nations that try to send men to the moon ought not to neglect a problem that touches, at some point or other, almost every man, woman, and child in this age of the cheap paperback, the motion picture, television, and other means of mass communication that are alleged to be also means of mass contamination. The point is that we do not know and should try to find out.

But there should be no illusion that, if such a study was accomplished, it could lead to an undoing of what has already happened. The books that have been cleared by the courts are available in millions of copies, and our future concern with community standards will be compelled to take this fact into account. Our children will live in a world which includes Fanny Hill, Candy, Lolita, Constance Chatterley; a world in which four-letter words in books produce no or little shock; a world in which *Playboy* nudes are seen at drugstores and supermarkets. No research and no laws can restore the old order; and it is the part of intelligence to look to the future hopefully rather than to the past nostalgically. Perhaps our children will be better "conditioned" against the effects of obscenity, whatever they may be, than were their fathers and mothers when they were young, curious, and ignorant.

Nor need we believe that, if research does one day establish indubitably a causal relation between obscene publications and social evils, the Court will be bound to apply to obscenity the clear-and-present-danger test. In *Cox* v. *Louisiana* (1965),[154] the Supreme Court unanimously held that the clear-and-present-danger test has no application to a statute that *absolutely bans* picketing and parading in or near courthouses with the intent of influencing the administration of justice. Whether or not the test has rational application to a certain type of expression is a difficult policy question, one that should be answered only after thorough exploration of the arguments and reasons, and such exploration is possible only when ignorance is replaced with knowledge. This does not mean that, as Justice Frankfurter said, "clear

d present danger" is only "a literary phrase."[155] It is a great deal
ore than that; but, as with any other legal doctrine or rule, its rele-
nce, application, and use must be determined not dogmatically but
the intelligence acting with a full awareness of its responsibility in
e light of explored facts, issues, and values.

There are critics of the Supreme Court who make the charge that
e Court's decisions went beyond prevailing community standards,
ough the Court professed to base its decisions on its "finding" of
hat those standards are. This is an argument used in support of the
rious constitutional amendments that have been proposed to give
nal authority to the states and local communities to determine for
emselves what is and what is not morally tolerable.

In the absence of reliable factual studies, there is no way to arbitrate
is dispute on objective grounds; whether the Court "found," or
nade," or partly "found" and partly "made" the community stand-
rds will continue to be the subject of fruitless debate. It is clear, how-
ver, that the decisions have had the effect of *validating* what the Court
as said *are* the contemporary community standards; and thus the
ecisions not only have been the effects of community forces, but have
so had a creative, causal role to play. The community standards are
ow what they are at least partly because the Court has said that these
re in fact the community standards.

The Court is not to be blamed for playing an active role. This role
inescapable from its judicial function. The controversy over this role
part of a wider debate over the nature of law. The Court's references
a contemporary community standard have echoes of the historical
chool of jurisprudence and Savigny's notion that law is the expression
f a particular people's *Volkgeist* and is rooted in the spirit of the
eople. I do not mean to suggest that the Justices of the Supreme
ourt are followers of Savigny—nothing could be further from the
uth—but in their professed search for the contemporary community
tandard, in the obscenity cases, they invite trouble for themselves. For
ey will be charged with usurping the role of the legislature as the
rgan of social consciousness in a democratic society; with imposing
nonexistent national community consciousness on the American
eople and displacing real and multiple popular moral standards.

The Court would have a hard time identifying the "community" that
talks about, which is a mental—or mythical—construct, like Rous-
eau's "general will," or President Johnson's "consensus." It would be
nore honest not to pretend to "find" a mysterious community standard

of the morally tolerable and intolerable—an action that suggests He. mann Broch's dilemma of "no longer and not yet": no longer Anthon Comstock and not yet Henry Miller. We would all be better off know that the Supreme Court has a creative role in lawmaking, an that the Court proposes to achieve social reforms by responding to fe social needs and by projecting social ideals against which existing inst tutions may be tested and found wanting. If it performed this constit tional function in the open and not under cover of fictions, myths, an evasions, responsibility could be properly focused and assessed.

It should be noted, however, that a considerable part of the Court creativity is in the reformation of legal principles and doctrines fo *which the Court was itself responsible*. Social reform is thus ofte achieved as a by-product of legal and judicial *self-reform*. Thus th Court in the school-segregation cases of 1954 abolished the "separat but equal" principle, which the Court itself had introduced into th Constitution in 1896. So, too, the *Hicklin* test, which dominated ob scenity cases after its formulation by Chief Justice Cockburn in 1868 was a judge-made doctrine, though it pretended to be an interpretatio of Lord Campbell's act of 1857. This self-reforming operation by th Court cannot be abrogated without stultifying the judicial proces Whether the Court follows the *Hicklin* test or replaces it with anothe in either case it is performing its judicial function on the basis of policy which the Court chooses for itself.

The Court has no way of discovering what are the prevailing com munity standards, for it cannot conduct opinion polls or engage in th Kinsey type of research. It really decides what the standards *should b* in the light of constitutional requirements, and trusts that the commu nity will, eagerly or reluctantly, agree to embody the constitutiona ideal, as formulated by the Court, in its institutions and value systems When the Court says that it "finds" the community standard, it mean thereby to express its sense of trust that society will not say that th burden of the law is too great to bear; to express the idea—as in th desegregation or reapportionment cases—that it speaks *for* the peopl as well as *to* them. Understood in these senses, the Court's "report" o contemporary community standards is philosophically and constitu tionally justified, and reasonable, provided we bear in mind that th Court's decisions themselves need to be taken into account as w discuss community standards, attitudes, and ideals.

In deciding what are the "contemporary community standards," Justice Frankfurter said, it is necessary for the Court to admit evidenc on this question. "Can it be doubted," he asked, at there is a great difference in what is to be deemed obscene in 1959 mpared with what was deemed obscene in 1859? The difference derives om a shift in community feeling regarding what is to be deemed prurient not prurient by reason of the effects attributable to this or that par- ular writing.

nd he added "that the literary, psychological or moral standards of community can be made fruitful or illuminating subjects of inquiry those who give their life to such inquiries," and it was for this ason, he said, that Parliament in 1959 provided for the admissibility expert testimony in obscenity trials.[156]

But the trouble is that we have no reliable evidence, but only preju- ces, guesses, and hunches, when it is a question of the "effects at- ibutable" to obscene writings in general, let alone "to this or that rticular writing"; and while community standards "can be made [a] uitful or illuminating" subject of inquiry "by those who give their fe to such inquiries," this work, on the whole, yet remains undone.

But the Court cannot refuse to decide an obscenity case because all e evidence on causation and on community standards is not before ; nor can it decide the case in 1959 as if it were sitting in 1859. It oes what it can; somehow it decides what "are" the "contemporary mmunity standards," but a large component of its "finding" is the ourt's view, in 1959, of what a free, pluralistic society, living under Constitution that includes the First Amendment, which enjoys a referential position among competing freedoms, must perforce freely llow or grudgingly tolerate. There is no escape from the compulsion make this value judgment; and it is very important, I believe, that e American people know and accept this fact of constitutional life.

Critics of the Court's decisions in the obscenity cases have com- lained that the Court has failed to define "obscenity" simply and learly. As we learned in the 1964 presidential election, many Ameri- ans believe that there are simple solutions for the most complex uestions. They in fact ask for doctrinaire answers, though the heavens all.

But Justice Frankfurter was right when he observed that "there is o external measuring rod for obscenity,"[157] and so, too, was Justice 3rennan when he said that what separates obscenity from constitution- lly protected expression is often only "a dim and uncertain line."[158] A long time ago Aristotle cautioned against looking for more precision a a discussion than the subject-matter will allow. The term "obscenity" cannot be defined in such a way that its application would ▮ mechanical. The term has a reach that goes far beyond its grasp; it h᷄ more nuances than denotative substance; it evokes feelings and imag which resist precise formulation. It is not a term that can please t᷄ tough-minded, who will be satisfied only with impersonal, cold, aᵣ rigorous argument, and who will scornfully rule out whatever does n᷄ meekly submit to rigid conceptualization.

"Obscenity" is a term of legal art, like "negligence," and what t᷄ Supreme Court has recently said about the latter applies to the form᷄ as well:

Surveyors can measure an acre. But measuring negligence is different. T᷄ definitions of negligence are not definitions at all, strictly speaking. . . Issues of negligence, therefore, call for the exercise of common sense aᵣ sound judgment under the circumstances of particular cases.[159]

The issue of negligence is decided by a jury; the issue of obscenity m᷄ ultimately be decided by the Supreme Court, after the book is read ᷄ the movie viewed by the Justices (except Justice Black, who, holdir that any exercise of censorship is unconstitutional, spares himself t᷄ trouble—or pleasure—of reading the books or seeing the motion pi᷄ tures).[160] Essentially the process is the same in both kinds of case᷄ The jury writes no opinion, gives no reason for its verdict; and in majority of the decisions since the Roth case the Supreme Court dec᷄ sions in obscenity cases have been without opinions.[161]

The process in the obscenity cases can be best understood if it subsumed under the constitutional process that was described by Ju᷄ tice Brandeis when he said that there are strong reasons for not relyin on *stare decisis* in cases that involve *applying*—as distinguished froᵣ *interpreting*—a provision of the Constitution to a set of facts. Thi᷄ he said,

is strikingly true of cases under the due process clause when the questi᷄ is whether a statute is unreasonable, arbitrary or capricious; of cases und᷄ the equal protection clause when the question is whether there is aᵣ reasonable basis for the classification made by a statute; and of cases und᷄ the commerce clause when the question is whether an admitted burde laid by a state upon interstate commerce is so substantial as to be deeme᷄ direct. These issues resemble, fundamentally, that of reasonable care i᷄ negligence cases, the determination of which is ordinarily left to t᷄ verdict of the jury. In every such case the decision, in the first instanc᷄ is dependent upon the determination of what in legal parlance is calle᷄ a fact, as distinguished from the declaration of a rule of law. When t᷄

iderlying fact has been found, the legal result follows inevitably. The
rcumstance that the decision of that fact is made by a court, instead of
a jury, should not be allowed to obscure its real character.[162]

As the decisions handed down on June 22, 1964, show, the Court
in split 6 to 3, as in the case involving *The Lovers,* or 5 to 4, as in
ιe case involving *Tropic of Cancer,* and cannot even agree on a ma-
·rity opinion in some obscenity cases. This may mean that there is
ιuch less agreement on the fundamentals involved in such contro-
ɛrsies than there is on the fundamentals involved in negligence suits;
t that, though there is substantial agreement on principles, such
greement is no guarantee that judges will reach the same conclusions
hen they try to apply the principles to a set of facts. Any volume of
·cent Supreme Court cases will show that the divisions in the Court
re by no means limited to obscenity cases, or to civil liberties cases.
he divisions in the Court do not alter, however, the nature of the
rocess applicable in the types of cases described by Justice Brandeis
ι the passage quoted above.

But since, as we have seen, the entire problem of obscenity is rela-
vely new in our legal system, and since the problem is one that more
asily generates heat than light, we can expect more Supreme Court
pinions in which the Justices try to express the principles and con-
iderations that push their thoughts one way or another. Many deci-
ions will be reached without opinions, yet also many opinions will be
·ritten; and the public should, I submit, have a basic sympathy for the
lourt as it faces difficulties that have no regard for the fact that they
re faced by men who wear judicial robes.

The process we have described has led to charges that the Court is
ow a "super censor." Justices Black and Douglas can easily make this
harge, for they are against censorship in any degree or form.[163] Chief
ustice Warren and Justice Clark have made the charge because they
re opposed to the Court's making its own independent, *de novo* judg-
ıent, based on its own reading or viewing of "the accused mate-
ial."[164] But there is a fatal defect in this approach. To obviate the
ιecessity of the Court's "sitting as the Super Censor of all the obscen-
ty purveyed throughout the Nation," says Chief Justice Warren,

nce a finding of obscenity has been made [in the trial court] below under
proper application of the *Roth* test, I would apply a "sufficient evidence"
tandard of review—requiring something more than merely any evidence
ut something less than "substantial evidence on the record [including the
llegedly obscene material] as a whole."[165]

The trouble with this approach is that, if the Court will not review the allegedly obscene book or movie, it will scrap the rule that a book or movie must be read or seen and judged *as a whole*. If the test of obscenity were still the language of selected passages or isolated scenes, then the Court could review the record, which would contain the allegedly obscene materials, and pay no attention to the rest of the book or the movie; but this would mean reversion to the *Hicklin* test. The Court cannot have it both ways: the rule that a book or movie must be judged as a whole and the rule that the Court should be satisfied with less than the whole book or movie. To see if the "sufficient evidence" standard of review has been met, the reviewing court is compelled to read the whole book or see the whole movie.

The Court is called enough bad names by outsiders without needing help from its own members in this respect. Nothing by way of clarification is gained by using such a pejorative term as "super censor." For, except from the point of view of an "absolutist," some censorship there must be; and it is far better, I think, that this function be ultimately performed by the Supreme Court than by the states or municipalities, where pressure groups will have their way. It was in the light of such considerations that the Supreme Court acted in *West Virginia State Board of Education* v. *Barnette*,[166] the second flag-salute case, in face of the charge that to do so would in effect make the Court "the school board for the country."[167] The answer to all such charges and epithets has been given by Justice Brennan:

Use of an opprobrious label can neither obscure nor impugn the Court's performance of its obligation to test challenged judgments against the guarantees of the First and Fourteenth Amendments and, in doing so, to delineate the scope of constitutionally protected speech. Hence . . . in "obscenity" cases as in all others involving rights derived from the First Amendment guarantees of free expression, this Court cannot avoid making an independent constitutional judgment on the facts of the case as to whether the material involved is constitutionally protected.[168]

In reaching a conclusion on the facts—on the publication alleged to be obscene—the Court does not try to subsume the facts under a definition of "obscenity." Obscene material, said the Court in the *Roth* decision, is "material which deals with sex in a manner appealing to prurient interest." This is not, of course, a definition, for, as Justice Harlan pointed out in the Manual Enterprises case, there are acknowledged masterpieces in literature and art whose "dominant theme" appeals to the "prurient interest" of the reader or observer. The refer-

ce to "prurient interest" in the Roth decision is only a sign that
ints in the direction in which the mind is to move when it seeks to
entify the obscene—as distinguished from the seditious, the libelous,
r any other kind of offensive material. In obscenity cases, then, we
ork not from but *toward* a definition; and the definition is found not
a verbal formula abstract from the obscene material, but in the
aterial itself: the configuration, the *Gestalt,* that is "obscene" "de-
nes" the "obscene," just as the facts of an automobile collision
define" "negligence," and just as the facts of a fair trial "define" "due
rocess of law."

But Justice Harlan's point is well taken that the term "obscene" con-
otes something "patently offensive"—so offensive as to be unaccept-
ble under the contemporary community standard. The term may not
ld anything that is not meant by reference to the contemporary com-
unity standard, but the term underscores that fact that obscenity
volves more than something unpleasant, unsuitable, indecorous, or
delicate. But of course the term "patently offensive" does not
define" "obscenity."

Nor does Justice Stewart's term "hard-core pornography," which
an only mean that the term obscenity should be reserved for *extreme*
ases. The phrase provides no easy, mechanical solution; four judges
f the New York Court of Appeals found *Tropic of Cancer* to be
hard-core pornography," while three judges said it was "a serious ex-
ression of views and reactions toward life. . ."; and when it came to
'anny Hill, four judges held that it was not obscene, while three judges
ondemned it as "hard-core pornography."

Other judicial efforts at definition have not proved more successful.
he majority of the New York Court of Appeals condemned *Tropic
f Cancer* as "dirt for dirt's sake" and "dirt for money's sake." But
vhether or not an author writes for money has nothing to do with the
uality of his books. Many of Sir Walter Scott's novels were written to
eep his creditors satisfied; and John Cleland, who was imprisoned for
lebt, wrote *Fanny Hill* to keep his creditors at a comfortable distance,
nd he probably wrote it to allure readers with a taste for erotica. But
notives and purposes of the *author,* while relevant for biography, do
ot play a dispositive role in our judgment of his *work.*

Nor is it helpful to think of obscenity as material that is—in
he language of Justice Harlan in the Roth case—"utterly without
edeeming social importance"; for the Constitution protects, he said,
'all ideas having even the slightest redeeming social importance. . . ."
The majority of the New York Court of Appeals found *Tropic of*

Cancer to be "devoid of theme or ideas"; and Chief Judge Desmor concurring, found in the book "no discernible artistic purpose, development of any theme or idea. . . ." One judge will find an "ide where another will find only "old-fashioned filth."

It would be better, I think, not to be concerned with "ideas" a their "social importance," for the publications that come before t courts are works of the imagination that do not address themselves the part of the mind that lives on logical argument. It would be silly judge *Tropic of Cancer* in the way one would judge *Marius the Epic rean*. As a matter of fact, much contemporary fiction deals with t realm of man's irrational experience, in which sex is encompassed. there are "ideas" in the novels, they are, like the acts, conditioned the character of the speaker and are not significant when abstract from his character. Thinker and thought are fused into an indissolub complexity.

Indeed, one of the most significant and enduring of the Supren Court's achievements in the censorship field is the secure place giv to works of the imagination; for the Court has treated them with t same care and respect that it has shown for works that appeal to t political or social intelligence or to the religious concern.

The Court in the Roth and later cases has said that obscene public tions are excluded from constitutional protection. It has taken this po tion not for the historical reasons it has given—there were strong historical reasons for excluding libelous publications from the constit tional guarantee of free press, but the Court overrode the historic considerations in the *New York Times* case[169] and in *Garrison Louisiana.*[170] The law reports are a repository of living law, but al a graveyard of discarded and deceased precedents. The Court's pos tion may be explained by two considerations: (1) an understandab reluctance to open the door to the use of the clear-and-present-dang test for allegedly obscene publications, in light of the fact that we kno so little about the effects of such publications on normal adults or c special audiences; and (2) an equally understandable reluctance say, bluntly, that obscene publications are constitutionally protecte

As to the latter, it may be that the Court would have overcome i hesitation had the Roth case followed rather than preceded the enac ment by Parliament of the Obscene Publications Act, 1959; for this a protects a publication *found to be obscene* if the court finds that it h literary or other merits. But I think that the Court was justified i seeking a way out of saying that the Constitution protects obscenit for that could easily have been twisted into the charge that the Court "approves" immorality and sin!

While the Constitution was kept out from the front door, it was let in through the back door—by providing "obscenity" ample "breathing space." The Court nowhere has said that it was giving obscenity "breathing space," but a careful review of the cases can leave no doubt that this, in effect, is what has happened. Obscenity is *in fact* protected constitutionally, for it is guarded by the following principles and rules:

(1) The Supreme Court itself reads or views "the accused material," just as it does when the publication is alleged to be seditious.

(2) The contemporary community standard is national rather than sectional or local, as in the case of any freedom guaranteed by the Constitution.

(3) The Court reads and judges the book as a whole and not by selected passages.

(4) The use of four-letter words does not make a book obscene.

(5) Nudity by itself is not obscene.

(6) Literary critics and other qualified witnesses may testify as experts as to the qualities of the publication.

(7) The test of obscenity is not what may be fit to be read by the young, but by the average, normal adult.

(8) Sex (or any aspect of sex, including homosexuality) and obscenity are not synonymous.

(9) The bookseller charged with criminal obscenity must be shown to have had knowledge of the contents of the offending book.

Important as these principles are, even more important is the fact that they culminated in the decision reversing the ban on *Tropic of Cancer*.

In the light of these principles or rules and in the light of what the Court has actually decided in the recent cases, as a practical matter it makes no difference whether the Court *says* that obscenity is or is not constitutionally protected; the Court *acts* as if it were thus protected. The dialectical process has been summarized by Justice Harlan:

Since it is only "obscenity" that is excluded from the constitutional protection, the question whether a particular work is obscene necessarily implicates an issue of constitutional law.[171]

What the Court takes away with one hand, it restores, with ample generosity, with the other.

It would be wrong to close this chapter leaving the impression that under the recent Court decisions every form of obscene publication has been protected. In this connection it is important to note that in the Roth case the Supreme Court *upheld a conviction* for mailing obscene literature, and in the Alberts case *upheld a conviction* for keeping for sale obscene books and publishing an obscene advertisement of them. States and local communities, and postal and customs authorities, are left with considerable power to deal with the commercial market in obscenity that transgresses the judicial standards.

The Post Office has been said to be the biggest distributor of smut; but the Post Office Department has not remained indifferent in the face of this claim. For many years it exercised administrative censorship of allegedly obscene mailings; but we have seen that its zeal was often misdirected to books by established and respected authors.

It was not until 1957 that the Post Office prescribed formal regulations.[172] After losing important cases in the Supreme Court for administrative usurpation or misuse of standards fixed by the Supreme Court, the Post Office concentrated on commercialized obscenity. In 1959 it went after the three largest mail-obscenity peddlers; in raids in New York City it picked up fifteen tons of materials; it took away a mailing list with a hundred thousand names;[173] but it also, at the same time, tried unsuccessfully to ban *Lady Chatterley's Lover*—its last assault on an important book.

In 1960 the Post Office received over seventy thousand complaints from parents and others who demanded action. One raid in New York City netted seized items valued at $800,000.[174] In 1961 there were 457 arrests for mailing obscene matter;[175] and in that year the Supreme Court denied certiorari in a case,[176] the effect of which action was to bring within the Roth decision advertising and photographs of a so-called "art" or borderline category. In 1962 there were 503 convictions for using the mails to send obscene materials.[177] In 1963 there were over 52,000 complaints, 761 arrests, and 637 convictions for violation of mail-obscenity laws; and in 1964 there were 805 arrests and 627 convictions.[178]

These statistics show that the Supreme Court decisions have by no means legalized all obscene publications; but critics of the Court, professing to be the watchdogs of the Constitution and morality, do not usually bother to find the facts.

Early in 1961, when the Kennedy administration took office, the Post Office Department instituted a radical change in procedure that is worthy of note. Postmaster General Day ordered that all cases brought to enforce the obscenity laws must thereafter be prosecuted through normal criminal procedures, and all administrative and civil procedures were to be abandoned.[179] A new spirit was clearly manifest. For the first time in history, the Post Office Department itself attacked administrative censorship and subjected itself to judicial guidelines and process. The statement of the Postmaster General describing the new attitude is important enough for us to quote from it as follows:[180]

The danger of censorship arises when the administrator takes the law into his own hands.

It has been the policy of this Department under this Administration [since February 1961] to leave judging to the judges. It is the function of the administrator to direct to the attention of the criminal authorities those cases where the law may have been violated. When an administrator attempts to determine what constitutes obscenity, too often justice is entangled in a maze of administrative procedures, stopgap remedies, appeals, and delays. . . .

The record of arrests and convictions scored in recent years [1961–1963], and the marked decline in unwarranted censorship charges against the Department, reinforce our conviction that the obscenity statutes are adequate and that the procedure we now follow in enforcing them is proper.

Previously it was standard procedure for the Postmaster General to ask Congress and its committees for new legislation, with additional powers. But now, for the first time, he asked Congress *not* to enact new laws:

Despite the well-intended concern of many persons who seek changes which, in their opinions, would strengthen the laws, we feel that no revision is necessary, and that any attempt at revision might, conversely, weaken the statutes.

And for the first time the Postmaster General openly rebuked the panic-mongers and those who would translate into enforceable law their own narrow and conventional moral attitude:

Our policy is to concentrate only on those cases that appear clearly within the scope of the test as laid down by the Supreme Court. We are not interested in "borderline cases" whose contents, though offensive to some, do not violate the law.

We will not dilute statutory enforcement with press-agentry. We will not jeopardize successful prosecution in pending cases by seeking headlines. We will not stimulate the previously disinterested to look for pornography by continually talking about it.

The Postmaster General stated that the Department knew that there existed, "in considerable quantity," "pornography—of the hard core prurient kind," but that the Department already possessed adequate and satisfactory power to deal with the problem—"without censorship."

The new procedure can be described briefly:

. . . when a possible violation of the mail obscenity laws comes to the attention of the Post Office Department, a postal inspector is assigned to thoroughly investigate the case. The inspector secures all available evidence concerning the circumstances of the mailing and the pertinent activities of the mailer. If it is determined that a probable violation has occurred, this evidence is then turned over to the appropriate U. S. Attorney for consideration of prosecution.

Should the U. S. Attorney determine that court action is warranted, a grand jury proceeding is undertaken, and if an indictment is returned the defendant has a right to trial by jury and appeal if convicted.

The record makes clear that despite the charges that recent Supreme Court decisions have benefited criminals by hampering law enforcement, under the new policy in 1963 and 1964 arrests and convictions for violation of the mail-obscenity laws were up 100 per cent over 1960,[181] the last year under the procedures of previous administrations.

Censorship has undergone radical changes when we see the Postmaster General publicly take a stand and say things which but a few years ago could have been expected only in statements critical of the attitudes and procedures of the Post Office Department. It is hard to believe that it was only as recently as 1959 that a Postmaster General made it his personal responsibility to ban from the mails *Lady Chatterley's Lover,* and to support his action by an opinion in which, borrowing a judge's words, he wrote of "the mystery of sex and procreation" as "sweet and sublime" and that "there is an underlying, perhaps universal, accord that there is a phase of respectable delicacy related to sex."[182] Now it is beyond any doubt that while a person has a constitutional right to believe and to say that sex and procreation are sweet and sublime mysteries, another person has an equal right to believe that it was the "mortal taste" of sex that

> Brought death into the world, and all our woe,
> With loss of Eden.

The Constitution leaves this and all other high and majestical questions to each man's mind, which "Can make a Heav'n of Hell, a Hell of Heav'n."

Two
Civil Rights

VI

Racial Equality and Democratic Government

1. The Vinson Court Prepares for the Warren Court

It is generally thought that the Supreme Court's unanimous decision in the main school-segregation case of 1954, *Brown* v. *Board of Education*,[1] was revolutionary in the sense that it was a sudden, complete change in the course of constitutional development, for which there were no warnings in the Court's previous decisions. The fact is, however, that in a series of cases preceding the Brown case the Court showed that it had no intention of lending its great prestige and power to a validation of racial segregation as it continued to accept unquestioningly and dogmatically the doctrine of "separate but equal." The N.A.A.C.P. attacked directly the doctrine of separate but equal in the Brown case because its attorneys had concluded, on the basis of the Court's precedents, that the Court in 1954 was ready to declare racial segregation in all schools unconstitutional. The Association had, needless to say, been ready for years to denounce racial segregation, equal or unequal, root and branch; but the constitutional attack had to be built up, step by step. The Brown case undeniably represents a great constitutional leap; but it was a leap for which the Justices, like athletes in a sports competition, had prepared themselves by running forward before bounding over the obstacle.

Before 1954 the Court, in case after case, showed displeasure and impatience with racial discrimination in education and interstate passenger transportation, with covenants limiting ownership or occupancy of real estate, with discriminatory practices in employment opportunity, with discrimination in the administration of justice, with denial of the rights of suffrage in general elections and in party primaries; and in the few years immediately preceding 1954 it became clear that the

Court was approaching the point where it would put an end to the grotesque constitutional doctrine of separate but equal facilities—a doctrine for which the Court itself was responsible by its decision in *Plessy* v. *Ferguson*[2] in 1896.[3]

We shall take as our point of departure the Sipuel case of 1948.[4] A Negro, concededly qualified to be admitted to the School of Law of the University of Oklahoma, was denied admission in 1946 solely because of her color. The state provided no law school for Negroes. The Supreme Court, in a brief *per curiam,* held that she was

entitled to secure legal education afforded by a state institution [in Oklahoma]. To this time [1946–1948], it has been denied her although during the same period many white applicants have been afforded legal education by the State. The State must provide it for her . . . *and provide it as soon as it does for applicants of any other group. . . .*

The italicized clause was crucial. The Oklahoma courts interpreted it as meaning, *inter alia,* that the state must proceed to establish a law school for Negroes. The N.A.A.C.P. again went to the Supreme Court and contended that the state courts' interpretation of the *per curiam* opinion and order was a subtle dodge or evasion, and that for the Negro petitioner time was of the essence—she had already lost two years waiting to start her legal education.

The Supreme Court held that the Oklahoma courts had not departed from the Court's mandate. But then, significantly, the Court's second *per curiam* opinion stated: "The petition for certiorari . . . did not present the issue whether a state might not satisfy the equal protection clause of the Fourteenth Amendment by establishing a separate law school for Negroes. On submission, we were clear it was not an issue here."

Justice Frank Murphy stated that he was not satisfied that the action of the state was not an evasion of the Supreme Court's mandate. But more important, as foreshadowing future developments, was Justice Rutledge's dissenting opinion. He said that the state obviously could not "over-night" establish a separate law school "capable of giving petitioners a legal education equal to that afforded by the state's long-established and well-known state university law school." Nor could the state take the "necessary time" to create a separate law school while continuing to delay the Negro petitioner's legal education in the meantime. It was obvious that to Justice Rutledge the state's constitutional duty to the Negro petitioner could be met in only one way: *by admitting her to the School of Law without regard to her race.*

The attorneys for the N.A.A.C.P. took the hints of both the *per curiam* and Justice Rutledge, and two years later challenged in the Supreme Court the idea that a segregated law school education ever could be "equal." This was not an attack on all aspects of the separate but equal doctrine, but it was a very significant start. Let us see what happened.

A Negro named Hemon Sweatt applied for admission to the University of Texas Law School for the February 1946 term. His application was rejected solely because of his race. At that time there was no law school for Negroes in Texas. He sued the University of Texas to compel his admission. The state court gave the state six months to supply him with substantially equal facilities. At the end of six months the state court denied Sweatt legal relief on a showing that the university intended to open a law school for Negroes in February 1947. Sweatt refused to apply for admission to the new school. He went back to the state court on the issue whether the new school met the test of separate but equal. The state court held that the school met this test. The Texas appellate courts upheld this decision. In 1949 the Supreme Court granted certiorari, and in June 1950, more than two years after its decision in the Sipuel case, the Court decided *Sweatt* v. *Painter*.[5]

Now, between February 1947 and June 1950 Texas had established a law school at the Texas State University for Negroes, which had acquired 5 professors, 23 students, a library of 16,500 volumes, a practice court, a legal aid association, and, by 1950, one alumnus.[6] Did this Negro law school fulfill the state's duty to supply "equal" though separate facilities?

It should be noted that the Supreme Court in June 1950 was not the "Warren Court." Frederick M. Vinson was Chief Justice from 1946 to his death on September 8, 1953. At the time of the Sweatt case, the Associate Justices were Black, Reed, Frankfurter, Douglas, Clark, Minton, Jackson, and Burton; one would hardly label a majority of them as "liberals.'" But it was this "Vinson Court" that ordered the University of Texas Law School to admit Sweatt.

In an opinion for a unanimous Court, Chief Justice Vinson pointed out that the University of Texas Law School was superior in the number of professors, variety of courses, opportunity for specialization, scope of library, size of student body, and other objective conditions; but, said the Court,

what is more important, the University of Texas Law School possesses to a far greater degree those qualities which are incapable of objective measurement but which make for greatness in a law school. Such qualities, to name but a few, include reputation of the faculty, experience of the administration, position and influence of the alumni, standing in the community, traditions and prestige.

The Court added that in view of the fact that a Negro lawyer must work, throughout his professional career, in a predominantly white society, a Negro law student in a segregated school would be precluded from associating with members of the white race who would form the large majority of his future colleagues, and would be shut off from the race which includes "most of the lawyers, witnesses, jurors, judges and other officials with whom petitioner will inevitably be dealing when he becomes a member of the Texas Bar." The Court expressly held that *a separate law school did not satisfy the constitutional requirement of equality.*

The Court thus agreed with the contention of the N.A.A.C.P. lawyers, first openly advanced in this case, that the separate-but-equal rule *inevitably results in discrimination.* The factors considered by the Court were not of the kind that are subject to measurement or other objective proof. The factors were intangible but such as anyone with common sense could "see." The Court in the Sweatt case unanimously vindicated the essential point of the dissenting opinion of Justice Rutledge in the Sipuel case. Sweatt, in 1950, was the first Negro ordered by the Supreme Court to be admitted to a state-operated school that was ordered to be instantly desegregated.

The Chief Justice said that the Court did not find it necessary to accept the N.A.A.C.P. contention "that *Plessy* v. *Ferguson* should be re-examined in the light of contemporary knowledge respecting the purposes of the Fourteenth Amendment and the effects of racial segregation." This re-examination was, in fact, only postponed. From this time on it was clear that thereafter the N.A.A.C.P. lawyers would be able to chip at the *Plessy* rule until it was fully repudiated.

In view of the attacks on the "Warren Court" for its decision in the Brown case, and especially for its statement that state-required school segregation has detrimental effects on the Negro children, and its citation, in footnote 11, of the writings of Myrdal and of other sociologists and psychologists, it is important to note that the N.A.A.C.P. brief in *Sweatt* v. *Painter* cited four of the authorities later cited by the Court in footnote 11. It was in *Sweatt* v. *Painter* that the N.A.A.C.P. first *expressly* asked the Court to re-examine and overrule *Plessy* v.

Ferguson.[7] The attack on racial segregation in this historically important brief went beyond the effects of such segregation on legal education; it attacked racial segregation in *all* schools and on *all* levels. The evils of segregation were described as follows:

First, segregation prevents both the Negro and white student from obtaining a full knowledge and understanding of the group from which he is separated. It has been scientifically established that no child at birth possesses either an instinct or even a propensity towards feelings of prejudice or superiority. . . . The very act of segregation tends to crystallize and perpetuate group isolation, and serves, therefore, as a breeding ground for unhealthy attitudes.

Secondly, a feeling of distrust for the minority group is fostered in the community at large—a psychological atmosphere which is most unfavorable to the acquisition of a proper education. This atmosphere, in turn, tends to accentuate imagined differences between Negroes and whites. . . .

Qualified educators, social scientists, and other experts have expressed their realization of the fact that "separate" is irreconcilable with "equality." There can be no equality since the very fact of segregation establishes a feeling of humiliation and deprivation to the group considered inferior. . . .

A definitive study of the scientific works of contemporary sociologists, historians and anthropologists conclusively documents the proposition that the intent and result of segregation are the establishment of an inferiority status. . . .

Obviously these words reach far beyond the facts of *Sweatt* v. *Painter* to undermine *all* school-segregation laws. The South was definitely on notice that from this time forth the N.A.A.C.P. would no longer come to court to ask for the "equality" that would fulfill the separate-but-equal rule, but would ask for the end of the rule, the end of segregation; and the Court's decision in this case should have been read in the South as handwriting on the wall foreshadowing the inevitability of the Brown decision.

A brief filed on behalf of more than two hundred professors of law also asked the Supreme Court expressly to overrule the Plessy decision as a precedent that was "seriously destructive of the democratic process in the United States."[8] Similar lines of attack were taken in briefs filed on behalf of the American Jewish Committee and the B'nai B'rith Anti-Defamation League, the American Jewish Congress, and the American Federation of Teachers. Of special significance was the brief for the United States as *amici curiae,* filed by Philip B. Perlman, Solicitor General, and Philip Elman, Special Assistant to the Attorney

General, which argued for the immediate desegregation of the University of Texas Law School by ordering the instant admission of Sweatt.

On the same day that the Court decided *Sweatt* v. *Painter,* it also decided the McLaurin case,[9] which was no less important. In this case, too, the opinion was by Chief Justice Vinson for a unanimous Court.

G. W. McLaurin, a Negro citizen of Oklahoma with an M. A. degree, applied to the University of Oklahoma to study for the doctorate in education. Obeying the state segregation laws, the university rejected his application. He went to the federal court for relief, and that court, relying on the Sipuel decision, held that the state had a duty to provide him with the education he sought as soon as it provided that education for whites; but the court withheld an injunction to afford the state an opportunity to meet the situation. Then the legislature met and amended the laws to permit the admission of Negroes to institutions of higher learning for such study as was not available in the Negro schools, but, the amendment provided, the Negro was to be admitted on a segregated basis.

Thereupon McLaurin was admitted to the University of Oklahoma Graduate School. But these were the conditions under which he was required to study and live—in the words of Chief Justice Vinson:

He was required to sit apart at a designated desk in an anteroom adjoining the classroom; to sit at a designated desk on the mezzanine floor of the library, but not to use the desks in the regular reading room; and to sit at a designated table and to eat at a different time from the other students in the school cafeteria.

McLaurin went back to the federal district court with the contention that these conditions violated his constitutional rights to equality, but that court denied his motion, and the N.A.A.C.P. took his case to the Supreme Court.

While the appeal was pending, the state authorities realized that it would be impossible for them to persuade the Supreme Court that Oklahoma was affording McLaurin "equality," so they made some changes, which Chief Justice Vinson described as follows:

For some time, the section of the classroom in which appellant sat was surrounded by a rail on which there was a sign stating, "Reserved for Colored," but these have been removed. He is now assigned to a seat in the classroom in a row specified for colored students; he is assigned to a table in the library on the main floor; and he is permitted to eat at the same time in the cafeteria as other students, although here again he is assigned to a special table.

The Supreme Court held that all these conditions were a denial of McLaurin's constitutional rights and, in effect, ordered the university to desegregate. The restrictions, said the Court,

impair and inhibit his ability to study, to engage in discussions and exchange views with other students, and, in general, to learn his profession.

It was argued by the state that the removal of these restrictions would not mean that McLaurin would not be set apart by the white students. But the Court said that this was irrelevant, for

there is a vast difference—a Constitutional difference—between restrictions imposed by the state which prohibit the intellectual commingling of students, and the refusal of individuals to commingle where the state presents no such bar . . . at the very least, the state will not be depriving appellant of the opportunity to secure acceptance by his fellow students on his own merits.

Briefs supporting McLaurin were filed by a number of organizations, including the American Civil Liberties Union, and a brief attacking segregation as a violation of the Fourteenth Amendment was filed for the C.I.O. by (later Justice) Arthur J. Goldberg. Especially important was the brief of the Solicitor General of the United States, which contended:

Racial segregation is itself a manifestation of inequality and discrimination. . . . The "separate but equal" theory of *Plessy* v. *Ferguson* is wrong as a matter of law, history and policy. The United States . . . urges the Court to repudiate the "separate but equal" doctrine as an unwarranted deviation from the principle of equality under law which the Fourteenth Amendment explicitly incorporated in the fundamental charter of this country.

Under the Constitution every agency of government, federal and state, must treat our people as *Americans,* and not as members of particular groups divided according to race, color, religion, or national ancestry. All citizens stand equal and alike in relation to their government, and no distinctions can be made among them because of race or color or other irrelevant factors. The color of a man's skin has no constitutional significance. . . .

"Separate but equal" . . . is derived not from the Constitution but from a judicial expression which did not make its appearance in the reports of this Court until 1896, and which is irreconcilable with the body of precedents which preceded and followed it. . . .

The proposition that all men are created equal is not mere rhetoric. It summarizes a rule of law embodied in the Constitution, the supreme law of the land, and thus is binding on the Federal and State governments and all their officials.[10]

The Solicitor General here was speaking for the United States Government, which for the first time openly and without reservations attacked *Plessy* v. *Ferguson* and every aspect of legally required or enforced racial segregation—and not merely segregation in higher education.

The facts in the McLaurin case dramatically showed how morally degrading racial segregation was in practice; for here was a reputable state university, and here was a Negro with a bachelor's and a master's degree and qualified to pursue studies for a doctor's degree, treated by educated persons as if he were an animal that had to be kept in a cage or an individual with some communicable disease—a member of a caste of untouchables. The effect on the Court of the spectacle presented by Oklahoma must have been deep and far-reaching.

This impression must have been confirmed by a third case decided on the same day, June 5, 1950, on which the Court decided the Sweatt and McLaurin cases.

The Henderson case[11] involved the practice of Jim Crow in interstate travel. Elmer Henderson, a Negro, was traveling as a first-class Pullman passenger on the Southern Railway from Washington, D. C., to Birmingham, Alabama, as a field representative of the President's Committee on Fair Employment Practices, War Manpower Commission. Henderson entered the diner soon after it opened at 5:30 p.m. and found white passengers at the two end tables which the railroad reserved conditionally for Negroes. But there was one vacant seat at these tables. The steward told him he could not then be served and promised to send him word in his Pullman car if the end tables became vacant. Henderson came back at 7:00 and again at 7:30 and white passengers were still at the end tables. He was never called by the steward, and the diner was detached from the train at 9:00 p.m.

The practice of the railroad was to draw curtains to separate the two tables nearest the kitchen from the other tables and to place "Reserved" cards on these two curtained tables. But if the other seats were occupied by white passengers before any Negro entered the diner, then the curtain and the cards were removed and white passengers were served at those tables.

The Henderson case started in 1942, when Henderson filed a complaint with the Interstate Commerce Commission. The Commission found the railway's regulations non-discriminatory; but the federal district court, to which he appealed, held that the regulations were discriminatory, for while tables were held for white passengers unconditionally, the two tables were held for Negroes only conditionally. The case then went back to the Commission for further hearings. At the new hearings the railway introduced new regulations, under which one table, nearest the kitchen, for four passengers, would be reserved exclusively for Negroes, and the curtain separating this table from the others would remain drawn and a "Reserved" card would be kept on it. All other tables were reserved for white passengers. The railway indicated that the curtain would soon be replaced by a permanent partition, five feet high. The Commission and the federal district court upheld these arrangements.

In 1950—eight years after Henderson had first started the proceedings—the case was before the Supreme Court on appeal. The Court, in an opinion by Justice Burton, unanimously held the regulations to be discriminatory in violation of Section 3 of the Interstate Commerce Act. Said the Court:

We need not multiply instances in which these rules sanction unreasonable discriminations. The curtains, partitions and signs emphasize the artificiality of a difference in treatment which serves only to call attention to a racial classification of passengers holding identical tickets and using the same public dining facility. Cf. *McLaurin* . . . , decided today.

In this case too the Solicitor General filed a brief—and this was the United States brief *against* a government agency, the I.C.C. Mr. Perlman's brief stated unequivocally:

"Separate but equal" is as much a contradiction in terms as "black but white": facilities which are segregated by law, solely on the basis of race or color, cannot in any real sense be regarded as equal. . . . Under the regulations here involved, persons traveling together, if they are of different color, cannot eat together regardless of their personal desires. Even if he so wishes, a white passenger is forbidden to sit at a colored table. In other words, the regulations do not merely carry out the prejudices of some members of the community; they compel everybody else to abide by such prejudices. . . .

One who is compelled to live in a ghetto, because of his color or creed, does not enjoy "equality," no matter how luxurious his abode. . . . A colored passenger who is set apart in a corner by himself is in no real sense being treated as an equal. The curtain or partition which fences Negroes off from all other diners exposes, naked and unadorned, the caste system which segregation manifests and fosters.

Rarely before or since has the case against segregation been put more forcefully than in this brief for the United States:

The colored passenger, paying the same price for his meal as other passengers, does not receive the same thing in return. True, he receives the same food, but the condition which is attached to receiving it is that he submit to having his mind bombarded with the message that he and all members of his race are classified as inferior, as constituting a lower social caste. This message of humiliation comes, not as a single voice, but with all the reverberations of the entire pattern of segregation and discrimination of which it is a part. . . .

It is bad enough for the Negro to have to endure the insults of individuals who look upon him as inferior. It is far worse to have to submit to a formalized or institutionalized enforcement of this concept, particularly when, as in this case, it carries the sanction of an agency of government and thus appears to have the seal of approval of the community at large. Such enforced racial segregation in and of itself constitutes inequality. In this situation the phrase "separate but equal" is a plain contradiction in terms.[12]

The brief for the United States specifically condemned Jim Crow laws because they "not only indoctrinate both white and colored races with the caste conception, but they solidify the segregation existing outside these laws and give it respectability and institutional fixity."[13]

The brief put it squarely to the Supreme Court that it was not the Constitution but the courts that supported racial segregation; that the Court could no longer evade responsibility for this denial of human dignity—and of constitutional equality. "So long as the doctrine of the *Plessy* case stands," said the brief,

a barrier erected not by the Constitution but by the courts will continue to work a denial of rights and privileges and immunities antagonistic to the freedoms and liberties on which our institutions and our form of government are founded. "Separate but equal" is a constitutional anachronism which no longer deserves a place in our law. . . . It is neither reasonable nor right that colored citizens of the United States should be subjected to the humiliation of being segregated by law, on the pretense that they are being treated as equals.[14]

The issue could not have been stated more unequivocally and directly; and it is historically important to note that it was in 1949–1950 that the United States Government, in the Truman administration, appealed to the Supreme Court squarely to overrule *Plessy* v. *Ferguson* and to bury the doctrine of "separate but equal." And it is also historically important to note that it was the "Vinson Court" that, in 1950, put the explosives under the Plessy decision, and that the explosives were there for all to see. It was only the ignorant or the willfully blind who could have honestly pleaded surprise when the explosives finally blew up in 1954. The basis for the Brown decision had been laid by the Sweatt, McLaurin, and Henderson cases.[15] On one side were the N.A.A.C.P., the leading civil rights and civil liberties organizations, the Jewish organizations, the American Federation of Teachers, the Congress of Industrial Organizations (C.I.O.), and, most important of all, the United States, represented by the Solicitor General and the Department of Justice. Opposed to them were the governments of the Southern states: in the Sweatt case the Attorneys General of eleven states that enforced segregation filed a brief in defense of the Plessy decision.[16] The opponents remained the same when the time came to litigate the Brown case before the Supreme Court.

2. The States Prepare Congress for the Civil Rights Act of 1964

Just as the decision in the Brown case was rooted in the Constitution and in judicial precedents, so, too, the Civil Rights Act of 1964 grew out of a soil that had been well prepared for it.

First of all, millions of Americans had been conditioned to think that the state has *an obligation* to prevent members of the white race from discriminating against Negroes in schools and in places of public accommodation. The theory was that while men may be *prejudiced* against others by reason of their race or color, they may not *act out* their prejudices in *public* life, and that the government has a *duty* to protect Negroes from such *acts*. Massachusetts deserves credit for enactment of the first civil rights statutes in the United States—and probably in world history. In 1855 the legislature of this state passed an act to provide that no school may make any distinction, in passing on admissions, "on account of race, color, or religious opinions of the applicant or scholar,"[17] and in 1865 Massachusetts put on its books a statute that banned discrimination on account of color or race "in any licensed inn, in any public place of amusement, public conveyance or public meeting [or theaters, added in 1866] in this commonwealth."[18] With these laws there was introduced into jurisprudence the "activist" principle in race and general intergroup relations; namely, that the state has a *positive* role to play in these relations, to protect the weak against the strong; to protect a man from suffering public indignity or humiliation; to prevent the development of a caste system, with superior and inferior social status in an order in which a man's place will be determined by his birth and not by his merits; to make discrimination an offense against the public order, just as physically attacking a man is such an offense.

New York and Kansas in 1874 followed the Massachusetts example. And Congress, in the first decade following the Civil War, assumed that civil rights should be protected by federal action and enacted a series of such acts. But the Supreme Court's decision in the civil rights cases of 1883 held the most important of these statutes— the Civil Rights Act of 1875—unconstitutional.[19] Then the states again proceeded to enact such statutes, so that by 1897 there were civil rights acts in eighteen Northern, Eastern, and Western states.

Then for fifty-six years no other state adopted such a measure. Oregon in 1953 restarted the trend. By the time Congress enacted the Civil Rights Act of 1964, there were thirty-one states with laws forbidding racial discrimination in public accommodations.[20] The exceptions were the eleven states that had been in the Confederacy and eight Border and Southwestern states.[21] These civil rights laws covered about two-thirds of the country's population, or about 120,000,000 people. Outside of the eleven Southern states, only about 14,500,000 people were not subject to state civil rights acts.[22] These figures tend to show how an American consensus had formed gradually in favor of civil rights in places of public accommodation.

In the early 1940s the nation began to see an important extension of the principle of civil rights. In 1941 A. Philip Randolph, Negro leader and president, since 1925, of the Brotherhood of Sleeping Car Porters, organized the March on Washington Movement in protest against job discrimination. The march was scheduled for July 1, 1941.[23] Randolph's movement is generally credited with causing President Roosevelt to issue Executive Order 8802 on June 25, 1941. The demonstration was canceled when the order was issued by the President. The order established the first Fair Employment Practices Committee, to promote the participation of all workers in defense industries without discrimination because of race, color, creed, or national origin. This F.E.P.C. was the first of a series of similar agencies in the Executive Office of the President. The 1941 F.E.P.C. was the first government agency set up to protect equality of employment opportunity, and thus a new civil right was born. Title VII of the Civil Rights Act of 1964 gave statutory recognition to this civil right, almost a quarter of a century after the March on Washington Movement, and the President's Committee on Equal Employment

Opportunity became absorbed by the statutory Equal Employment Opportunity Commission, of which Franklin D. Roosevelt, Jr., became the first chairman.

On the state level, prior to the 1940s laws in thirteen states prohibited discrimination in certain areas of *public* employment, and a New York law of 1935 required all public works contracts to provide a clause against discrimination[24]—the pattern for the chief concern of President Truman's Committee on Government Contract Compliance (which under President Eisenhower became the Committee on Government Contracts).

The major breakthrough, however, came in New York in 1945, when the legislature enacted the first state fair employment practices act in the United States, and perhaps in the world. The Ives-Quinn law—for which the late Irving M. Ives deserved most of the credit—created a State Commission against Discrimination, with power to prevent and to stop discrimination in employment because of race, color, creed, or national origin. Employers, unions, and employment agencies were subject to the terms of the law, which expressly declared opportunity for employment without discrimination to be a civil right. By the time Congress enacted the Civil Rights Act of 1964, there were F.E.P. acts in twenty-five states.[25] While there were numerous differences among them, they all were based on recognition of the fundamental principle of the Ives-Quinn law. The twenty-five states with F.E.P. laws had about two-thirds of the population of the country. Outside of the eleven Southern states, only about 18,000,000 Americans were not subject to such state laws.

The spread of state civil rights and fair employment practices statutes must be credited with helping to prepare all the branches of the federal government for a comprehensive and far-reaching federal law, such as Congress enacted in 1964. These state laws were often only halfheartedly enforced,[26] but they nonetheless were a clear expression of public policy and morality, and experience with them provided Congress with plans and ideas to follow, modify, or reject.

The states themselves showed a willingness to learn from experience and to experiment with new methods. In 1949 New Jersey became the first state to carry over to its public-accommodations law the administrative machinery originally established to handle only F.E.P. cases, and thus imposed on a public agency the duty to investigate complaints of racial discrimination. The New Jersey experiment was then followed by Connecticut, Massachusetts, New York, and other states.[27]

And some of the states established civil rights divisions in the offices of their attorneys general.[28] In this respect the states followed the example of the United States Department of Justice. When he was Attorney General of the United States, Frank Murphy (later Justice of the Supreme Court) in 1939 set up a Civil Rights Unit (or Section) in the Criminal Division of the Department of Justice.[29] In 1957 a Civil Rights Division was set up in the Department, with an assistant attorney general in charge. The record made by Burke Marshall as he filled this office in the crucial years from 1961 to 1965 showed how important this position could be when held by an able and dedicated public servant in an administration committed to enforcement of the laws.

The historic report of 1947 by President Truman's Committee on Civil Rights—*To Secure These Rights*—stated that the record made by the Civil Rights Section (now Division) during its first eight years was a "remarkable one." The report went on to say:

In many instances during these eight years, the Section, the FBI and the United States Attorneys in the field have done invaluable work. They deserve the highest praise for the imagination and courage they have often shown.[30]

This record of achievement has been sustained over the years since 1947.

While Congress deserves credit for enactment of the Civil Rights Act of 1964, it may be seriously doubted if this would or could have happened had not most Americans been schooled *by their states* to believe that there is a governmental duty to prevent and to punish violations of civil rights, broadly defined to include equality in places of public accommodation and in schools, and opportunity in public-supported and in private employment, and had not the states experimented with new methods in implementing such rights. All the creative work in this area was done by the states—with the exception of the pioneering work of Frank Murphy in the Department of Justice, and what President Truman did in the armed forces.

3. Desegregation of the Armed Forces

It is hard to see how the civil rights movement could have taken the course it took after 1954 if in the few years immediately preceding the Brown case the armed forces had not become desegregated. No clearer, more dramatic expression of public policy was possible, on a national level, than this momentous step, taken by President Truman in 1948.

Looking back over the past several decades, it is now almost unthinkable that the annual report of the N.A.A.C.P. for 1943 should have opened as follows:

I
THE ARMED FORCES

Together with employment opportunities, the treatment of the Negro in the armed services continued to be the principal item in the race relations picture during 1943.

The NAACP renewed on several occasions its demands that the War Department establish a voluntary mixed unit, composed of white and colored enlisted men and officers, but the War Department continued to refuse with the excuse that this kind of change was inexpedient in war time.[31]

In its 1947 report, *To Secure These Rights,* the President's Committee on Civil Rights stated that the record showed that members of minority groups,

fighting and dying for the survival of the nation in which they met bitter prejudice, found that there was discrimination against them even as they fell in battle.[32]

The report called attention to the fact that Negroes faced an absolute bar against enlistment in any branch of the Marine Corps other than the steward's branch; that the Army had a ceiling of 10 per cent for Negro personnel; and that discrimination in recruiting practices was apparent from the fact that Negroes were only 4.4 per cent of the strength of the Navy and only 4.2 per cent of the Coast Guard. In the Army less than one Negro in seventy was commissioned, while there was one white officer for every seven white enlisted men. In the Navy there was one white officer for every seven white enlisted men, but there were only two Negro officers in a ratio of less than one to ten thousand Negro enlisted men. In the Marine Corps there was not one Negro among the 7798 officers; and in the Coast Guard there was one Negro among the 2981 officers.[33] These were typical facts which —as recently as 1947—manifestly showed the extent of racial discrimination practiced in and by the armed forces.

Negroes had by no means been silent about the facts, and some fine sentiments had been expressed on behalf of the various services, but the discrimination remained essentially unchanged. The evidence, said the report of the President's Committee on Civil Rights, leaves no doubt that we have a long way to go. The armed forces, in actual practice, still maintain many barriers to equal treatment for all their members. . . . Morally, the failure to act is indefensible.[34]

The objections to action were the stereotypes that one frequently heard during World War II when the problem was discussed: integration will lead to inevitable friction; integration will lower standards; whites will object to taking orders from Negroes; integration will create social problems; Negroes prefer to be by themselves.[35] These attitudes unfortunately were the basis on which national policy was established; and in 1940 the policy appeared to be so firmly fixed that the Secretary of the Navy, Frank Knox, could state without apology that Negroes would not be accepted in the Navy in any other capacity than as mess attendants.[36]

In 1945 the so-called Gillem Board, composed of Army general officers, headed by Lieutenant General A. C. Gillem, Jr., spent more than three months studying the question of Negro personnel in the Army. Its conclusion was that the Army should maintain segregated units and restrict the percentage of Negroes in the Army to their ratio in the whole population, i.e., a *numerus clausus* of 10 per cent for Negroes. The board tried to mitigate this racist pattern by advocating more skilled jobs for Negroes and experimenting with Negro battalions and companies assigned to white groupings—for example, a Negro infantry regiment to be assigned to a white infantry division.[37] The recommendations of the Gillem Board were put into effect for three years.

Then President Truman reacted to the racial situation in the armed forces as it was described in the report of the President's Committee on Civil Rights, and on July 26, 1948, he issued the historic Executive Order No. 9981,[38] in which he stated:

It is hereby declared to be the policy of the President that there shall be equality of treatment and opportunity for all persons in the armed services without regard to race, color, religion or national origin. This policy shall be put into effect as rapidly as possible, having due regard to the time required to effectuate any necessary changes without impairing efficiency or morale.

In the history of civil rights in the United States, this order ranks among the most important steps taken to end racial discrimination.

President Truman by the same order set up the President's Committee on Equality of Treatment and Opportunity in the Armed Services, headed by Charles Fahy, former Solicitor General of the United States and later a judge of the United States court of appeals. The committee's report, *Freedom to Serve,* published in 1950, deserves to be linked with *To Secure These Rights* as among the most influential documents in the struggle for civil rights. The Fahy Committee was authorized to act for the President in examining procedures and practices in order to determine how these should be altered to carry out the President's order. The committee worked intimately with the armed services to reach decisions mutually agreed upon. The results were revolutionary.

The Fahy Committee, when it started to work, found that the racial practices were defended on two grounds: (1) that the Negro could not match the white in intelligence and skill, and (2) that social custom commanded the segregation of the Negroes. The committee insisted that men were to be judged and classified as *individuals,* and not on the basis of any supposed *general* racial characteristics or intelligence, and that, if this policy was followed, men would be accepted for their personal qualities, skills, and worth.

From 1949 to 1950 the Army dropped its 10-per-cent quota; it opened all jobs and courses to Negroes; it assigned Negroes to all units; and it ended the practice of requiring Negroes to live in separate barracks and eat in separate messes.

The Korean War (from June 1950 to July 1953) was the first war involving the United States in which Negroes were in service on a nonsegregated basis. A study of the experience, conducted in 1951 for the Defense Department, showed that all the misgivings and fears previously expressed had been without foundation.[39]

Members of the armed forces continue to run into racial discrimination on overseas duty. This was true, for example, at the bars frequented by American GIs in the towns and villages in West Germany where American troops were based; but by 1965 the reports were that things had changed for the better.

The reserve service, however, remained the one area where progress seemed relatively slow. The National Guard is federally supported, and one may serve in it in fulfillment of one's military obligations under federal law; but the Guard is an organ of the states in peacetime, when not placed on federal service by the President (as in 1957, when President Eisenhower placed 10,000 members of the Arkansas National Guard on federal service to put down the mob in Little Rock).

President Kennedy ordered studies of the question of segregation in National Guard units and at overseas areas, and appointed a Committee on Equal Opportunity in the Armed Forces, headed by Gerhard A. Gesell. The committee's reports in June 1963 and November 1964 concluded that there was no racial discrimination in the assignment of men for overseas service (some 22 per cent of all men in uniform were overseas in 1964); that some elements of discrimination persisted on overseas bases, against which the Secretary of Defense had issued new regulations and had taken corrective steps (following the committee's report of June 1963); that off-base discrimination existed, especially in Germany and the Far East, against which the Department of Defense had issued new directives in July 1963.

As to the National Guard—nearly 500,000 men, in over 4000 units, located in some 2500 communities in every state—the President's committee found that there was discrimination against Negroes attempting to enroll or serving in the National Guard in some states. In its final report, the committee said:

In some states . . . there is complete or almost complete absence of Negroes in officer ranks. Similarly, the participation of Negroes in enlisted ranks in the case of some states is still only on a token basis, a condition that carries special emphasis where such states with a large Negro population and units are not at full authorized strength.[40]

The final report pointed out that, since the National Guard is a federally assisted program, Section 601 of the Civil Rights Act of 1964 could be used to cut off federal funds to units that continued to discriminate.

On December 29, 1964, the chief of the National Guard Bureau, Major General Winston P. Wilson, said:

I can now confirm [that] the National Guard of all the states, the District of Columbia and Puerto Rico is now integrated and that all restrictions, whether by law or administrative regulation barring membership for race, religion or national origin, have been eliminated in the National Guard.[41]

The last two states to abandon racial discrimination in their National Guard units were Alabama and Mississippi (the latter on December 1, 1964); but the federal authorities noted that in some Southern states there was only token desegregation. On March 31, 1965, there were only 380 Negroes in the National Guard in the 11 Southern States.

The Pentagon, in December 1964, made known its plan to place all members of the Army Reserve either in the National Guard or in a pool of fillers, and to abolish the units of the Army Reserve. But the Senate Appropriations Committee killed the merger plan in September 1965; the Johnson administration indicated, however, that it would continue to push for it. The opposition of the Southern Governors Conference in September 1965, and of Senator John Stennis of Mississippi, chairman of the Senate Preparedness Subcommittee, probably played an important part in the defeat. A larger degree of racial integration in the National Guard would be only a by-product of the plan; the purpose of the merger, according to the Secretary of Defense and the Army Chief of Staff, was to improve war plans and to increase readiness of top-priority divisions and brigades. If this plan ever is adopted, the pace of desegregation in the Guard units is bound to accelerate.

The experience in the armed services is significant in that it served as an example of what can be accomplished by effective Presidential leadership. As Lee Nichols put it in his study of "one of the biggest stories of the Twentieth Century":

By knocking down its racial barriers, the military had shown it could be done; that Negroes and whites, despite a long history of sharp separation and frequently deep-seated antagonism, would work, live and play together with little or no concern once they got used to the idea.

Secondly, . . . men leaving service were taking back to civilian life at least some of their new experience . . . ; from all available evidence the great majority of men in integrated units took home a fresh slant on race free from the basic concept of segregation that once dominated the American scene. . . .

A third impact was in direct military contacts with outside communities. Integration was spilling over uncontrollably. Churches, USO clubs, cafes and taxicabs, in the North and South, here and there began voluntarily to admit Negroes on an equal or near-equal basis with white service-men.[42]

A fourth effect, hard to measure, was that on the Negro GIs. Integrated life in the armed forces must have provided many of them with the will never again to accept segregation and discrimination supinely. Some of this determination must have been channeled into the civil rights struggle of the late 1950s and the 1960s.

Discussing the effects of his Executive Order No. 9981, President Truman in 1953 said: "It's the greatest thing that ever happened to America."[43] It was certainly *one* of the greatest things, and, as Hubert H. Humphrey said in 1954, "the first truly effective step that has been made in implementing the Emancipation Proclamation."[44]

4. Conclusion

But how many Americans knew anything, after only ten or fifteen years, of Executive Order No. 9981? or about the desegregation decisions of 1950 by the "Vinson Court"? or of the Ives-Quinn law of 1946? or of the dozens of state civil rights and F.E.P. acts? Yet these were milestones in the civil rights movement, without which there could have been no nonviolent resistance movement among Negroes, and no school-desegregation cases of 1954, and no Civil Rights Act of 1964.

Walter Bagehot once asked who among his contemporaries knew anything about Bolingbroke or the Peace of Utrecht which he negotiated. Yet several generations of their fathers had quarreled violently over the character and acts of Bolingbroke. There is no help for it. Wellington displaced Marlborough, and Churchill will displace Wellington. The "Warren Court" of 1954 displaced the "Vinson Court" of 1950, and the Civil Rights Act of 1964 displaced a century of state legislation, and the role of John F. Kennedy in the civil rights struggle pushed out the record made by Harry S. Truman. But if piety is, as Santayana put it, loyalty to the sources of our being, it is only a simple act of piety to record and remember the significant events that were, in and for their time, breakthroughs in the struggle for freedom and equality for the Negro.

Other events also helped in this struggle. Certainly a contribution was made by the independence won by the Africans, as Africa's thirty-six colonies became sovereign nations.[45] All this happened from March 1957 to February 1965, at a dizzying pace; and the presence in New York, at the U.N. and its agencies, of these countries' delegations, and their ministries and embassies in Washington, and their travel in the United States, could not but influence the American Negro, public opinion, and the federal government. And the role of Dr. Martin Luther King, Jr., and the nonviolent resistance movement (which we consider in a separate chapter) was inestimable in influencing Congress and all other agencies of government, as well as the local communities.

In retrospect, perhaps the least credit goes to Congress. In 1957 and 1960 it passed civil rights acts, but they were the first congressional enactments since 1875, a period of over eighty years, and these two enactments[46] were extremely limited in scope. The enactment of 1964 is certainly one of the most important in American history; but the action of the 88th Congress does not wipe out the do-nothing record of the 44th Congress, or the 45th, right on up to the 88th.

This fact about Congress has disturbing implications for the theory of democracy that places primary stress on the legislature, and for idealistic theories of law that are oblivious of such profane things as economic and political power. The Civil Rights Act of 1964 was not freely given by but wrested from Congress by the power exerted by Presidents Truman, Kennedy, and Johnson; by the social forces let loose by the Supreme Court under Chief Justices Vinson and Warren; by the forces exerted by the spreading network of state civil rights and F.E.P. acts; by the Negroes acting as a pressure group; and by the international community observing us and freely commenting on what it saw.

Thanks to this confluence of forces, achievements in civil rights have been momentous. In the struggle from 1960 to the beginning of 1966, the civil rights movement has had nearly thirty martyrs— among them Medgar Evers; the four Negro children who died in the Birmingham church bombing; the three civil rights workers who were murdered in Mississippi; Jimmie Lee Jackson, who was killed on February 18, 1965, at Marion, Alabama, as state troopers broke up a civil rights march; the Reverend James J. Reeb, a Unitarian minister from Boston, who was murdered in Selma in March 1965; and Mrs. Viola Liuzzo, murdered on the road between Selma and Montgomery. Of course there should have been no martyrs at all; but the United States record is immeasurably better than that of India, for example, the home of Gandhi and the mother country of mass nonviolent movements, where in three weeks in January and February 1965 sixty-one persons were killed in the language riots of Madras.[47]

Having said this, one must at once take measures against smugness, for besides the lives lost there were other heavy costs that one ought not to forget—the beatings from sheriffs, policemen, state troopers, possemen; the failure of Southern courts to vindicate the Negro's rights; the mortification from insults hurled by shrieking and spitting men, women, and children; the countless testings and teasings; the hurt to the body, to the pride, and to the dignity; and the successive defeats that left the Negro with little reason to trust the political process and the effect of reasoning on human behavior. President Johnson likes to quote the verse from the prophet Isaiah: "Come now, let us reason together." But what if the governor of the state, and the mayor of the city, and all the "good," "solid" citizens refuse to come and refuse to listen? The miracle has been that only a small minority of Negroes chose, in the face of a mountain of troubles, to say: "And why not do evil that good may come?"[48]

The only other events in our history with which the civil rights struggle may be compared are those in the struggle of workers to win the rights of self-organization and of collective bargaining. But the workers faced the hostility of the courts; "government by injunction" was perhaps the most formidable obstacle that labor had to overcome. The first breakthrough for labor, and the most significant, was the passage by Congress in 1932 of the Norris-LaGuardia Act, which limited the powers of the courts in labor disputes. The Wagner Act of 1935, which set up procedures for the establishment of unions as bargaining agents, and which specifically acknowledged the right of unions to insist on collective bargaining, was almost anticlimactic; for, once the courts' powers were sharply reduced, the great gains of labor for many years continued to depend on their own energies in strikes, picketing, and other self-help measures. But, among the three branches of the federal government, the workers, perhaps because they had the vote in the industrial states and cities, made their influence felt most directly and effectively in Congress and least of all in the Supreme Court and the courts generally. The opposite was, as we have seen, true of the Negro's struggle, to whom the Supreme Court and the President reached out helping hands before Congress could be stirred to action.

It cannot all be explained in terms of centers of power, voting and other kinds; for the Negro had no power in the Supreme Court except the power of conscience, and it may be seriously doubted that President Truman's position on civil rights in his second term of office could be rationally explained in terms of power. In the election of 1948, we should recall, the thirty-nine electoral votes of Alabama, Louisiana, Mississippi, South Carolina, and Tennessee were cast for the States' Rights Democrats, Thurmond for President and Wright for Vice-President. Harry Truman's stand on civil rights could hardly have been a calculated bid for power. Civil rights leaders who knew President Truman personally felt that no President had been as dedicated to their cause as he was. While he was anxious to win the election, he was not one to gather grapes of thorns or figs of thistles.

VII

The First Amendment and Civil Rights Demonstrations

1. Sit-in Demonstrations and Free Speech

Late one morning in March 1961, 187 Negro high-school and college students in Columbia, South Carolina, met at the Zion Baptist Church. At about noon they left the church and walked, in groups of fifteen, to the State House grounds, an area of two city blocks. Their purpose was to submit a protest to the citizens of the state and to the legislators, expressing, as they put it,

our feelings and our dissatisfaction with the present condition of discriminating actions against Negroes, in general, and to let them know that we were dissatisfied and that we would like for the laws which prohibited Negro privileges in this State to be repealed.

When they reached their destination there were already on the State House grounds thirty or more police officers, who had advance notice of what was to happen. On arrival, each group was told by the officials that they had a right to go through the grounds "as long as they were peaceful." The students walked for the next thirty to forty-five minutes in the same groups, single file or two abreast, in an orderly fashion. Each group carried placards that read "I am proud to be a Negro" or "Down with segregation."

During this time some two hundred to three hundred onlookers gathered in the area and on the adjacent sidewalks. There were no threatening remarks or other hostile manifestations from the crowd; nor was pedestrian or vehicular traffic obstructed.

The police officers told the students that they would have to disperse within fifteen minutes or they would be arrested. The students, however, did not leave but listened to a religious talk, sang patriotic and religious songs, stamped their feet, and clapped their hands. At the end of the fifteen minutes all 187 students were arrested and marched

267

off to jail. They were charged with breach of the peace, convicted, and sentenced with fines from $10 to $100 or five to thirty days in jail. The convictions were appealed to the state supreme court, where they were affirmed.

The United States Supreme Court, in *Edwards* v. *South Carolina*,[1] reversed, holding that "under the circumstances disclosed by this record, South Carolina infringed the petitioners' constitutionally protected rights of free speech, free assembly, and freedom to petition for redress of their grievances." In an opinion by Justice Stewart, the Court said that the facts show "an exercise of these basic constitutional rights in their most pristine and classic form."

Following this decision, the Supreme Court in 1963 overturned the convictions of 373 Negro students on charges of breach of the peace after a demonstration march in Orangeburg, South Carolina,[2] and in 1964 it took the same action in a case arising out of a demonstration in front of the city hall in Rock Hill, South Carolina, in which 65 students were convicted.[3] In the latter case the Court, in a unanimous *per curiam* opinion, noted that the students had assembled in a place where they had not been forbidden by law, and that they had engaged, as in the Edwards case, in the "peaceful expression of unpopular views." Said the Court in the Rock Hill case:

They assembled in a peaceful, orderly fashion in front of the City Hall to protest segregation. They carried signs to that effect and they sang patriotic and religious songs. Although white onlookers assembled, no violence or threat of violence occurred and traffic was not disturbed. After 15 minutes of this, they were arrested for failure to disperse upon orders. . . .
Edwards established that the "Fourteenth Amendment does not permit a State to make criminal the peaceful expression of unpopular views."

One of the distressing things that these and similar cases disclose is the "hardness of heart," the sheer inhumanity—forgetting for the moment the constitutional aspects—of the state judges who imposed and upheld sentences of $50 fines or 30 days in jail on each of the 373 students in the Orangeburg demonstration, and the equally severe penalties imposed in the Edwards case. If the word "peaceful" means anything at all, all these student demonstrations were certainly peaceful.

But there was method in this madness. Throughout the South, after several years had passed, the legal import of the school-segregation cases of 1954 came to be understood, and public officials at last realized that they could no longer *openly* claim that they would enforce racial segregation. They knew that the Supreme Court would not uphold the enforcement of any segregation statute, ordinance, or regulation. Faced with this exigency, as we saw in an earlier chapter, Southern officials turned their fire against the N.A.A.C.P. But there were other things that they could do, and one of them was to arrest demonstrators and to charge them—not with violating segregation laws, but with breach of the peace or creating a public disturbance.[4] In this respect there is no essential difference between these assembly-petition cases and the lunch-counter sit-ins that we shall soon consider. Since "segregation," when constitutionally considered, had become a dirty word, other words had to be used by the arresting officers and the judges, and among the circumlocutions "breach of the peace" and "disorderly conduct" soon became favorites. In not one of the three South Carolina cases was there a showing of *acts* that made the students disorderly persons. They were against the social order but that is not the same thing as *acting disorderly*.

A key case—but one that had, when it was decided, nothing to do with protests and demonstrations—was *Thompson* v. *Louisville*.[5] When it was decided by the Supreme Court in 1960, hardly anyone paid any attention to it, but in due course its significance became apparent. On its facts, the case could hardly have been less important —it involved only a fine of $10 on each of two convictions—but, unforeseeably, it became the foundation for the hundreds and thousands of demonstrators who claimed the protection of the Constitution.

Sam Thompson was forty-six years old and lived alone in a small house in a suburb of Louisville, Kentucky. He was a Negro, but this fact appears nowhere in the record, and his race or color was not claimed to have had any legal significance in the case.[6] He made a living by doing odd jobs as a handyman. On a Saturday evening, at 6:20, Thompson went into a café that sold food and beer. There were other patrons in the café. After he had been there about half an hour, two Louisville policemen came in on a routine check. They saw Thompson on the floor shuffling his feet. One of the police officers went up to the manager and asked how long Thompson had been there and if he had bought anything. The manager answered that Thompson had been there a little over a half-hour and had not bought anything. The officer then walked up to Thompson and asked him what he was doing there. Thompson said that he was waiting for a bus. The officer told Thompson that he was under arrest, and he took Thompson outside. This was the loitering charge against Thompson, and this was the case against him on that charge.

After going outside, the officer testified in court, Thompson "was very argumentative—he argued with us back and forth and so then we placed a disorderly conduct charge on him." This was all the testimony there was on the charge of disorderly conduct.

This was the total case against Thompson for loitering and disorderly conduct, except a record of fifty-four previous arrests. But this time it was different because he now had as his attorney Louis Lusky, a distinguished lawyer with an interest in civil liberties;[7] for a citizen of Louisville, for whose family Thompson had worked for over thirty years, agreed with Thompson that the time had come to put a stop to his harassment by the police, and asked Lusky to defend Thompson.

Lusky's examination of Thompson at the trial brought out that Thompson had bought from a café employee, other than the manager, a dish of macaroni and a glass of beer, and that he remained in the café waiting for a bus to go home; he had with him a bus schedule that showed that a bus was due, about half a block away, at 7:30. He had money with him at the time of his arrest. He owned two lots of land; for over thirty years he had worked one or more days a week for the same family, and worked as well for others at odd jobs; he paid no rent for the house where he lived, and his meager income was sufficient to meet his needs. The café manager testified that Thompson had frequently patronized the café and that he had never told him that he was not welcome; that he had seen Thompson in the middle of the floor tapping his foot—Thompson had put a coin in the juke box—and had no objection to anything he was doing; and there was no testimony that any patron had objected to anything Thompson had done.

The judge found Thompson guilty on both charges—loitering and disorderly conduct—and fined him $10 on each charge. Since in Kentucky police-court fines of less than $20 on a single charge are not appealable or otherwise reviewable, Thompson took his case directly to the United States Supreme Court. The Court, impressed that the constitutional questions were substantial, granted certiorari. (Perhaps this was the first time since 1886 that the Court had agreed to review a case so trivial from the monetary point of view; in that year it decided the famous case *Yick Wo* v. *Hopkins*,[8] which involved a $10 fine.)

On the oral argument before the Supreme Court, the attorney for the city of Louisville was asked about one of the reasons for Thompson's arrest, namely, that "he could not give a satisfactory account of himself." Justice Frankfurter asked: "Would it not have been within Thompson's constitutional rights to tell the interrogating officer, 'It's none of your business what I'm doing'?" The attorney had no answer.

On the disorderly conduct charge, the municipal attorney was asked to explain how an argument with a police officer warranted arrest and conviction. "Do you really put a man in jail for arguing with a police officer?" Chief Justice Warren asked. Justice Brennan wanted to know at what point an argument becomes disorderly conduct. "Any argument tends to lead to disorder," the attorney said. "You are making an argument now, aren't you?" asked Justice Brennan. "Do you see any signs of disorder?"

The Court, obviously interested in the case and its implications, allowed more time for questioning and argument than was permitted by the rules and then, by unanimous decision, reversed the convictions.

The city ordinance under which Thompson was charged provides:

It shall be unlawful for any person . . ., without visible means of support, or who cannot give a satisfactory account of himself, . . . to sleep, lie, loaf, or trespass in or about any premises, building or other structure in the City of Louisville, without first having obtained the consent of the owner. . . .

The Court's opinion, written by Justice Black, pointed out the inapplicability of the terms of the ordinance to the facts in the case on the charge of loitering. The record was "entirely lacking in evidence to support" this charge. Regarding the other charge, Justice Black said that merely "arguing" with a policeman could not possibly constitute "disorderly conduct." As a matter of fact, he said, under Kentucky law a person, unless he objects to his arrest, waives the right to complain later that the arrest was unlawful. The Court concluded that it was "a violation of due process to convict and punish a man without evidence of his guilt."

Quite apart from the important use of the decision in the later sit-in cases that we shall soon consider, the Thompson case is important for shaking the constitutional basis of the countless statutes and ordinances that make it a crime *to be* a loiterer, a loafer, a vagrant, a disorderly person, a tramp—offenses "defined in terms of *being* rather than in terms of *acting*"[9]—a problem that we discussed in Chapter IV, where we were concerned with the attempt to make *being* a Communist a criminal offense.

In a case before the Supreme Court in 1953,[10] in a dissenting opinion Justice Black called the Court's attention to the fact that the defendant in that case had been convicted in California for *being* a "dissolute" person. The trial judge had charged the jury that the defendant was not accused of any particular act but of being a person of "a certain status," for "vagrancy [a dissolute person was a vagrant under the California vagrancy statute] is a status or a condition and it is not an act." He said:

One is guilty of being a vagrant at any time and place where he is found, so long as the character remains unchanged, although then and there innocent of any act demonstrating his character. . . . His character, as I said before, is the ultimate question for you to decide.

The defendant was given a ninety-day jail sentence after a trial in which the state's witnesses made it clear that they did not like what he had said in many speeches he had made in a Los Angeles park, in which he discussed political and economic questions and made attacks on the local police force—speeches that were involved in the vagrancy prosecution.

Prosecutions such as these, based on a crime of status or condition rather than acts, which was the essence of the grievance against Sam Thompson and the defendant in the California case—men of "bad character" in the eyes of the police, though no criminality attached to what they *did*—are disposed of unceremoniously by the thousands in American city or police courts, and there is no outcry over them, and there is no Louis Lusky to take them to the Supreme Court.

Yet Americans showed interest when a similar case somehow leaked out of Russia. Early in 1964 Iosif Brodsky[11] was sentenced in Leningrad to five years at hard labor for being a "parasite" and writing and reading in public his own "decadent" poetry. At the trial the prosecutor wanted to know how Brodsky could live and buy clothing on his scanty earnings as a poet and translator, and especially since for four months (out of some seven years) he had not worked at all. Brodsky said: "I live very modestly. I have one old suit and it's enough for me." His attorney pleaded: "He is not a vagrant. He has a permanent home and he can be reached at any time." A defense witness argued:

The law under which Brodsky was brought to trial, namely, Paragraph 22 about vagrancy, was directed against people who work too little, no against those who earn little. . . . You cannot call a parasite a man who works with such fervor and tenacity as Brodsky does, but who is not concerned about the amount of his earnings. He lives very modestly. . . .

Let us now trace the effect of *Thompson* v. *Louisville* on the sit-in cases.

The school-segregation cases[12] were decided in 1954. One evening in December 1955—a year and a half later—Mrs. Rosa Parks, a Negro seamstress, took a seat near the front in a section reserved for whites on a bus in Montgomery, Alabama. A white passenger got on. The bus driver told Mrs. Parks to get up and give the seat to the white man. She refused, was arrested, and ordered to appear for trial five days later. The charge was violation of the segregation laws. The next night leaders of the Negro community—Montgomery had some fifty thousand Negroes—met in the Baptist church to which Mrs. Parks belonged and of which Martin Luther King, Jr., was minister, and a few days later the historic bus boycott got under way. It lasted for more than a year. Normally Negroes comprised 65 per cent of the bus passengers, and for over a year the buses rode through the streets of Montgomery almost empty as Negroes walked, took taxis, or rode in the automobiles of a three-hundred-car pool. The response to Dr. King's plea for nonviolent direct action was an extraordinary manifestation of sustained discipline on a mass scale.

While the direct protest action was on, the Montgomery Negroes went to court, in a case that involved another Negro woman who had refused to move to the rear of the bus to a section segregated for Negro passengers. In November 1956 the Supreme Court held that bus segregation was unconstitutional.[13] No doubt the legal outcome would have been the same even if there had been no Montgomery bus boycott, but the Negro would not have been the same; for the Montgomery movement, under Dr. King's leadership, assumed transcendent ends. A Negro woman in Montgomery was asked how she could walk four miles to work every day, month after month. Her answer became the title of Montgomery's freedom song: "My feet is tired but my soul is rested."[14] The direct action freed the Negro from fear, gave him well-earned self-respect and self-reliance, and dramatized for the whole world the Negro's struggle for freedom, equality, and justice.

The meaning of the Montgomery bus boycott was grasped only tentatively and superficially at first. In 1958 high-school units of the N.A.A.C.P. in Oklahoma City launched a campaign of sit-in demonstrations to secure service at lunch counters in chain stores. By 1960 fifty-six eating places in the city were opened to Negroes. The idea of nonviolent direct action against lunch-counter segregation spread to other cities in Oklahoma and Kansas.[15] In April 1959 twenty Negro and white students, members of the Congress of Racial Equality (CORE), sat down at Grant's lunch counter in Miami, Florida, and continued to sit there after they were refused service. The sit-in campaign continued until August 1960, by which time all dime-store lunch counters were open to all customers regardless of color.[16] Important as these demonstrations were, they were only local skirmishes.

It was at Greensboro, North Carolina, in 1960, that a student sit-in set off a movement that achieved importance next only to Montgomery's bus boycott. Anthony Lewis reported on what happened there:

On January 31, 1960, a Negro college freshman in Greensboro, North Carolina, Joseph McNeill, tried to get something to eat at the bus terminal in downtown Greensboro. Like other Negroes at lunch counters throughout the South and through much of the border area, he was turned down: We do not serve Negroes. But the humiliation that so many others had experienced for so long this time set off a spark.

That night, in his dormitory, McNeill asked his roommate, Ezell Blair, Jr., "What can we do?" Then he answered his own question: "Let's have a boycott. We should go in and ask to be served and sit there until they do."

The next day McNeill, Blair and two of their classmates, David Richmond and Franklin McCain, sat down at the lunch counter in Woolworth's. When they were not served, they continued to sit there. When they finally left after several hours, they had still not had a cup of coffee, but they did not feel let down.[17]

They returned to Woolworth's the next morning, and *The New York Times* and other newspapers began to take note. By the fourth day the four students had been joined by others from the area, and

outside of Greensboro the power of what they were doing began to be recognized. Other students sat at other lunch counters, and a movement was born. It was an extraordinary movement, displaying as really nothing else had the suffering in the soul of the Negro. When young people, without money or influence, risked literally everything to demonstrate for equal treatment as human beings, it was impossible for the South to talk convincingly about "outside agitators" or northern politicians or the Supreme Court as the source of the "trouble."[18]

Greensboro, Louis Lomax wrote, "happened by itself; nobody planned it, nobody pulled any strings. Negro students simply got tired and sat down."[19] As white opposition increased, the students called for help, and the N.A.A.C.P. and CORE sent their representatives, and Dr. King left Montgomery and came to Greensboro, and a national movement was born.

Surely the award of the Nobel Peace Prize to Dr. King four years later was meant to embrace symbolically also the tired seamstress of Montgomery and the four Negro students of Greensboro who "simply got tired and sat down."

It took just six months to open the [lunch] counter at Woolworth's in Greensboro to all races. Hundreds of other stores began serving Negroes by the end of 1960 and hundreds more in succeeding years.[20]

A great deal of respectability was added to the sit-in movement when John F. Kennedy, in a campaign speech at Los Angeles on September 9, 1960, told the American people that the President should use the force of his office "to help bring about equal access to public facilities —from churches to lunch counters—and to support the right of every American to stand up for his rights—even if that means sitting down for them."[21] Three years later—in a televised speech on the night of June 11, 1963, the day on which Governor George C. Wallace stood in front of the door to prevent two Negro students from entering to register at the University of Alabama—President Kennedy said to the nation:

If an American, because his skin is dark, cannot eat lunch in a restaurant open to the public; . . . if, in short, he cannot enjoy the full and free life which all of us want, then who among us would be content to have the color of his skin changed and stand in his place? . . . Are we to say to the world—and much more importantly, to each other—that this is the land of the free, except for the Negroes . . .? We face, therefore, a moral crisis as a country and a people.[22]

But the country faced also a legal, constitutional crisis, for there were many hundreds of sit-ins,[23] participated in by tens of thousands of demonstrators, and thousands were arrested. Were the sit-ins legal, or were thousands of Negroes (and some whites) to be branded as criminals and sent to jail? Local judges imposed jail sentences and fines, the state courts of last resort upheld the convictions, and at the end of 1961 the first sit-in cases reached the Supreme Court.[24]

The first cases came up from Louisiana and were decided by the Supreme Court, in December 1961, in *Garner* v. *Louisiana*.[25] Because the cases varied only slightly on the facts, the Court consolidated them and disposed of them in one opinion.

They all involved lunch-counter demonstrations in Baton Rouge. A typical situation was the following: Seven Negro college students went to the Kress Department Store, where Negroes were welcome as customers, except that the lunch counter was segregated. They took seats at the white counter. The store manager, who was also seated there, told the waitress to tell the Negroes that they could be served at the counter across the aisle. She did. They remained in their places, quietly. The manager finished his lunch and telephoned the police, saying that some Negroes were seated at the white counter. The police came and ordered the students to leave. When they showed no signs of complying, they were arrested and taken to the police station, where they were charged with disturbance of the peace. They were tried and convicted and sentenced to four months' imprisonment, three months of which would be suspended upon payment of a $100 fine by each. The state supreme court upheld the convictions.

The state's law under which the students were convicted provided as follows:

Disturbing the peace is the doing of any of the following in such a manner as would foreseeably disturb or alarm the public:
   (1) Engaging in a fistic encounter; or
   (2) Using of any unnecessarily loud, offensive, or insulting language; or
   (3) Appearing in an intoxicated condition; or
   (4) Engaging in any act in a violent and tumultuous manner by any three or more persons; or
   (5) Holding of an unlawful assembly; or
   (6) Interruption of any lawful assembly of people; or
   (7) Commission of any other act in such a manner as to unreasonably disturb or alarm the public.

The state could not, by 1960 or 1961, charge the students with violation of any statute or ordinance *compelling* racial segregation; for by then it was absolutely clear that racial segregation *commanded by law* was unconstitutional. It was, therefore, necessary to charge the sit-in demonstrators with the violation of some other law, and the statutes punishing "disturbing the peace" were resorted to in hundreds of arrests.

In the Garner case the Supreme Court looked at other cases in which the Louisiana supreme court had construed the statute, and found that the provisions were not intended to punish peaceful conduct. Acting "in such a manner as would foreseeably disturb or alarm the public" meant "conduct which is violent or boisterous in itself, or which is provocative in the sense that it induces a foreseeable physical disturbance." For example, in a Louisiana case, the evidence was that thirty Jehovah's Witnesses approached a town to distribute their literature and solicit contributions. They were warned by the mayor and the police that their presence would cause trouble and were asked to stay out. They entered the town and stopped passers-by on a street. For this they were convicted under the statute; but the state supreme court reversed the convictions for breach of the peace, holding that they had not committed any unlawful act or pursued any disorderly course of conduct which would tend to disturb the peace. This earlier decision of the state's court was summarized by Chief Justice Warren for the Supreme Court in the Garner case in this significant language:

That peaceful conduct, even though conceivably offensive to another class of the public, is not conduct which may be proscribed by Louisiana's disturbance of the peace statute without evidence that the actor conducted himself in some outwardly unruly manner.

Chief Justice Warren said that the facts in the Garner case and the other cases which were consolidated with it showed that the students "not only made no speeches, they did not even speak to anyone except to order food; they carried no placards, and did nothing, beyond their mere presence at the lunch counter, to attract attention to themselves or to others." Citing the Thompson case, the Court held that since there was no evidence of the students' guilt, their convictions for breach of the peace deprived them of due process of law.

The Warren opinion brought out a number of interesting facts, which appeared also in other lunch-counter sit-in cases:

(1) No one connected with the business establishment had asked the students to leave the counter or the store.

This is understandable, for Negroes were consumers and customers, and the owners were therefore anxious not to insult or antagonize the students and through such conduct lose the trade of the Negro community. Often in such cases there was not even a *refusal* to serve, but only a *failure* to serve; for the stores did not want the Negro community to feel that segregation was the company's own policy, which it aggressively enforced. Therefore, the management acted politely, almost as if it only failed to act.

An important circumstance was also the fact that the stores were often part of a national chain. The company had no desire to stir up a Negro boycott of its stores in the North—or anywhere—so its employees tried hard to avoid giving Negroes any offense. Tied in with this consideration was the existence of some pressure on the company from stockholders, who either had some sympathy for the students' movement or were reluctant to see the company hazard a loss in business.

(2) In the Kress case the manager telephoned the police, but he did not file charges against the students. In the other cases no one connected with the company called the police; others notified the police. In all the Baton Rouge cases the same police officers came to arrest the students in all the demonstrations. Apparently this was their special assignment.

These circumstances show that the stores tried not to associate themselves closely with the police action, so as not to antagonize the Negro community.

But the lack of prosecuting zeal on the part of the owners also shows that they did not think that there was *in fact* a disturbance of the peace. There was a similar circumstance in the Thompson case, where no one connected with the café complained against Sam Thompson. The police action against him was the policemen's own benevolent inspiration; they saw him in the café and proceeded to arrest him. The café was a private business; the lunch counters were in privately owned stores. Whose peace was breached when the police made the arrests?

The decision in the Garner case was unanimous, though Justices Frankfurter, Douglas, and Harlan each wrote concurring opinions. While this was obviously a civil rights case, it was also obviously a free-speech case; for the students who occupied the seats at the lunch counter were there to *protest* against the policy of racial segregation and to *plead,* by their action, for a change of heart. The purpose of nonviolent resistance, Dr. King has written,[26] is to work on the conscience of the opponents. "It is the method," he wrote,

which seeks to implement just law by appealing to the conscience of the great decent majority who through blindness, fear, pride or irrationality have allowed their consciences to sleep. . . . We will not obey unjust laws or submit to unjust practices. We will do this peacefully, openly, cheerfully—because our aim is to persuade. . . . We will try to persuade with our words—but if our words fail we will persuade with our acts.

The fact is that, according to the Department of Justice, in 1963 alone lunch counters were desegregated in over three hundred cities; and in almost as many cities hotels and theaters were desegregated;[27] and this came to pass before Congress enacted the Civil Rights Act of 1964. The Tuskegee Institute reported that the Chamber of Commerce n at least five cities in the South in 1963 exerted influence on city officials and on business firms to end segregated service, and that in hat year eating facilities were desegregated in almost every Southern tate.[28] The Southern Regional Council reported that during a thirty-day period in the summer of 1963 at least fifty cities and towns in the South made some changes in racial segregation practices; and *The New York Times* reported that Negroes were especially pleased with he changes that were effected at that time in Birmingham:

Lunch counters and other facilities in many downtown department and variety stores have been desegregated. Negroes have been promoted to other than menial positions and still others have been hired. City officials have reopened public parks on a desegregated basis.[29]

In the light of the impressive record of success that desegregation achieved *without the aid of legislation,* can there be any doubt that he Negro demonstrations were a form of speech or assembly—an exercise of First Amendment freedoms, whether they were in the orm of a march to the State House grounds, as in the Edwards case, or in the form of a lunch-counter sit-in, as in the Garner case?

This aspect of the sit-ins was not touched on by the Chief Justice, but the reversal of the convictions by a unanimous Supreme Court must have been read by Negroes as an implied legitimization of the sit-ins as a peaceful form of speech or assembly. Had the convictions been affirmed, the jails and prisons in the South would have been too small to hold all the demonstrators, and the decision would have been a blow to civil rights, but no less to freedom of speech and assembly.

In his concurring opinion, Justice Frankfurter touched on the speech element, but only tangentially. He said: "It is not fanciful speculation . . . that a proprietor who invites trade in most parts of his establishment and restricts it in another may change his policy when non-violently challenged." But Justice Harlan's concurring opinion did go into this aspect of the Garner case. There was more to the conduct of the students, he said,

han a bare desire to remain at the "white" lunch counter. . . . Such a demonstration . . . is as much a part of the "free trade in ideas" . . . as is verbal expression, more commonly thought of as "speech." It, like speech, appeals to good sense and to "the power of reason as applied through public discussion," . . . just as much as, if not more than, a public oration delivered from a soapbox at a street corner. This Court has never limited the right to speak . . . to mere verbal expression. . . . If the act of displaying a red flag as a symbol of opposition to organized government is a liberty encompassed within free speech . . . , the act of sitting at a privately owned lunch counter with the [implied] consent of the owner as a demonstration of opposition to enforced segregation, is surely withi the same range of protections.

A half-year later the Court had before it the Taylor case, whicl developed out of the "freedom ride" launched in 1961.[30] Fou Negroes went into the white waiting room at a Louisiana bus termina to take a bus to Mississippi. The chief of police asked them to go int the colored waiting room. When they refused, they—and two othe Negroes waiting in a car outside—were arrested and charged witl violation of the breach of the peace statute. They were given fines an jail terms. In a *per curiam* opinion, the Supreme Court pointed ou that, as in the Garner case,

There was no evidence of violence. The record shows that the petitioner were quiet, orderly, and polite.

The convictions were reversed.[31]

From the standpoint of the purpose of the Negroes' actions, ther was no essential difference between Negroes' sitting at a white luncl counter waiting to be served and their entering a white waiting roon to wait for a bus. In each instance their purpose was to "demon strate": to protest and to appeal for a change in attitude and conduct

So, too, in *Wright* v. *Georgia*,[32] decided in 1963, in which th Court considered the conviction of six Negroes under Georgia' breach of the peace statute. These young Negroes had gone into public park in Savannah one afternoon in 1961 and played on basketball court. The only trouble with their innocent play was tha the park was for whites only. A woman who saw them called th police. The officers ordered the boys to leave. When they refused, the were arrested. They were charged with assembling "for the purpos of disturbing the public peace" and not dispersing at the comman of the police. They were convicted, and five were sentenced to pa a fine of $100 or serve five months in prison; the sixth boy was fine $125 or given six months in prison. The Georgia supreme cour affirmed.

In the light of the Garner and Taylor cases, the Supreme Court had no difficult time in unanimously reversing the judgments.

2. The Clear and Present Danger Doctrine

In the Wright case it was contended that the boys were guilty of breach of the peace because their being in the park was likely to cause a breach of the peace by others—white persons who might react violently. Said the Court: "The possibility of disorder by others cannot justify exclusion of persons from a place if they otherwise have a constitutional right . . . to be present." The police had made the same point in the lunch-counter sit-in cases and in the Taylor (freedom ride) case, and the Court met this argument in its opinions, but only here did it make its point sharply.

The point is crucial in free-speech and -assembly as well as in civil rights cases. May the police justifiably deny to a person his constitutional rights because *other persons* in the community may resort to violence or disorder if he should insist on exercising his rights?

A number of civil rights cases, apart from those of Garner, Taylor, and Wright, have contributed toward an answer to this sticky problem. Its importance calls for our consideration of these precedents.

Following the decision in the school-segregation cases of 1954, the school board of Little Rock, Arkansas, formulated a school-desegregation program which was judicially approved as compliance with the decision in these cases. Then the governor and the legislature of Arkansas took the position that the state was not bound by the Supreme Court decision, and the Little Rock school board applied to the federal district court for leave to suspend its desegregation program for two and a half years, and the court granted this petition. The Supreme Court, in *Cooper* v. *Aaron*,[33] unanimously reversed the judgment.

Now, the school board's petition for postponement rested on the ground that extreme public hostility, engendered largely by the official attitudes and actions of the governor and legislature, had made implementation of the board's desegregation program impossible. The Supreme Court, in refusing to suspend the board's plan, said (in an opinion by Chief Justice Warren for all the Justices):

The constitutional rights of respondents are not to be sacrificed or yielded to the violence and disorder which have followed upon the actions of the Governor and Legislature. As this Court said some 41 years ago in a unanimous opinion in a case involving another aspect of racial segregation [by a zoning ordinance]: "It is urged that this proposed segregation will promote the public peace by preventing race conflicts. Desirable as this is, and important as is the preservation of the public peace, this aim cannot be accomplished by laws or ordinances which deny rights created or protected by the Federal Constitution." *Buchanan* v. *Warley,* 245 U. S. 60 [1917]. Thus law and order are not here to be preserved by depriving the Negro children of their constitutional rights.

While Justice Frankfurter joined in the Chief Justice's opinion, he wrote a concurring opinion in which he argued that to approve the school board's petition would mean that the law was bowing to force. "To yield to such a claim," he said, "would be to enthrone official lawlessness, and lawlessness if not checked is the precursor of anarchy. . . . Violent resistance to law cannot be made a legal reason for its suspension without loosening the fabric of our society."

The Court in *Cooper* v. *Aaron* shed no tears over the plight of Arkansas, for it was the government of the state that had created the difficulties faced by the Little Rock school board. Arkansas was in the position of the man who had murdered his parents and then pleaded for mercy as an orphan. Is the principle of the case limited to such a situation—i.e., that the rights of the Negroes are not to be sacrificed or postponed because of threatened violence or disorder by whites *if the state has fomented or substantially contributed to the threatened dangers*? This seems to be the holding of *Cooper* v. *Aaron*.

But the Court quoted from *Buchanan* v. *Warley,* in which the Court in 1917 had held unconstitutional a municipal ordinance which established separate residential districts for Negroes and whites. The rationale of the ordinance was that it would promote racial peace. The Court held that racial peace may not be acquired by the denial of constitutional rights. There was nothing in that case to show that the state or city had created the racial unrest that was to be undone by the racial zoning law.

We know from tragic events all over the country what may happen when a Negro family decides on a "dwell-in" demonstration at a location where the reaction of the neighbors is summarized in the phrase: "But not next door!" The racial zoning ordinance that was before the Court in *Buchanan* v. *Warley* was adopted by Louisville to prevent racial conflicts caused when Negroes move into white areas.[34] In holding the ordinance unconstitutional, the Court said:

That there exists a serious and difficult problem arising from a feeling of race hostility which the law is powerless to control, and to which it must give a measure of consideration, may be freely admitted. But its solution cannot be promoted by depriving citizens of their constitutional rights and privileges.

No one now can argue that the police can charge a Negro with a criminal offense because he refuses to abandon his home in order to satisfy or placate a hostile neighbor or a mob. Should the rule be different when the Negro is in a bus terminal waiting for a bus, or in a public park playing ball, or at a lunch counter—whether he is engaged in a peaceful, orderly "freedom ride," or sit-in, or kneel-in, or wade-in, or play-in?

In 1963 the Supreme Court had before it the case of *Watson* v. *Memphis*,[35] in which Negro residents of the city of Memphis had brought an action in 1960 to desegregate public parks and public recreational facilities from which Negroes were excluded. The city did not try to justify segregation but only urged "the need and wisdom of proceeding slowly and gradually in its desegregation efforts." The lower federal courts agreed with the city and ordered it to submit, within six months, a plan for gradual desegregation. The Supreme Court unanimously reversed.

In the Court's opinion by Justice Goldberg it was pointed out that the case was before the Court nine years after the decision in *Brown* v. *Board of Education* and eight years after the Court had applied the principle of the Brown decision to public recreational facilities.[36]

In the Brown decision the Court did not immediately frame a decree that all public schools be desegregated at once. The Court recognized that a local school board may have complex problems arising from the physical condition of the school plant, the school transportation system, personnel, revision of school districts, and similar circumstances, and so it laid down the guidelines for the lower courts and directed that desegregation must proceed with "all deliberate speed."[37] Justice Goldberg recalled, however, that the Court in that case expressly excluded delay in desegregation because of disagreement with the Supreme Court's decision. "Hostility to the constitutional precepts underlying the original decision [in *Brown*]," said Justice Goldberg, were "expressly and firmly" excluded as a delaying or postponing factor.

Furthermore, in the case of public parks and other recreational facilities, the difficulties connected with schools are absent. Significantly, Justice Goldberg said the following—for a unanimous Court:

Most importantly, of course, it must be recognized that even the delay countenanced by *Brown* was a necessary, albeit significant, adaptation of the usual principle that any deprivation of constitutional rights calls for prompt rectification. The rights here asserted are, like all such rights, *present* rights; they are not merely hopes to some *future* enjoyment of some formalistic constitutional promise. The basic guarantees of our Constitution are warrants for the here and now and, unless there is an overwhelmingly compelling reason, they are to be promptly fulfilled. . . .

The claims of the city to further delay . . . cannot be upheld except upon the most convincing and impressive demonstration by the city that such delay is manifestly compelled by constitutionally cognizable circumstances warranting the exercise of an appropriate equitable discretion by a court. In short, the city must sustain an extremely heavy burden of proof.

The Court held that this burden had not been sustained by the city.

The city contended that gradual desegregation was necessary "to prevent interracial disturbances, violence, riots, and community confusion and turmoil." The Court said simply and emphatically:

The compelling answer to this contention is that constitutional rights may not be denied simply because of hostility to their assertion or exercise. See *Wright* v. *Georgia* . . .; *Brown* v. *Board of Education* . . .; *Talyor* v. *Louisiana.* . . .

And the Court quoted from *Cooper* v. *Aaron* and *Buchanan* v. *Warley* some of the passages that we have quoted above, and concluded that the "controlling principle" is that "constitutional rights are to be promptly vindicated."

The cases we have thus far considered all arose in a civil rights context; but the basic principles are not limited by this circumstance. These principles have been applied, though with less clear articulation, in free-speech and freedom-of-assembly situations that were not meshed with racial segregation.

Consider, for example, the interesting situation in *Terminiello* v. *Chicago*,[38] decided in 1949. Arthur Terminiello, a Catholic priest under suspension by his bishop, came from Birmingham to Chicago to address a gathering, under the auspices of Christian Veterans of America, on "Christian Nationalism or World Communism—Which?" One of the sponsors of the meeting was Gerald L. K. Smith, leader of the anti-Semitic Christian Nationalist Crusade. The auditorium was filled to capacity with over eight hundred people. Some were turned away. Outside, a crowd of about a thousand persons gathered to protest against the meeting—a crowd that was "angry and turbulent." A cordon of policemen tried to maintain order, but there were several disturbances. Police escorted Terminiello into the building through the pickets and crowd. There were police officers inside near the stage and at the back door. The crowd broke about twenty-eight windows. About seventeen persons of the group outside were arrested.

In his long speech Terminiello referred to the crowd outside as "scum"; he said that the twelve years of the New Deal were the build-up for the power of Communists of all shades; that the mob outside wanted a Communist revolution; that Eleanor Roosevelt was a Comnunist; that Franco was "the savior of what was left of Europe." He attacked "Zionist Jews" and asked: "Do you wonder they were persecuted in other countries in the world?" "I speak," he said, "of the Communistic Zionistic Jew, and those are not American Jews. We don't want them here; we want them to go back where they came from."

Members of the audience shouted their approval with such outcries of: "Yes, send the Jews back to Russia!" and "Kill the Jews!"

Terminiello was arrested and charged with breach of the peace. He was tried before a jury, which received the following instruction from the trial judge:

Misbehavior may constitute a breach of the peace if it stirs the public to anger, invites dispute, brings about a condition of unrest, or creates a disturbance, or if it molests the inhabitants in the enjoyment of peace and quiet by arousing alarm.

He was found guilty, and the appellate courts of Illinois affirmed.

The Supreme Court, by 5 to 4, reversed the judgment. The reason for the reversal was one that made it unnecessary for the majority opinion, written by Justice Douglas, to go into the facts of the case; it found the charge to the jury, as set forth above, an unconstitutional restriction on free speech. The instruction was an authoritative construction of the ordinance under which Terminiello was convicted. But an ordinance written in these terms would be clearly unconstitutional.

If changes in our government or society are to be brought about peacefully, there must be, said Justice Douglas, free debate, free exchange of ideas. "Accordingly," he said,

a function of free speech under our system of government is to invite dispute. It may indeed best serve its high purpose when it induces a condition of unrest, creates dissatisfaction with conditions as they are, or even stirs people to anger. Speech is often provocative and challenging. It may strike at prejudices and preconceptions and have profound unsettling effects as it presses for acceptance of an idea. That is why freedom of speech, though not absolute, . . . is nevertheless protected against censorship or punishment, unless shown likely to produce a clear and present danger of a serious substantive evil that rises far above public inconvenience, annoyance, or unrest.

The majority of the Justices, looking not at the facts but only at the charge to the jury, said:

The ordinance as construed by the trial court seriously invaded this province [of free speech]. It permitted conviction of petitioner if his speech stirred people to anger, invited public dispute, or brought about a condition of unrest. A conviction resting on any of those grounds may not stand.

The Court's position in this case, and its position in the civil rights demonstration cases considered in this chapter, is one and the same: persons may speak, demonstrate, protest, or otherwise assert their First Amendment freedom of speech or assembly, without regard to the possibility that others may resent their action or become distressed or annoyed or even be stirred to anger. This is what the First Amendment guarantees, whether free speech or assembly is enjoyed through a sit-in demonstration at a lunch counter, a march to the state-house grounds, a freedom ride on a bus, a play-in in a public park, or an intemperate harangue. Just as public hostility cannot prevent, or even delay, desegregation, so, too, it may not be a basis for denial of a First Amendment freedom. Just as racial peace may not be achieved by depriving Negroes of their constitutional rights and privileges, so, too, social or communal peace may not be achieved by depriving some persons—regardless of the reasons for their unpopularity—of their constitutional rights and privileges. For constitutional rights are "*present* rights; they are not merely hopes to some *future* enjoyment of some formalistic constitutional promise." Negroes cannot be punished as disorderly persons if, by exercising their constitutional rights, they "invite dispute," or induce "a condition of unrest," or create "dissatisfaction," or even stir people "to anger"; nor can a speaker be punished if his talk has any of these effects.

Under a desegregation plan approved by a federal court, a few Negro children were to be admitted to Central High School in Little Rock, Arkansas, in September 1957. On September 23 some five hundred persons gathered near the school. They shouted and talked and acted like an unruly mob asking for a fight. Six Negro girls and three Negro boys arrived and entered the school. The crowd surged toward the school building but was held back by police officers. By ten o'clock the crowd had grown to a thousand persons, and by noon it had become even greater, and it ignored the police. Shortly after noon the Negro pupils were taken out through a side door and were escorted in police cars to their homes. No attempt was made on the next day to get the children to the school. President Eisenhower then ordered a thousand paratroopers to Little Rock and placed ten thousand members of the Arkansas National Guard on federal service to keep the mob from depriving the nine Negro children of their rightful places in the Central High School schoolrooms. It was the first time since Reconstruction that federal troops had been in the South to protect the rights of Negroes. On Wednesday, September 25, the nine Negro pupils were back in school, the mob was dispersed, and paratroopers patrolled the school. Some soldiers remained at the school the whole of that school year.[39] When the school board went to court to ask for a delay of the desegregation plan, they were told by a unanimous Supreme Court, as we have seen, that "Law and order are not here to be preserved by depriving the Negro children of their constitutional rights."

A similar drama was enacted in September 1962, when President Kennedy called into federal service Mississippi's National Guard and dispatched troops to assure the admission of James H. Meredith into the University of Mississippi. Meredith was driven to the campus in a convoy of automobiles and military trucks, and on the campus he was protected by three hundred federal marshals and a large force of state troopers carrying riot clubs and tear-gas cartridges. Students on the campus rioted against the federal marshals, and cars filled with whites came onto the grounds and moved in against the marshals. Federalized Guardsmen and regular Army units arrived to help. Two men were killed, however, before the armed forces arrived. The riot lasted fifteen hours. The next day 5000 soldiers and Guardsmen were in Oxford, Mississippi, a town with a population of 6500, but Meredith attended the university, and his safety was protected by federal troopers and marshals who remained on the campus.[40]

The facts concerning Little Rock and the University of Mississippi have been recalled here because they give substance and meaning to the proposition that public order is not to be preserved by calling on Negroes to forfeit their constitutional rights. In the light of what the federal government accomplished by its vigorous actions in these two instances, it is difficult to imagine a situation that would be an exception to the constitutional rule, an exception justified by "an overwhelmingly compelling reason"—to use the phrase from Justice Goldberg's opinion in *Watson* v. *Memphis*.

The same approach would, it seems, be taken if the exercise of religious liberty were imperiled by a showing or threat of public hostility. Suppose, for example, a community were up in anger to prevent a religious service in a church or synagogue because of its hatred for the religion or sect. The federal government would then need to use force to protect the worshipers, just as it protected the Negro high-school pupils and Meredith.

Would the government have the same duty to insure the safety of

Terminiello if a mob were to prevent him from speaking at a meeting of his followers? Would it be constitutionally necessary to provide him with armed protection so that he might exercise his freedom of speech and his followers their freedom of assembly and of speech?

The Court did not, as we have seen, go into the facts in the Terminiello case, but the majority opinion, by Justice Douglas, did state that freedom of speech is protected "unless shown likely to produce a clear and present danger of a serious substantive evil that rises far above public inconvenience, annoyance, or unrest." Now, a riotous mob, as in Little Rock or at the University of Mississippi, threatens physical violence and endangers property and life. Such consequences rise, one would say, "far above public inconvenience, annoyance, or unrest." The Terminiello decision leaves the door open to censorship (prior restraint) or punishment where the speech creates a clear and present danger of such consequences.

But, under the precedents, such action may be taken against the speaker only if it is shown that *he* was at fault *because of the character of his speech*. If Terminiello, though notorious for his racist and anti-Semitic views, were to do nothing more than read to his audience the Declaration of Independence or a half-dozen Psalms, he could not be punished, though a mob outside the meeting hall rioted because he was in there speaking. Constitutionally, then, the character of a speech is crucial.

It was on this point that several Justices dissented in the Terminiello case. Chief Justice Vinson argued that the Illinois courts did not have before them the judge's instructions to the jury as an issue, and that the Illinois courts had construed the Chicago ordinance as punishing only the use of "fighting words" used by a speaker. Justice Jackson's dissenting opinion (with which Justices Frankfurter and Burton agreed, in varying degrees) went extensively into the facts and contended that the Illinois courts had not been concerned with abstract conceptions but "with a riot and with a speech that provoked a hostile mob [outside] and incited a friendly one [inside the auditorium], and threatened violence between the two." According to Justice Jackson, the trial judge in his instruction "was saying to the jury, in effect, that if this particular speech added fuel to the situation already so inflamed as to threaten to get beyond police control, it could be punished as inducing a breach of peace." Terminiello's speech, said Justice Jackson, was made in a context of violence and disorder, and in that context it was "a provocation to immediate breach of the peace," and was therefore not entitled to constitutional immunity from punishment.

Justice Jackson, like Justice Douglas, referred to the test of a clear and present danger. He said:

Rioting is a substantive evil, which I take it no one will deny that the State and the City have the right and the duty to prevent and punish. Where an offense is induced by speech, the Court has laid down and often reiterated a test of the power of the authorities to deal with the speaking as also an offense. "The question in every case is whether the words *used are used in such circumstances* and are of *such a nature* as to create *a clear and present danger* that they will bring about the substantive evils that Congress [or the State or City] has a right to prevent." [Emphasis supplied.] Mr. Justice Holmes in *Schenck* v. *United States,* 249 U. S. 47 [1919]. No one ventures to contend that the State on the basis of this test . . . was not justified in punishing Terminiello.

According to Justice Jackson, the evidence proved beyond dispute that there was a "clear, present and immediate danger" of rioting and violence "in response to the speech."

To give a proper constitutional evaluation of Terminiello's speech, it is necessary to bear in mind that the First Amendment does not protect "fighting words." The basic precedent on this point is *Chaplinsky* v. *New Hampshire,*[41] in which Justice Murphy—as we noted in Chapter V—said for a unanimous Court:

There are certain well-defined and narrowly limited classes of speech, the prevention and punishment of which have never been thought to raise any Constitutional problem. These include the lewd and obscene, the profane, the libelous, and the insulting or "fighting" words—those which by their very utterance inflict injury or tend to incite an immediate breach of the peace.

The rationale for the exclusion of these classes of speech from the protection of the First Amendment was, again in the words of Justice Murphy, that

such utterances are no essential part of any exposition of ideas, and are of such slight social value as a step to truth that any benefit that may be derived from them is clearly outweighed by the social interest in order and morality.

Chaplinsky was punished under a statute of New Hampshire which, as construed by the state courts, prohibited a person from calling another person, in a public place, by any offensive or derisive name—the use of such words as would lead ordinary men to fight, causing a breach of the peace. The Court unanimously upheld the conviction of Chaplinsky for throwing at an officer the epithets "damn racketeer" and "damn Fascist." Such words, spoken to a man on the street, said Justice Murphy, are "likely to provoke the average person to retaliation, and thereby cause a breach of the peace."

Now, said Justice Jackson, Chaplinsky's words were mild in comparison to the epithets which Terminiello "hurled at an already inflamed mob of his adversaries": "slimy scum," "snakes," "bedbugs," and the like.

Justice Jackson was, one can say, right in stating that on the merits the state was justified in punishing Terminiello—if the record showed that his audience included men to whom he referred in fighting words, or that he incited his adherents to attack those outside.

Whether or not the majority was right in avoiding a review of the case on the merits is not a question relevant to our discussion. As the case comes to us, it is illuminating both for the majority decision and opinion and for the dissents.

Several other Supreme Court decisions contribute to an understanding of the problems and their principled resolution. In the 1930s, when the Russellites became Jehovah's Witnesses, and in the 1940s, when their Kingdom Halls could be seen going up in many cities and towns, members of this sect were about as welcome in many communities as were representatives of the Negro civil rights groups in Alabama or Mississippi fifteen or twenty years later. With their talk about the battle of Armageddon and the urgent, immediate need for repentance if sinners were to be saved, with their identifying of government as the work of Satan and their refusal to salute the flag or to bear arms or to participate in the affairs of state or government, and with their vitriolic attacks on all churches and especially the Roman Catholic Church and the Pope, their very presence was often regarded as a "clear and present danger" to our most cherished institutions and their respected symbols. Walter Chaplinsky was a Jehovah's Witness.

So was Jesse Cantwell, who got into trouble in New Haven. On the day of his arrest he was engaged in going from house to house, equipped with books and pamphlets, and with a phonograph and a set of records that described the literature. Cantwell asked the person who responded to his call for permission to play a record. If he received permission, then he offered the book described on the record for a price or a contribution.

Cantwell engaged in missionary work in a neighborhood that was 90 per cent Roman Catholic. He stopped two men on the street and asked for permission to play the record for them. They consented, and he played a record which attacked the Roman Catholic Church and religion. They were both Catholics and were incensed and tempted to strike him unless he collected his wares and went on his way. He left. No insulting words passed between them. Cantwell was arrested and convicted of the common-law offense of inciting a breach of the peace.

The Supreme Court unanimously reversed the judgment.[42] In his opinion for the Court, Justice Owen J. Roberts said that breach of the peace may include words "likely to produce violence in others." Incitement to riot or to physical attack may be punished. "When clear and present danger" of such effects is shown, the speaker may be punished. But here there was no showing that Cantwell had created a clear and present danger. His conduct was not "noisy, truculent, overbearing or offensive." He had no intention to insult or affront his listeners. (On the contrary, he wanted to win them over, to get their willing assent.) What they heard was offensive to them because it was an attack on their religion, but no "profane, indecent, or abusive remarks [were] directed to the person of the hearer." There was no "personal abuse," "no intentional discourtesy," "no truculent bearing." "In the realm of religious faith," said the Court,

and in that of political belief, sharp differences arise. In both fields the tenets of one man may seem the rankest error to his neighbor. To persuade others to his own point of view, the pleader, as we know, at times, resorts to exaggeration, to vilification of men who have been, or are, prominent in church or state, and even to false statement. But the people of this nation have ordained, in the light of history, that, in spite of the probability of excesses and abuses, these liberties are, in the long view, essential to enlightened opinion and right conduct. . . .

The recording played by Cantwell "not unnaturally aroused animosity," but it was not "a clear and present menace to public peace and order."

Cantwell's "speech" could have stirred—to borrow language from the later Terminiello case—listeners to anger or dispute or could have brought about "a condition of unrest," but the speech did not call on listeners to riot or engage in violence or otherwise to act as a riotous, unruly mob; nor did the speech address epithets of personal insult or abuse to the *listeners,* such as "*You* are a damn Fascist" and a "damn racketeer" ("fighting words," as in the Chaplinsky case).

These cases, as we see, are not inconsistent; they fall into an intelligible order.

In the light of the Court's unanimous decisions in the libel cases of

1964—*The New York Times* case and *Garrison* v. *Louisiana*—and in the light of the recent cases on obscenity which we discussed in Chapter V, we can no longer accept Justice Murphy's oft-quoted statement in the Chaplinsky opinion that "certain well-defined and narrowly limited classes of speech" do not raise any constitutional problems. The concept of "breathing space" has altered the Court's view of libel, at least insofar as the defamation relates to official conduct; and it is safe to say that the majority view in the Terminiello case and the Court's decision in the Cantwell case are consistent with and clarified by the "breathing space" doctrine of the Button decision. For freedom to speak or publish the truth can be enjoyed only if one has the freedom to misstate facts, exaggerate events and issues, vilify men and institutions, say things that will make men angry or stir them to dispute —in short, engage in "excesses and abuses." One does not need to say that error has its rights. It is enough if we see that the truth has no rights unless error too has rights. There is wisdom in Pareto's saying: "Give me a fruitful error any time, full of seeds, bursting with its own corrections, and you can keep your sterile truth for yourself." He said this of Kepler, but it applies equally to many others. In 1864 Pope Pius IX made known what he considered the eighty "principal errors" of his time. The eightieth, and greatest, error, he said, was the opinion that the Pope "can and should reconcile himself to and agree with progress, liberalism, and modern civilization." And in the same year he announced his intention to convene the First Vatican Council. But a hundred years later the Second Vatican Council met to achieve a reconciliation between the ancient Church and the modern world. Errors and truths, heresies and orthodoxies, the ugly and beautiful, the "natural" and the "unnatural," the conventional and the new have been seen to change places. The Constitution guarantees that the changes and transitions shall take place peacefully, without violence.

The Clear and Present Danger Doctrine—when coupled with a commitment to the "preferred" position of fundamental liberties and the concept of "breathing space" for these liberties—is sufficient to assure that the changes and transitions will be effected with a minimum of social disruption. The Clear and Present Danger Doctrine standing alone, however, is insufficient to accomplish this end. Standing alone, it can be emasculated, as it was in the Dennis case, or lead to sophistical rationalizations for decisions that in fact deny the fundamental liberties, as in *Schenck* v. *United States,*[43] *Frohwerk* v. *United States,*[44] and *Abrams* v. *United States.*[45] It can be said that in recent years Justice Frankfurter contributed to a downgrading of the doctrine. For example, he spoke of it as being only a "felicitous phrase,"[46] as an " 'oversimplified judgment.' "[47]

The doctrine continues, however, to have appeal and vitality. As recently as 1961 Justice Harlan used the doctrine as a constitutional test.[48] And Justice Jackson said of the doctrine:

I would save it, unmodified, for application as a "rule of reason" in the kind of case for which it was devised [by Justices Holmes and Brandeis]. When the issue is criminality of a hot-headed speech on a street corner, or circulation of a few incendiary pamphlets, or parading by some zealots behind a red flag, or refusal by a handful of school children to salute our flag, it is not beyond the capacity of judicial process to gather, comprehend, and weigh the necessary materials for decision whether it is a clear and present danger of substantive evil or a harmless letting off of steam. It is not a prophecy, for the danger in such cases has matured by the time of trial or it was never present.[49]

One should not, however, limit the usefulness of the doctrine to the types of free-speech situations referred to by Justice Jackson. It may have a legitimate role in some other kinds of First Amendment cases, provided it is not used in isolation from such other constitutional principles as those summarized by the phrases "preferred" freedoms and "breathing space" for freedoms.

But the doctrine is pre-eminently useful in the situations referred to by Justice Jackson; as, for example, in *Feiner* v. *New York*.[50]

A young college student in Syracuse stood on a large box on a street corner and spoke over loudspeakers mounted on a car. His purpose was to publicize a meeting of the Young Progressives of America[51] to be held that evening. He spoke in a section of the city predominantly Negro, and his audience was composed of about seventy-five persons of both races. The police received a complaint, and two policemen were sent over.

Feiner's purpose, as we have said, was to give publicity to the meeting. That meeting was originally scheduled in a public school auditorium, but the permit had been revoked, and so it was shifted to a hotel. These facts may explain the reason for some of his vituperative statements. He said:

Mayor Costello [of Syracuse] is a champagne-sipping bum. . . .
President Truman is a bum.
Mayor O'Dwyer [of New York] is a bum.
The American Legion is a Nazi Gestapo.
The Negroes don't have equal rights; they should rise up in arms and fight for their rights.

There were some angry mutterings and some pushing and shoving. But there were no fights, and the record was bare of testimony that the speaker was heckled.

After Feiner had spoken for about thirty minutes, a man in the crowd said to one of the policemen, "If you don't get that son of a bitch off, I will go over and get him off there myself." The police then ordered Feiner to stop speaking, and, when he refused, they arrested him. He was convicted of disorderly conduct and sentenced to thirty days in jail.

The Supreme Court, by 5 to 3, affirmed. Chief Justice Vinson's opinion for the Court said that the trial judge "heard testimony supporting and contradicting the judgment of the police officers that a clear danger of disorder was threatened," and the trial judge concluded that the officers were justified in taking action to prevent a breach of the peace. The arrest was made, said Chief Justice Vinson, not because the speaker made derogatory remarks concerning public officials or the American Legion; he was arrested and punished not for making a speech, nor for its content, but only because of "the reaction which it actually engendered." This was within the "bounds of proper state police action." The Court, said Chief Justice Vinson, "respects, as it must, the interest of the community in maintaining peace and order on its streets."

The Court said that a speaker may not be silenced because of the "ordinary murmurings and objections of a hostile audience," but here the trial judge had found that the speaker had gone beyond "the bounds of argument or persuasion" and had undertaken "incitement to riot."

Dissenting, Justice Black said:

It is neither unusual nor unexpected that some people at public street meetings mutter, mill about, push, shove, or disagree, even violently, with the speaker. . . . Nor does one isolated threat to assault the speaker forbode disorder. Especially should the danger be discounted where, as here, the person threatening was a man whose wife and two small children accompanied him and who, so far as the record shows, was never close enough for petitioner to carry out the threat.

Furthermore, he said, the police have an obligation to protect a speaker; but here the police officers did nothing to discourage the one person who threatened assault, "when even a word might have sufficed."

It is difficult to find the slightest justification for the majority position in this case—unless "the interest of the community in maintaining peace and order on its streets" wipes out the interest of the community in maintaining freedom of speech. If the "threat" of one member of an audience can effectively silence a speaker, then there is no such thing as free speech. Vituperative language concerning public officials cannot be the subject of a criminal complaint. "This is," the Court said in *The New York Times* case,[52] "the lesson to be drawn from the great controversy over the Sedition Act of 1798, . . . which first crystallized a national awareness of the central meaning of the First Amendment."

And the loose talk about the need of the Negro to "rise up in arms" was not even considered by the Court as a possible "incitement to riot." People are not that volatile. Negro and white racists and hate-mongers have learned that it takes more than loose talk to motivate listeners to resort to arms or violence.

The Court said that it could not condemn the judgment of the New York courts, "approving the means which the police, faced with a crisis, used in the exercise of their power and duty to preserve peace and order." Peace and order were preserved, but free speech was not, though the American hypothesis is that free speech is the true foundation for peace and order.

The testimony was that, before asking the speaker to step down, one of the police officers had called headquarters, and only after his telephone conversation did he go up to Feiner and demand that he stop. Obviously, if there was an opportunity to discuss the matter over the telephone, there was time to ask for additional officers if they were needed. For the Court to describe this petty situation as a "crisis" was to exaggerate beyond all reason.

This was the kind of case in which the Clear and Present Danger Doctrine could have played a role if it had been coupled with an acceptance of the "preferred" freedoms position; for then the Court could not have given overriding weight to the "interest of the community in maintaining peace and order on its streets."

But a case such as *Feiner* v. *New York* is rare in the recent history of the Supreme Court. There were the cases involving the activities of Communists, such as *Herndon* v. *Lowry*,[53] decided in 1937; and the Smith Act and McCarran Act cases, discussed in Chapter IV. None of these involved just making a speech. Then there were the Jehovah's Witnesses cases, that of Cantwell, in which a man played a record for two men on the street, and that of Chaplinsky, who addressed "fighting" words to one man, a police officer. These cases obviously fall into a special class. This leaves us with the Terminiello and Feiner cases, only two cases of persons addressing audiences in settings that suggest Justice Holmes's classic statement of the clear-and-present-danger test.[54]

Decisions on only two cases in a quarter of a century or longer hardly support the pervasive fear—among judges, lawyers, law-enforcement agencies, and laymen—of speech that incites to riot. The fear is misplaced. The causes of riots and disturbances run deeper than street-corner oratory.

In a paper read before the annual meeting of the American Historical Association at the end of 1965, Professor Elliott M. Rudwick noted that the Black Muslim talk about violence seems to function as a psychological safety valve rather than as a triggering of actual violence; that a James Baldwin character who speaks of the gun as enjoying equal place with the Bible in the Negro's struggle for advancement in fact shows no sign of setting other than rhetorical fires or of shooting any but verbal game. He noted that in the riots of 1964 and 1965 the violence was directed at the white man's property rather than his life. In part, he observed, this was due to the tendency to dream and talk violence rather than to practice it.

Admittedly, we know very little about the psychological roots of violence, about the motivation and background of people who resort to violence. At the end of 1964 an institute was established at Brandeis University to study why violence starts and how it can be controlled. Maybe after some years of study we will be in a position to talk about it with a measure of justifiable self-assurance. Meantime, however, it can be said that Justice Jackson had no foundation of facts for his assertion in the Terminiello case:

But we must bear in mind . . . that no serious outbreak of mob violence, race rioting, lynching or public disorder is likely to get going without help of some speech-making to some mass of people. A street may be filled with men and women and the crowd still not be a mob. Unity of purpose, passion and hatred, which merges the many minds of a crowd into the mindlessness of a mob, almost invariably is supplied by speeches. . . .

Justice Jackson simply assumed, uncritically, that speeches account for the actions of mobs. The events of the early 1960s, in which hundreds of thousands of Negroes and their white sympathizers participated in mass actions, show that speech kept men and women *from becoming mobs.* Roy Wilkins, Martin Luther King, Jr., James Farmer, Bayard Rustin, Whitney M. Young, Jr., John Lewis, A. Philip Randolph, and other Negro leaders spoke responsibly, and, even when they were not physically present to address a crowd, they always provided a conscience for their followers. It was rather Negroes and whites *who would not listen* who precipitated public riots and who violently fought for "mastery of the streets"; lynch mobs work in secret, and at night, and accomplish their murderous purposes in silence. The men in Mississippi who conspired to lynch the three civil rights workers on June 21, 1964, were not, as far as we know, incited by a speech on a street corner in the town of Philadelphia. In March 1964 Negro mobs poured into the streets in Jacksonville, Florida, and for two days there was an "orgy of violence, arson and vandalism."[55] Their mood was typified by a Negro postman of Jacksonville, who spoke of his second-class citizenship as the reward for his military service in World War II, and said: "I am ready to go to war for this country again. But I am also ready to go to war in this country. I am a peaceful man but I can be moved."[56] But he did not mean that he could be moved by speeches. He probably had had his bellyful of talk.

On August 28, 1963, the nation's capital saw the biggest demonstration in its history, when over 200,000 persons, mostly Negroes, but including thousands of whites, gathered from all parts of the country to show their support of Negro demands for full civil rights immediately. It was a peaceful, orderly demonstration, and it was seen or heard with awe by many millions on television and radio. So, too, on November 20, 1965, when some eight thousand opponents of the war in Vietnam marched from the campus of the University of California at Berkeley to Oakland, whose officers had been forced to permit the march by an order of a federal district court. There were no incidents.

Admittedly, there are demagogues, rabble-rousers, white and black racists, anti-Semites, men and organizations that peddle hatred of their fellow men. There are the Ku Klux Klan, the Christian Nationalist Crusade, the Christian Educational Association, the White Citizens Councils, and similar organizations of bigots and racists, whose existence and actions ought not to be ignored. But the record does not show that anti-Semitic vandalism like the swastika epidemic of 1960,[57] or the burning of some forty Negro churches in Mississippi in 1964,[58] was incited by speeches.

The claim of the police in the Feiner case that the officers were acting, in arresting the speaker, to maintain peace and order should have been interpreted by the Court against the background of American history, in which the police do not generally win acclaim as zealous respecters of civil liberties. In racial disturbances, the police have not been generally known to be impartial. If they did not stand aside, they sometimes joined the attacks on Negroes. In 1951, for example, the police chief of Cicero, Illinois, was convicted on charges of helping white rioters.[59] In 1943 the riot in Harlem was said to have been sparked by a rumor that a Negro soldier had been killed by a policeman. In 1964 in Rochester, New York, Negro men and women at a dance turned into a mob when word spread that policemen had dragged a Negro to a prowl car. The rumors and reports may have exaggerated or even falsified the facts, but the resentments against the police were so strong that a minor incident set off an explosion of force and violence. One can suggest that police dogs and fire hoses, and the attitude that Negroes can be addressed and treated as if they were idiots or mere things, have a much greater claim to creating clear and present dangers than have street-corner speeches.

Following riots in seven cities between the middle of July and Labor Day in 1964, President Johnson asked the F.B.I. to prepare a report on the events, to see if they showed a "particular pattern."[60] According to the F.B.I. report,[61] six of the city riots (in Rochester, New York; Jersey City, Elizabeth, and Paterson, New Jersey; Dixmoor, a Chicago suburb; and Philadelphia, Pennsylvania) developed

from a minor incident, normal in character. Similar incidents, usually routine arrests for disorderly conduct, had happened hundreds of times in most communities involved and in other cities throughout the country. For some reason there suddenly occurred a rupture of the cords that normally bind people to decent conduct and respect for law and the rights of their fellow citizens.

Whatever the cause, in each instance there was first violent interference with the policemen on the scene, followed by the gathering of a crowd. Then, either because of exhortation of rabble-rousers or further incidents caused by the disturbance, the crowd was increased by the arrival of youths looking for excitement or violence or worse. As mob spirit swept through the crowd it became increasingly unruly, began storming police officers and civilians and the ominous surge of a mass of violent people bent on destruction spread through the streets.

In each of the six riots, then, passions became inflamed although no one had made a speech. The passions probably were let loose by seeing or hearing what police officers were doing. If there were rabble-rousers, they were there as part of the mob; mobs did not gather attracted by rabble-rousers. In every mob there are probably men and women who impulsively cry out that the crowd should do this or that; the occasion turns them into "leaders" of the rabble that is already aroused. They are not rabble-rousers in the sense that Terminiello and Feiner were.

The events in the Harlem riot—which was the first of the seven city riots—were somewhat different. The F.B.I. report states that the initial incident happened on July 16, when a police lieutenant was attacked with a knife by a fifteen-year-old Negro boy. The officer fired one warning shot, and then two which were fatal. The shooting received "nationwide publicity and [provoked] wild charges of police brutality." For several days after the shooting, however, there were no disturbances; then on July 19 there were riots in Harlem and in the Bedford-Stuyvesant section of Brooklyn, which continued for five days. What happened between July 16 and 19? The F.B.I. report mentions agitation by a Communist splinter group, known as the Progressive Labor Movement, which is oriented toward the Chinese Communist line. This group distributed thousands of copies of a handbill containing a photograph of the police lieutenant under the caption: "Wanted for Murder." A mass demonstration was announced for July 25, to demand prosecution of the police officer. An officer of this Communist group on July 18 harangued a street meeting, announcing that

there was going to be a demonstration, "not necessarily peaceful," that he and his followers "were going to kill cops and judges," that "no revolution can be won by peaceful means" and that this state must be smashed "totally and completely."

But the report does not say how many persons heard this talk, who they were, and what, if any, was the effect on them.

On July 19 a former organizer for the Communist Party issued a "public call" for "a hundred skilled black revolutionaries who are ready to die" to correct what he called "police brutality." But the report does not describe the "public call"—how it was made, or to whom.

There is obviously very little in the report that points toward demagogic speeches as incitement of the riots. It states that two individuals "with histories of Communist affiliation" "were instigators and leaders of the riots in at least two of the cities in New Jersey," yet "neither of them started the riots but they capitalized on them and tried to continue them"; there is no indication, however, that they made any speeches. There are in the report other references to agitators, but in no instance is an agitator pointed to as having incited a riot. One of the conclusions in the report is as follows: "While adult troublemakers often incited the riots, the mob violence was dominated by the acts of youths. . . ." When this is read in the light of the specific facts related in the report, it must mean that after the crowd interfered with the police with force and violence, in some instances this was followed by "exhortation of rabble-rousers." Another conclusion in the F.B.I. report is that "No evidence was found that the riots were organized on a national basis by any single person, group of persons, or organization." The report also noted that riot situations are rare in the United States. This fact gains in significance when one notes, as the report states, that the "social and economic conditions in which much of the Negro population lives are demoralizing."

The report might have pointed out, too, something that was put forcefully by Dr. Karl Menninger when he said at a conference: "Ladies and gentlemen, we not only tolerate violence, we love it. We put it on the front pages of our newspapers. One-third or one-fourth of our television programs use it for the amusement of our children. Condone! My dear friends, we love it."[62]

On December 20, 1965, William Epton, a leader of the Progressive Labor Movement, was convicted in a New York City court of conspiring to riot, of advocating the overthrow of the New York State government, and of conspiring to overthrow it. These criminal anarchy charges were under a state statute enacted in 1901 following the assassination of President McKinley in Buffalo. Epton was accused of circulating, during the Harlem riots, posters reading: "Wanted for Murder," referring to the policeman who had shot and killed the fifteen-year-old Negro, and he was charged with trying to inflame the emotionally tense situation in Harlem by a street-corner speech two days after the killing—the incident referred to in the F.B.I. report. He was arrested while leading a march on a police station in Harlem. This case, like the Feiner case, is rare in American law, and it will not be possible to evaluate it until the trial record is made available to the appellate courts, and perhaps eventually to the United States Supreme Court.

The commission, headed by John A. McCone, appointed by Governor Edmund G. Brown of California to investigate the riots in the Watts district of Los Angeles in August 1965, reported that the specific cause of the riot stemmed from the arrest of a twenty-one-year-old Negro on a reckless driving charge. The officers were at the scene where the arrest was made for some forty minutes. A large mob gathered, fired by rumors of police brutality. Negroes then started to stone passing automobiles. On the following afternoon the Los Angeles County Human Rights Commission called a meeting to cool off emotions in the Watts area. While a placating speech was being made, a high-school boy grabbed the microphone and shouted that rioters would attack the adjacent white neighborhoods that night. The mood of the meeting changed instantly, and that night, August 12, the rioting intensified. The McCone Commission concluded that there was "no reliable evidence of outside leadership or pre-established plans for the rioting." But once the rioting was under way, several extremist groups moved into action to spread the ongoing disorder.*

A great many pages have been written by judges and commentators who seem to be burdened with the fear that the First Amendment may be used to keep out of prison men who have the compulsion to shout "Fire!" in crowded theaters when there are no fires. There is much less cause for this fear than is generally assumed. Among the things that inflame the passions of men sufficiently to convert them into raging, destructive mobs, soap-box or platform speech probably ranks near the bottom of the list. After a crowd becomes a mob, speech may direct the rioters toward one objective or another; but no case in our system of law has raised First Amendment questions in such a factual setting. Because of this relatively baseless fear, Feiner, the college student in Syracuse, was sent to jail with the blessings of a Supreme Court majority. The clear-and-present-danger rule, when coupled with the "preferred position" and the "breathing space" doctrines, can serve to keep the courts from succumbing too easily to fears that are more rooted in emotions than in facts. The ideas that may incite to action create no "clear" and no "present" danger. Their work is slow, devious, and invisible, and is beyond the reach of the law and its processes. When ideas openly incite, more often they incite persecution of the speaker rather than the action intended and hoped for by him.

3. Demonstrations and the Rule of Law

The civil rights demonstrations in the early 1960s, partly because young people from the universities and high schools predominated in them, have aggravated fears of "mob rule" and general lawlessness. A typical expression of this fear is the following passage from a newspaper column:

Many incidents in the current year [1964] indicate a drift toward mob rule. The racial strife with its organized demonstrations, sit-ins and kin-

*From *Violence in the City—an End or a Beginning,* Report by the Governor's Commission on the Los Angeles Riots (December 2, 1965), pp. 13, 22, 23.

dred tactics on the one side, and Ku Klux Klanism on the other, and more recently the student (plus faculty) ruckus at the University of California [at Berkeley], are straws in the wind showing how it is blowing. . . . In other words, if the crowd wants a certain result, it should be allowed to achieve it, regardless of what it is, and if immediate compliance is not granted, use mob pressure. And mob pressure tends to generate mob violence. . . .

If mob pressure can force the change of regulations at a university, why not apply it also to the courts, demanding either acquittals or verdicts of guilty, according to the sympathies of the mob, rather than the legal merits in the case?[63]

There are several things seriously wrong with this line of argument: In the first place, there is the logical fallacy that Professor Sidney Hook has called the "slippery slope" argument, which he describes as follows:

This mode of thinking takes its point of departure from the fact that conflict of principles or values sometimes compels us to take a necessary risk whose dangers are manifest. It then asks: where does one stop? And since in advance no one can indicate a specific stopping point, it assumes that one can never stop but that once we step on the slippery slope we must descend at an accelerated speed into the dread abyss of catastrophe, however conceived.[64]

This logical fallacy is one that traps even the best of minds. Madison, for example, said the following—words that have been frequently quoted in Supreme Court opinions:

It is proper to take alarm at the first experiment on our liberties. . . . [Who does not see] that the same authority which can force a citizen to contribute threepence only of his property for the support of any one [religious] establishment, may force him to conform to any other establishment in all cases whatsoever?[65]

Of course, it does not follow that if we find no fault with the Negro lunch-counter demonstrations we "logically" would be compelled to approve "mob pressure" on a court to issue a specific verdict.

Second, the attack against the Negro demonstrations as replacing the rule of law with "mob rule" is so on-sided, so partial, as to suggest prejudice, for the judgment of condemnation is made in the face of overwhelming evidence of the massive *frustration* of the rule of law by *whites* in the South. The young Negros were not taught respect for law and order by the example of the white neighbors. The white South did everything possible to show contempt for the Constitution,

he Supreme Court, and the President. How could one, with a straight
ace, talk to the Negro about the need to move only through legislation
and litigation when he was every day denied the fruits of his court
victories and when remedial legislation was for years made impossible
by the Senate filibuster? It is not possible to talk about "law and
order" to a Negro who cannot get out of his memory the countless
times when Southern governors, judges, legislators, sheriffs, police
officers, and ordinary citizens thumbed their noses at the law and the
Constitution and paid respect to the Confederate flag, the symbol of
racial slavery and of rebellion against constitutional authority. Compared with Eugene "Bull" Connor of Birmingham, Governor George
C. Wallace of Alabama, Governor Orval Faubus of Arkansas, and
Governor Ross Barnett of Mississippi, the Negro student demonstrators were angels. The street and campus riots in the South were
chiefly riots of white men, women, and children, and at "white" state
universities.

If Feiner was sent to jail for a street-corner speech that created—
allegedly—danger of a riot, what should have been done with governors of Southern states for *their* speeches that aroused the worst and
deepest instincts and sent ugliness and brutality into the faces of
shrieking women and girls?

If there are speeches that in fact create clear and present dangers,
they apparently are beyond reach of the law. The speeches that were
links in a chain of causation that ended in the murder of Medgar Evers,
the murder of four little girls killed when a Negro church in Birmingham was bombed, the murder of Mrs. Viola Liuzzo, and many others
—these speeches have not and perhaps never will be punished.

When one hears or reads attacks on the Negro student demonstrations and the stereotyped argument about respect for law and order,
what presses forward to consciousness is Governor Wallace's statement when he was told that the federal district court had ordered the
admission of two Negro students to the University of Alabama—in
1963, *nine years* after the Supreme Court's decision in the school-
segregation cases: "I am," he said, "the embodiment of the sovereignty
of this state and I will be present to bar the entrance of any Negro who
attempts to enroll at the University of Alabama." And whoever saw
it on the television screen on June 11, 1963, will not forget the spectacle of the governor—despite a plea from President Kennedy to stay
away from the campus at Tuscaloosa—standing in front of the auditorium door to bar Vivian Malone and James Hood from registering.

And attacks on the demonstrations in the name of law and order inevitably force one to think back to Birmingham, where there could be no demonstration without a permit, and where Bull Connor kept all the permits for himself and then obtained from a *state* court an injunction against such demonstrations. Dr. King refused to abide by the injunction, and on Good Friday (1963) he led a march to protest the exclusion of Negroes from worship in "white" churches. It was a peaceful demonstration, and as the Negroes walked and sang hymns they were met by Connor and his police force and a squad of snarling police dogs. Three Negro ministers were arrested—Martin Luther King, Jr., Ralph D. Abernathy, and Fred Lee Shuttlesworth—and placed in jail. (For Dr. King it was the thirteenth time in jail.)

The objections to demonstrations in the name of "law and order" fail to distinguish three radically different situations:

(1) There are demonstrations that take place without permits, and thus violate city or town ordinances. Technically, such demonstrations appear to be violative of law and public order. But many of these ordinances are unconstitutional on their face, or are unconstitutional because administered in discriminatory ways.

The classic case on this point is still the Hague case,[66] decided by the Court in 1939. An ordinance of Jersey City, New Jersey, prohibited public assembly on the streets or in the public buildings of the city without a permit, and the licensing official was authorized to refuse to issue a permit in order to prevent "riots, disturbances or disorderly assemblage." Alleging that the individuals applying for permits were Communists, the police denied numerous persons the right to hold public assemblies. The Court held the ordinance unconstitutional, for the ordinance could be used as an "instrument of arbitrary suppression of free expression of views . . . for the prohibition of all speaking will undoubtedly 'prevent' such eventualities [that is, riots, disturbances or disorderly assemblage]." The Court held that the ordinance was "void on its face." In other cases, some of them brought by Jehovah's Witnesses, the Court consistently held to this position.[67]

Had Dr. King and his two associates litigated their arrests in Birmingham through the federal courts, up through the Supreme Court, it is not risking much to say that their right to demonstrate would have been vindicated.

(2) The situation described is closely linked with the philosophy of nonviolent resistance. In his speech at Oslo, when he accepted the Nobel Peace Prize, Dr. King said:

The nonviolent resisters can summarize their message in the following simple terms: We will take direct action against injustice despite the failure of governmental and other official agencies to act first. We will not obey unjust laws or submit to unjust practices. We will do this peacefully, openly, cheerfully, because our aim is to persuade. We adopt the means of non-violence because our end is a community at peace with itself. We will try to persuade with our words, but if our words fail, we will try to persuade with our acts. We will always be willing to talk and seek fair compromise, but we are ready to suffer when necessary and even risk our lives to become witnesses to the truth as we see it.[68]

Nonviolent resistance, Dr. King said, has meant "non-cooperation with customs and laws which are institutional aspects of a regime of discrimination and enslavement."

Thus, by marching in the streets of Birmingham on Good Friday, the Negroes violated an ordinance which was one of the "institutional aspects" of the city's regime of racial discrimination; but they did this peacefully—i.e., they used no violence but voluntarily exposed themselves to possible attacks by police officers and police dogs and made themselves subject to arrest.

The purpose of the march, however, was not to protest against the licensing ordinance; it was to influence the community to end the immorality and injustice of racial segregation in the churches and in all other aspects of public life. If this meant the violation of "unjust laws" or the breach of "unjust practices," the demonstrators were ready to suffer the penalties that such acts might entail. For while they would not submit to unjust laws, they were prepared to submit to the penalties provided by these unjust laws.

The philosophy of nonviolent resistance is far removed from nihilism, philosophical anarchism, or Pauline antinomianism. By willing, even eager, subjection to the punishment provided by the breached law, the nonviolent resister affirms the rule of law; but by breaching the law he means to bear witness to the law's injustice—to a specific unjust law, or an unjust practice supported by law.

If one assumes the absolute sanctity of each and every law or legal judgment, then the philosophy of nonviolent resistance is a vicious doctrine, subversive of law and order, and those who preach or practice this doctrine should be abhorred and placed with Communists among the enemies of our society. But this is not what the generality of mankind believes. *Law itself is subject to the moral judgment; and justice, human dignity, and human rights are more fundamental than law.* The Universal Declaration of Human Rights, adopted by the General Assembly of the United Nations in 1948, is a better, more truthful witness on this matter than is Ross Barnett or George Wallace.

It must be stressed that nonviolent resistance means to affirm the general legal order and the rule of law; and that by trying to purify that order, to remove from it an intolerable evil, it acts to conserve rather than to destroy. By reminding us that laws must be just if they are to deserve respect and observance, nonviolent resistance refreshes the living mainsprings of law and order.

Nonviolent resistance must manifest, Dr. King has written,

a willingness to accept suffering without retaliation, to accept blows from the opponent without striking back. "Rivers of blood may have to flow before we gain our freedom, but it must be our blood," Gandhi said to his countrymen. The nonviolent resister is willing to accept violence if necessary, but never to inflict it. He does not seek to dodge jail. . . .[69]

This position is common to all proponents of nonviolent resistance. Thoreau went to jail and was not happy when an anonymous friend paid the tax and secured his liberty. Socrates repulsed his friends who urged him to make his escape, for which they had secured the cooperation of the jail warden. Antigone, in Sophocles' drama, went to her death with an eagerness that confounded Creon and Ismene. And Gandhi in 1922, when he faced the British judge in Ahmedabad, after the indictment was read, rose and declared: "I am here . . . to invite and cheerfully submit to the highest penalty that can be inflicted upon me for what in law is a deliberate crime and what appears to me to be the highest duty of a citizen." Gandhi time and again stressed the idea that civil disobedience entails "suffering in your own person by inviting the penalty for the breach of the law."[70]

Perhaps the first recorded instance of mass nonviolent resistance is to be found in *A History of the Jewish War* by Josephus. He relates that the emperor Gaius sent Petronius with an army to Jerusalem to place his statues in the Temple. If the Jews refused to admit the statues, Petronius had orders to slay all who opposed him and to enslave the rest. The Roman army arrived at Ptolemais (Acre), and there a large assembly of Jews, with wives and children, approached and supplicated Petronius not to violate their laws, which prohibited images as idols. Petronius listened and, leaving the legions at Ptolemais, he went himself to Galilee and summoned the most important people to Tiberias. He told them that their request was unreasonable and that the vengeance of the emperor would be great; and he pointed out that, since all other subject nations had accepted statues of the emperor, the action of the Jews would be nothing less than rebellion. The Jewish leaders answered that they must obey the laws of God.

Petronius then said to them words that Nazi war criminals have made familiar: "But am I, too, not compelled to observe the law of my master? If I disobey him and spare you, I shall be justly destroyed. Not I but he who sent me will make war against you; for I, just like you, am subject to his authority." At this point, the answer of the Jews was a cry "in unison that they were prepared to suffer for their law."

When the clamor subsided, Petronius asked: "Will you then make war against the emperor?" They answered that they were loyal subjects and made sacrifices twice daily for the emperor and the Roman people. "But," they went on, "if he wishes to put up these statues, he must first sacrifice the entire Jewish nation; and we herewith present ourselves, with our children and wives, ready for the slaughter."

Josephus reports that Petronius pleaded and threatened, but to no avail, and, being a decent man, in the end gave in and assumed the risk of himself suffering the fury of the emperor.[71]

Mass action that exemplifies nonviolent resistance to unjust laws or decrees is not the concoction of a demagogue. It is rooted in conscience and in history. The masses of harijans led by Gandhi were no different from the masses at Ptolemais or Tiberias some two thousand years ago; and the masses of Negroes led by Dr. King were no different from the masses of Indians led by Gandhi.[72]

Nonviolent resistance, as we see, is a form of protest that is older than the American nation and the First Amendment. The civil rights movement did not originate it, and it will be used by other movements and in other lands. In the years to come it will be such demonstrations, rather than street-corner speeches, that will test the meaning of the First Amendment freedoms of speech, assembly, and petition.

(3) The constitutional issue will in part take the form of free speech *versus* trespass, rather than the traditional concept of incitement to riot.

The history of this clash of values—between the right to protest and private property—in our time goes back to 1936, when rubber workers began a sitdown strike at the Firestone plant over the disciplining of a shop steward and a failure to adjust piece rates. This was soon followed by a sitdown strike at the Goodyear plant.[73] Toward the end of 1936 the sitdown was taken over by the auto workers, first at a Bendix plant in South Bend, Indiana, where the workers held the premises for six days. Almost immediately thereafter sitdown strikes swept the automobile industry. The major sitdown was at General Motors, where some 1700 workers remained in the plants. A Michigan state court judge issued an injunction but it was not used. The company, after several weeks, turned off water and heat (this was in January 1937), and a five-hour battle followed, in which twenty-four men were hurt. Governor Frank Murphy (later to become a Justice of the Supreme Court) ordered the National Guard to stand ready for duty. Municipal judges issued warrants against hundreds of sitdown strikers, while union members and sympathizers gathered to aid the embattled strikers. The sitdown had the effect of closing fifty plants, employing over 125,000 workers. After forty-four days the strike ended in a victory for the workers. Governor Murphy could have used troops to oust the strikers, but he refused to take such strong measures and insisted on a peaceful settlement.[74]

The new tactic spread rapidly and widely to other industries and to other parts of the country. In the United States Senate, James Byrnes (also later a Justice of the Supreme Court) offered a bill declaring sitdowns illegal, but the measure was defeated; and a proposal in the House of Representatives to conduct an investigation of the sitdowns was also defeated.[75]

As happens repeatedly in major social-policy crises, it was left to the Supreme Court to tangle with the complicated issues and to offer a principled resolution of them. In 1939 the Court considered the Fansteel case.[76]

In 1937, in response to unfair labor practices by the Fansteel Metallurgical Corporation, the union decided on a sitdown strike. Employees occupied the buildings, as fellow union members brought them food, blankets, and cigarettes. Then the employer got an injunction ordering the workers to leave. They refused. They were then cited for contempt. Upon their refusal to submit, a pitched battle ensued, and the strikers succeeded in resisting ouster and arrest. Finally, with reinforcements, the sheriff got the men out of the factory buildings and into jail for violating the injunction. The occupation had lasted nine days.

When production was resumed, the company refused to take back some of the employees who had engaged in the sitdown. The National Labor Relations Board, in a proceeding brought by the union, held that, since the strike was against an unfair labor practice by the employer, the strikers were entitled to reinstatement, with back pay, despite their illegal conduct while on strike.

The Supreme Court, in an opinion by Chief Justice Hughes, held that the seizure and retention of the plant were unlawful. "It was," said the Court, "a high-handed proceeding without shadow of legal right." If the company was guilty of an unfair labor practice, the union had its remedy under the National Labor Relations Act. The company's wrong did not make it an outlaw or deprive it of its legal rights to its property. "The employees had the right to strike but they had no license to commit acts of violence or to seize their employer's plant." Whether the workers did or did not injure the plant, the "seizure and holding of the buildings was itself a wrong. . . ." The Court condemned the sitdown in the sternest terms:

To justify such conduct because of the existence of a labor dispute or of an unfair labor practice would be to put a premium on resort to force instead of legal remedies and to subvert the principles of law and order which lie at the foundations of society.

The Court said that the ousting of the owner from lawful possession was not essentially different from an assault upon the officers, or seizure and conversion of the company's goods, or the despoiling of its property or other unlawful acts.

The employer had "the right to discharge the wrongdoers from its employ," and, said the Court, there was nothing in the National Labor Relations Act that could be reasonably construed as a congressional intention to deny this right to the employer. The employees did not exercise "the right to strike"; for the original intention was to take over and hold the buildings. The action of the workers, said the Court,

was not a mere quitting of work and statement of grievances in the exercise of pressure recognized as lawful. It was an illegal seizure of the buildings in order to prevent their use by the employer in a lawful manner and thus by acts of force and violence to compel the employer to submit. . . . There is not a line in the statute to warrant the conclusion that it is any part of the policies of the Act to encourage employees to resort to force and violence in defiance of the law of the land.

Justices Reed and Black dissented, contending that the N.L.R.B. acted within its statutory authority when it ordered the reinstatement of the sitdown strikers. This, they said, did not, however, mean that the strikers were beyond reach of the law, for they could still be punished for their unlawful activity through the normal processes of the criminal law.

Now, there are some important differences between the Fansteel sitdown and the civil rights sit-ins, as follows:

(1) The sitdown strikers used force and violence to retain possession of the plant. These workers were not followers of Gandhi's philosophy of nonviolent resistance. The seizure of the buildings, and the use of force and violence to hold on to their positions, were uncom-

fortable reminders of events in the Russian Revolution of 1917, instigated by the Bolsheviks, and the theories of syndicalists and the Wobblies.

(2) The sitdown striker had no intention of submitting to legal punishment for their acts.

(3) The sitdown strikers were not demonstrating for any general change of heart, or change of policy, law, or custom. The strikers were not part of a movement. They had grievances against their employer, but no large social views or ends.

(4) The strikers had a remedy at law. A purpose of the National Labor Relations Act was to substitute an orderly procedure before the N.L.R.B. for self-help measures that disrupt production.

(5) The strikers were engaged in an economic contest with their employer. Such a struggle, though it has high value in our day, is not comparable in moral dignity to a struggle for racial equality.

Before passage of the National Labor Relations Act of 1935, workers theoretically had the right to form unions and engage in collective bargaining, and they could resort to peaceful measures of self-help to attain these ends.[77] But there was no statutory machinery to which employees could resort to compel an employer to recognize a union or to bargain collectively.

It was a situation comparable to that in the area of civil rights in the years between the decision in the Brown case in 1954 and the enactment of the Civil Rights Act of 1964. In that decade states could not compel segregation in places of public accommodation. In nineteen states there was a legal no-man's land: the states did not prohibit segregation through state civil rights statutes, nor could they enforce segregation.[78] The field was, therefore, left open for peaceful self-help measures.

Just as "Congress was not required to ignore" the right of employees "but could safeguard it"—to use the language of Chief Justice Hughes regarding the National Labor Relations Act of 1935[79]—so, too, Congress in 1964 acted to safeguard the rights of Negroes.

Racial equality has a much clearer constitutional charter than can be claimed for the rights of labor. We say this not in terms of theoretical considerations or abstract rights, but in light of the record of constitutional history. Until Congress acted in 1935, labor was subject to "government by injunction," and there was no clear constitutional guarantee to which labor could point as its Magna Carta.[80] But the Negro *could* point to the Civil War Amendments as his—in a special sense *his*—Magna Carta.[81] Since the adoption of these amendments, the Negro was constitutionally entitled to *equality* under the law. The only ones who could dispute this were those who attacked the constitutionality of the Civil War Amendments.

Before the decision in the school-segregation cases, the states could satisfy the Constitution by providing "separate but equal" facilities because segregation was not held to be a denial of equality. But the requirement, the standard, always was equality, "the equal protection of the laws." The Court in 1954 decided that, as a matter of fact, "separate" was not "equal"; but the constitutional guarantees on behalf of the Negro were always the same after the Civil War Amendments were adopted.

I would suggest that, in a philosophic consideration of human rights, economic rights should be given a place inferior to racial equality or the First Amendment freedoms. In the Universal Declaration of Human Rights, adopted by the U. N. General Assembly, our First Amendment freedoms are formulated in Articles 18, 19, and 20; and while the United States Constitution makes no mention of workers and their unions, the U. N. document devotes Article 23 to a statement of their rights. But Articles 1 and 2 provide for equality of rights and equal human dignity.

It can be said that in a *constitutional* consideration of human rights the First Amendment freedoms and human equality have a "preferred" position. Economic rights—the rights of management and the rights of employees—however, are subject to legislative regulation, as the National Labor Relations Act of 1935, the Taft-Hartley Act of 1947, and the Landrum-Griffin Act of 1959 bear eloquent witness. But a law regulating free speech raises no presumption of constitutional validity,[82] and racial classifications are "constitutionally suspect" and subject to the "most rigid scrutiny."[83]

There is, however, one significant similarity between the Fansteel sitdown and some of the civil rights and other sit-in demonstrations, i.e., the invasion—real or only apparent—of property rights.

For sixty-eight days pickets representing the Congress of Racial Equality occupied the press room at a building in Manhattan owned by Governor Rockefeller. They were picketing the Joint Committee on Equal Job Opportunity. The pickets were orderly, except on one day when seven demonstrators blocked the building entrance by squatting in the doorway. They were arrested for trespass. But their occupancy of the press room for over two months was tolerated. They were there on a round-the-clock basis. They sent out for food or replacements and were permitted to use the washroom. They gave up the press room voluntarily; and when they did this Governor Rockefeller stated that he would ban demonstrators in his office.[84]

On July 29, 1963, three demonstrators were arrested as they blocked the entrance to Mayor Wagner's office section at the City Hall of New York. The demonstrators were charged with disorderly conduct. Before the demonstrators were removed, persons were forced to step over them to get through the gate to the Mayor's executive offices.[85]

In July 1963 CORE representatives blocked the entrance to the building of the New York City Board of Education. They linked arms and blocked the passage of people.[86]

In 1964 fourteen persons, who said they had cancer, staged a sit-in at the office of the Secretary of Health, Education and Welfare. They were protesting the government's ban on a certain drug. They were arrested by federal guards on the charge of unlawful entry.[87]

On March 6, 1964, a small group of demonstrators sat down on the roadway of the Triborough Bridge in New York City, blocked all traffic, and littered the area with garbage.[88]

These are all typical illustrations of the taking over of public or quasi-public property[89] by demonstrators seemingly dedicated to non-violent resistance (though strewing garbage on the bridge was a breach of discipline). The 814 persons who occupied the administration building at the University of California at Berkeley in December 1964 belong to the same category. Such occupancy was unlawful. Because a place is public property, it does not follow that it may be occupied for purposes other than those for which it was dedicated. A public library may belong to the town or city; but this does not mean that a group of men may move into it and use it as their residence or place of business. The governor of a state or the mayor of a city is provided with offices where he may attend to his public duties. If persons take over the waiting room or his office, the public business may be seriously hampered. So, too, occupying a bridge and stopping traffic is a misappropriation of public property and is unlawful.

The arrest and punishment of persons engaged in such demonstration offer no constitutional difficulties. The demonstrators have the guarantee of free speech, petition, and assembly, but this does not mean a guarantee of any and every place as their platform. The guarantee of freedom of the press allows no one to try to take over the Government Printing Office, or the *Congressional Record*. Because we have the guarantee of free speech, it does not mean that any citizen may walk into a classroom of a state university and proceed to lecture to a class. Although this should be obvious, discussion of demonstrations often discloses a failure to understand these propositions.

There seems to be no legal or constitutional difference between the seizure of private property, as in the Fansteel case, and the seizure of public property, as in the instances we have cited, insofar as the invasion of property rights is concerned. This does not mean that the law "prefers" property over free speech or freedom of the press. Because the constitutional guarantee of freedom of the press does not give one the right to walk into the office of the editor of *The New York Times* and to oust and replace him, it does not mean that freedom of the press is inferior to property rights. As we have noted, freedom of the press is to a degree dependent upon private property—as part of its "breathing space." The Constitution does not guarantee to every man a private press, or a platform, or a television channel; nor does it give demonstrators a right to oust the governor or mayor from his office, or citizens from waiting rooms, or automobiles from bridges, or university administrators from their offices.

Furthermore, the examples we have cited are all cases of demonstrations which might just as well have taken place elsewhere. In India, the untouchables swept the highways but were not permitted to walk on them. Under Gandhi's leadership the untouchables demonstrated their protest against their degradation by walking on the highways. This was a case of mass nonviolent resistance to an unjust law or custom. These demonstrations were *themselves* violations of the very laws or customs against which they were directed. Walking on the pavement was not a means to an end, but was the end sought. Sitting at lunch counters was not a means to an end, but was the end sought.

But men who sit on a bridge, or occupy an official's office, like the workers who occupied the Fansteel plants, seek ends that transcend their actions. *These actions are not themselves those which they seek to make lawful.* Gandhi's harijans wanted the right to walk on the highways—and they did, despite law and punishment. But the men who sat on the bridge did not want to win the right to sit on bridges, and the students who occupied the university's administration building did no seek to win the right to occupy the administration offices.

This is an important distinction. The upper-caste Indians could not say to the harijans that they could make their protest against untouchability in other ways than by walking on the highways, for the harijans had decided, with Gandhi, that they would not obey laws or customs that were unjust and that deprived them of their human dignity. But we could say to the men on the bridge that they *could* find another forum for *their* protest.

This brings our discussion back to the lunch-counter sit-in demonstrations. There were several sets of sit-in cases in the Supreme Court. We discussed the first series of such cases—the Garner case, decided in 1961—earlier in this chapter. In the Garner case, it will be recalled, the lunch-counter demonstrators were charged with disturbance of the peace, and on conviction were sentenced to four months' imprisonment. The Supreme Court reversed and held that, since the defendants had conducted themselves peacefully, their convictions for disturbance of the peace could not stand under the Due Process Clause of the Fourteenth Amendment. In essentials, the Garner case followed the Thompson case.

Now, these lunch-counter sit-in demonstrators were like the harijans who defied Indian law and custom by walking on the highway near the temple at Viakom—a road on which they had no right to walk. Like them, the sit-in demonstrators protested *by breaking the very pattern against which they protested.*

They were also like the absolutists among pacifists, to whom everything connected with war is morally wrong. They refuse, therefore, to cooperate with the evil—to register for the draft, to get into a military uniform, or in any other way to acknowledge the lawfulness of conscription. So, too, the sit-in demonstrators: they refused to recognize by any action the lawfulness of racial segregation. Their actions exemplified their belief in noncooperation with evil.

In the sit-in cases decided by the Supreme Court, the defendants, when placed under arrest, went voluntarily with the police officers to the police wagon and the police station.

There were also instances where demonstrators passively waited to be carried out by the police. Such demonstrators wrongly followed the pattern set by the pacifist absolutists, who argued that if cooperation with conscription was wrong, "then cooperation to assist in imposing penalties for refusal to cooperate with conscription was also wrong."[90] The extremists were utterly passive and refused to cooperate with the prison system; some of them even refused to take food. They simply wished to show that they would not cooperate *in any way* with the law that implemented conscription for military service. If this is madness, there is certainly method in it; and the absolutist, by his absolutism, places himself beyond the realm of rational discussion. He says with Luther: "I can do no other." The 814 young men and women who went limp when they were arrested in the administration building on the Berkeley campus certainly showed mettle and discipline, for many of them were hurt as they were dragged through the halls and down the steps; but it was a case of misapplied absolutism.

One should not, however, judge too harshly the mistakes that have been made in some sit-in demonstrations. For the fact remains that often the authorities and the public simply would not hear the spoken word. When people will not listen, men with grievances must then find another way of exercising their right of petition for redress of grievances. This in part explains what happened at Berkeley, where the administration and the faculty were separated from the students by a wide gulf over which the human voice apparently would not carry. When the students demonstrated as they did, then everyone began to ask: "What are they saying? What is the message? What do they want?" So, too, in Selma, Alabama, where 13,000 whites disfranchised 15,000 Negroes, and where the sheriff, James G. Clark, and his helmeted posse terrorized the Negro community; but no one paid attention until the Negroes, led by Martin Luther King, Jr., marched and demonstrated, and 3400 Negroes, including Dr. King, were put in jail, and 165 Negro youths were taken on a forced march by Sheriff Clark and his deputies with night sticks and electric cattle prods. Then, and only then, did the rest of the nation listen, and only then did the President of the United States strongly denounce infringement of voting rights and pledge vigorous legal action, and state that he would ask Congress for new legislation to eliminate barriers to the right to vote. At last the Negroes of Selma had *effectively* exercised their constitutional right to petition the government for redress of grievances. Of course ordinary speech should be the vehicle for rational discourse; but if people will not listen to such speech, we should not judge harshly the aggrieved when they turn to other means of peaceful, nonviolent, but more dramatic forms of communication. Thousands of years ago prophets found that men would not listen even to the words spoken in the name of God, and they sought other ways of conveying their message; so it was that Jeremiah bought a potter's earthen flask to break in the sight of men, and made himself thongs and yoke-bars and put them on his neck. Jeremiah and Dr. King were separated by twenty-six centuries, but they were united by the problems they faced.

For this reason it can be said that the Supreme Court, in *Cox* v. *Louisiana* (1965), put the argument in favor of communication by "pure speech" too strongly. "We emphatically reject," said the Court, the notion . . . that the First and Fourteenth Amendments afford the same kind of freedom to those who would communicate ideas by conduct such as patrolling, marching, and picketing on streets and highways, as these amendments afford to those who communicate ideas by pure speech.

This is to emphasize the letter, at the cost of the spirit, of the free-speech guarantee. For if the First Amendment freedoms "need breathing space to survive," the Court must give to the word "speech" the meaning that time and circumstance may require. If motion pictures are "speech," men in motion—or men sitting silently on stools at lunch counters—are also men using "speech." If there are tongues in trees and sermons in stones, it is because men sometimes will listen, not with their ears, but with their hearts and spirits.

No doubt the sit-in technique may be misused. But what tool may not be misused? Who will say that Sheriff Clark did not misuse the powers of his office? Yet this does not mean that we should abolish the office of sheriff. Because he was afraid that publishers and authors would abuse the right to publish, Henry VIII instituted a licensing system. Today we, too, know that freedom of the press may be abused by publications that are seditious, or libelous, or obscene, or otherwise offensive; but there are calculated risks that free men are bound to take, and we find ways to discourage or to punish abuses of rights and misuses of gifts. Of course the Court should be no more "absolutistic" with respect to the communication of ideas through peaceful demonstrations than with respect to "pure speech," and certainly there are differences that the Court is bound to recognize between one form of communication and another; there are significant differences, too, between distributing a hundred copies of a pamphlet and broadcasting to millions of listeners, between publishing a twenty-volume encyclopedia and releasing a movie. The differences between peaceful demonstrations and "pure speech" are no greater, and they should be recognized and weighed in the measure. *But there is an identity, too,* and it too deserves to be recognized and weighed in the measure provided by the First and Fourteenth Amendments. This is simply, following the advice of Justice Holmes, that we must take the provisions of the Constitution not as mathematical formulas, which have their essence in their very form, but as organic living institutions, with a significance that is vital rather than formal.

4. The Sit-in Cases of 1963 and 1964

The second series of sit-in cases was decided in 1963. In *Peterson* v. *Greenville*,[91] ten Negro boys and girls entered the S. H. Kress store in Greenville, South Carolina, and seated themselves at the lunch counter. The manager asked an employee to call the police, turn the lights out, and declare the lunch counter closed. City and state police officers came, and the boys and girls were arrested. It is important to note that the manager did not ask that the defendants be arrested. He asked them to leave because, he said, integrated service was contrary to local customs and in violation of a city ordinance. He testified that the defendants were clean, orderly, and peaceful, and that Negroes were welcome in all other parts of the store. The defendants were convicted of trespass and each was sentenced to a fine of $100 or thirty days in jail.

The Supreme Court reversed the convictions on the ground that the Kress management had acted in obedience to the segregation ordinance, which was unconstitutional. The state argued that the store would have acted as it did independently of the ordinance; but the Court said that "The State will not be heard to make this contention," for the convictions had the effect of enforcing the city ordinance.[92]

On June 22, 1964, the Supreme Court decided the third set of sit-in cases and some of these involved the most difficult constitutional challenges to sit-in demonstrations, and issues that will survive the struggle over lunch-counter service.

By the time these cases came up, it was clear to the Southern officials that they could not successfully prosecute lunch-counter demonstrators if the record showed a statute or ordinance or some other official statement or policy *requiring* racial segregation; nor could convictions for breach of the peace or disorderly conduct be sustained where the demonstrators acted peacefully and quietly. This left the Southern officials with only one more possible line of attack, and that was to prosecute demonstrators for *criminal trespass*. The cases would need to be wholly "pure" in this respect: the facts must clearly show that the proprietor of the shop refused to serve Negroes; that his refusal was entirely an expression of his own, *private* will and policy; and that the police, in arresting the demonstrators, were merely responding to the wishes *of the proprietor,* and were not acting on their own or carrying out a state policy.

To do this, there would need to be a statute that would cover such situations. This necessity of an adequate statute involves a nice point, for the Negroes were not trespassers when they went into the drugstores or novelty shops. They were welcome as customers. The only part of the business premises where they were not welcome was the area of the "white" lunch counters. Now the traditional, common-law conception of trespass looked only at an unlawful entry, and criminal trespass statutes were generally drawn with only unlawful entry in view. The situation faced by the Southern shopkeepers was largely unanticipated by the legislators.

Virginia, for example, discovered in 1960 that its criminal trespass statute was inadequate in this respect and hastily amended the statute to provide that it shall be a criminal offense to enter upon "the lands, *buildings* or premises of *another, or any part, portion or area thereof,* . . . after having been forbidden to do so, either orally or in writing. . . ." (Words italicized represent the amendment.) The statute also contained the following telltale provision: "An emergency exists and this act is in force from its passage."[93]

In *Bouie* v. *Columbia,*[94] two Negro college students entered a drugstore in Columbia, South Carolina, and took seats in a booth in the food department and waited to be served. No one spoke to them or came over to take their order. Then an employee put up a chain with a "no trespassing" sign attached. They remained in their places for fifteen to twenty minutes, each with an open book before him. During this time white customers were served.

The store manager called the police. When they arrived, he asked the students to leave because, he said, he was not going to serve them. They remained seated. The chief of police then asked them to leave. "For what?" one of the students asked him. "Because it is a breach of the peace . . .," he replied. The student again asked the chief of police, "For what?" The chief of police then took him by the arm and pulled him out of his seat; he then seized him by the belt, frisked him, and marched him out of the store. The student offered no resistance.

The Negro students were convicted of trespass and sentenced to pay a fine of $100 or serve thirty days in jail. In addition, the student who had asked, "For what?" was convicted of resisting arrest, and a similar sentence was added to the one imposed on the trespass conviction, the two sentences to run consecutively. They were also charged with breach of the peace but were not convicted on this charge. The state supreme court affirmed only the trespass convictions.

The South Carolina trespass statute prohibited only entry after notice from the owner prohibiting such entry. The defendants argued that there was no evidence on which to convict them under the terms of the statute, and relied on the Thompson case. The South Carolina supreme court, however, construed the trespass statute to cover not only entry but also the act of *remaining* after receiving notice to leave; i.e., it rewrote the statute to make it fit the facts of the case.

The United States Supreme Court, by 6 to 3, reversed the convictions. In the Court's opinion by Justice Brennan, the Court held that a basic due process requirement is that a criminal statute must give "fair warning" of the conduct that it condemns as a crime. The trespass statute, on its face, accomplished this in precise language, but it was "unforeseeably and retroactively" rewritten and expanded by the state court; and so the statute as judicially construed became "void for vagueness." The defendants did not violate the statute as written. Remaining on premises after being asked to leave was a different offense from unlawful entry, and was not provided for by the state's laws. Justice Brennan called attention to the fact that although the trespass statute had been on the books for ninety-five years, it was not until 1961 that the South Carolina supreme court held that it applied to remaining on the premises after having been asked to leave.

On the same day the Supreme Court also decided *Barr* v. *Columbia*,[95] in which five Negro college students entered a drugstore in Columbia, South Carolina, and, after some of them had made some purchases, sat down at the lunch counter and waited for service. In anticipation, the manager had on the preceding day arranged for the police to come and arrest sit-in demonstrators who refused to leave. As a result, three officers were waiting at the drugstore when the students arrived. The manager went with the officers to the students and asked them to leave, and when they refused they were arrested and charged with criminal trespass and breach of the peace. They were convicted on both counts, and the state supreme court affirmed.

As to breach of the peace, the state argued that the mere presence of the students, seated at the lunch counter, might have tended to provoke onlookers to commit acts of violence. The Supreme Court reversed. The opinion for a unanimous Court on this issue, by Justice Black, pointed out that the defendants were polite, quiet, and peaceful from the time they entered to the time they left. Significantly, the Court said:

And further, because of the frequent occasions on which we have reversed under the Fourteenth Amendment convictions of peaceful individuals who were convicted of breach of the peace because of the acts of hostile onlookers, we are reluctant to assume that the breach-of-peace statute covers petitioners' conduct here.

As to the trespass convictions, the Court, by 6 to 3, reversed as in the Bouie case.

Robinson v. *Florida*[96] involved a statute that made it a misdemeanor to remain at a hotel or restaurant after being asked to leave if the guest was intoxicated or conducted himself in a way that disturbed the peace, or if the person was one "who, in the opinion of the management, is a person whom it would be detrimental to such hotel, . . . restaurant, . . . for it any longer to entertain." In effect, this was a trespass-after-entry statute but specified the reasons for which a person might be asked to leave. The case involved nine Negroes and whites, who went as a group to a restaurant in a department store in Miami and seated themselves at tables. The manager told them that they would not be served, called the police, and with a police officer went to each table and again told them that they would not be served and requested them to leave. When they refused, they were all arrested and convicted.

The Court unanimously reversed. In an opinion by Justice Black, the Court avoided passing on the use of the refusal-to-leave statute, for it found this case to follow the pattern of *Peterson* v. *Greenville,* in which the trespass convictions were reversed because Greenville had a segregation ordinance. In the Florida case, the state had a Board of Health regulation that required restaurants to have separate toilet facilities for Negroes "where colored persons are employed or accommodated." Only a month before the arrests in this case, the state had issued a manual in which this provision was stated to be a "basic requirement." This requirement, the Court held, imposed a burden that was "bound to discourage the serving of the two races together," and so was an unconstitutional "state action."

It was in *Bell* v. *Maryland*[97] that the Court gave the fullest consideration to the trespass issue. The case involved twelve Negro students who went into a restaurant in Baltimore. In the lobby they were told by the hostess: "I'm sorry, but we haven't integrated as yet." They went on and took seats at tables. The manager told the leader of the group that the company's policy prohibited service to Negroes. The manager called the police. The state trespass statute was read to them, and the manager went to a police station and obtained warrants for their arrest. They were found guilty of unlawfully entering the restaurant after having been duly notified by the owner's agent not to do so.

While a minority of Supreme Court Justices, as we shall see, went into the trespass issue, a majority of Justices bypassed this issue and reversed the convictions on the ground that after the convictions Baltimore enacted an ordinance that prohibited segregation in places of public accommodation, and this was followed by a statute enacted by the legislature to the same effect. These enactments came after Maryland's court of last resort had affirmed the convictions but before their final disposition by the United States Supreme Court—before the convictions became "final."

Justice Brennan, in his opinion for the Court, argued that the state and the city had substituted "a right for a crime," and a legislature that so acted "probably did not desire that persons should still be prosecuted and punished for the 'crime' of seeking service from a place of public accommodations which denies it on account of race." Five Justices voted for this disposition of the case: Justice Brennan, Chief Justice Warren, and Justices Clark, Stewart, and Goldberg.

While this decision by a majority disposed of the case as a practical matter, the concurring and dissenting opinions raised significant constitutional questions on the merits. Because of the profound policy issues involved, these opinions require consideration.

Justice Goldberg's concurring opinion (in which Chief Justice Warren and Justice Douglas joined) argued that the Civil War Amendments do not permit denial of access to places of public accommodation solely because of race or color. At least since the Brown case, the Constitution is color blind. We cannot, he said,

blind ourselves to the consequences of a constitutional interpretation which would permit citizens to be turned away by all the restaurants, or by the only restaurant, in town. The denial of the constitutional right of Negroes to access to places of public accommodation would perpetuate a caste system in the United States.

Justice Goldberg agreed with the contention of Archibald Cox, Solicitor General, who in his brief in this case stated that

it is an inescapable inference that Congress, in recommending the Fourteenth Amendment, expected to remove the disabilities barring Negroes from the public conveyances and places of public accommodation with which they were familiar, and thus to assure Negroes an equal right to enjoy those aspects of the public life of the community.

This was, said Justice Goldberg, "the contemporary understanding of the general public," i.e., that "freedom from discrimination in places of public accommodation was part of the Fourteenth Amendment's promise of equal protection." Equal treatment in places of public accommodation was not then conceived of as a "social" but rather as a "civil" right, and it was understood that Negroes would enjoy the same civil rights as white persons. This was the understanding at the heart of the Fourteenth Amendment's guarantee of equal protection— that the states by legislation or common law were obligated to guarantee *all* citizens access to places of public accommodation. "For it was assumed that under state law, when the Negro's disability as a citizen was removed, he would be assured the same public civil rights that the law had guaranteed white persons," and white citizens, by common law of the states, enjoyed a remedy against any unjust discrimination in public places.

Justice Goldberg—and Chief Justice Warren and Justice Douglas—in sum, then, agreed with the dissenting opinion of the first Justice John M. Harlan in the civil rights cases of 1883,[98] "that it was understood that under the Fourteenth Amendment the duties of the proprietors of places of public accommodation would remain as they had long been [before the amendment was adopted] and that the States would now [after the adoption of the amendment] be affirmatively obligated to insure that these rights ran to Negro as well as white citizens"; and that if states withdrew or denied these rights, the judicial power of the United States could be used to achieve them; and Justice Goldberg stressed the fact that Justice Joseph P. Bradley's opinion for the Court in the 1883 case rested on the assumption, explicitly stated in the opinion, "that a right to enjoy equal accommodation and privileges in all inns, public conveyances, and places of public amusement [as stated in the Civil Rights Act of 1875], is one of the essential rights of the citizen which no State can abridge or interfere with." Thus the "inaction" of the state, in failing to protect the right of the Negro students who sought service at lunch counters, was "state action" within the meaning of the Fourteenth Amendment.[99] But Maryland was doing even more to hurt its Negro citizens: it was actively prosecuting them for attempting to exercise their right. The decision of the state's court of last resort sustaining the convictions for trespass cannot, said Justice Goldberg,

be described as "neutral," for the decision is as affirmative in effect as if the State had enacted an unconstitutional law explicitly authorizing racial discrimination in places of public accommodation. A State, obligated under the Fourteenth Amendment to maintain a system of law in which Negroes are not denied protection in their claim to be treated as equal members of the community, may not use its criminal trespass laws to frustrate the constitutionally granted right. Nor, it should be added, may a State frustrate this right by legitimating a proprietor's attempt at self-help. . . . As declared in *Cooper* v. *Aaron*, . . . "law and order are not . . . to be preserved by depriving the Negro . . . of [his] constitutional rights."

Justice Douglas, in a separate concurring opinion (in which Justice Goldberg joined), also argued the merits of the basic constitutional issue, just as he had done in one of the 1963 sit-in cases.[100] More than Justice Goldberg, he addressed himself to the argument that, since the restaurant was private property, the trespass convictions were merely judicial recognition of the owner's rights. But, said Justice Douglas,

The property involved is not, however, a man's home or his yard or even his fields. Private property is involved, but it is property that is serving the public. . . . Here it is [a] restaurant refusing service to a Negro. But so far as principle and law are concerned it might just as well be a hospital refusing admission to a sick or injured Negro, . . . or a drug store refusing antibiotics to a Negro, or a bus denying transportation to a Negro. . . .
The problem with which we deal has no relation to opening or closing the door of one's home. The home, of course, is the essence of privacy, in no way dedicated to public use. . . . The facts of these sit-in cases have little resemblance to any institution of property which we customarily associate with privacy. . . .
Restaurants in the modern setting are as essential to travelers as inns and carriers.
Are they not as much affected with a public interest? Is the right of a person to eat less basic than his right to travel . . . ? In these times, that right is, indeed, practically indispensable to travel either interstate or intrastate.

Justice Douglas found the trespass convictions to be "state action":

Maryland's action against these Negroes was as authoritative as any case where the State in one way or another puts its full force behind a policy. The policy here was segregation in places of public accommodation; and Maryland enforced that policy with her police, her prosecutors, and her courts. . . .
Segregation of Negroes in the restaurants and lunch counters of parts of America is a relic of slavery. It is a badge of second-class citizenship. . . . When the state police, the state prosecutor, and the state courts unite to convict Negroes for renouncing that relic of slavery, the "state" violates the Fourteenth Amendment.

Justices Black, Harlan, and White dissented in the Barr, Bouie, and Bell cases in an opinion by Justice Black.[101] Like the three concurring members of the Court, these Justices too wanted a decision on the constitutional merits. Justice Black contended that the Fourteenth

Amendment does not forbid a state to prosecute for "crimes" committed against a person's "property," however prejudiced the complaining "victim" may be. The state does not, by prosecuting for the crime, assimilate to itself the victim's bigotry or prejudice. A "tranquil and orderly society" would be impossible if a citizen, because of his prejudices, could not call for the aid of the police. Addressing himself to the arguments of Justice Goldberg, Justice Black said that he did not believe that the Fourteenth Amendment

was written or designed to interfere with a storekeeper's right to choose his customers or with a property owner's right to choose his social or business associates, so long as he does not run counter to valid state or federal regulation. . . . The Fourteenth Amendment, standing alone, does not prohibit privately owned restaurants from choosing their own customers. It does not destroy what has until very recently been universally recognized in this country as the unchallenged right of a man who owns a business to run the business in his own way so long as some valid regulatory statute does not tell him to do otherwise.

Then Justice Black turned to a consideration of the free-speech aspect of the sit-in demonstrations. The Negro students contended that they had a right to sit in the restaurant, to communicate thereby to the owner their objections to his racial policy, particularly since they made no speeches, passed out no handbills, carried no picket signs, and otherwise did not conduct themselves objectionably; that the form of their communication was appropriate to the time and place.

But Justice Black rejected this view. "The right to freedom of expression," he said,

is a right to express views—not a right to force other people to supply a platform or a pulpit. . . .

A great purpose of freedom of speech and press is to provide a forum for settlement of acrimonious disputes peaceably, without resort to intimidation, force, or violence. The experience of ages points to the inexorable fact that people are frequently stirred to violence when property which the law recognizes as theirs is forcibly invaded or occupied by others. Trespass laws are born of this experience. . . .

Justice Black was right in his observations on the free-speech aspect of the lunch counter sit-ins—*if* he was also right on the trespass question. But if he was wrong on the trespass question, then his argument on the free-speech issue was irrelevant.

And regarding the trespass convictions Justice Black was, one can say, wrong, for the reasons stated by Justices Goldberg and Douglas. I have elsewhere gone at some length into the historical background of the Fourteenth Amendment and have shown that the dissenting opinion of Justice Harlan in the civil rights cases of 1883 was supported by constitutional history, constitutional policy, and logic.[102] To reach his conclusion, Justice Black truncated the principle of *Shelley* v. *Kraemer*,[103] so that it stood for a rather narrow, almost sterile proposition, one that could hardly overflow its factual confines.

If a majority of the Court had agreed with Justice Black, and the convictions for trespass had been affirmed, it would have been an obvious signal for the Southern states to proceed to enforce racial segregation through prosecutions for trespass. Such prosecutions could have been just as effective as were the segregation statutes. Nothing would have been changed but the noises that Southern prosecuting attorneys could constitutionally make in the courts. The Southern states could not say anything about segregation statutes or ordinances; they could not use the disorderly conduct or breach of the peace statutes; they could not keep the N.A.A.C.P. out of the South. But they needed only *one* good legal weapon to sustain racial segregation, only *one* stick with which to beat the Negro; and trespass could have served this purpose beautifully, for trespass calls up images that are dear and venerable: defense of private property, defense of privacy, defense of free enterprise. What the South could not accomplish through racist legislatures, it could just as easily, and with much less of a bad odor, achieve through its criminal courts. Would racial segregation then be more palatable to the Negro, less offensive to sentiments of liberty and equality, and less the result of "state action"?

There are in Justice Black's dissenting opinion some fine phrases about the rule of law and about law and order. He lectured the sit-in demonstrators on some points of public morality. The Constitution, he said, "does not confer upon any group the right to substitute rule by force for rule by law." The "constitutional rule of law," he said, "has served us well." Surely Justice Black, when he took this line of argument, must have forgotten that from 1883 to 1954 the Negro suffered from a "constitutional rule of law" that the Supreme Court had imposed on him by writing into the Constitution the rule of "separate but equal" facilities. Surely he must have forgotten that the Negro, more than anyone else in our history, had suffered from the substitution of "rule by force for rule by law." Generally the law gave the Negro the short end; but when the law was on his side, he and the law were crushed by mob rule, and by large conspiracies in which all elements and agencies of society and the state participated actively or by passive consent.

The Negro has a right to ask, time and again, when he is told about law and order and about the rule of law: *Whose* law? *Whose* order? Yes, and until 1954 he could even ask: *Whose* Constitution? Is there a lack of "order" and "law" in the Republic of South Africa? Was there a lack of "law" and "order" in Nazi Germany? Is it from an absence or insufficiency of "law" and "order" that the Russian people suffer?

Justice Black's concluding paragraph quotes from the Preamble to the Constitution: our course is to "establish Justice, insure domestic tranquillity . . . and secure the Blessings of Liberty to ourselves and our Posterity." But there is not a word in his opinion about the Negro's claim for justice, and the Negro's claim for liberty. His opinion is focused only on the need for tranquillity—and especially the tranquillity of owners of restaurants and lunch counters. This obsessive concentration on the tranquillity of property and business is odd in a case that involves some fundamental human questions—such as the right to humiliate men publicly by excluding them from the tables where men sit down to break bread, as if they were cattle that had to be served elsewhere; and it is especially odd on the part of a member of the Court who had made an "absolute" out of freedom of speech and press —a freedom which, more than any other, has the capacity to replace tranquillity with clear and present dangers to property, to every law, and to every kind of order.

The logical inference that can be drawn from this dissenting opinion is that all the thousands of Negroes who participated in the sit-ins really belonged in the jails of the South. It was not their merits or rights that kept them free but the stupidity and incompetence of the Southern lawyers. Directly after the Brown decision, the lawyers should have advised the state legislatures to repeal all segregation laws, and at the same time the states should have carefully revised their trespass statutes. Had this been done, and had the prosecutors based their cases against the Negroes on the trespass statutes, the jails and prisons could have been filled to capacity with the young demonstrators; there would have been "standing room only" in the jails and prisons, and racial segregation would have continued as the "rule of law"—only legally one could not mention the subject but only talk about trespass!

Justice Black must have forgotten that the Supreme Court's "rule of law" was that school desegregation was to be accomplished with "all deliberate speed," and yet, at the end of 1963, only 1 per cent of the Negro children in the eleven Southern states were in desegregated schools. The ratio became 2 per cent by the end of 1964; but in Alabama, Arkansas, Georgia, Mississippi, and South Carolina—five out of eleven states—the percentage was, at the end of 1964, still less than 1.[104] And even this record of "achievement" came about only as the result of countless suits and court orders—and countless Negro demonstrations.

Of course one cannot blame the Supreme Court for this shameful record; but the record can hardly be expected to make the American Negro jump with national pride when he hears talk about law and order and the rule of law.[105]

As we have seen, in the sit-in cases decided by the Court before *Bell* v. *Maryland* in June 1964, the Court stressed the fact that the Negro students had behaved peacefully at the lunch counters—that they did not argue, shout, or make other noises, or use force in any way. Certainly those decisions must have persuaded many Negroes that the Court would solidly support them as long as they pursued the policy of nonviolent resistance. There was not a single word in the Court's opinions that the Negroes had been in places where they had no right to be, that in some way their actions were unlawful. And Justice Black participated in all the earlier sit-in cases. Yet in June 1964 he wrote in his opinion: "A great purpose of freedom of speech and press is to provide a forum for settlement of acrimonious disputes peaceably, without resort to intimidation, force, or violence." But now he gave these words a meaning that heretofore they did not have: sitting at a lunch counter peacefully, without arguing or threatening, is *by itself* the use of intimidation, force, and violence. Now, if this is what a peaceful sit-in is, what is wrong with calling it disorderly conduct or breach of the peace? Surely if the actions amount to criminal trespass, *a fortiori* they could be called by some milder names! The Thompson case was analogous to the sit-ins only if the demonstrators were as guiltless of wrongdoing as was Sam Thompson when he shuffled his feet on the floor of the café without the slightest objection from the owner. But now it turns out that Justice Black all along must have thought that the demonstrators were not at all as innocently engaged as was Sam Thompson; that the Court was only playing some secret game of anagrams—it was waiting for the Southern lawmen to cry out the magic word: "Trespass!" Everything Justice Black said in his opinion in the Bell case about the rationale of trespass, why society should want to punish acts of trespass, shows that trespass is made a serious criminal offense because it may lead to breaches of the peace if not legally punished. "The experience of ages points to the inexorable fact that people are frequently stirred to violence," said Justice Black, "when property which the law recognizes as theirs is forcibly invaded or occupied by others. Trespass laws are born of this experience." Could not an act that stirs to violence be a breach of the peace or disorderly conduct?

The earlier sit-in cases were, I believe, correctly decided; they did not involve disorderly conduct or breaches of the peace, just as the cases decided in June 1964 did not involve criminal trespass. In fact, the sit-ins that were strictly peaceful were *in no way* criminal, for the reasons given by Justices Goldberg and Douglas.

Justice Black had a choice in the Bell case and the associated cases. He could have accepted the arguments of Justices Goldberg and Douglas and Chief Justice Warren. In the 1963–1964 term the Court split in six cases involving internal security, immigration, or nationality, and in all six cases Justice Black voted with Chief Justice Warren and Justices Douglas and Goldberg. The same pattern appeared in the five freedom-of-expression cases in which the Court divided.[106] Indeed, if the law is, as Justice Holmes described it, the "prophecies of what the courts will do in fact, and nothing more pretentious,"[107] it should have been relatively easy to foretell Justice Black's vote in civil rights or First Amendment cases. I say this not to disparage but to underscore the great debt that the nation owes him for the integrity of his principled position. But all the more for this reason is his dissenting opinion in the Bell case a deep and hurtful disappointment. It shows even less moral sensitivity than was shown by the judge of the Baltimore criminal court who, in the Bell case, fined the defendants only $10, suspended the fines, and said: "These people are not law-breaking people; . . . their action was one of principle rather than any intentional attempt to violate the law."[108]

Justice Black is an "absolutist" not only with respect to the First Amendment freedoms, but with respect to *all* liberties and rights guaranteed by the Constitution; and he has used the term "Bill of Rights" broadly "as including all provisions of the original Constitution and Amendments that protect individual liberty . . ."; and he also believes that "by virtue of the Fourteenth Amendment, the first Ten Amendments are now applicable to the States. . . ."[109] The Fourteenth Amendment prohibits a state from making or *enforcing* "any law" that abridges the privileges or immunities of United States citizens; or from depriving any person of his liberty without due process; or from denying to any person the equal protection of the laws. No exceptions or qualifications are to be found in these clauses—they are written in terms that are "absolute." These clauses are no less "absolute" than are those in the First Amendment. And these clauses of the Fourteenth Amendment were adopted with an eye on the Negro. The Supreme Court in 1873—*only five years* after the Fourteenth Amendment was adopted—wrote:

The one pervading purpose found in . . . all these [Civil War Amendments], lying at the foundation of each, and without which none of them would have been even suggested; we mean the freedom of the slave race, the security and firm establishment of that freedom, and the protection of the newly-made freeman and citizen from the oppressions of those who had formerly exercised unlimited dominion over him.[110]

Yet in the 1964 sit-in cases Justice Black found it necessary to review the history of the Fourteenth Amendment so as to give it a restricted—far from an "absolute"—meaning. He has not read the history of the First Amendment in this way, so as to read into its "absolute" terms exceptions, such as obscene or libelous publications.

Finally, Justice Black directed some of his strongest blows against a windmill. The Fourteenth Amendment, he contended, was "directed at state action only" and "did not displace the power of the state and federal legislative bodies to regulate the affairs of privately owned businesses." But all that was involved in the sit-in cases was the *enforcement* of a *state's* criminal trespass law to continue racial segregation in places of *public* accommodation. It was a *state's* criminal law that was *enforced* by the *state's judicial process* against the demonstrators. The owner of the place of business was not before the Supreme Court; it was Florida in the Robinson case, Maryland in the Bell case, and South Carolina in the Bouie case that stood before the bar of the Supreme Court. In legal contemplation, the owners of the lunch counters had no more standing than has the victim of any other crime— rape, arson, or theft. Trespass is no more and no less a crime than these. It is an attack on a man's property, just as an attack on his person may be assault and battery. If he wants to vindicate his *private* right, he can sue for damages. But through the criminal law *society* vindicates *its* rights—the rights of the *public*.

From this point of view one may well ask if it is not *state action* when a state—as, for example, South Carolina—lets it be known that it stands fully ready, with its police and courts, to act upon a signal from any and all owners of places of public accommodation, to punish Negroes who venture to ask for unsegregated service. All that the owner needs to do is to shout: "Trespass!"—and the floodgates of the law would be opened to flush out the Negro "criminals." Only the owners must be sure *not* to use such words as "disorderly conduct" or "breach of the peace"; *that* could spoil everything. The magic word is *"trespass."*

I have dealt with Justice Black's opinion at some length precisely because it was he who wrote it, and not Justice Harlan or Justice White, who joined him; for he is the senior Justice of the Supreme Court, where he has served with great distinction since 1937, and where he has led in the effort to win maximum support for fundamental human rights and liberties. His place in American history will be a notable and honorable one.

But the place of the sit-ins in American history will also be a notable and honorable one; for through them voluntary desegregation was achieved in hundreds of cities and towns; without them, it is doubtful if Congress would have enacted the Civil Rights Act of 1964; without them, it is hard to see how the Negro could have gained a new and vital sense of his own dignity; without them, the Negro would have no conception of the meaning of nonviolent resistance to unjust laws or customs, and only heaven knows what directions would have been given to his accumulated feelings of despondency and anger.

Despite all that Justice Black said about the rule of law as the guarantor of liberty and equality, the Negroes in the high schools and colleges saw daily with their own eyes that the Constitution and the law had done very little for them. They were often used *against,* and not *for,* them and their rights to liberty and equality.

In the light of the historical record, it is hard to believe in the immaculate conception of rights and liberties. Aldous Huxley somewhere wrote that "liberties are not given; they are taken." Americans *took* their liberties by fighting for them in 1776. The Civil War Amendments were written in the blood of a war that brought death to more Americans than did any other war, including World War II. Unfortunately, ideal aspirations have seldom achieved their ends without the aid of material forces. "The great transitions [in history]," Alfred North Whitehead wrote, "are due to a coincidence of forces derived from both sides of the world, its physical and its spiritual natures"— and among the former he listed such things as "senseless forces, floods, barbarians, and mechanical devices." Great ideas, like liberty or equality, sometimes even "enter reality with evil associates," but "the greatness remains, nerving the [human] race in its slow ascent."[111] Fortunately for America, in the 1950s and early 1960s the great ideas of liberty and equality entered reality with associates who were far removed from evil and who, by using their bodies, by sitting peacefully at lunch counters, provided the "physical forces" that were needed as midwives. The Negro's body was more than a physical force; it was his tongue, it was his plea, his petition. The Negro students gave new meaning to the words of the prophet Isaiah, "Their strength is to sit still," for their sitting was a form of speech that showed "the spirit of wisdom, and understanding, the spirit of counsel and might, the spirit of knowledge and of the fear of the Lord."[112]

A half-year after the decision in the Bell, Robinson, and Bouie cases, the Court had before it two important civil rights cases, to which we now turn our attention.

On December 14, 1964, the Court decided the Atlanta Motel case,[113] in which it unanimously upheld the constitutionality of the public-accommodations provisions of the Civil Rights Act of 1964, which came into force on July 2, 1964, several weeks after the Supreme Court's decisions in the Bell and related sit-in cases. The act, in Title II, provides that any establishment that provides lodging to transient guests "affects [interstate] commerce" *per se*; that restaurants and other eating places "affect commerce" if they offer to serve interstate travelers or if a substantial portion of the products they serve have "moved in commerce"; and there are similar provisions respecting other places of public accommodation the operations of which "affect commerce." Segregation is prohibited in all such places. While the act carried no congressional findings of fact, it was clear that Congress considered racial discrimination a damaging burden upon interstate commerce.

Justice Clark, in his opinion for the Court, held that the Constitution gave Congress plenary power to regulate interstate commerce; that Congress had a "rational basis" for finding that racial discrimination by motels affected such commerce, and that the means selected by Congress to eliminate this evil were reasonable and appropriate.

It is hard to think that there was in the country a single lawyer with a knowledge of constitutional law who for a moment expected any other decision.

Justice Black wrote a concurring opinion which only elaborated on some of the points covered in Justice Clark's opinion but added nothing that was new.

Justices Douglas and Goldberg wrote concurring opinions which, however, went beyond the Court's position and attempted to give the act a broader base than is provided by the power to regulate interstate commerce. Their opinions have a pathos that casts a dark shadow on the status of some basic human rights as conceived under the United States Constitution.

Agreeing that the Commerce Clause vests power in Congress to regulate commerce "in the interests of human rights," Justice Douglas argued, however, that the right to be free from racial discrimination "occupies a more protected position in our constitutional system than does the movement of cattle, fruit, steel and coal across state lines."[114] He would have preferred to rest the decision on Section 5 of the Fourteenth Amendment, which gives Congress the power to enforce, by legislation, the provisions of that amendment; for "the right to be free of discriminatory treatment (based on race) in places of public accommodation—whether intrastate or interstate—is a right guaranteed against state action by the Fourteenth Amendment. . . ."

Justice Goldberg, also agreeing that the action of Congress in passing the act was within its power under the Commerce Clause, stressed that the primary purpose of the act "is the vindication of human dignity and not mere economics," and that the act is also constitutional under Section 5 of the Fourteenth Amendment.

These two concurring opinions are, I think, entirely justified, and it would have been a morally cleansing act if the entire Court had openly recognized the fact that the Civil Rights Act of 1964 intended to accomplish something more important than merely the removal of certain obstacles to and burdens on commerce between the states. The occasion called for something better than resort to a legal fiction or crutch.

There is, of course, language in the act that was put in to make sure that the act would be valid under the Commerce Clause; but this is because only a minority of Justices have been willing to give to the Privileges and Immunities Clause and to other provisions of the Fourteenth Amendment sufficient breadth to comprehend all basic human rights. Justices Bushrod Washington, Bradley, Stephen J. Field, Noah H. Swayne, Harlan, Murphy, and Jackson[115] in the past, and Justices Douglas and Goldberg, and to a lesser degree Chief Justice Warren, have shown a willingness to read the Fourteenth Amendment in a way that would maximize the enjoyment and security of all fundamental rights; but the Atlanta Motel case shows that the Court continues to think in such a way that fundamental rights, such as those protected by the Civil Rights Act of 1964, can best come into the Constitution through, as it were, the kitchen door, with the man who delivers eggs, meat, and milk. It is a tragic fact that the Court, in validating the Civil Rights Act, bypassed the amendments that were adopted precisely with the view to assuring the Negro of all the rights, privileges, and immunities that go with being a "person" and a "citizen"—what he was not when he was a slave. It is odd, indeed, that the Court, since 1937, has had no difficulty in giving to the Commerce Clause the broadest possible interpretation, so that under its power Congress may fix minimum wages, set minimum prices on the sales of milk, control labor-management relations, and do many other things that were certainly beyond the contemplation of the Framers of the Constitution, *and is even willing to let "commerce between the states" comprehend civil rights,* yet drew back from the opportunity to place civil rights squarely under the Thirteenth and Fourteenth Amendments, where historically and morally civil rights belong.

The sense of something very important having been compromised or lost is aggravated as one reads some of the opinions in the sit-in cases decided on the same day in December 1964 as the Atlanta Motel case.

In *Hamm* v. *Rock Hill* and *Lupper* v. *Arkansas,*[116] which were consolidated, the sit-in demonstrators were convicted of criminal trespass under the laws of South Carolina and Arkansas. By 5 to 4 the Court reversed. The majority opinion by Justice Clark held that the convictions—like that in *Bell* v. *Maryland*—had abated. In light of the new act of Congress, enacted before these judgments were reviewed by the Supreme Court, "there is no public interest," said the Court, "to be served in the further prosecution of the petitioners." Since the act of Congress intervened before the convictions were "finalized," and since the act substituted "a right for a crime," and since its purpose was "to obliterate the effect of a distressing chapter of our history," the Court held that the situation called for the application of "a normal rule of statutory construction to strike down pending convictions inconsistent with the purposes of the Act."

Justices Black, Harlan, Stewart, and White dissented in separate opinions, in which the following arguments were made: that the doctrine of abatement cannot be applied in the construction of a *federal* act to apply to *state* legislation; that there is no evidence showing that giving effect to *past* state convictions for trespass would result in any burden on *present* interstate commerce; that congressional silence on the question of abatement between the decision in *Bell* v. *Maryland* on June 22, 1964, and passage of the act on July 2, 1964, points to a conclusion of congressional intent opposite to that reached by the Court; and that had Congress intended to ratify "massive disobedience to the law," it would have said so in clear language.

Some three thousand convictions were, in effect, reversed by these decisions.[117] Some demonstrators were under severe sentences for trespass convictions—for example, a student of Connecticut College was fined $1000 and sentenced to eighteen months in jail for violating Georgia's trespass law;[118] in one of the cases before the Supreme Court in the Lupper case, the defendants were fined $500 each and sentenced to thirty days' imprisonment for violation of the Arkansas Trespass Act.

There is "logic" of a sort in the argument that, if an act was criminal when it was done, the convicted defendant should be punished for it, and that a later change in the law having the effect of a repeal has no bearing on the guilt or innocence of the defendant.

But logic needs to be tempered by common sense, and by a sense of morality, and by a sense of practicality. Here the law was changed before the convictions were reviewed by the court of last resort, while the cases were still pending. Here the "crime" was in fact an act that in some thirty states was recognized expressly as a "right"; an act that President Kennedy had in mind when he said to the nation: "It ought to be possible for American consumers of any color to receive equal service in places of public accommodation . . . without being forced to resort to demonstrations in the street,"[119] and regarding which President Johnson said, in a formal State of the Union Message: "Today Americans of all races stand side by side in Berlin and Vietnam. They died side by side in Korea. Surely they can work and eat and travel side by side in America."[120] The "crime" of which the defendants were convicted was in fact an act that the Senate Commerce Committee had in mind when it spoke of "the deprivation of personal dignity that surely accompanies denials of equal access to public establishments."[121] In the context of the cases, for the dissenting Justices to speak of the "crime" as if a murder or some other outrage of public decency had taken place—as if the act in question were *malum in se*—was to engage in a dangerous form of abstractionism. Had the three thousand young Negro men and women been put in jail after the enactment of the Civil Rights Act, the moral sense of the American people, and of the world, would have been outraged, and the ideal of the rule of law would have been imperiled.

The law, according to the famous phrase of Lord Coke, is the "perfection of reason." It is not the perfection of logic; for reason is more, much more, than logic. "The misuse of logic . . . begins," said Justice Benjamin N. Cardozo, "when its method and its ends are treated as supreme and final."[122] By abstract and literalistic reasoning, the four dissenting Justices were brought to a conclusion that was absurd and morally indefensible. They obviously disregarded the *caveat* expressed by Justice Bradley, that what may be reasonable in one class of cases may be entirely unreasonable in another.[123] Above all, they seem to have forgotten that just as the Court has in its keeping its precedents and rule of law, so, too, it has in its keeping the conscience of the law. The equity jurisdiction of courts had its origin and development in the conviction of the common law that moral considerations and conscience at times override the letter of the law. This meant that courts could, when necessary, use legal methods and conceptions with flexibility in place of rigidity. Speaking for the Court in a case decided in 1944, Justice Douglas said:

The qualities of mercy and practicality have made equity the instrument for nice adjustment and reconciliation between the public interest and private needs as well as between competing private claims.[124]

These qualities had a special role when the Court was faced with the question whether some three thousand Negroes should be put behind bars and marked for the remainder of their lives as persons with criminal records. There was no need for Congress to mention expressly the thousands of Negroes, including Martin Luther King, Jr.,[125] who had been arrested and sentenced for trespass, for the purpose of the statute enacted by Congress was to vindicate the rights and privileges of the demonstrators. In the Atlanta Motel case the Court said that in framing Title II of the act "Congress was also dealing with what it considered a moral problem."

The disposition of the Hamm and Lupper cases bears out the position taken by Justices Goldberg and Douglas in the Atlanta Motel case, that, as the former wrote, the "primary purpose" of the 1964 act was "the vindication of human dignity and not mere economics," and it must have been for *this* reason, though unexpressed, that the Court, in the Hamm and Lupper cases, reversed the trespass convictions.

The speeches and messages of Presidents Kennedy and Johnson, the action of Congress in passing the Civil Rights Act of 1964, and the decisions of the Court on December 14, 1964, collectively bear testimony to the fact that the peaceful sit-ins were effective as a form of petition for the redress of grievances. For a hundred years the grievances had been suffered with unexampled submissiveness. Not until 1950—as we saw in Chapter VI—did Negroes openly attack the "separate but equal" interpretation of the constitutional guarantee of racial equality. But the decisions of the Supreme Court, from 1950 on, attacked segregation only when it was found to have been supported "under color" of a law. There was no indication that the Court could be relied on to go beyond a rather narrow view of what constitutes "state action," and some of the law-review writings on *Shelley* v. *Kraemer* probably tended to retard the march of civil rights through litigation. Progress was made by two factors:

(1) The incompetence—or misfortune—of Southern states' attorneys, who prosecuted demonstrators on records that could not stand up when examined closely, especially after the decision in the Thompson case in 1960; and when the states lost their cases in 1961, 1962, and 1963, the Negroes won the precious time that they needed.

(2) The exploitation by the Negroes of this "borrowed time" to involve many thousands of young persons in peaceful sit-in demonstrations. Eventually the trespass issue was bound to arise, and there was real concern as to how the Court would resolve the question. In oral argument before the Court in 1962, some questions and comments from Justice Black were obvious danger signals. At one point he asked Jack Greenberg, N.A.A.C.P. counsel, who was arguing about "state action":

Assuming that the owner does have a legal right to choose who can come into his place, do you argue that the state has no right to protect his right?

At another point, Justice Black said from the bench:

Does the Constitution protect the power of property in selecting his customers? That's the issue.

He also said at the time that the owner of a store may follow the local custom of racial segregation not out of state coercion but simply to "make more money"—implying that the owner was free to do so and to invoke the police power of the state in enforcing his decision without the state's thereby violating the Constitution.[126]

Thus, though no one could have planned it this way, the civil rights forces in effect played for time, and the time won through the Court was used, through the sit-in demonstrations (primarily, though, of course, not exclusively), to persuade the President and Congress that only a broad and effective federal civil rights statute could end the unrest. As merchants voluntarily agreed to integrate their public facilities, they, no less than the Negroes, needed the federal act to end any possible competitive advantages gained by the obstinately resisting merchants, so that all lunch counters and other public places would be equally placed competitively.

The sit-in demonstrators held, therefore, the key to the future public policy of the United States with respect to racial practices in places of public accommodation. In retrospect, the history of the events can make one feel as if there were a pre-established harmony. The events meshed, though there was no plan that manipulated irreconcilable forces. In a sense, the reconciliation was effected by the thousands of young, immature, anonymous Negroes, boys and girls in high school and college, who assumed the burden of bearing witness, by sitting mutely and with moral courage, petitioning not only the manager of the store, but beyond him the American people and their President, their Congress, and their courts. These village Hampdens were eloquent in their silence, and their victory brings to mind the lines of Gray:

> Th' applause of list'ning senates to command,
> The threats of pain and ruin to despise, . . .
> And read their hist'ry in a nation's eyes.

Regarding school segregation, the Court in 1958 said that the rights of Negro children

can neither be nullified openly and directly by state legislators or state executive or *judicial officers,* nor nullified indirectly by them through evasive schemes for segregation whether attempted "ingeniously or ingenuously."[127]

In the light of the record of prosecutions of sit-in demonstrators on one ground or another, in an anxious search for a substitute for the Black Codes, there can be no question that the convictions for trespass were judicial attempts—"ingeniously or ingenuously" contrived —to retain segregation in places of public accommodation. That four Justices of the Court refused to see through the cry of "trespass" to the ugly fact of state-enforced segregation is in itself a sufficient reason to avoid exclusive reliance on the courts for vindication of fundamental human rights. The vote of a single judge can hardly be expected to settle the destinies of a race or a nation. Jefferson was willing to accept the idea that "a little rebellion now and then is a good thing," and that "the tree of liberty must be refreshed from time to time with the blood of patriots and tyrants."[128] We have no need for such extreme measures. But the history of labor and of civil rights in the United States shows that, as Justice Frankfurter wrote,

Particularly in legislation affecting freedom of thought and freedom of speech much which should offend a free-spirited society is constitutional. Reliance for the most precious interests of civilization, therefore, must be found outside of their vindication in courts of law. Only a persistent positive translation of the faith of a free society with the convictions and habits and actions of a community is the ultimate reliance against unabated temptations to fetter the human spirit.[129]

The lunch-counter sit-in demonstrations, and their final vindication in the Supreme Court by the contingency of a single vote, despite their previous vindication in an act of Congress, have given a fresh significance to these words. Laws are made and unmade by legislators and judges, but also by "free-spirited" men and women willing to act out their convictions through nonviolent resistance to "habits and actions of a community" which degrade the dignity of man and debase his self-esteem and estate.

But one's last word on this subject must be a recognition of the inestimably great contribution that the Court, under Chief Justice Warren, has made to the struggle for civil rights—a struggle that would not have been possible if the Court had not shown itself to be ready to test the claims of justice in cases that involved only $10 fines; and the claims of equality made by boys and girls, many of whom could barely spell the word; and the claims for the First Amendment freedoms on behalf of men and women who were eloquent as they sat mute and by their silence asserted their freedom to speak and to petition for the redress of their grievances, grievances against customs, against laws, and even against the Constitution if it should—God forbid!—fail them.

Nor can we leave the subject without recognizing the contribution of Congress. In breaking the Southern filibuster in the Senate and in enacting the broadly conceived Civil Rights Act that was offered by the Kennedy administration, Congress went far toward completion of the work that was begun by Lincoln when he issued the Emancipation Proclamation and by Congress when it passed the Fourteenth Amendment and sent it to the states for ratification. This act will stand in importance and dignity next to the Civil War Amendments among the great documents of American history.

In passing the act when it did, Congress sought to bring to an end one of the greatest social, political, and moral crises ever faced by the American people, and it also saved the Supreme Court from an ordeal such as it has not suffered since President Roosevelt's attack on it in February 1937. For if the act had not been passed, the Court would have had to decide the Hamm and Lupper trespass cases on their merits. We know that Justices Douglas and Goldberg, and very likely Chief Justice Warren, would have voted for a reversal of the convictions. We know that Justices Black, Harlan, Stewart, and White would have upheld the convictions. We do not know how Justice Clark or Justice Brennan would have voted. On the basis of their past voting records in civil rights and civil liberties cases,[130] one might hazard the thought that Justice Brennan would have voted for reversal and Justice Clark for affirmance; and thus the decision would have been 5 to 4 to let the trespass convictions stand. One hates to think of the social unrest, or even upheaval, that would have been the effect of such a decision. It is doubtful if the Negro leaders could have restrained the masses of Negroes that would have taken to the streets. The seven major riots that occurred in the summer of 1964 all happened *after* July 2, 1964, when Congress passed and President Johnson signed the act. Only heaven knows what might have happened had the three thousand Negroes gone to jail and had countless thousands of others invaded lunch counters, restaurants, and theaters to let themselves be arrested and jailed. The storm over the Supreme Court would have shaken its moral position and would have brought immeasurable harm to the nation's respect for law and to our trust in judges as constituting uniquely a "fellowship of reconciliation."

Fortunately, this crisis for the Supreme Court was avoided, and all branches of the federal government acted in a way that brought increased esteem for the Constitution and renewed faith in the health of our political, moral, and social order—an order which serves the spiritual destinies of those who participate in its life by not neglecting their duties.

VIII

"With Liberty and Justice for All"

1. Americans of Chinese and Japanese Descent

The dramatic events of the struggle to end discrimination against the Negro have been related in two chapters and touched on in other chapters as well; but the United States has, unfortunately, a record of discrimination against other minorities too, and with respect to these minority groups—racial and national—some commendable events have happened, though without the *Sturm und Drang* that have accompanied the struggle over the Negro's rights.

Although some forty-two million men and women have come to our shores, the American record in reception and treatment of aliens leaves much to be desired from the standpoint of human rights. This is especially true regarding the immigration of Orientals or Asians.

Starting in 1882, Congress passed numerous acts to exclude Chinese. In the Chinese Exclusion case[1] in 1889, the Supreme Court unanimously upheld the power of Congress to pass such exclusion acts even when they contravene formal treaties. The attitude of the United States Government toward Chinese immigrants was stated by the Supreme Court in an earlier case, in 1884:

A restriction upon their further immigration was felt to be necessary, to prevent the degradation of white labor and to preserve to ourselves the inestimable benefits of our Christian civilization.[2]

At the time Congress passed the anti-Chinese acts, there were very few Chinese outside the states on the West Coast, and members of Congress from other parts of the country knew about the Chinese immigrants only what the West Coast propagandists chose to tell them. China was at that time too weak to shake a big stick at us. After Reconstruction came to an end in 1877, a voting pattern developed in Congress: Southern members of Congress voted for anti-

Chinese measures in return for votes by members from the West on anti-Negro measures.

Before the turn of the century California race-purists started to clamor for the exclusion also of Japanese, although in 1890 there were only 2039 Japanese in the United States and the state was sparsely settled. But the United States had no desire to affront Japan, which was not a hat-in-hand nation. In 1907 Theodore Roosevelt succeeded in effecting the so-called Gentlemen's Agreement, which virtually stopped Japanese immigration. But this did not stop the Californians from wanting an act of Congress; and so, when the Quota Act came up in 1924, they succeeded in getting provisions for the exclusion of Japanese. Had the Japanese been given a quota, it would have meant an annual immigration of about one hundred persons.[3]

With our knowledge of what happened at Pearl Harbor on December 7, 1941, there was prescience in the message of Charles Evans Hughes, then Secretary of State, to the House Committee on Immigration as it was considering the 1924 act:

The practical effect of section 12(b) is to single out Japanese immigrants for exclusion. The Japanese are a sensitive people, and unquestionably would regard such a legislative enactment as fixing a stigma upon them. I regret that I feel compelled to say that I believe such legislative action would largely undo the work of the Washington Conference on Limitation of Armament. . . .[4]

An immigration law of 1917 contained a barred-zone provision, which had the effect of an exclusion act, to keep out immigrants from India, Siam (Thailand), Java (now part of Indonesia), Ceylon, and certain other Asian countries.

Not only were Asians singled out for exclusion; the few who were legally admitted found that our naturalization laws barred them from citizenship. Thus we had laws that were both discriminatory and cruel, for they relegated certain persons, though legally here, to a status of permanent alienage.

In 1922 the Supreme Court, interpreting the naturalization law of 1790, held that naturalization was open only to an alien who is "a free white person," and, under a law of 1870, to an alien of African nativity or descent; and the Court held that Japanese were excluded from American citizenship because they were not Caucasians.[5] In another case decided in the same year the Supreme Court held that aliens from India, though admittedly Caucasians, were barred from citizenship because they were not "white" persons.[6] Thus Japanese were excluded from American citizenship because they were not Cauca-

342 | EXPANDING LIBERTIES

sians—a racial test; and aliens from India were excluded because they were not white—a color test. These decisions were used by federal courts to deny naturalization to Koreans and other people from Asia. An exception was made in favor of Filipinos if they had served for at least three years in the armed forces of the United States.[7]

The first break in this pattern of discrimination came in 1943 when President Roosevelt, in a message to Congress, asked for repeal of the Chinese exclusion laws. We were then engaged in World War II, and China was our ally and was to be one of the Big Five of the United Nations, enjoying permanent membership in the Security Council and the veto power. "By repeal of the Chinese exclusion laws," said the President, "we can correct a historic mistake and silence the distorted Japanese propaganda."[8] Congress repealed the exclusion acts, and China was given an annual quota of 105 immigrants. In 1946 Congress passed an act to give India an annual quota of 100 immigrants.[9] Also in 1946, Congress passed acts providing for the admission and naturalization of Filipinos. Then in 1952 a new Immigration and Nationality Act ended all racial and color bars on naturalization; and this statute ended all overt racial and color discrimination in our immigration policy; yet provisions in this law subtly yet clearly discriminated in the admission of immigrants of Chinese ancestry who had non-Chinese nationality and in the admission of Negroes from the West Indies.[10]

Surely it is disturbing to recall that it took a World War, a Cold War, and a Korean War to bring to an end racial discrimination in our immigration and naturalization policies. Had the Chinese, the Japanese, the Indians, and the other nations of Asia been given quotas on a basis of equality with some European peoples, our quota laws would have given them an annual total of approximately a thousand immigrants,[11] which has been their combined quota since 1952, with no visible ill effects on the American people; yet monstrous events had to take place before Congress could be moved to perform an act that had more symbolic than tangible reality.

It is not possible to pass over in silence what "is now widely regarded as the most serious violation of the rights of citizens and of peaceful resident aliens ever actively sponsored by the federal government"[12]—the exclusion of Americans of Japanese ancestry from a certain area of the West Coast, under an evacuation order in 1942, and their internment.[13] Two-thirds of those affected were American citizens. After the war, over half of the evacuees returned to the West Coast. They are said to have lost between $350,000,000 and

$500,000,000—though no person of Japanese ancestry had been charged with sabotage or espionage.

Since the end of World War II, despite our lack of relations with Communist China, there has been no ostensible discrimination against the approximately one million aliens and Americans of Oriental or Asian descent. In part this may be owing to the transfer of prejudice to Negroes and Mexicans. We still have problems, but the vexing and explosive problem of prejudice against the Oriental has, providentially, been largely ended.

We can, too, look back to 1965 as the year in which the offensive Nordic-supremacy features of our immigration laws—first enacted in the 1920s and codified in the Immigration and Nationality Act (McCarran-Walter) of 1952—were erased by Congress. In a message to Congress on January 13, 1965, President Johnson called for priority consideration of this problem. He said that the national-origins quota system is "incompatible with our basic American tradition." He pointed out that the quota system discriminates not only against potential immigrants but also against *American citizens* whose ancestry is disparaged because they are told that others are more desirable citizens simply because they or their ancestors came from other countries. The total number of immigrants would not be substantially changed if the discriminatory provisions were taken out of our immigration laws; the total of authorized immigrants would be 158,361, an increase of less than 7000. But the change in our laws would be a reaffirmation of our belief that a man should be judged, "and exclusively judged," said President Johnson, "on his worth as a human being."

On October 3, 1965, Congress responded to this challenge and enacted H.R. 2580, which provides for the ending of national quotas on June 30, 1968. Thereafter, no person will receive any preference or priority or be discriminated against in the issuance of an immigrant visa because of his race, sex, nationality, place of birth, or place of residence. The act is not perfect but it wipes out a form of discrimination that was an affront to millions of Americans and to democratic ideals.

2. New Deal to New Trail for American Indians

In his State of the Union Message of January 8, 1964, President Johnson said that federal-local effort must end poverty wherever it exists, in city slums, in small towns, in sharecroppers' shacks or in migrant worker camps, *on Indian reservations,* among whites as well as among Negroes....[14]

This was, it seems, the first time in many years that the Indians had been mentioned by a President in a State of the Union Message. Significantly, however, they are mentioned in connection with the nation's problem of the underprivileged, of those who suffer from lack of economic opportunity and its consequences.

Contrary to common impression, the American Indians are not disappearing. In the 1950 census, there were 357,000 Indians; in 1960 their number was 523,000.[15] The Indians are increasing at a higher rate than that for the total population. It is estimated that in 1975 the Indian population will be 720,000.[16] Yet their living conditions could be described only as deplorable. In 1964 the unemployment rate on the reservations was from 40 to 50 per cent, the average *family* income was $1500 (the average *per capita* personal income in the United States was almost double this amount); the average age at death was forty-two (the average for the United States was seventy; in 1900 it was forty-seven—in 1963 the Indians were five years behind *that* figure); 90 per cent of their housing was substandard.[17] One needs to go to underdeveloped, backward countries in Asia or Africa for comparable conditions and statistics.

In 1961 the Kennedy administration announced a "New Trail" for Indians. To understand its meaning one needs to have some background. We can only sketch in broad strokes a highly complicated history.

In 1830 Congress enacted the Indian Removal Act,[18] which was based on the assumption that segregation of the Indians in Western territory would be best for both races. At the same time, white men were hungry for the lands held by Indians, and there was a desire to throw the Indians into the general "melting pot," so that they would become culturally, socially, and economically assimilated. Under the Dawes Act of 1887[19] it was possible to individualize Indian land holdings and to permit Indians to dispose of their lands. By 1933 they had lost two-thirds of the lands they had held in 1887.

Their legal status was described by the Supreme Court in these terms:

They are communities dependent on the United States; . . . dependent for their political rights. They owe no allegiance to the States, and receive from them no protection. Because of the local ill feeling of the people, states where they are found are often their deadliest enemies. . . .[20]

This was said in 1885; but it reads almost like an eternal truth, for the situation, while fluctuating, seems hardly to change in essentials.

While the Fourteenth Amendment, in 1868, conferred citizenship on all Negroes born in the United States, Indians had to wait for an act of Congress in 1924 to become citizens.[21] This was affirmed by the Nationality Code of 1940.[22] Until as recently as 1948, Indians were denied the right to vote in Arizona and New Mexico; in 1950 they could not vote in Maine and in 1956 they could not vote in Utah.[23]

John Collier, Commissioner of Indian Affairs from 1933 to 1945, described the plight of the Indian as it was in 1928:

The Indians, by and large, were the most poverty-stricken population in the country. For most of the tribes the land base was severely inadequate or non-existent. Four-fifths of the residual Indian land, in value or potential yield, was unusable by the Indians because of the results of allotment in severalty and of fractionalization through descent to heirs. In most of the tribes all forms of human organization had been killed by the positive or negative official policies of seventy years. A high birth rate was slightly overreached by a very high death rate. The processes of "liquidation," material, biological, psychic and social, were moving forward with steady acceleration. And as a final, all-registering and all-embracing condition, propaganda and the course of events had blanketed the Indian's mind with a deep fatalism. He believed that as a social being he had to die; and other than as a social being, the tribal Indian did not want to live.[24]

Collier drew this devastating picture as of 1928 because the Hoover administration witnessed, as he said, "a gentling of spirit in the Indian service." But the first breakthrough really came in 1934, in the Roosevelt administration, when Congress enacted the Indian Reorganization Act,[25] the most important statute since the Dawes Act of 1887. The act of 1934 introduced a new policy and a new spirit. Under its terms land holdings were increased and land-conservation measures introduced; the organization of Indian tribes was reinvigorated, and tribal customs and laws were given dignity and power; liberal credit policies were established to aid the tribes and individual members; Indian cultural life and institutions were encouraged, and Indian arts and crafts sustained. In spirit, if not in letter, this act of 1934 was a model for the Economic Opportunity Act of 1964.

In his annual report for 1938, Collier defined the New Deal's Indian policy as follows.

So productively to use the moneys appropriated by the Congress for Indians, as to enable them, on good, adequate lands of their own, to earn decent livelihoods and lead self-respecting, organized lives in harmony with their own aims and ideals, as an integral part of American life. Under such a policy, the ideal end result will be the ultimate disappearance of any need for Government aid or supervision. This will not happen tomorrow; perhaps not in our lifetime; but with the revitalization of Indian hope . . . that aim is a probability, and a real one.[26]

Secretary of the Interior Harold Ickes, Collier, William Zimmerman, Assistant Commissioner of Indian Affairs, and Felix S. Cohen, an authority on Indian law, based their activities on the principle that the Indians must be given opportunities *to decide for themselves* what is best for Indians, and that no one has a right to decide for the Indians that they should die out as a people and that their native culture, their forms of social life and consciousness, and their arts and crafts should not be encouraged and used. They assumed that there was nothing "un-American" in a group not wanting to become totally assimilated—that the ideal of cultural pluralism, formulated by Horace M. Kallen in the early 1920s, must be understood to accommodate the Indian tribes who freely wanted to continue their forms of communal existence and life; that just as America is not impoverished by Old Order Amish and other Mennonite communities and by utopian settlements, in which men live by the spirit that possesses and moves them, so, too, the Indians might be afforded opportunities in freedom to work and to live productive lives according to their own rhythm and social and spiritual patterns.

The spirit of the Indian Reorganization Act was the government's policy until about 1950. The Eisenhower administration started a new epoch and brought to an end previous programs and policies. Steps were taken to get the Indians off the reservations; and Indians, bewildered by bureaucratic zigzags, reversals, and confusions, became divided among themselves. Huge blocks of land, involving millions of acres, have gone out of trust. Individual allotments were made and disposed of without regard to their effect on the tribal holdings or on the individual Indians, who found themselves migrants in cities where they were not wanted, and whom the government needed to relocate, as if they were wartime refugees from some foreign oppression. The policy of the Eisenhower administration—and of the Congress of the 1950s, though perhaps to a lesser degree, it is hard to say definitely—seems to have been to liquidate the Indian question by liquidating the Indian himself.

There are in the Southwest villages of Spanish-Americans. There are Mennonite settlements in Pennsylvania. There are settlements of Orthodox Jews in New York State and New Jersey. There are some scattered utopian communites. Are they "un-American"? Would it not be a form of cultural genocide for the government to adopt policies and practices that would have the effect of liquidating them? Yet this was often the policy of the federal government respecting Indian life before 1934 and it became again the policy in the 1950s— a policy which Oliver La Farge described as follows:

Ending tribal ownership of property and encouraging the breakup of solid blocks of Indian land into fragments accompanied by measures to weaken or destroy tribal governments, frustrate Indian leadership, and . . . to cut young Indians off from their cultures and languages or to instill in them contempt for their elders and their tradition. . . . We did not, however, make the subjects over into white men, mentally, morally, or physically; what we did was nearly to destroy the Indian economic base, reduce tens of thousands to landless beggary, and prepare the desolate mess that many now want to sweep under the rug by means of "termination."[27]

The spirit of the policy of "termination" is clearly conveyed by the terms of the resolution of Congress, passed in 1953, that provided that "at the earliest possible time," all the tribes and the individual members thereof located in New York, California, Florida, and Texas, and certain other named tribes, should be freed from all federal supervision and control, and that the offices of the Bureau of Indian Affairs in these states should be abolished.[28]

But fortunately the Kennedy administration resumed the essentials of the policies that obtained through the Roosevelt and Truman years and directed its efforts primarily toward rehabilitation and development of the reservations.

In February 1961, Stewart L. Udall, Secretary of the Interior, set up a Task Force on Indian Affairs, which included Philleo Nash, who became Commissioner of Indian Affairs; and when a report was issued later that year Mr. Udall accepted and endorsed its major recommendations. The most important of these was to shift emphasis from termination of federal trust relationship toward development of the human and natural resources on the reservations, except for "Indians with substantial incomes and superior educational experience, who are as competent as most non-Indians to look after their own affairs," and except for participation in programs under the Social Security Act and the Area Redevelopment Act and similar programs, under which Indians and non-Indians alike may benefit.[29]

The report also recommended vigorous efforts to attract industries to reservations; an expanded program of vocational training and placement; negotiation with states and counties, and resort to courts, to make certain that off-reservation Indians suffer no discrimination and enjoy the rights and privileges of citizens; and more effort to inform the public about the status of the Indians and their problems.

Mr. Udall, in his 1962 report to President Kennedy, said that probably the most significant passage in the Task Force report was the following:

. . . the proper role of the Federal Government is to help Indians find their way along a new trail—one which leads to equal citizenship, maximum self-sufficiency, and full participation in American life. In discharging this role, it must seek to make available to Indians a greater range of alternatives which are compatible with the American system, and, where necessary, to assist Indians with choosing from among these alternatives. . . .[30]

Soon after his election President Kennedy turned his attention to the Indian and said:

We want every group which is now unable to make its full contribution to American strength to be given the opportunity to do so. It is in this spirit that we shall approach our work on Indian reservations, and it is in this spirit, I am sure, that Indians throughout the country will work together for a better life. . . .[31]

And in the summer of 1962, as if to symbolize the "New Trail" spirit, President Kennedy received at the White House the first group of ten Indian and Eskimo young men from Alaska who had completed an eighteen-month course of electronics training in New York City and were on their way to high-paying positions in their native state.[32] Congress has responded with increased appropriations for training and other programs.[33]

As we have seen, President Johnson made special mention of the Indians in his message on poverty; and Hubert H. Humphrey, when he was Senator, stated that the logical starting place for the first battle against poverty would be on pilot projects on Indian reservations; and Secretary Udall agreed with Senator Humphrey.[34] Thus it may well be that the most important accomplishment for Indians, since the New Deal act of 1934, may be the "New Trail" that they may find in the Economic Opportunity Act of 1964.[35]

Congress appropriated, for fiscal 1965, $85,000,000 for Alliance for Progress grants in Latin-American countries. A substantial part of this sum would, without doubt, be used to aid the Indian populations of Ecuador, Peru, Bolivia, and Chile, where many Indians live in total or semi-servitude. Would it not be strange if it were to turn out that the federal government was able to accomplish more for the Indians of Latin America than for its own?

At a conference in 1961, of 460 Indians of 90 tribes, the Indians drew up a statement which concluded as follows:

When Indians speak of the continent they yielded, they are not referring only to the loss of some millions of acres in real estate. They have in mind that the land supported a universe of things they knew, valued, and loved.

With that continent gone, except for the few parcels they still retain, the basis of life is precariously held, but they mean to hold the scraps and parcels as any small nation or ethnic group was ever determined to hold to identity and survival.

What we ask of America is not charity, not paternalism, even when benevolent. We ask only that the nature of our situation be recognized and made the basis of policy and action.

In short, the Indians ask for assistance, technical and financial, for the time needed, however long that may be, to regain in the America of the space age some measure of the adjustment they enjoyed as the original possessors of their native land.[36]

Surely a nation that proposes to lift Asians from a state of abject poverty, disease, and ignorance to a life of abundance and human dignity—as President Johnson offered to do in his address on Vietnam at Johns Hopkins University in April 1965[37]—may reasonably be expected to help effectively a half-million Indians, who are American citizens, to attain "the adjustment they enjoyed as the original possessors of their native land."

Three
Human Rights

IX

American Policy in International Protection of Human Rights

On July 22, 1963, President Kennedy sent to the United States Senate a letter[1] of such great historic importance that its text ought to be read in its entirety:

I have today transmitted to the Senate three conventions with a view to receiving advice and consent to ratification. These are:

1. The Supplementary Convention to the Abolition of Slavery, the Slave Trade, and Institutions and Practices Similar to Slavery, prepared under the direction of the United Nations in 1956, to which 49 nations are now parties.

2. The Convention on the Abolition of Forced Labor, adopted by the International Labor Organization in 1957, to which 60 nations are now parties.

3. The Convention on the Political Rights of Women, opened for signature by the United Nations in 1953, to which 39 nations are now parties.

United States law is, of course, already in conformity with these conventions, and ratification would not require any change in our domestic legislation. However, the fact that our Constitution already assures us of these rights does not entitle us to stand aloof from documents which project our own heritage on an international scale. The day-to-day unfolding of events makes it even clearer that our own welfare is interrelated with the rights and freedoms assured the peoples of other nations.

These conventions deal with human rights which may not yet be secure in other countries; they have provided models for the drafters of constitutions and laws in newly independent nations; and they have influenced the policies of governments preparing to accede to them. Thus, they involve current problems in many countries.

They will stand as a sharp reminder of world opinion to all who may seek to violate the human rights they define. They also serve as a continuous commitment to respect these rights. There is no society so advanced that it no longer needs periodic recommitment to human rights.

The United States cannot afford to renounce responsibility for support of the very fundamentals which distinguish our concept of government from all forms of tyranny. Accordingly, I desire, with the constitutional consent of the Senate, to ratify these Conventions for the United States of America.

This letter marked the end of a ten-year period in which the United States had stood aloof from the efforts of international agencies to make respect for human rights a matter of international concern and international law through the ratification of binding conventions.

The United States was by no means isolationist during the years of the Eisenhower administration; it was deeply involved and committed in the United Nations, in Europe, and elsewhere throughout the world. As Secretary of State, John Foster Dulles formulated, in these years, the American policy of "containing" communism, upholding the Chinese Nationalist defense of Formosa and the islands off the coast of Communist China, maintaining the independence of Middle Eastern nations, protecting the interests of all Western nations, and fostering inter-American cooperation. It was within this period of time that the President of the United States intervened in the Sinai campaign by Israel and the occupation of the Suez Canal Zone by British and French forces and insisted that, in the conduct of international relations, force must be replaced by the rule of law. It was only when it came to making human rights matters of international law that the United States took an isolationist position.

This isolationism was a break with the past. Just as President Wilson was the chief builder in the establishment of the League of Nations at the Paris Peace Conference in 1919, so President Franklin D. Roosevelt was the chief figure in the establishment of the United Nations. It was Roosevelt who, in 1941, coined the phrase "United Nations," though he used it then to describe the countries fighting against the Axis; and it was also Roosevelt who in 1941, in a message to Congress, urged that the United States must help the Four Freedoms—freedom of speech, freedom of worship, freedom from want, and freedom from fear—prevail everywhere in the world. Later that year these were substantially incorporated in the Atlantic Charter, the joint program of peace aims enunciated by Churchill and Roosevelt.

The Charter of the United Nations, drafted at San Francisco in 1945, stated in the Preamble the determination "to reaffirm faith in fundamental human rights, in the dignity and worth of the human person, in the equal rights of men and women, and of nations large and small"; and Article I stated that a principal purpose of the U.N. shall be "To achieve international cooperation . . . in promoting and encouraging respect for human rights and fundamental freedoms for all without distinction as to race, sex, or religion." By Article 55 the U.N. committed itself to promote "universal respect for and observance of, human rights and fundamental freedoms for all without distinction as to race, sex, language or religion"; and by Article 56 all members pledged themselves "to take joint and separate action in cooperation with the Organization for the achievement of the purposes set forth in Article 55." The Charter also vested power in the Economic and Social Council to make recommendations with respect to human rights, to establish a commission on human rights, and to exercise other powers in this area. Thus, the furtherance of human rights was not a merely incidental concern of the U.N. It was a primary objective. And no wonder that this was so when one recalls the ideology and the horrors and atrocities of the Nazi and Fascist powers. The U.N. interest in and concern with human rights were not window-dressing or merely theoretical; they were vital and urgent and central to its purposes.

In 1946 Eleanor Roosevelt was made chairman of the Commission on Human Rights, which at once undertook to frame a declaration on human rights. A Commission on the Status of Women and a Sub-Commission on the Prevention of Discrimination and the Protection of Minorities were also appointed.

On December 10, 1948, the General Assembly adopted the Universal Declaration of Human Rights, to set "a common standard of achievement for all peoples and all nations." The United States and forty-seven other members voted for its adoption; the U.S.S.R., five of its East European satellites, Saudi Arabia, and the Union (now Republic) of South Africa abstained, for obvious reasons; there were no dissenting votes.

The declaration was not meant to be legally binding. It was to be followed by conventions which, when ratified by the governments, were to have the effect of legally binding treaties. But the declaration has exerted great moral influence. Perhaps next only to the charter, it has been more frequently referred to than any other international instrument; and many new nations have followed it as a model when they drafted their constitutions—displacing our own Bill of Rights as the model for framers of constitutions.[2]

Articles 3 to 21 of the declaration cover civil and political rights; articles 22 to 27 cover economic, social, and cultural rights. When the Commission on Human Rights came to consider a convention, the United States urged that there be two separate conventions, along the division just mentioned; for, it was argued, while a government can bind itself to insure observance of civil and political rights, it cannot bind itself in the same way respecting economic, social, and cultural rights, which may be dependent upon stages of a country's development. This makes sense; but it has also been said that the position of the United States can be explained by the fear that the Senate would react unfavorably to a convention that would embody economic, social, and cultural rights—conceptions that went beyond the current conception of rights claimed by Americans. Our view, historically rooted, was that we can claim negative rights against government restriction or interference with respect to civil and political liberties, but that we have no positive rights that are dependent on the government's becoming vested with duties and powers in the economic, social, and cultural spheres. We have been changing in this respect— witness our new concern with the arts, the war on poverty, the preservation of wilderness and seashore, urban redevelopment, federal funds for education on all levels, Medicare, concern with recreation and leisure-time living, and other recent developments that indicate an evolving belief that there is a legitimate sphere for government in respect to social and cultural needs. But these developments have not yet fallen into the consciousness of the average American citizen. Be that as it may, the Commission on Human Rights acceded to the American view.

The United States played a leading role in proposing and setting up the trials for war crimes at Nuremberg in 1945. These crimes were defined as including atrocities against civilian groups, especially genocide (a term coined in 1944) or the intentional destruction, in whole or in part, of a racial, religious, or ethnic group. The charter of the Nuremberg Tribunal—to which the United States, Great Britain, France, and the U.S.S.R. subscribed—listed racial or religious persecution as a war crime for which the subscribing states would try Nazi and other offenders. It established the principle of individual responsibility and accountability of officials carrying out extermination policies. The Nuremberg trial led to death sentences for Göring, Ribbentrop, Streicher, and other arch-criminals; and in 1946–1947 a similar trial conducted by an eleven-nation tribunal in Tokyo ended in death sentences for Tojo and other major war criminals in Japan.

It was natural that the General Assembly of the U.N. should in 1946 adopt a resolution condemning genocide as a crime under international law; and the United States took a leading position in drafting the Genocide Convention, which the General Assembly unanimously approved December 9, 1948, on the day preceding adoption of the Declaration of Human Rights. Two days later the United States appended its signature. On June 16, 1949, President Truman transmitted the convention to the Senate, asking for its ratification, which was essential to give it the effect of a binding treaty. A subcommittee of the Senate Foreign Relations Committee held public hearings early in 1950, at which the representative of the State Department pleaded for approval of the convention. In May 1950 the subcommittee reported the convention favorably to the full committee, but with four "understandings" or "reservations" and one "declaration"—regarded by many as unnecessary because self-evident.

But this was three months after Senator Joseph R. McCarthy had already launched McCarthyism with his speech at Wheeling, West Virginia, in which he charged that the State Department had been infiltrated by Communists. Now a recommendation from the State Department meant only that the recommended convention was suspect as part of a Communist plot against the Constitution and the government. The new nativism was opposed to the U.N. and all other international agencies. The full committee never got around to acting on the Genocide Convention, and so it never reached the floor of the Senate.

As of early 1966, the convention still languished in the files of the Foreign Relations Committee. But, having been ratified by the requisite number of nations, it had gone into effect in 1951, and by 1966 it had been ratified by sixty-seven nations.

Early in 1952 the new nativism found a rallying point—the so-called Bricker Amendment,[3] offered by Senator John Bricker, who had been a strong contender for the Republican Party's presidential nomination in 1940 and was the party's candidate for Vice-President in 1944, and fifty-six other Senators. Intended as an expression of the Senate's dissatisfaction with the foreign policy of the Truman administration, its stance and tone were continued into and pervaded the Eisenhower administration, which took office in January 1953.

The joint resolution offered by Bricker called for an amendment to the Constitution to provide that

No treaty or executive agreement shall be made respecting the rights of citizens of the United States protected by this Constitution, or abridging or prohibiting the free exercise thereof.

No treaty or executive agreement shall vest in any international organization or in any foreign power any of the legislative, executive, or judicial powers vested by this Constitution in the Congress, the President, and in the courts of the United States, respectively.

No treaty or executive agreement shall alter or abridge the laws of the United States or the Constitution or laws of the several States unless, and then only to the extent that, Congress shall so provide by Act or joint resolution.

Although the Bricker Amendment never won sufficient support to pass the Senate, its spirit dominated the State Department during the Eisenhower years. The administration policy was clearly stated by the Secretary of State, John Foster Dulles, in his testimony before the Senate Judiciary Committee on April 6, 1953:

The present Administration intends to encourage the promotion everywhere of human rights and individual freedoms, but to favor methods of persuasion, education, and example rather than formal undertakings which commit one part of the world to impose its particular social and moral standards upon another part of the world community, which has different standards. . . . Therefore, while we shall not withhold our counsel from those who seek to draft a treaty or covenant on Human Rights, we do not ourselves look upon a treaty as the means which we would now select as the proper and most effective way to spread throughout the world the goals of human liberty to which this nation has been dedicated since its inception. We therefore do not intend to become a party to any such covenant or present it as a treaty for consideration by the Senate.

With respect to the Genocide Convention, Mr. Dulles told the committee that it "could better be reconsidered at a later date."

An interpretation of this position is that the administration, eager to see the Bricker Amendment defeated, offered to the Senate the sacrifice of human rights treaties as a temporizing measure of appeasement. But after the 1954 elections the Democrats were again in control of Congress; the Bricker measure had no chance of approval; in December 1954 the back of McCarthyism was broken with the Senate passage of the motion of censure against McCarthy; and the election on November 4, 1958, gave the Democrats in Congress the largest margin since the Roosevelt victory in 1936, and Senator Bricker and other right-wing Republicans were defeated. But these events seemed to have no important effect on the next two years of the Eisenhower administration; it continued to turn its back on international cooperation in the protection of human rights.

The break with this essentially isolationist-nativist policy did not come until July 22, 1963, when President Kennedy asked the Senate to ratify three human rights conventions: on the political rights of women (1953), by 1965 ratified by forty-three nations; the 1956 supplementary convention on the abolition of slavery, the slave trade, and related practices, ratified by fifty-five nations; and the I.L.O. convention on forced labor (1957), ratified by sixty-eight nations. By 1966, however, the Senate had not yet acted on the conventions.

Also in July 1963 the President's deputy special counsel told congressional leaders that the President wanted the Senate to ratify the Genocide Convention. But nothing further happened. In February 1964 a group of ten Senators, headed by Senator Hugh Scott, wrote to President Johnson, asking his help to get the Senate to act and said: "It is generally recognized that only a strong appeal from the President will bring this measure to debate and a vote in the Senate." As of early 1966, as we have noted, no progress was made regarding this convention.

On June 14, 1963, Secretary of State Dean Rusk said:

We do favor ratification of the Genocide Convention. . . . It is the intention of the Administration to ratify the Genocide Convention if it receives the advice and consent of the Senate, and we hope that this situation in the Senate may develop to a point where this will be possible.

The inference from remarks made by Mr. Rusk before the American Jewish Committee on April 30, 1964, is that the Johnson administration hesitated to push the human rights conventions because it was not certain that they would have the necessary two-thirds vote for ratification, and a losing vote would more seriously hurt the prestige of the United States than would a continuation of the no-action record.

Respecting the International Covenants on Human Rights, the Third Committee of the General Assembly has already adopted the substantive articles of both convenants[4] and has begun work on the difficult implementation provisions. Together with the dozen or more other human rights conventions completed by 1965 (including the several sponsored by the I.L.O. or UNESCO) these covenants and conventions constitute a considerable body of international law that attempts to explicate and implement the Four Freedoms and other basic human rights, and represent a significant consensus among diverse nations of the meaning of human dignity, equality, and freedom.

While the United States delegations took practically no part in the debates on human rights conventions for about ten years, in the 1960s these delegations ended their policy of virtual abstention. The new policy was clearly shown in the consideration given to the Declaration on Racial Discrimination, a document worthy of special note in the light of our civil rights struggle.

On October 28, 1963, the General Assembly's Third (or Social) Committee adopted the declaration by a vote of 89 to 0, with 17 abstentions. The United States, together with the British Commonwealth and Western European countries, abstained. The objection centered on Article 9, which provided that

all states shall take immediate and positive measures including legislative and other measures to prosecute and/or outlaw organizations which promote racial discrimination or incite to or use violence for the purpose of discrimination based on race, color or ethnic origin.[5]

The United States argued that this provision went too far by possibly invading constitutionally guaranteed free speech and freedom of the press, but expressed wholehearted support of the declaration otherwise. Asian and African delegations, however, contended that free speech "can go too far." The debate dragged on over twenty-five meetings, at which over eighty amendments were discussed.

A month later, on November 20, 1963, the General Assembly, with only the Republic of South Africa voting against, approved the declaration. In its final form as adopted by the General Assembly, the provision cited above was amended to read: ". . . to prosecute and/or outlaw organizations which promote *or incite* racial discrimination. . . ." (Words in italics were added by the amendment.) Adlai E. Stevenson, voting for the declaration as amended, said that the United States approved with a formal reservation, since the amended text "still calls for an invasion by the government of the right of free speech"[6] by subjecting to legal prosecution those who simply "promote racial discrimination."[7]

The measure acted upon was only a declaration. The next step was the drafting of an international convention. On December 21, 1965, the General Assembly, by a vote of 104 to 0, adopted a convention to eliminate racial discrimination. The convention, in twenty-four articles, is sweeping in scope. Governments that ratify the convention would be bound to condemn racial bias and to render illegal racist acts and the spreading of race hatred and racist ideas. Governments would be bound to ban organizations that promote such sentiments. To become operative, the convention must be ratified by twenty-seven countries. Optional enforcement machinery is provided.

Arthur J. Goldberg, (who left the Supreme Court to succeed Mr. Stevenson as United States Ambassador to the United Nations), in urging adoption of the convention, called the attention of the Third Committee to the fact that the United States would interpret the convention in the light of the following considerations:

The opening paragraph of Article IV provides that in carrying out certain obligations of the Convention, the States that are parties to it shall have "due regard to the principles embodied in the Universal Declaration of Human Rights and the rights expressly set forth in article V of this Convention."

As we know, these principles and rights include freedom of speech and of association. Nonetheless, we find that subparagraph (a) of Article IV holds that the dissemination of ideas based on racial superiority or hatred shall be declared an offense punishable by law.

It is the view of the United States, therefore, that Article IV does not obligate a state to take action that would prohibit its citizens from freely and fully expressing their views on any subject no matter how obnoxious they may be or whether they are in accord with government policy or not.

We believe that a government should only act where speech is associated with, or threatens imminently to lead to, action against which the public has a right to be protected. Our Supreme Court, in *Yates vs. United States*, emphasizes "the distinction between advocacy of abstract doctrine and advocacy directed at promoting unlawful action." In our view, therefore, a state should act under the terms of Article IV only if the dissemination of obnoxious ideas is accompanied by, or threatens imminently to promote, the illegal act of racial discrimination.

Under our system of government, moreover, there must be an imminent danger of illegal action before speech becomes unlawful. Justice Brandeis stated the reason for this succinctly: "If there be time to expose through discussion the falsehood and fallacies, to avert the evil by the process of education, the remedy to be applied is more speech, not enforced silence."

The same considerations apply to our interpretation of the obligations in sub-paragraph (b) of Article IV. In accordance with the right of freedom of speech and freedom of association, it is our view that organizations cannot be declared illegal if they merely attempt to win acceptance of their beliefs by speech alone. However, if such organizations go beyond advocacy of their views and engage, or attempt to engage, in the illegal act of racial discrimination itself, they come within the purview of the Convention.

It is noteworthy that Morris B. Abram, American member of the sub-commission that drafted the convention on racial discrimination, played a major role in proposing the draft and in the debate that culminated in its unanimous approval. It may be that President Johnson's attack on the Ku Klux Klan will help mold American opinion in favor of this and similar international human rights measures.

American differences with the U.S.S.R. came out prominently in connection with the U.N. Declaration on the Elimination of All Forms of Religious Intolerance, which the same sub-commission forwarded to the Commission on Human Rights in January 1964. The debate over this declaration lasted thirteen weeks and was often sharp and bitter. The U.S.S.R. delegate, while insisting on language protecting atheists, including a right to propagandize for atheism, argued against a comparable clause favorable to religious groups. The Soviet member also opposed a provision affirming the right of parents to decide the religion in which their children should be reared. He asked for a provision prohibiting religious groups from engaging in political activities, by which he meant more than merely partisan activities. He objected to a provision, applicable to countries where the state controls all means of production, requiring the government to help religious groups to import articles needed for religious observances.

In February 1965 the sub-commission approved a convention on the Elimination of All Forms of Religious Intolerance and submitted the document to the Commission on Human Rights. The U.S.S.R. and Mexico voted against the document, and Poland, which supported the U.S.S.R. in the debate, abstained. (Mexico took the position that the state has the right to monopolize secular education, to prevent religious groups from attempting to exert any political influence, to control the property of religious bodies, and to impose its law in matters relating to marriage, burial, and the administration of oaths, and insisted on a provision for total church-state separation.)

In view of the record of religious discrimination and persecution in the U.S.S.R. and other countries, it is significant that an important U.N. agency has formally declared that governments have the obligation to guarantee to everyone:

(1) freedom to worship, to assemble, and to establish and maintain places of worship or assembly;

(2) freedom to teach, to disseminate, and to learn his religion or belief and its sacred language or traditions, and to train personnel intending to devote themselves to the performance of its practices or observances;

(3) freedom to practice his religion or belief by establishing and

maintaining charitable and educational institutions and by expressing the implications of religions or belief in public life;

(4) freedom to observe the rituals, dietary and other practices of his religion or belief and to produce or if necessary import the objects, foods, and other articles and facilities customarily used in its observances and practices;

(5) freedom to make pilgrimages and other journeys in connection with his religion or belief whether inside or outside his country;

(6) equal legal protection for his places of worship, for his rites, ceremonies, and activities, and for the burial places associated with his religion or belief;

(7) freedom to organize and maintain local, regional, and national associations, and to participate in international associations in connection with his activities and to communicate with his coreligionists and believers;

(8) freedom from compulsion to take an oath of a religious nature;

(9) freedom from compulsion to undergo a religious marriage ceremony not in conformity with his religion or belief.

The active participation of the American members in the drafting of these declarations and conventions relating to the prevention of racial and religious discrimination and in the debates—often acrimonious—over specific proposals has been a significant step toward the ending of American isolationism in regard to the international interest in and protection of human rights. While such active participation is important, it is likely to prove embarrassing should years go by without ratification by the Senate of the three conventions submitted by President Kennedy—as well as of the Genocide Convention, submitted by President Truman, and other and more recent and equally important human rights conventions.

Of course no one is naïve enough to think that ratification will have the automatic effect of converting a totalitarian nation into a democratic one, but American promotion of human rights internationally can be beneficial in at least these ways:[8]

First, United States ratification can stimulate other nations to adhere to these conventions and can augment their impact among countries already parties to them. The United States will thus be encouraging the implementation of these basic human rights standards within foreign countries.

Second, ratification will put the United States in a better legal and moral position to protest infringement of these human rights in countries that have ratified the conventions but failed to implement them in practice.

Third, ratification will increase United States influence in the continuing

United Nations process of the drafting of legal norms in the field of human rights. So long as the United States fails to ratify any human-rights conventions, its views will carry less weight than they deserve.

Americans often think of themselves as being far in advance of other people in adherence to the conception of a world rule of law. The fact is, however, that our professions of faith have at times been contradicted by our actions; and it has happened that other nations, making less stir in the world, have acted more consistently in the interests of establishment of a legal world order that would protect and enforce human rights. Three examples may be cited:

(1) Chapter 14 of the U.N. Charter established the International Court of Justice at The Hague. The court consists of fifteen judges chosen by the U.N. General Assembly and the Security Council. The court has jurisdiction to render judgment in certain disputes between states. A dispute may be brought to the court by consent of the parties in a particular case or by virtue of an advance formal declaration automatically to accept the court's jurisdiction.

The United States, as a condition to accepting the compulsory jurisdiction of the court, in 1946 imposed the restrictive condition (the Connally reservation) which excludes all disputes that concern domestic matters from the court's jurisdiction, and reserves to the United States the right unilaterally to determine what matters it will choose to regard as domestic—notwithstanding the fact that the competence of the court is limited to disputes between states concerning the interpretation of treaties, questions of international law, breaches of international obligation, and the amount of reparations due for such breaches.[9]

Now other nations, seeing the example of the United States, also stipulated such a reservation. But in 1958 Great Britain withdrew its reservation, and in 1959 France and India deposited new declarations accepting compulsory jurisdiction and omitting their previously stipulated reservations.

Our State Department has asked for repeal of the Connally reservation, and resolutions to this effect have often been introduced in the Senate, but the reservation is still in effect. Perhaps the change in the American attitude toward international cooperation on the human rights front will have the effect eventually of removing the reservation.

(2) A month after the establishment of the North Atlantic Treaty Organization (NATO) in Washington, in April 1949, the original ten European nations signed in London the statute of the Council of Europe. A condition of membership was acceptance of the rule of law

and the enjoyment, by all persons within its jurisdiction, of human rights and fundamental freedoms. By 1965 the council, with headquarters at Strasbourg, had eighteen members, including Great Britain, France, the Netherlands, and the German Federal Republic.

In 1950 the Council adopted the European Convention for Protection of Human Rights and Fundamental Freedoms, modeled after the Universal Declaration of Human Rights, but having the binding effect of a treaty. In 1959 the Council established the European Court of Human Rights and the European Commission of Human Rights to enforce the convention. The most significant feature of the enforcement machinery is the provision that *individuals* shall have the right to bring complaints against their own governments for denial of a human right or fundamental liberty, accepted by eleven nations.[10]

This step was a radical break with traditional legal conceptions, which contemplated actions only between states. Thus, only sovereign states may be parties in cases before the International Court of Justice at The Hague. The approach of the Council of Europe is as far removed from the position represented by the Connally reservation or the Bricker Amendment as one pole is from the other, and is far in advance of anything done by or proposed for a U.N. convention on human rights. With this daring break with tradition, European nations are helping to establish a "common law of mankind."[11] And this new law applies on behalf of any person, whether he be a citizen, an alien, or a stateless person.

Fifteen members of the Council of Europe are, in 1966, legally bound by the Convention of Human Rights; and ten of the members have, by treaty, submitted themselves to the jurisdiction of the Court of Human Rights.[12] Belgium, Norway, and Austria have modified their laws to conform to the convention; and while the case record for the first few years is not impressive, the European approach represents the third important breakthrough—next to the Nuremberg Tribunal and the Universal Declaration of Human Rights—for the international recognition and implementation of human rights and fundamental freedoms.

(3) A similar though less spectacular development has taken place among the American nations. In 1948 the Organization of American States (O.A.S.) was created as a regional agency of twenty-one American republics, with headquarters at Washington. The organization adopted the American Declaration of the Rights and Duties of Man; and membership in the O.A.S. was made conditional upon the adoption of a democratic form of government and a guarantee of the

fundamental rights of man. It was partly for violation of these conditions that Cuba was expelled in 1962. O.A.S. early in its existence directed the Inter-American Juridical Committee to draft a statute on an Inter-American Court of Human Rights, and this direction was renewed in 1960 and coupled with instructions to prepare a Convention on Human Rights. Without, however, waiting for these developments, O.A.S. in 1960 created the Inter-American Commission on Human Rights, which at once began to work. Unfortunately, however, the United States served notice that it will not be possible for it to participate in multilateral conventions of this nature.[13] This policy will probably be changed to reflect the new position introduced by President Kennedy's submission of three human rights conventions for ratification by the Senate.

The United States has not ratified the U.N. Conventions on Genocide (1948), on the Status of Refugees (1951), on the Status of Stateless Persons (1954), on the Political Rights of Women (1953), on the Nationality of Married Women (1957), on Reduction of Statelessness (1961), the Supplementary Convention on Abolition of Slavery (1956), and several others. It has not ratified the I.L.O. Conventions on Forced Labor (1930 and 1957), on Freedom of Association and Protection of the Right to Organize (1948), on Right to Organize and Collective Bargaining (1949), on Discrimination in Employment and Occupation (1958), and other conventions affecting rights of workers, women, and children. Nor has the United States ratified the UNESCO convention against Discrimination in Education (1960).[14]

Obviously the United States has much ground to recover if it is to resume the position of leadership that it enjoyed when it took the initiative to proclaim the Four Freedoms, the human rights ideals of the Atlantic Charter and of the United Nations Charter, the principles of the Nuremberg war crimes trials, the provisions of the Universal Declaration of Human Rights, and the fundamental-freedoms ideals of the O.A.S. Charter—which were no mean achievements. Our own struggle over civil rights, the veto power exercised for years by Southern members of Congress, the difficulties of the McCarthy period, the strength of conservative, right-wing, nativist, and isolationist elements throw light on our withdrawal from the world-wide struggle to secure and protect human rights and fundamental freedoms through international cooperation. Liberals in the United States have not been deeply involved in this struggle, perhaps because of concentration on winning the struggle at home through legislation, executive action, and Supreme Court decisions. But the United States, as President Kennedy recognized, cannot any longer turn its back to the rest of the world in regard to international law on human rights. Domestically we are at the opposite pole from the U.S.S.R. and the Republic of South Africa, and no other nation can match us on our record, our historical roots, or our ideals in the matter of fundamental freedoms; for while the nations, new and old, now look to the Universal Declaration of Human Rights as a model, our own Declaration of Independence and our own Bill of Rights were models for the U.N. Declaration.

We have seen in the United States that insistence on states' rights was often a cover for the denial of basic human rights and freedoms, and that only federal action could promise a remedy through legislative, executive, and judicial action. Although more complicated, the problem among nations must be approached in the same way. The approach may be easier among the homogeneous nations of a region, as in Europe, than it is on a world-wide scale, but the task is not an impossible one; and the least that may be expected is that the United States should not place itself in a position where it could be blamed for not helping the forces of history to move in the direction of universal recognition and protection of human rights and fundamental freedoms under a common law of mankind.

The World of Interdependent Ideals

When President Johnson, on March 20, 1965, ordered troops in Alabama to protect the civil rights demonstrators as they marched from Selma to Montgomery, a Negro woman in Selma remarked that now the President saw that a society must first be *free* before it can become *great*. First things must be done first.

Thinking back to the Athens of Pericles, one might concede that, in the perspective of history, it was possible for a society based on slavery to become great. But one must put such a thought in the past tense and push the possibility, if it is conceded, back some twenty-five hundred years. Few today would concede this possibility for the pre-Civil War South. While we can view the dim past amorally, or even romantically—thereby paying our remote ancestors the dubious compliment of assimilating them to natural history—we judge ourselves or our near forefathers more stringently. It is difficult to argue that the Republic of South Africa can become a great society while it adheres to the principle of apartheid. We may agree with Reinhold Niebuhr that one cannot always make equally high moral demands of society and of the individual; still we find it impossible to exclude altogether the moral dimension from our judgment of a society. Most Americans would agree with the Negro woman of Selma that a society that is not free cannot be great.

But must first things always be done first? Here again history would show that this is not how life has been organized, for if it had been organized on such a rational principle human society would look quite different today; humanity would have moved by logical steps from high to ever higher points along clear lines of progress. But the history of mankind shows indescribable complexity. Humanity has followed no order of priorities. For example, the tiny, weak Massachusetts Bay Colony founded Harvard University in 1636, with a grant from the

General Court, before the settlement had made provision for a water supply or a garbage-disposal system. Many of our cities have fine public libraries and museums, while their public schools and hospitals languish from indifference and inadequate support. People buy cars before they put their houses in order, and they spend more money on cosmetics than on books. First things are not always done first, and only in a rigidly organized totalitarian society could the situation be different. And so President Johnson would be right were he to answer the Negro woman of Selma that, when he speaks of the Great Society, he means of course to include the American ideals of liberty and equality; for the President asked Congress to enact the Civil Rights Act of 1964 with the same fervor with which he asked for passage of the Economic Opportunity Act of 1964. Certainly in the United States of the second half of the twentieth century freedom and greatness interact and are inextricably intertwined.

For in our time we have seen that the man who is held down will no longer wait indefinitely for a chance to straighten up. If the oppressor will not get off the other man's back voluntarily, he will be knocked off. The tactic of nonviolent resistance essentially involves the making of such a noise of protesting, moaning, and pleading under the burden, that those on top will get off, or society will force them to.

In effect the demonstrator says, with Saint John: "Behold, I stand at the door, and knock."[1] And he adds: "I will stand, and I will knock, until I am heard. If the man inside will not open the door, then his neighbors will come and open it for him. But the door will be opened." The demonstrator appeals first of all to the oppressor, but beyond him to the wider community, for "a decent respect to the opinions of mankind." He seems to have learned well the lesson that Emerson addressed to all who might feel the need to become martyrs for the cause of abolition:

Take care, O ye martyrs. . . . Reserve your fire. Keep your temper. Render soft answers. Bear and forbear. Do not dream of suffering for ten years yet. Do not let the word *martyrdom* ever escape out of the white pearl of your teeth. Be sweet and courtly and merry these many long summers and autumns yet, and husband your strength, so that when an authentic, inevitable crisis comes, and you are fairly driven to the wall, . . . you may then at last turn fairly round on the baying dogs, all still—with all Heaven in your eye—and die for love, with all heroes and angels to friend.[2]

For a long time we assumed that, since all men had certain "unalienable rights," all Americans had them, just as they had air to breathe and water to drink, and nothing more needed to be done. We thought that occasionally a man might be deprived of what was his own, but for such exceptional cases we had police forces and courts; we had a system which saw to it that force and fraud, which Hobbes called "the two cardinal virtues" in war, should not operate in civil society in a time of peace. But in the last quarter century we have seen, in big events and in small, that the rights of man are not "unalienable" but are, in fact, hard-won and painfully kept.[3]

We saw Hitler and Nazi Germany, the war lords of Japan, and Italy under the dictatorship of Mussolini plan to reduce man to a wild beast of prey; we saw the Soviet Union under Stalin commit acts of mass oppression almost unmatched for wanton cruelty in the annals of history, and we saw the Soviet Union advance into Eastern and Central Europe and plan to transform life for humanity into an endless series of unbearable crises. Every vestige of human right or dignity would have been crushed had these forces not been destroyed or "contained." More than that, had they had their way, all the memorials of man's freedom would have been destroyed in a universal book-burning, and history would have been rewritten in such a way that new generations would have no knowledge of the fact that once men were free and of the fact that humanity's scriptures, philosophy, literature, and politics had defined man as a free being. Man's very nature and his conception of himself—of his nature and destiny—would have been radically changed. Mankind had never faced greater threats and challenges to its very being.

These events could not have left humanity untouched. First of all, we all learned much more than we had ever known about the possibility of evil, the potentiality of man to act cruelly, his capacity to re-enter a state of nature in which man to man is a wolf. We saw that we hold on to our humanity precariously, that the enemies lurk inside us as well as outside. We learned a great deal about the nature of communism—even before Nikita Khrushchev delivered his "secret" report to the Twentieth All-Union Party Congress (1956) on the crimes of Stalin and "The Personality Cult and Its Consequences."

As before in history, the ruling ideals of freedom, equality, human rights, and human dignity found secret assistance in brute forces such as war, hunger, cruelties, commerce, and machinery; and reason found assistance in instincts, and faith found assistance in insight and tradition.[4]

And so humanity, as in the story of Samson, found honey in the carcass of the lion. The nations of the world united for peace, the furtherance of human rights, and the development of a common law of nations and of mankind. The nations of Western Europe created political, judicial, and economic agencies for a united Europe. Britain withdrew from India and from what is now Pakistan, and from Burma, Malaya, Cyprus, Ceylon, Palestine, and other countries. France was forced to give up Indochina, and other empires were liquidated. Thirteen independent Arab nations came into existence in the Middle East and North Africa; and Israel became the third commonwealth in Jewish history. In 1945 Liberia and the Union of South Africa were the only free states in Africa, but the war brought to an end Italian domination of Ethiopia; it was not until 1956, when the British evacuated the Suez Canal Zone, that Egypt, after several thousand years, achieved at last complete independence. Then, starting with Ghana in 1957 and Guinea in 1958, one after another, the African colonies achieved national independence. The United Nations Charter was signed, in 1945, by 50 nations. At the end of 1965 the membership of the U.N. was 117.

The ending of colonialism, the emergence of nations which had never before existed, the steps toward unification of Western Europe, and the efforts to create an international common law of mankind and of nations, must be considered among the great events of world history.

These events—the new nationalisms and the fall of national barriers, the process of individualization and the process of universalization—have taken place against the Soviet penetration of Eastern and Central Europe and the emergence, during 1949 and 1950, of Communist China, and the threat of Communist wars of aggression and of revolutions in all parts of the world.

These threats have, however, been somewhat mitigated by the development of a rift, if not enmity, between the U.S.S.R. and Communist China, by the de-Stalinization movement in the Soviet Union since 1956, and by the loosening of ties with the Soviet Union among the Communist countries of Eastern and Central Europe since the Soviet armed suppression of the anti-Communist revolution in Hungary in 1956 and the uprising of masses of Polish workers and students in Poznań in the same year.

Underneath the turmoil, however, democratic forces were at work almost everywhere, and freedoms about which men had for long centuries dreamed came to life. Only the most significant developments can be mentioned.

(1) Everywhere, even in the Moslem world, women began to assert their right to political, economic, and social equality, and in many countries they won the right to vote, to own property, to appear in public without the veil (purdah), to assert their nationality, and to enter the professions, public office, and the public service. It surely must seem a startling fact to recall that in France women voted for the first time in 1945, in the first election after World War II; that Belgium granted suffrage to women only in 1946, Japan in 1945, Argentina and Mexico in 1946.

Symbolic of this development were the announcement in September 1964 that women would be admitted—though only as "auditors"—at some sessions of the Ecumenical Council in Rome, and the homily of Pope Paul VI in which he expressed reservations on the cloistered life of nuns and noted that the life of the approximately sixty international orders for women had been the refuge of "weak and timid minds," but that today their life must be "the workshop of strong, constant and heroic hearts."[5]

The revolution in the status of women was seen in dramatic form in the civil rights demonstration in Selma, Alabama, in March 1965, when white nuns were in the front line of the march, alongside Martin Luther King, Jr., and Ralph J. Bunche;[6] and it was the murder of a woman civil rights worker, Mrs. Viola Liuzzo, that led to President Johnson's attack on the Ku Klux Klan. These events were important not only for the civil rights struggle but also as symbols of women's struggle for equality everywhere in the world.

(2) While forced labor camps existed in the Soviet Union under Stalin, and slavery lingered on in parts of the Arab world, no one anywhere dared to defend these atrocities that had behind them ancient traditions and a long history of social convention and approval. Freedom from slavery and peonage was everywhere acknowledged as a human right. For the first time in history no voice was heard to defend the notion that some human beings may be used as mere means to an end.

The universal outlawing of slavery, peonage, and forced labor entailed recognition of the workers' freedom of association in unions of their own choosing, and the right of collective bargaining. Through the work of the International Labor Organization, which became affiliated with the U.N. in 1946, and which had in 1965 a membership of 115 member states, nations everywhere became aware of the legitimate claims of labor for higher—and ever higher—standards of working and living conditions. Through the 115 or more conventions on labor standards and labor relations, the voice and the strength of labor penetrated into areas and corners of the world in which workers had never had rights except those given to them by their masters. Now, for the first time in history, the common man had the acknowledged right to dignity, a defense against subjection to the arbitrary will of employers, and an awareness of legitimate goals within his reach.

These changes in the status and rights of workers meant more than changes in physical and economic conditions; they meant a change in spirit, a change in the very nature and destiny of the common man. No longer will he be the man whom Edwin Markham, as recently as 1899, could describe as a creature degraded and exploited, with the "emptiness of ages in his face."[7]

In 1949, when India became a sovereign republic, it adopted a constitution modeled after that of the United States, with a provision that outlawed untouchability and that brought to an end the existence of pariah castes. Some fifty million pariahs became harijans, children of God, as Gandhi had called them, who from then on were protected by law from all degrading and disabling discriminations. This event dramatized the ideal of equality that had won universal recognition throughout the world.

Only the Republic of South Africa and Rhodesia have openly avowed a purpose to perpetuate domination by their white minorities on a caste basis. But world opinion has condemned South Africa, which in 1961 felt forced to withdraw from the British Commonwealth on this issue, and the rebel government of Rhodesia, set up on November 11, 1965, was at once declared to be "illegal" and "treasonable" by the British government, and on the following day the U.N. Security Council called on all nations to refrain from recognizing "this illegal racist minority regime." The total isolation of these countries strikingly marks the universal condemnation of the idea that castes can be inferior or superior to one another in the enjoyment of basic human and democratic rights.

(3) The struggle in South Africa, was, however, more than an attempt to end a form of economic exploitation; it was part of a worldwide revolt by the peoples of Asia and Africa against racial inequality and racist ideologies. The concept of the right to equal dignity and equal rights and privileges, without regard to race or color, was everywhere a dominant force. In the nineteenth century many men were impressed with Gobineau's theory of Nordic supremacy and the anti-

democratic and anti-Semitic arguments in his *Essai sur l'inégalité des races humaines,* published just before the Civil War broke out in the United States; and at the turn of the century Houston Stewart Chamberlain, who was born an Englishman and became a German citizen, continued the teaching of the racist doctrine by glorifying the Teutons, whom he credited with all the achievements of civilization. That those ideas had great appeal should not surprise us if we recall that slaves in the British dominions were not emancipated until 1833; and that only about a century ago there were in the United States some four million Negro slaves, and that our Supreme Court could at that time state that the American nation believed that the Negro race was unfit to have social or political relations with the white race and that "the Negro might justly and lawfully be reduced to slavery for his benefit."[8]

The anti-democratic, anti-Semitic, racial-supremacy ideas found their way into the mind of Adolf Hitler, who reshaped them into an ideology of "racial purity" and other vicious racial doctrines of Nazi Germany and of the cult of Führer-worship, and they gave the Germans the mission to achieve supremacy for themselves as the world's "master race."

The German tyranny, the mass extermination of six million Jews, the extermination of civilian populations of "inferior" "races," the use of slave labor, and the murder of prisoners of war, removed from racism and anti-Semitism whatever pretense to serious consideration they may ever have had—except as aspects of criminality. Only those who operate in the underground of insanity and criminality dare to attach respectability to any theory of racial superiority or to anti-Semitism. The murder of the Jews in Europe helped to loosen the colonial bonds of the Negroes of Africa and of the peoples of Asia, and "the white man's burden" was put in the lumber room of historical monstrosities and eccentricities.

(4) Though coming after the achievement of racial liberation in Asia and Africa, the encyclical *Mater et Magistra,* issued in 1961 by Pope John XXIII, the convening of the Second Vatican Council in 1962, and his encyclical *Pacem in Terris* in 1963 (and the schema on the rights of religious conscience, adopted by the Council in 1965), contributed to the enhancement of the idea of religious liberty and equality. Pope John's advocacy of social reform, assistance to underdeveloped nations, support for all measures contributing to social welfare, the legitimation of social, intellectual, and religious diversity, the primacy of conscience, the unequivocal recognition of the right of religious liberty of all men, the equal dignity and rights of all races,

and the explicit discrediting and rejection of anti-Semitism, has cer-
tinly added spiritual vitality to the forces of freedom and equality.

"Every human being," wrote Pope John in *Pacem in Terris,* "has
the right to honor God according to the dictates of an upright conscience, and therefore the right to worship God privately and publicly." With this one sentence the Pope built a bridge that connected
the Roman Catholic Church with the Act of Toleration of 1689, with
John Locke, Roger Williams, William Penn, Thomas Jefferson, James
Madison, and the First Amendment of the United States Constitution.
And Pope John, as if fearing that the full import of what he was saying
might be missed—since for centuries Catholic writers had thought
that, while they believed in freedom of religion, error had no rights—
wrote: "Moreover, one must never confuse error and the person who
errs. . . . The person who errs is always and above all a human being,
and he retains in every case his dignity as a human person; and he
must always be regarded and treated in accordance with that lofty
dignity." The world has recognized that in these and other passages
Pope John spoke not only for and to the Roman Catholic Church, but
for and to mankind. "Only in recent times has it been practicable,"
he said, "for men to extend their fellowship to all humanity."

Religious liberty and equality are by no means everywhere recognized, but today no people or church openly avows or dares to justify
religious persecution or discrimination. Of the Four Freedoms proclaimed by President Roosevelt in 1941, and substantially incorporated into the Atlantic Charter—freedom of speech, freedom of worship, freedom from want, and freedom from fear—none has won the
degree of acceptance achieved by freedom of worship—or freedom of
religion and the rights of conscience.

In its march toward freedom, humanity follows a zigzag course, and
no one can feel sure that what has been won will not be lost. Germany
under the Nazis and the U.S.S.R. under Stalin demonstrated the
possibility of reversion to barbarism. In the face of this recent history
it is hard to be a Pollyanna; but at the same time it would be equally
wrong not to recognize the gains of the postwar years, howsoever precariously held. History should still record the fact that in these years
the world was changed by at least four developments of inestimable
importance: the victory of women in their struggle for equal dignity
and equal rights; the worldwide recognition of racial equality, and the
rejection of any notion of racial superiority or the right to practice
racial discrimination; the universal rejection of slavery, peonage, economic castes, or the right to exploit one group for the economic advan-

tage of another; and acceptance of the idea that religious persecution and coercion of the conscience cannot be justified in the name of religion or on behalf of the claims of any social order.

These ideals, the fruit of "a slow and hard-won growth," are, in the words of Josiah Royce, written in 1892,

nobody's arbitrary invention, no gift from above, no outcome of a social compact, no immediate expression of reason, but the slowly formed concretion of ages of blind effort, unconscious, but wise in its unconsciousness, often selfish, but humane even in its selfishness. The ideals win the battle of life by the secret connivance, as it were, of numberless seemingly un-ideal forces. Climate, hunger, commerce, authority, superstition, war, cruelty, toil, greed, compromise, tradition, conservatism, loyalty, sloth— all these cooperate, through countless ages, with a hundred other discernible tendencies, to build up a civilization. And civilization itself is, in consequence, a much deeper thing than appears on the surface of our consciousness.[9]

As we talk about the ideals, we in a way falsify them and our experience by abstracting them from the historical, social, and even natural forces which generated and sustain them. We project them as if they were the products of pure reason; and then we debate their meanings as if they were nothing but constructs of the conceptualizing faculty. This cannot be helped if they are to be discussed. But still we must always bear in mind that they are also the expressions of the will, and of the desires, wants, assertions, and longings, of living and willing human beings with memories of hunger, humiliation, hurts, indignities, fears, and fights; human beings with hopes, desires, hates, and loves, and, perhaps above all else, with the consciousness of promises and of a freedom of the will that turns man's eyes toward a future, for his children if not for himself—the awareness of life as striving, becoming, for which freedom is as necessary as air, food, drink, and sleep. Since World War II humanity seems, through processes that are more instinctive than rational, to have reached a consensus on four basic freedoms: freedom from discrimination because of race, freedom from discrimination because of sex, freedom from discrimination because of religion, and freedom from economic discrimination. They all point to an affirmance of equality and the radical freedom of man as man.

In the United States these four freedoms no longer have a revolutionary ring. Yet the evolution of their promise has made ours a time of great excitement if not of revolutions. It takes many books and many minds to develop, to unfold the ideas hidden in a word, and when the word is "justice," or "love," or "liberty," or "equality," or a phrase such as "due process of law" or "equal protection of the laws," or "the rule of law," the process of explication is endless, for no sooner is a position reached than it is discovered that, while it may be an answer to an earlier question, it itself generates other questions. And so the process goes on. Only a fundamentalist is sure that he possesses the full meaning; only the totalitarian is sure that he knows enough not to want to hear any more. A free man is, however, committed to the process of finding more and more meaning, and a free society will always have more tasks on its agenda than it will have time and will to achieve. This can easily be seen when we look briefly at the posture of these four freedoms in the United States since World War II. As religious liberty and racial equality were considered at length in earlier chapters, we may at this point look briefly at equal rights for women and, more elaborately, at economic freedom and equality.

When the Nineteenth Amendment was adopted in 1920, it was assumed that women, having won the right to vote, would quickly win full equality in all important social and economic relations. Yet in December 1961—more than forty years later—President Kennedy found it necessary to establish, by Executive Order 10980, the President's Commission on the Status of Women. This order stated, among other things, that

prejudices and outmoded customs act as barriers to the full realization of women's basic rights . . .; [that] in every period of national emergency women have served with distinction in widely varied capacities but thereafter have been subject to treatment as a marginal group whose skills have been inadequately utilized. . . .

The commission was charged with responsibility

for developing recommendations for overcoming discriminations in government and private employment on the basis of sex and for developing recommendations for services which will enable women to continue their role as wives and mothers while making a maximum contribution to the world around them. . . .[10]

By the very terms of the President's order, the commission has an endless task if our ideal is—as it must be—that women, like men, should live and work in a society that will allow them to make "a *maximum* contribution to the world around them." For a "maximum" attained at one time is only a way-station to a new "maximum."

In addition to the report of the commission,[11] its committees, headed by Mrs. Eleanor Roosevelt until her death in November 1962, have published reports on civil and political rights, education, federal employment, private employment, home and community, protective labor legislation, and social insurance and taxes. The subjects of these committee reports merely point up the fact that the suffrage amendment of 1920, while an answer to a problem, by no means meant—as we know now—the total emancipation of women. There is much unfinished business, which in part will be met by Title VII of the Civil Rights Act of 1964. This bars discrimination in employment by reason of sex, no less than by reason of race, color, religion, or national origin.

The Thirteenth Amendment, adopted in 1865, permanently outlawed slavery and involuntary servitude. It was not, however, until Congress enacted the National Labor Relations Act of 1935 (the Wagner Act) that workers won the statutory right to organize into unions of their own choosing and to compel employers to engage in collective bargaining. The Taft-Hartley Act of 1947 and the Landrum-Griffin Act of 1959 have not seriously affected these two basic rights. Thus, insofar as concerns legal relations, legal forms and rights, American workers are free and enjoy equality before the law; they too, like the owners of business and industry, are free to combine, and to assert their combined strength against their employers. In upholding the constitutionality of the Wagner Act, Chief Justice Hughes stated the underlying philosophy of the legislation:

Long ago we stated the reason for labor organizations. We said that they were organized out of the necessities of the situation; that a single employee was helpless in dealing with an employer; that he was dependent ordinarily on his daily wage for the maintenance of himself and family; that if the employer refused to pay him the wages that he thought fair, he was nevertheless unable to leave the employ and resist arbitrary and unfair treatment; that union was essential to give laborers opportunity to deal on equality with their employer.[12]

It all sounded so simple and logical in 1937, when this was said by the Supreme Court. But a quarter of a century later it was realized that this approach left out of account economic and social conditions, affecting "equality," that went beyond the reach of collective bargaining and the union's conventional self-help measures. Even before 1935, the Supreme Court had said:

The ethical right of every worker, man or woman, to a living wage, may be conceded. One of the declared and important purposes of trade organizations is to secure it.[13]

But what if the "ethical right" is not fully implemented by the law because of forces toward which the law was not directed?

The launching of the Marshall Plan in 1947, to bring massive economic aid to Europe, marked the beginning of a new American policy: to use our economic and technical resources to aid disadvantaged— and, later, underdeveloped—countries to build themselves up to a level of economic self-support or even prosperity. American money, materials, manpower, and skills soon began to flow to countries in Asia, Africa, and Latin America.

It was inevitable that before long Americans would begin to think that, if we can do these things for others, why can we not do them also for ourselves, here at home? For we too had "underdeveloped" cities and regions; we had hard-core poverty; we had a constant stream of untrained youth looking for nonexistent jobs; we needed some 25,000 *new* jobs to be opened up *each week* in order to take care of the *new* entrants into the labor force. If America had an obligation to help the distressed, the dispossessed, and the disinherited in remote parts of the world, how long could we ignore our own people who seemed helpless in the face of their adversities? Were we to "love" our "neighbor" only if he was *not* our "neighbor"?

But how were we to convert the abstract "ethical right of every worker, man or woman, to a living wage" into a tangible reality? Traditionally we were stuck with the approach of modified poor laws, which assumed that poverty was not society's concern unless poverty became pauperism; and there was a general belief that pauperism stemmed from an unwillingness to work in jobs that were available if only the pauper would shake himself free from his sloth. Even when poor-law relief became a welfare program, we could not, generally, free ourselves from the poor-law philosophy and so insisted that relief must always be at levels below that earned by the poorest workers. The New Deal had introduced unemployment compensation and old-age pensions, but they were rightly regarded as preventive and cushioning measures.

The first important breakthrough came when, in 1961, a task force reported to President Kennedy the need of an area redevelopment program and named the Appalachian region as an area for priority consideration. Later that year Congress passed the Area Redevelopment Act. In 1963 President Kennedy appointed the President's Appalachian Regional Commission to plan the economic development of the region (which includes all of West Virginia and parts of ten other states, with over 15,000,000 people, for whom the per capita income is $1400—$500 below the national average—and with an unemployment rate 50 per cent above the national rate). Now at last we had an agency that proposed that we do for Americans what for years we had done for foreign countries under the Point Four program, started in 1950, and its successive agencies (T.C.A., A.I.D.). In 1964 President Johnson sent a bill to Congress to carry out the commission's recommendations; and on March 3, 1965, Congress passed the bill and authorized a billion dollars to develop the economy of the depressed eleven-state Appalachian region.[14]

In his first State of the Union Message[15] President Johnson declared "unconditional war on poverty in America." It will not be, he said,

a short or easy struggle, no single weapon or strategy will suffice, but we shall not rest until that war is won. The richest nation on earth can afford it. We cannot afford to lose it.

That the "ethical right" to a living wage may entail social action on many fronts was made clear by the President, for the lack of a job and money may be, he said, not a cause of poverty but a symptom, for the cause

may lie deep in our failure to give our fellow citizens a fair chance to develop their own capacities, in a lack of education and training, in a lack of medical care and housing, in a lack of decent communities in which to live and bring up their children.

On August 20, 1964, President Johnson approved the Economic Opportunity Act of 1964,[16] which made provision for a job corps and other youth programs to train young men and young women, aged sixteen through twenty-one; for urban and rural community action programs, to be developed, conducted, and administered—significantly —"with the maximum feasible participation of residents of the areas and members of the groups served"; for special programs to combat poverty in rural areas, and for cognate purposes.

In 1960 Kennedy, campaigning for the Presidency, acted on a suggestion of Hubert H. Humphrey and announced that, if elected, he would recruit young Americans for service in foreign countries as ambassadors of peace. A few months after he took office, President

Kennedy established the Peace Corps, a body of trained men and women sent overseas to help foreign countries meet their pressing needs for trained manpower. In September 1961 Congress established the Peace Corps as a permanent organization.[17] Following the enactment of the Economic Opportunity Act, at the end of 1964 the government launched Vista, a volunteer *domestic* Peace Corps, to work on poverty-related programs.

The multiple anti-poverty programs, combining idealism and realism in ways almost uniquely American, have their roots in many earlier policies, including some of the Reconstruction acts which tried to provide the freed Negroes with an educational and economic base for the freedom they had won through the Emancipation Proclamation and the Thirteenth Amendment. But nearer in time was the Employment Act of 1946,[18] a cornerstone of President Truman's Fair Deal and one of the most important legislative enactments in the twentieth century; for by this act the federal government committed itself to maintain conditions of maximum production, full employment, and maximum purchasing power. In 1949 Truman called for an economic expansion program with proposals that anticipated, in essentials, the program of Kennedy and Johnson.[19]

Two other contributing causes should be mentioned:

(1) Michael Harrington's *The Other America: Poverty in the United States,* published in 1962, had an eye-opening effect somewhat similar to that achieved by John Steinbeck's *The Grapes of Wrath* when it was published in 1939 and made Americans aware of the plight of the "Okies" on their way to the "promised land" of California.

(2) A less obvious yet significant impetus to consider the problem of the poor came from a series of Supreme Court decisions relating to the administration of justice. The story cannot be told in detail here, but the highlights are too important in this context to be omitted.

Historically, the basis of an accused's right to counsel varied according to whether the prosecution was in a federal or in a state court. In the former instance, the Sixth Amendment—which provides that "in all criminal prosecutions, the accused shall enjoy the right . . . to have assistance of counsel for his defense"—was pertinent. In 1946 the Federal Rules of Criminal Procedure implemented this provision by providing:

If the defendant appears in [federal] court without counsel, the court shall advise him of his right to counsel and assign counsel to represent him at every stage of the proceedings unless he elects to proceed without counsel or is able to obtain counsel.[20]

The difficulty was mainly with regard to state cases, for as to them there was only the broad language of the Fourteenth Amendment that no state shall deprive any person of life, liberty, or property without due process of law. A minority of the Supreme Court, led by Justice Black, contended that the Fourteenth Amendment incorporated, *sub silentio,* the guarantee of the Sixth Amendment,[21] so that all persons charged with crime are entitled to counsel, without regard to the jurisdiction in which they are prosecuted.

Griffin v. *Illinois,*[22] decided in 1956, brought out into the open the hidden economic inequalities that were built into this seemingly technical question of federal-state jurisdiction in the administration of justice. The defendants in the Griffin case had been convicted of armed robbery in a state court. They asked for a certified copy of the record; but as they were without funds to pay for the transcript, their request was denied. Under Illinois law, indigent defendants may obtain a free transcript to get appellate review of constitutional questions, but, except for capital cases, not of other trial errors, such as sufficiency or admissibility of evidence. The defendants in the Griffin case, having been denied a free copy of the trial record, were unable to perfect their appeal. They then petitioned the state courts under a special act, alleging that the refusal to afford them appellate review *because of their poverty* was a denial of due process and equal protection. When their petitions were denied by the state courts, the Supreme Court heard their petition and, by 5 to 4 vote, vacated the state judgment.

The dissenting opinion of Justice Burton articulated the economic issue. Illinois, he said,

is not bound to make the defendants economically equal before its bar of justice. For a State to do so may be a desirable social policy, but what may be a good legislative policy for a State is not necessarily required by the Constitution of the United States. Persons charged with crimes stand before the law with varying degrees of economic and social advantage. Some can afford better lawyers and better investigations of their cases. Some can afford bail, some cannot. Why fix bail at any reasonable sum if a poor man can't make it?

The Constitution requires the equal protection of the law, but it does not require the States to provide equal financial means for all defendants to avail themselves of such laws.

The minority—Justices Burton, Harlan, Minton, and Reed—wanted the law of the Court to stand as it had stood before this case came up. The majority—Chief Justice Warren, Justices Black, Douglas, Frankfurter, and Clark—thought that the Fourteenth Amendment should be read as a pledge of "a fairer and more nearly equal application of criminal justice." The Constitution does not, they said, tolerate "invidious discrimination between persons and different groups of persons." Said Justice Black:

Both equal protection and due process emphasize the central aim of our entire judicial system—all people charged with crime must, so far as the law is concerned, "stand on an equality before the bar of justice in every American court." . . . In criminal trials a State can no more discriminate on account of poverty than on account of religion, race or color. Plainly the ability to pay costs in advance bears no rational relationship to a defendant's guilt or innocence and could not be used to deprive a defendant of a fair trial. . . . There can be no equal justice when the kind of trial a man gets depends on the amount of money he has. Destitute defendants must be afforded as adequate appellate review as defendants who have money enough to buy transcripts.

In a concurring opinion, Justice Frankfurter observed that the position of Illinois reminded him of Anatole France's quip: "The law, in its majestic equality, forbids the rich as well as the poor to sleep under bridges, to beg in the streets, and to steal bread." The state, added Justice Frankfurter, "is not free to produce such a squalid discrimination."

The ideal of equal justice was a basic Biblical commandment; for example, "You shall do no injustice in judgment; you shall not be partial to the poor or defer to the great, but in righteousness shall you judge your neighbor."[23] And Justice Black, in the Griffin case, recalled that Magna Carta pledged that "To no one will we sell, to no one will we refuse, or delay, right or justice." But only now, in the 1950s and 1960s, has this fundamental principle of justice moved up to a position of constitutional dignity.

The most dramatic development of this principle came in 1963 when the Supreme Court, in *Gideon* v. *Wainwright,*[24] overruled contrary precedents and held that the Due Process Clause of the Fourteenth Amendment makes applicable to the states the Sixth Amendment's guarantee of an accused's right to the assistance of counsel in criminal prosecutions.

To understand this very important decision, we must look briefly at a case decided in 1942, *Betts* v. *Brady.*[25] Smith Betts was prosecuted for robbery in a Maryland court. He was indigent and asked the judge to appoint counsel to represent him. The judge told him that the practice was to appoint counsel for indigent defendants only in prosecutions for murder and rape. Betts then did his best without a lawyer: he elected to be tried without a jury; he summoned witnesses, whom he examined, and he cross-examined the state's witnesses. He was found guilty and sentenced to eight years' imprisonment.

The Supreme Court upheld the conviction and held that the Sixth Amendment applied only to trials in federal courts. Justices Black, Douglas, and Murphy dissented. In his dissenting opinion, Justice Black pointed out that Betts was a farm hand, out of a job and on relief, and a man of little education. A practice, he said,

cannot be reconciled with "common and fundamental ideas of fairness and right," which subjects innocent men to increased dangers of conviction merely because of their poverty. . . . Denial to the poor of the request for counsel in proceedings based on charges of serious crime has long been regarded as shocking to the "universal sense of justice" throughout this country.

No man, he concluded, should be deprived of counsel merely because of his poverty.

In the Gideon case, two decades later, the Court unanimously overruled the Betts decision, and it was Justice Black who wrote the opinion for the Court.

Clarence Gideon was charged in a Florida court with breaking into and entering a poolroom with intent to commit a misdemeanor. He was without funds and asked the court to appoint counsel for him. The judge told him that under Florida law he could appoint counsel only when an accused was charged with a capital offense. He was tried before a jury; he conducted his own defense; he was found guilty and sentenced to five years in the state prison. Gideon asked the Supreme Court for a writ of certiorari. This was granted, and the Court appointed Abe Fortas (now a Justice of the Supreme Court) to represent him and to argue the question whether *Betts* v. *Brady* should be reconsidered.

Overruling the Betts decision, the Court said that it was in fact returning to older and better precedents, and that

reason and reflection require us to recognize that in our adversary system of criminal justice, any person haled into court, who is too poor to hire a lawyer, cannot be assured a fair trial unless counsel is provided for him. This seems to us to be an obvious truth. Governments, both state and federal, quite properly spend vast sums of money to establish machinery to try defendants accused of crime. Lawyers to prosecute are everywhere deemed essential to protect the public's interest in an orderly society. . . .

That government hires lawyers to prosecute and defendants who have the money hire lawyers to defend are the strongest indications of the widespread belief that lawyers in criminal courts are necessities, not luxuries. . . . This noble ideal [that every defendant stands equal before the law] cannot be realized if the poor man charged with crime has to face his accusers without a lawyer to assist him. . . . "He requires the guiding hand of counsel at every step in the proceedings against him. Without it, though he be not guilty, he faces the danger of conviction because he does not know how to establish his innocence."

The Supreme Court's concern with the rationing of justice contributed to a growing public awareness of the problem of poverty and to the development of a poverty program by the Kennedy and Johnson administrations. It also provoked the Department of Justice and the American Bar Association to look seriously into the problems involved. The A.B.A. estimated that about 150,000 defendants charged with serious state crimes each year cannot afford lawyers, and it was revealed that over 10,000 federal cases each year involve indigents. It was also revealed that of the 34,000 persons accused of federal offenses in 1963 a substantial number spent considerable time in prison awaiting their trials because they were too poor to provide bail. The Vera Foundation has shown that many a defendant awaiting trial could be relied on to appear for trial without society's needing to look to his financial capacity to ransom himself through bail; for reliance could reasonably be placed upon the defendant's ties to his job, to his family, and to his community to get him to appear in court.

Early in 1961, Attorney General Robert F. Kennedy appointed a Committee on Poverty and the Administration of Federal Criminal Justice, and two years later this committee submitted a comprehensive report with detailed recommendations.[26] In August 1964 President Johnson signed the Criminal Justice Act of 1964,[27] which makes specific provision for defendants "financially unable to obtain an adequate defense." And in March 1965 twenty-one Senators introduced the Omnibus Bail Reform Bill (S. 1357) to take advantage of the experience of the Vera Foundation and other studies to provide more equitable release procedures.

Thus by a slow and painful process, taking generations and centuries, we are forced to look at the implications of what seems superficially to be a simple, and even trite, proposition: "the ethical right of every worker, man or woman, to a living wage." We are forced to see living, even passionately living connections between the Thirteenth Amendment, the National Labor Relations Act, the Bible, Magna

Carta, the Sixth Amendment, the Fourteenth Amendment, the Employment Act of 1946, a poor man in Florida named Gideon, the constitutional philosophies of Supreme Court Justices, the social ideals and the practical sense of Presidents and members of Congress, the spirit of the times—and the Economic Opportunity Act of 1964 and the Criminal Justice Act of 1964. They all make a seamless web, and they are all part of an endless process, in which the spirit sees how freedoms do not exist in separate compartments but are interfused, and how the ideals of freedom, equality, justice, and truth are interdependent.

Notes

Index

Notes

CHAPTER I: RELIGIOUS LIBERTY

1. *Permoli* v. *New Orleans*, 3 How. 589 (1845).
2. *Watson* v. *Jones*, 13 Wall. 679 (1872).
3. E.g., *Kedroff* v. *St. Nicholas Cathedral*, 344 U.S. 94 (1952).
4. *Plessy* v. *Ferguson*, 163 U.S. 537 (1896).
5. Case cited supra, note 3, opinion by Justice Reed, p. 116.
6. Ibid. and footnote 20 on p. 115.
7. *Reynolds* v. *United States*, 98 U.S. 145 (1878).
8. The other two cases were *Davis* v. *Beason*, 133 U.S. 333 (1890), and *Church of Jesus Christ of Latter-Day Saints* v. *United States*, 136 U.S. 1 (1890).
9. See "Adoption of the Bill of Rights" in M. R. Konvitz, *Fundamental Liberties of a Free People* (1957), pp. 345–61.
10. *Church of the Holy Trinity* v. *United States*, 143 U.S. 266 (1892).
11. *Bradfield* v. *Roberts*, 175 U.S. 291 (1899).
12. *Meyer* v. *Nebraska*, 262 U.S. 390 (1923). *Pierce* v. *Society of Sisters*, 268 U.S. 510 (1925).
13. *Arver* v. *United States*, 245 U.S. 366 (1918); *United States* v. *Macintosh*, 283 U.S. 605 (1931); *Hamilton* v. *Regents of University of California*, 293 U.S. 245 (1934). Cf. *United States* v. *Schwimmer*, 279 U.S. 644 (1929).
14. *Quick Bear* v. *Leupp*, 210 U.S. 50 (1908).
15. *Cochran* v. *Louisiana State Board of Education*, 281 U.S. 370 (1930).
16. 60 Stat. 230, § 4, 11 (d)(3), 42 U.S.C. § 1753, 1759 (1946).
17. In addition to the fifteen cases, there were two later ones involving Jehovah's Witnesses: *Niemotko* v. *Maryland* 340 U.S. 268 (1951), and *Fowler* v. *Rhode Island*, 345 U.S. 67 (1953). In addition there were many cases involving members of the sect under military service laws, which we are not considering.
18. The free-speech cases were: *Lovell* v. *Griffin*, 303 U.S. 444 (1938); *Schneider* v. *Irvington*, 308 U.S. 147 (1939); *Chaplinsky* v. *New Hampshire*, 315 U.S. 568 (1942); and *West Virginia State Board of Education* v. *Barnette*, 319 U.S. 624 (1943).
    The religious-liberty cases were: *Cantwell* v. *Connecticut*, 310 U.S. 296 (1940); *Minersville School District* v. *Gobitis*, 310 U.S. 586 (1940), overruled by the Barnette case (1943), supra; *Cox* v. *New Hampshire*,

312 U.S. 569 (1941); *Jones* v. *Opelika*, 316 U.S. 584 (1942) and 319 U.S. 103 (1943); *Murdock* v. *Pennsylvania*, 319 U.S. 105 (1943); *Martin* v. *Struthers*, 319 U.S. 141 (1943); *Taylor* v. *Mississippi*, 319 U.S. 583 (1943); *Jamison* v. *Texas*, 318 U.S. 413 (1943); *Prince* v. *Massachusetts*, 321 U.S. 158 (1944); *Follett* v. *McCormick*, 321 U.S. 573 (1944); *Marsh* v. *Alabama*, 326 U.S. 501 (1946); *Niemotko* v. *Maryland*, 340 U.S. 268 (1951); *Fowler* v. *Rhode Island*, 345 U.S. 67 (1953).

19. *Gitlow* v. *New York*, 268 U.S. 652 (1925).
20. *Cantwell* v. *Connecticut*, cited in note 18, supra.
21. Dissenting opinion in *West Virginia State Board of Education* v. *Barnette*, cited in note 18, supra.
22. Justice Jackson for the Court, ibid.
23. For his address, see *N. Y. Times*, March 16, 1965.
24. *Everson* v. *Board of Education*, 330 U.S. 1 (1947).
25. *McCollum* v. *Board of Education*, 333 U.S. 203 (1948).
26. *Zorach* v. *Clauson*, 343 U.S. 306 (1952).
27. See supra, note 18.
28. *Engel* v. *Vitale*, 370 U.S. 421 (1962).
29. 36 U.S.C. § 172 (1954).
30. 36 U.S.C. § 185 (1952).
31. 36 U.S.C. § 170 (1931).
32. *School District of Abington* v. *Schempp*, and *Murray* v. *Curlett*, 374 U.S. 203 (1963).
33. Passage from Engel case quoted in Schempp and Murray cases.
34. *Peterson* v. *Greenville*, 373 U.S. 244 (1963).
35. Opinion of Justice Brennan in case cited supra, note 32.
36. Ibid., footnote 60.
37. See ibid., footnote 78, for tax exemption of an Ethical Culture Society and a Humanist Fellowship.
38. See *Sherbert* v. *Verner*, 374 U.S. 398 (1963), decided the same day as the Bible-reading cases.
39. See *McGowan* v. *Maryland*, 366 U.S. 420 (1961); *Gallagher* v. *Crown Kosher Super Market*, 366 U.S. 617 (1961); *Two Guys from Harrison–Allentown* v. *McGinley*, 366 U.S. 582 (1961); *Braunfeld* v. *Brown*, 366 U.S. 599 (1961).
40. *Lewis* v. *Allen*, 379 U.S. 923 (1964).
41. See supra, note 29.
42. See supra, note 30.
43. 39 U.S.C. § 368a (1956).
44. 31 U.S.C. § 324a (1955).
45. S. J. Res. 87, 83rd Cong. 1st sess., June 1, 1953.
46. Sec. 511 of Internal Revenue Code of 1954, as amended.
47. *Gregory* v. *Helvering*, 293 U.S. 465 (1935).
48. See *National Observer*, Feb. 18, 1963; *Wall Street Journal*, Oct. 29, 1963. See also "Business Practices of Churches," *Social Action*, May 1961.
49. *Relations Between Church and State*, Adopted by the 175th General Assembly, May 1963, Philadelphia, Pa., pp. 15–16.
50. *World Almanac* (1965), p. 625.
51. Op. cit. supra, note 49, p. 17. The report contains the statement that "The historical support our Church has given to conscientious objectors be reaffirmed."
52. Ibid., p. 18.

53. Ibid., p. 7.
54. Report, National Study Conference on Church and State, Columbus, Ohio, Feb. 4–7, 1964, National Council of Churches of Christ in U.S.A., p. 17.
55. Ibid., p. 21.
56. Ibid., pp. 25–26.
57. See M. R. Konvitz, chapter on "Inter-Group Relations," in *The American Jew: A Reappraisal*, Oscar Janowsky, ed. (1964).
58. *Otis* v. *Parker*, 187 U.S. 606 (1902).
59. Memorandum, American Jewish Congress, June 3, 1958.
60. See cases cited supra, note 39.
61. Op. cit. supra, note 49, pp. 10–11.
62. Op. cit. supra, note 54, pp. 34–35.
63. See op. cit. supra, note 57; also George Kellman, "Religious Freedom and Public Affairs," National Conference of Christians and Jews (1965).
64. See Kellman, op. cit. supra, note 63; also *The Dialogue*, Bulletin 29, May 1964, National Conference of Christians and Jews; Leo Pfeffer, CLSA Report, Feb. 15, 1964. *Proposed Amendments to the Constitution Relating to School Prayers, Bible Reading*, etc., Staff Study, Committee on Judiciary, 88th Cong., 2d sess. (1964); *Report from the Capital*, April-May 1964, Baptist Joint Committee on Public Affairs; *School Prayers*, Hearings before House Judiciary Committee, 88th Cong., 2d sess., in 3 Parts (1964); *Interreligious Newsletter*, American Jewish Committee and B'nai B'rith Anti-Defamation League, Feb. 1963.
65. Paul Tillich, *The Protestant Era* (1957), p. 185.
66. The statement, originally published in the *Atlantic Monthly*, is reprinted in *Living Ideas in America*, H. S. Commager, ed. (1964), p. 520.
67. *N. Y. Times*, Sept. 14, 1960.
68. See American Jewish Committee, *Politics in a Pluralistic Democracy* (1963); "The 'Catholic Vote'—a Kennedy Staff Analysis," *U. S. News & World Report*, Aug. 1, 1960; P. Barrett, "Religion and the 1960 Election," *Social Order*, June 1962; Irving Spiegel, *N. Y. Times*, Nov. 4, 1963; "The 1960 Election Campaign," *Facts*, March 1961, B'nai B'rith A. D. L.; A. B. Wildavsky, "The Intelligent Citizen's Guide to the Abuses of Statistics," in *Politics and Social Life*, Polsby, Dentler, and Smith, eds. (1963); "Who Elected Kennedy?" *U. S. News & World Report*, May 1, 1961; G. Lensk, *The Religious Factor* (1961); John Wicklein, *N. Y. Times*, Feb. 18, 1962.

CHAPTER II: FREEDOM OF ASSOCIATION

1. Arthur M. Schlesinger, "Biography of a Nation of Joiners," 50 *American Historical Review* (1944), p. 1; reprinted in Schlesinger, *Paths to the Present*, 1949, p. 23.
2. Alexis de Tocqueville, *Democracy in America*, the Henry Reeve Text, Phillips Bradley, ed. (1945), Vol. I, p. 191.
3. Schlesinger, op. cit. supra, note 1, p. 11.
4. Tocqueville, op. cit. note 2, Vol. I, p. 192.
5. Ibid., Vol. II, p. 106.
6. Ibid., Vol. II, pp. 109–10.
7. James Bryce visited the United States in 1870, in 1881, and a third time in 1883–1884. The first edition of *The American Commonwealth* was published in 1888, by which time the population had grown to 60,000,000.

8. Bryce, *The American Commonwealth* (1920 ed.), Vol. II, pp. 281–82.
9. From *Max Weber: Essays in Sociology*, H. H. Gerth and C. Wright Mills, eds. (1946), p. 310; cf. p. 57.
10. Robert C. Angell, *The Integration of American Society* (1941), p. 3.
11. Robin M. Williams, Jr., *American Society: A Sociological Interpretation* (1961), p. 501.
12. Max Lerner, *America as a Civilization* (1957), p. 630.
13. See Samuel Beer, "Pressure Groups and Parties in Britain," 50 *American Political Science Review* (1956), p. 3; Bernard E. Brown, "Pressure Politics in France," 18 *Journal of Politics* (1956), p. 718; and generally *Interest Groups on Four Continents*, Henry W. Ehrmann, ed. (1958); Frank H. Hankins, "Fraternal Orders," 6 *Encyclopedia of the Social Sciences*, p. 423.
14. For a different view, see Charles R. Wright and Herbert H. Hyman, "Voluntary Association Memberships of American Adults," 23 *American Sociological Review* (1958), p. 284.
15. Tocqueville described freedom of association as "this perilous liberty." Op. cit. supra, note 2, Vol. I, p. 195.
16. *N.A.A.C.P.* v. *Alabama*, 357 U.S. 449 (1958).
17. Freedom of association was, however, mentioned in some earlier decisions, notably *Whitney* v. *California*, 274 U.S. 357 (1927); *Bryant* v. *Zimmerman*, 278 U.S. 63 (1928); *Bridges* v. *Wixon*, 326 U.S. 135 (1945). See Charles E. Wyzanki, Jr., "The Open Window and the Open Door," 35 *California Law Review* (1947), p. 338.
18. For a brief history of the adoption of the Bill of Rights, see M. R. Konvitz, *Fundamental Liberties of a Free People* (1957), pp. 345–61.
19. *The Federalist* (1787), No. 10.
20. Farewell Address, Sept. 17, 1796, in 1 *Messages and Papers*, J. D. Richardson, ed., p. 213.
21. The drafts are in *The Writings of George Washington*, W. C. Ford, ed., Vol. 13.
22. Thomas Hobbes, *Leviathan* (1651), Part 2, Ch. 22. See Robert A. Horn, *Groups and the Constitution* (1956), pp. 5–6. Charles E. Rice, *Freedom of Association* (1962), pp. 6–8. Wyzanki, op. cit. supra, note 17, pp. 344–45.
23. *Leviathan*, Ch. 22.
24. George H. Sabine, *A History of Political Theory* (1961), p. 475.
25. The quotations are from John Locke, *Second Treatise of Civil Government* (1689) and *A Letter Concerning Toleration* (1689).
26. Horn, op. cit. supra, note 22, p. 8, states: "Most important, Locke assumes that the individual has a natural and inalienable right to associate." This, I think, goes beyond what Locke's writings warrant.
27. J. J. Rousseau, *The Social Contract* (1762), Book 2, Ch. 3, in *The Social Contract and Discourses* (Everyman ed., 1913), p. 23.
28. The "Great Society"—did this phrase flow into the vocabulary of President Johnson in 1964 directly or indirectly from Rousseau? The phrase is also found in Walter Lippmann, *The Good Society* (1937), p. 311.
29. Rousseau, *A Discourse on Political Economy* (1758), in *The Social Contract and Discourses*, pp. 237–38.
30. Ibid., p. 238.
31. Op. cit. supra, note 27, p. 23. The French seem to have followed Rousseau's position. In 1791 the French Assembly banned associations; and freedom

of association was not recognized until 1901. See Rice, op. cit. supra, note 22, pp. 15–16.

32. *The Complete Madison: His Basic Writings,* Saul K. Padover, ed. (1953), p. 306.

33. *Western Turf Association* v. *Greenberg,* 204 U.S. 363 (1907). See also *Northwestern National Life Insurance Co.* v. *Riggs,* 203 U.S. 243 (1906).

34. *Louis K. Liggett Co.* v. *Baldridge,* 278 U.S. 105 (1928); *Smyth* v. *Ames,* 169 U.S. 466 (1898). But see dissenting opinion of Justice Black in *Connecticut General Life Insurance Co.* v. *Johnson,* 303 U.S. 77 (1938), and dissenting opinion of Justice Douglas in *Wheeling Steel Corp.* v *Glander,* 337 U.S. 562 (1949).

35. 263 U.S. 510 (1925).

36. Italics supplied.

37. Justice Black in *Connecticut General Life Insurance Co.* v. *Johnson,* 303 U.S. 77 (1938), dissenting opinion.

38. Ibid.

39. *Wheeling Steel Corp.* v. *Glander,* 337 U.S. 562 (1949). The case involved the Equal Protection Clause of the Fourteenth Amendment.

40. 307 U.S. 496 (1939). Justices McReynolds and Butler dissented.

41. "State Control Over Political Organizations: First Amendment Checks on Powers of Regulation," 66 *Yale Law Journal* (1957), p. 545.

42. See Justice Douglas's opinion in case cited supra, note 39.

43. Locke, *Second Treatise of Government,* Sec. 6.

44. Ibid., Sec. 123.

45. Ibid., Sec. 173.

46. Madison, 1792, in op. cit. supra, note 32, pp. 267–69.

47. *Grosjean* v. *American Press Co.,* 297 U.S. 233 (1936). See A. P. Sindler, *Huey Long's Louisiana* (1956), pp. 89–90.

48. *Bridges* v. *California* 314 U.S. 252 (1941). The decision was by 5-to-4 vote.

49. In 1937 three-fourths of the daily and Sunday newspapers were published by corporations. See op. cit. supra, note 41, p. 549.

50. Cf. Robert G. McCloskey, "Economic Due Process and the Supreme Court," *1962 Supreme Court Review* (1962), pp. 34, 45 ff.

51. Cf. *Kedroff* v. *St. Nicholas Cathedral,* 344 U.S. 94 (1952), discussed in Konvitz, *Fundamental Liberties for a Free People,* pp. 92–97.

52. That corporations are "persons" under the Equal Protection Clause, see note 39 supra.

53. *Burstyn, Inc.* v. *Wilson,* 343 U.S. 495 (1952)—the so-called *"Miracle* case."

54. *Hale* v. *Henkel,* 201 U.S. 43 (1906); *United States* v. *White,* 322 U.S. 694 (1944); *Wilson* v. *United States,* 221 U.S. 361 (1911); *Oklahoma Press Publishing Co.* v. *Walling,* 327 U.S. 186 (1946); *Rogers* v. *United States,* 340 U.S. 367 (1951).

55. On the other hand, a corporation may invoke the rule against the admission of evidence seized in violation of the Fourth Amendment. *Silverthorne Lumber Co.* v. *United States,* 251 U.S. 385 (1920).

56. See note 35 supra. Italics supplied.

57. Congress in drafting the Civil Rights Act of 1964—Public Law 88–352, 88th Cong., H.R. 7152, 78 Stat. 241 (July 2, 1964)—had in mind the fact that the public-accommodations provisions in Sec. 201 would of course be challenged in the courts and it anticipated the constitutional

difficulties that would be encountered in the light of Supreme Court precedents that go back to the nineteenth century and that had not—by July 2, 1964—been overruled.

58. Case cited supra, note 16. For factual account of case, see George R. Osborne, "The NAACP in Alabama," in *The Third Branch of Government*, C. Herman Pritchett and Alan Westin, eds. (1963), pp. 149 ff.
59. *NAACP Annual Report, 1962*, p. 21.
60. Ibid., p. 86.
61. *Browder* v. *Gayle*, 142 F. Supp. 707, 1 Race Rel. L. Rep. 668 (1956), affd. *per curiam*, 352 U.S. 903 (1956). See M. R. Konvitz and T. Leskes, *A Century of Civil Rights* (1961), pp. 132–33.
62. *Brown* v. *Board of Education*, 347 U.S. 483 (1954); *Bolling* v. *Sharpe*, 347 (1954).
63. *Brown* v. *Board of Education*, 349 U.S. 294 (1955).
64. In Selma, Alabama, 29 members of the N.A.A.C.P. signed a petition requesting the board of education to consider desegregating the public schools. Within a few days it became known that sixteen of the signers had been discharged from their jobs. See op. cit. supra, note 58, pp. 161–62. See also N.A.A.C.P. Brief on Petition for Writ of Certiorari, filed with U.S. Supreme Court, October Term 1956, pp. 19–25.
65. Brief cited in note 64, p. 23.
66. Ibid., pp. 25–31. Italics supplied.
67. Italics supplied.
68. Matthew 22: 20–21.
69. *Bates* v. *Little Rock*, 361 U.S. 516 (1960).
70. 371 U.S. 415 (1963). The decision was 6 to 3, with Justices Harlan, Clark, and Stewart dissenting. The dissenters took the position that the Virginia statute constitutionally regulated the litigating activities of the N.A.A.C.P
71. Italics supplied.
72. Zechariah Chafee, Jr., *The Blessings of Liberty* (1956), p. 75. This statement is true not only of the A.C.L.U. and the N.A.A.C.P. but of other organizations that have worked zealously on behalf of civil liberties and civil rights, such as the American Jewish Committee, the American Jewish Congress, the Workers Defense League, and the American Association of University Professors.
73. "The South's Amended Barratry Laws: An Attempt to End Group Pressures through the Courts," 72 *Yale Law Journal* (1963), p. 1638, note 97.
74. Correspondence of N.A.A.C.P. with the author.
75. Op cit. supra, note 73, pp. 1642–43.
76. Ibid., p. 1638.
77. See, for example, the story about the civil rights case in Baton Rouge, La., reported in *N. Y. Times*, Nov. 30, 1962. *Johnson* v. *Virginia*, 373 U.S. 61 (1963): courtroom segregation is unconstitutional.
78. See *Hamilton* v. *Alabama*, 156 So. 2d 926 (1963), reversed by U.S. Supreme Court, 11 L. ed. 979 (1963).
79. See report by Claude Sitton in *N. Y. Times*, Oct. 30, 1961. See also Barbara Carter, "A Lawyer Leaves Mississippi," *The Reporter*, May 9, 1963, p. 33; Charles Morgan, Jr., *A Time to Speak* (1964); Bruce M. Galphin, "When a Negro Is on Trial in the South," *N. Y. Times Magazine*, Dec. 15, 1963, p. 17. Cf. *Jordan* v. *Hutcheson*, 323 F. 2d 597

(1963). See report "Law Enforcement in Mississippi," Southern Regional Council, 1964.

80. Editorial. "Lawyers and Racial Unrest," 49 *A.B.A. Journal*, Nov. 1963, p. 1083. See also article on composition of the A.B.A. Committee in *N. Y. Times*, July 3, 1963. See also Criminal Justice Act of 1964, Public Law 88–455, Aug. 20, 1964.

81. *N. Y. Times*, Aug. 15, 1963.

82. Op. cit. supra, note 73, p. 1619, note 32.

83. Ibid., p. 1613.

84. Ibid., pp. 1616–17. See also *Assault Upon Freedom of Association—A Study of the Southern Attack on the N.A.A.C.P.*, by American Jewish Congress (1957).

85. N.A.A.C.P., *Annual Report*, 1957, p. 42.

86. *N.A.A.C.P.* v. *Alabama*, 84 S. Ct. 1302 (1964). For summary of proceedings in this case, see 5 Race Rel. L. Rep. 809 (1960); 6 Race Rel. L. Rep. 497 (1961); 9 Race Rel. L. Rep. 526 (1964). The injunction against the N.A.A.C.P. was finally lifted and the Association was granted permission to operate in the State of Alabama as of Oct. 9, 1964—more than six years after the decision of the Supreme Court. (Letter from the Association to the author.)

87. Quoted by Anthony Lewis, "Campaign: The Supreme Court Issue," *N. Y. Times*, Oct. 11, 1964.

88. Benjamin N. Cardozo, *Growth of the Law* (1924), p. 87.

89. Case cited supra, note 86.

90. See report by Claude Sitton, "Alabama Compiling Files on Civil Rights Advocates," *N. Y. Times*, Feb. 17, 1964.

91. *N. Y. Times*, Sept. 16, 1964.

92. *Uphaus* v. *Wyman*, 360 U.S. 72 (1959), and 364 U.S. 388 (1960). See Willard Uphaus, *Commitment* (1963), written while the author was in prison.

93. 350 U.S. 497 (1956). Justices Reed, Burton, and Minton dissented. Bills were introduced in Congress as reactions to the Nelson decision, but none was enacted.

94. See Chief Justice Warren's opinion in the Nelson case.

95. See Emerson and Haber, 1 *Political and Civil Rights in the United States* (1958), pp. 428 ff.; *Digest of the Public Record of Communism in the United States* (1955).

96. See Walter Gellhorn, *The States and Subversion* (1952), pp. 382–383; and Ch. VII, where the state and municipal laws are summarized.

97. 364 U.S. 388 (1960).

98. 372 U.S. 539 (1963). The Court also distinguished the relatively early case *New York ex rel. Bryant* v. *Zimmerman*, 278 U.S. 63 (1928), in which the Court upheld as constitutional a New York statute that required associations with oath-bound memberships to file lists of their members with a state officer. It was aimed at the Ku Klux Klan and its activities, "involving acts of unlawful intimidation and violence." The Court in *N.A.A.C.P.* v. *Alabama* distinguished this case on the same basis.

99. Italics in original.

100. Cf. Wilson Record, *Race and Radicalism: The NAACP and the Communist Party in Conflict* (1964).

101. 366 U.S. 293 (1961).

396 | NOTES

102. Justice Goldberg's language in the Gibson case.
103. Concurring opinion in the Gibson case.
104. Justice Brennan in the Button case.
105. Justice Douglas, concurring opinion in the Gibson case.

CHAPTER III: ACADEMIC FREEDOM

 1. Samuel Eliot Morison, *Freedom in Contemporary Society* (1956), p. 107. See Richard Hofstadter and Walter P. Metzger, *The Development of Academic Freedom in the United States* (1955); Robert M. MacIver, *Academic Freedom in Our Time* (1955).
 2. Comment, 46 *Yale Law Journal* (1937), pp. 670, 671, quoted in William P. Murphy, "Academic Freedom—an Emerging Constitutional Right," 28 *Law and Contemporary Problems,* summer 1963, p. 447. The entire issue is devoted to academic freedom.

 Meyer v. *Nebraska,* 362 U.S. 390 (1923) may be cited as a forerunner of the cases decided in the 1950s. The plaintiff was convicted of violation of a Nebraska statute of 1919 by teaching the German language. The Supreme Court reversed the judgment, holding that the state may not prohibit the teaching of subjects that are not injurious to health or morals.
 3. 342 U.S. 485 (1952).
 4. 344 U.S. 183 (1952). Justice Jackson did not participate. Justice Black wrote a concurring opinion in which Justice Douglas joined.
 5. 354 U.S. 234 (1957). Justice Whittaker did not participate. Justices Clark and Burton dissented.
 6. But it should be noted that the Uphaus case was decided in 1959 and 1960, several years after the Sweezy case.
 7. 360 U.S. 109 (1959).
 8. Italics supplied.
 9. 364 U.S. 479 (1960).
10. Justices Clark, Harlan, and Whittaker agreed with Justice Frankfurter's opinion. Justice Harlan also wrote a dissenting opinion, in which the other dissenters joined.

 There is a suggestion in Justice Harlan's opinion that the statute may have been intended as a weapon against N.A.A.C.P. members in the teaching profession; and so "unremitting vigilance" on the part of the courts was demanded—yet the statute was constitutional. It is hard to know what "unremitting vigilance" means in such a context.
11. R. W. Emerson, essay on "Worship"—*Conduct of Life* (1860).
12. Cf. John Dewey, *Quest for Certainty,* (1929), passim.
13. *McAuliffe* v. *New Bedford,* 155 Mass. 216, 29 N.E. 517 (1892). Cf. *United Public Workers* v. *Mitchell,* 330 U.S. 75 (1947); *Slochower* v. *Board of Education,* 350 U.S. 551 (1956).
14. See, for example, W. E. Hocking, *The Lasting Elements of Individualism* (1937), p. 81.
15. Case cited supra, note 4.
16. See the issue of *Law and Contemporary Problems* on academic freedom, summer 1963, especially the articles by Ralph F. Fuchs, William P. Murphy, Thomas I. Emerson and David Haber, and Louis Joughin. See

Annual Reports of A.C.L.U., which summarize the organization's activities in all fields, including academic freedom.

17. American Civil Liberties Union, *Academic Freedom and Civil Liberties of Students in Colleges and Universities* (1961, rev. 1963). Louis M. Hacker was chairman of the committee.
18. American Association of University Professors, *Statement on Faculty Responsibility for the Academic Freedom of Students* (draft, March 1964).
19. *Wieman* v. *Updegraff*, cited supra, note 4.
20. *A Report on Campus Censorship*, spring 1962. Whitney North Seymour, Jr., was chairman of the committee.
21. Ibid., pp. 4 and 5. See also Andrew Hacker, "Academic Freedom—How Much Is There?" *N. Y. Times Magazine*, June 7, 1964, pp. 25 ff.; William W. Van Alstyne, "Banning the Campus Speaker," *The Nation*, March 30, 1963, pp. 267.
22. Case cited supra, note 4.
23. The study was due to be completed late in 1964. Reynold A. Neuwein directed the study and made public some preliminary findings in April 1964. *N. Y. Times*, April 3, 1964.
24. See three articles by Gene Currivan in *N. Y. Times*, May 4, 5, and 6, 1964.
25. This, incidentally, has been the Jewish pattern. The Hebrew school—Talmud Torah—starts to teach late in the afternoon, after the children leave their public schools. Now there are also "all-day" schools under Jewish auspices, attended by some 50,000 children in 1964. They are not referred to as "parochial" schools because they divide the day and the curriculum into two separate parts—generally the morning is devoted to the religious and Hebrew subjects, and the afternoon to the secular subjects. For the latter, public-school textbooks are used. Thus, even the all-day schools are so organized and oriented that the pupils receive religious teaching only *in addition* to that provided by the public schools.

    As we have noted, Roman Catholic schools have begun to rely on public-school texts, and lay teachers are being used more and more. In time perhaps these schools too will look more like "all-day," and less like the traditional "parochial," schools. Before 1950 nuns and members of male religious orders constituted 90 to 95 per cent of all teachers in Roman Catholic schools. In 1964 about 30 per cent of the teachers were lay teachers.

    Some Roman Catholic schools have become coeducational. In some dioceses there are now lay school boards. See report in *U.S. News & World Report*, Feb. 3, 1964. See also Wilber G. Katz, *Religion and American Constitutions* (1964), pp. 81–82.
26. Sidney Hook, *Education for Modern Man* (1963), pp. 90–91.
27. Case cited supra, note 4.
28. Cf. Hook, op. cit. supra, note 26, p. 55, for a fine statement of the ends of education.
29. 268 U.S. 510 (1925).
30. Cf. released-time case, *Zorach* v. *Clauson*, 343 U.S. 306 (1952).
31. In 1960 the enrollment in Roman Catholic elementary schools was 4,400,000, attending 10,622 schools. There were 2426 Roman Catholic secondary schools, with an enrollment of 885,000. There were in these schools 153,000 teachers. See Memorandum of Legal Department of

National Catholic Welfare Conference, in 52 *Georgetown Law Journal* (1961), p. 399.

There are some 3500 Jewish schools, with an enrollment of 600,000. About half of the schools are for after-school, weekday instruction; the other half are Sunday schools. In addition to these types of school, there are about 250 all-day schools, with an enrollment of 50,000. See supra, note 25. See Alexander Dushkin and U. Z. Engelman, *Jewish Education in the United States* (1959); *The American Jew—a Reappraisal,* Oscar Janowsky, ed. (1964), pp. 135, 143.

32. Statement published in full in *N. Y. Times,* Nov. 15, 1958.
33. Walter Lippmann, *The Good Society* (1937), pp. 308–12.

CHAPTER IV: THE COMMUNIST PARTY AND FREEDOM OF ASSOCIATION

1. U.S. Dept. of State, Bureau of Intelligence and Research, Intelligence Report No. 4489-R-14, *World Strength of the Communist Party Organizations* (Jan. 1962).
2. Ibid., p. 2.
3. *Internal Security Manual,* revised, Senate Document No. 126, 86th Cong., 2d sess. (1961).
4. Published, in 1955, by the Fund for the Republic.
5. Smith Act, 18 U.S.C. § 2385 (Supp. 1952).
6. Espionage Act of 1917, 40 Stat. 219 (1917); 1918 amendment, 40 Stat. 553 (1918); revision of 1948—18 U.S.C. § 2388 (Supp. 1952).
7. Zechariah Chafee, Jr., *Freedom of Speech* (1920); *Free Speech in the United States* (1941). James P. Hall, "Free Speech in War Times," 21 *Columbia Law Review* (1921), p. 526.
8. Conspiracy provision is 18 U.S.C. § 371 (Supp. 1952).
9. 86 *Congressional Record* (1940), pp. 9032 ff.
10. *Dunne* v. *United States,* 138 F. 2d 137 (1943), certiorari denied, 320 U.S. 790 (1943).
11. Sec. 9(h) of Labor-Management Relations Act of 1947, popularly known as Taft-Hartley Act. This section was eliminated by the Landrum-Griffin Act, the Labor-Management Reporting and Disclosure Act of 1959.
12. For Harry Bridges, see M. R. Konvitz, *Civil Rights in Immigration* (1953), pp. 114 ff.
13. The Cominform was dissolved in 1956 as a gesture of reconciliation when Tito seemed to have been won back by the Russian Communists under Nikita Khrushchev.
14. The Order is published in *Digest of the Public Record of Communism in the United States,* p. 43. President Roosevelt's Executive Order 9300 (1943) establishing an interdepartmental committee to consider cases of subversive activity by federal employees is published in the *Digest,* p. 42. See Eleanor Bontecou, *The Federal Loyalty-Security Program* (1953).
15. The Dies Committee, which was in existence from 1938 to 1944, expired with the 78th Congress. The action of the House of Representatives in 1945, setting up the standing committee, was sudden and unexpected. Robert K. Carr, *The House Committee on Un-American Activities 1945–1950* (1952), p. 17. See August R. Ogden, *The Dies Committee* (1945).

16. The witnesses were successfully prosecuted for contempt. See cases cited by Carr, op. cit. supra, note 15, p. 35.
17. For the Chambers-Hiss story, see W. A. Jowitt, *The Strange Case of Alger Hiss* (1953); Whittaker Chambers, *Witness* (1952); Alger Hiss, *In the Court of Public Opinion* (1957); Ralph de Toledano and Victor Lasky, *Seeds of Treason* (1950).
18. Committee report, Dec. 31, 1948, *Soviet Espionage within the United States: Second Report*, p. 1, quoted by Carr, op. cit. supra, note 15, p. 129.
19. H. R. 5852.
20. *Schenck* v. *United States*, 249 U.S. 47 (1919). See M. R. Konvitz, *Fundamental Liberties of a Free People* (1957), pp. 280 ff.
21. See Konvitz, op. cit. supra, note 20, for full discussion of the doctrine's history and use. Justice Frankfurter in his concurring opinion in the Dennis case also went into the history of the doctrine in Supreme Court cases; the Appendix to Justice Douglas's opinion is also relevant. See also annotations in 93 L. ed. 1159 and 95 L. ed. 1196.
22. *Dennis* v. *United States*, 341 U.S. 494 (1951). Justice Clark did not participate. Justices Frankfurter and Jackson each wrote a concurring opinion. Justices Black and Douglas each wrote a dissenting opinion.
23. 18 U.S.C. § 2384 punishes conspiracy to overthrow, put down, or destroy by force the Government of the United States.
24. Communication to author from Department of Justice, April 1963. The aliens ordered deported were Williamson and Potash. The bail jumpers were Thompson, Winston, Potash, and Green.
25. Report of Committee on Foreign Relations, *State Department Employee Loyalty Investigation*, 81st Cong., 2d sess., Senate Report No. 2108 (1950), p. 2. Italics supplied.
26. Ibid., p. 3.
27. Ibid.
28. Ibid., p. 6.
29. See James Rorty and Moshe Decter, *McCarthy and the Communists* (1954); Report of Committee on Privileges and Elections, *Investigations of Senators Joseph R. McCarthy and William Benton* (1952), published also by Beacon Press, Boston, 1953; William F. Buckley, Jr., and L. B. Bozell, *McCarthy and His Enemies* (1954); Telford Taylor, *Grand Inquest* (1955).
30. *Diversity in International Communism: A Documentary Record 1961–1963*, Alexander Dallin et al., eds. (1963); *Polycentrism: The New Factor in International Communism*, Walter Laqueur and Leopold Labedz, eds. (1962); George F. Kennan, *On Dealing with the Communist World* (1964).
31. *Digest of the Public Record of Communism in the United States*, p. 579.
32. Ibid., p. 550.
33. David Lawrence's syndicated newspaper column, March 27, 1962.
34. Arthur Herzog, "A Specter Haunts the American Communist Party," *N. Y. Times Magazine*, Oct. 25, 1964, p. 61.
35. Ibid., p. 54.
36. Jack Levine, article in *The Nation*, Oct. 20, 1962. *Newsweek*, Oct. 29, 1962, p. 24; editorial in *N. Y. Times*, Oct. 23, 1962. In 1964 the Party expelled William Albertson, high-ranking member, for allegedly being a "police agent" and "informer" for the F.B.I. *N. Y. Times*, July 8, 1964. He was one of the Communists convicted on Aug. 20, 1953; but on

Sept. 13, 1957, his indictment was dismissed on motion of the government after the credibility of a key witness came under doubt.

37. Op. cit. supra, note 1, pp. 5, 7.

38. Sidney Hook, *Heresy, Yes—Conspiracy, No* (1953), Ch. 5; for a study of legal safeguards of the country's security, see Library of Congress, *Federal Case Law Concerning the Security of the United States*, 83d Cong., 2d sess., Senate Committee on Foreign Affairs, 1954.

39. The facts regarding the cases are taken from memoranda prepared by the Department of Justice in April 1963 and December 1964. Some of the cases appear also in op. cit. supra, note 31, pp. 202–205.

40. 354 U.S. 298 (1957). Justices Brennan and Whittaker did not participate. Justices Clark and Burton dissented, though between them there was no complete agreement. Justice Black wrote a separate opinion, concurred in by Justice Douglas.

On June 19, 1962, Congress amended the Smith Act by providing that the terms "organizes" and "organize" shall include the recruiting of new members, the forming of new units, and the regrouping or expansion of existing groups. Public Law 87–486, 87th Cong., H.R. 3247; 76 Stat. 103 (1962).

41. *Alabama State Federation of Labor* v. *McAdory*, 325 U.S. 450 (1945); *N.L.R.B.* v. *Jones & Laughlin*, 301 U.S. 1 (1937).

42. *Winter* v. *New York*, 333 U.S. 507 (1948).

43. *Lightfoot* v. *United States*, 355 U.S. 52 (1957).

44. Op. cit. supra, note 31, p. 579, where the membership is given for 1953.

45. *Scales* v. *United States*, 355 U.S. 1 (1957).

46. *Scales* v. *United States*, 367 U.S. 203 (1961).

47. *Noto* v. *United States*, 367 U.S. 290 (1961).

48. Department of Justice communications to author, April 1963 and December 1964.

49. Theodore Draper in *N. Y. Times*, Feb. 7, 1962.

50. *N. Y. Times*, April 6, 1962; also editorials Feb. 7 and June 14, 1962.

51. Alexander Pope, "Epistle to Dr. Arbuthnot."

52. *Sacher* v. *United States*, 343 U.S. 1 (1952). Justice Clark did not participate. Justices Black, Frankfurter, and Douglas dissented.

53. *Re Disbarment of Abraham J. Isserman*, 345 U.S. 286 (1953). Justice Clark did not participate.

54. Harold Sacher, another of the defense attorneys in the Dennis trial, was subjected to professional discipline. He was ordered disbarred from the federal district court for the southern district of New York. The Supreme Court, by 6 to 2, held that permanent disbarment was too severe and remanded the case. Justices Burton and Reed dissented from the *per curiam* opinion. Justice Clark did not participate. *Sacher* v. *Association of the Bar*, 347 U.S. 388 (1954).

55. *Re Disbarment of Abraham J. Isserman*, 348 U.S. 1 (1954). Chief Justice Vinson and Justice Clark did not participate. The dissenting Justices were Burton, Reed, and Minton.

56. 50 U.S.C. § 781 ff.; 64 Stat. 987 (1950).

57. Under the Emergency Detention Act, when the President declared an Internal Security Emergency, the Attorney General was to apprehend persons who were likely to engage in espionage or sabotage, who were to be detained in special camps. Such facilities were maintained for several

years with funds authorized by Congress for this purpose. About 1956 or 1957 the camps were discontinued and no funds were further appropriated for this purpose. (Letter from Bureau of Prisons to author.)

58. Kennan, *On Dealing with the Communist World*, p. 37.

59. Published in 1964 by American Bar Association.

60. Ibid., pp. xvi, xvii.

61. *N. Y. Times*, Feb. 26, 1964. See R. Lowenthal, "The Prospects for Pluralistic Communism," *Dissent*, winter 1965.

62. This provision was declared unconstitutional. *Aptheker* v. *Rusk*, 12 L. ed. 2d 992 (1964).

63. The message is found in Commager, *Documents of American History* (7th ed., 1963), Vol. 2, p. 564.

64. Subversive Activities Control Board [S.A.C.B.], *13th Annual Report, 1963*, p. 6.

65. Op. cit. supra, note 31, pp. 403 ff. Such statutes are probably invalid under *Pennsylvania* v. *Nelson*, 350 U.S. 497 (1956).

66. 68 Stat. 775 (1954), Public Law 637.

67. Such organizations are not required to register. They are required to comply with certain provisions and are denied certain benefits under the National Labor Relations Act.

68. *Communist Party* v. *Subversive Activities Control Board*, 351 U.S. 115 (1956). Justices Clark, Reed, and Minton dissented. See H. L. Packer, *Ex-Communist Witness* (1962).

69. *Communist Party* v. *Subversive Activities Control Board*, 367 U.S. 1 (1961). Chief Justice Warren and Justices Black, Douglas, and Brennan wrote dissenting opinions.

70. 52 Stat. 631; 22 U.S.C. § 611–21. *Viereck* v. *United States*, 318 U.S. 236 (1943).

71. *N. Y. Times*, March 16, 1962.

75. S A C. B., *13th Annual Report*, 1963, p. 7; *N. Y. Times*, June 1, 1962;

73. 12 L. ed. 2d 737 (1964). Court of appeals opinion in *U.S. Law Week*, Dec. 24, 1963.

74. *N. Y. Times*, Aug. 24, 1964.

75. S. A. C. B., 13th *Annual Report*, 1963, p. 7; *N. Y. Times*, June 1, 1962; Attorney General, *Annual Report*, 1963, pp. 261–63; Report of Attorney General to President and Congress With Respect to Subversive Activities Control Act, June 1, 1964. Memorandum of Attorney General, Oct. 12, 1964. *Albertson and Proctor* v. *Subversive Activities Control Board*, 86 S. Ct. 194 (1965). Editorial in *N. Y. Times*, Nov. 16, 1965.

When the top twelve party leaders were indicted as co-conspirators under the Smith Act, ten of them were also indicted, at the same time, under the membership clause, but they were never tried on the latter charge, and fifteen years later the government moved that the indictments be dropped. *N. Y. Times*, May 30, 1963.

76. *N. Y. Times*, Sept. 20, 1964; Attorney General, *Annual Report*, 1963, p. 261.

77. Report of Attorney General to President and Congress, cited supra, note 75.

78. S. A. C. B., *13th Annual Report*, p. 8.

79. Ibid., p. 11.

80. 12 L. ed. 2d 185, 1043 (1964).

81. 85 S. Ct. (1965).
82. Memorandum of Department of Justice, Nov. 15, 1963; Attorney General, *Annual Report*, 1962, p. 231.
83. Attorney General, *Annual Report*, 1963, p. 255. *N. Y. Times*, Nov. 16, 1965.
84. S. A. C. B., *12th Annual Report*, p. 6; *13th Annual Report*, pp. 8–9; *11th Annual Report*, p. 9; Report of Attorney General to President and Congress, cited supra, note 75. *N. Y. Times*, Nov. 16, 1965.
85. *Communist Domination of Certain Unions*, Senate Document No. 89, 82d Cong., 1st sess. (1951), Ch. 8. Also *The Communist Party and the CIO*, Senate, 82d Cong., 2d sess. (1952).
86. See S. A. C. B., *9th Annual Report*, p. 10, regarding the United Electrical, Radio and Machine Workers of America.
87. *Guide to Subversive Organizations and Publications*, House Committee on Un-American Activities, revised and published Dec. 1, 1961.
88. Ibid., p. 10.
89. Walter Gellhorn, *Security, Loyalty, and Science* (1950), pp. 129, 138. The list in 1948 contained 82 organizations; by 1953 the list had grown to over 250. See Appendix II in *Guide to Subversive Organizations and Publications*. Peter Edson's column, Newspaper Enterprise Association, June 11, 1962.

Executive Order 10450 took the place of Executive Order 9835 on May 27, 1953. On April 29, 1953, rules of procedure were prescribed regarding notice, hearing, and designation of organizations. All organizations designated under 9835 were redesignated under 10450, and 62 organizations were notified under the 1953 rules of procedure that their designation was proposed. Attorney General, *Annual Report*, 1953, p. 15.

In 1958 the Attorney General removed three organizations from the list on their initiative and after investigation and hearings. These were the Independent Socialist League, the Socialist Youth League, and the Workers Party. Attorney General, *Annual Report*, 1958, pp. 250–51; 1959, pp. 258–59.

In 1957 the Attorney General proceeded to list the National Lawyers Guild but rescinded the proposal on Sept. 11, 1958. Attorney General *Annual Report*, 1958, p. 251; 1959, p. 259.

In 1958–1959 the Department of Justice reviewed 439 organizations, and in 1959–1960 it reviewed 471 organizations, but no new listings were made. Attorney General, *Annual Report*, 1959, p. 260; 1960, p. 263. In his *Annual Report* for 1963, p. 273, the Attorney General said that there are "no known Communists on the rolls of the Executive Branch at the present time."
90. 341 U.S. 123 (1951).
91. Ibid., concurring opinion. See also *Dombrowski* v. *Pfister*, 85 S. Ct. 1116, p. 1125 (1965). The regulations for the listing by the Attorney General were revised, after the Joint Anti-Fascist Refugee Committee case, to comply with Supreme Court requirements. See Attorney General, *Annual Report*, 1954, p. 14.
92. Text in full in *N. Y. Times*, Oct. 8, 1956.
93. Op. cit. supra, note 31, p. 299.
94. Robert K. Murray, *Red Scare: a Study in National Hysteria 1919–1920* (1955), p. 234.
95. *Communist Party* v. *Moysey*, 141 F. Supp. 332 (1956); *Publishers New*

Press v. *Moysey*, 141 F. Supp. 340 (1956); *Communist Party* v. *Commission of Internal Revenue*, 332 F. 2d 325 (1964); *N. Y. Times*, March 20, 1962, Sept. 20, 1962, and March 23, 1965.

96. *N. Y. Times*, Sept. 26, 1964.

97. *N. Y. Times*, June 4, 1964.

98. *N. Y. Times*, Jan. 4, 1964.

99. *N. Y. Times*, Nov. 1, 1964; see letter in *N. Y. Times*, Nov. 17, 1964, and full-page advertisement, Oct. 27, 1964; *N. Y. Times*, Dec. 13, 1964. In the 1964 election, the Socialist Workers Party candidates received 28,510 votes; see also *N. Y. Times*, Oct. 30, 1962.

100. *N. Y. Times*, May 1, 1963.

101. Op. cit. supra, note 1, pp. 14–15.

102. Ibid., pp. 10–11.

103. Ibid., pp. 8–9.

104. Ibid., pp 22–23.

105. "The Enemy Within Our Gates," *U.S. News & World Report*, May 4, 1964, p. 108; "Treason Unpunished," ibid., Nov. 29, 1965, p. 116.

106. See Alan F. Westin, "The John Birch Society," in *The Radical Right*, Daniel Bell, ed. (1964), pp. 239 ff.

107. Op. cit. supra, note 1.

108. Attorney General, *Annual Report* 1963, pp. 381–82; *World Almanac* (1964), p. 312.

109. *United States* v. *E. C. Knight Co.*, 156 U.S. 1 (1895).

110. Op. cit. supra, note 1, pp. 12–13.

111. Ibid.

112. *N. Y. Times*, Nov. 25, 1964.

113. See Harry and Bonaro Overstreet, *The Strange Tactics of Extremism* (1964); Arnold Forster and Benjamin R. Epstein, *Danger on the Right* (1964); *The Radical Right*, Daniel Bell, ed.

114. 370 U.S. 660 (1962). Justice Frankfurter did not participate. Justices Clark and White dissented.

115. *Lanzetta* v. *New Jersey*, 306 U.S. 451 (1939). Justice Frankfurter did not participate. See F. W. Lacey, "Vagrancy and Other Crimes of Personal Condition," 66 *Harvard Law Review* (1953), p. 1203. See also *Edelman* v. *California* 344 U.S. 357 (1953), dissenting opinion of Justice Black, in which Justice Douglas concurred.

116. *State* v. *Gaynor*, 119 N. J. L. 582, 197 A. 360.

117. The Supreme Court gave additional grounds for holding the New Jersey act unconstitutional, but they are not relevant to our discussion.

118. *United States* v. *Buffalino*, 285 F. 2d 408 (1960).

119. *Barenblatt* v. *United States*, 360 U. S. 109 (1959), dissenting opinion.

120. *Aptheker* v. *Rusk*, 12 L. ed. 992 (1964). Justices Clark, Harlan, and White dissented.

121. Ibid., footnote 13 in Justice Goldberg's opinion for the Court, quoting from the government's brief in case cited supra, note 73.

CHAPTER V: CENSORSHIP OF LITERATURE

1. *West Virginia Board of Education* v. *Barnette*, 319 U.S. 624 (1943), dissenting opinion.

2. Engels' letters to Schmidt, Starkenburg, Bloch, and Mehring, 1890–94, in

Sidney Hook, *Towards the Understanding of Karl Marx* (1933), Appendix.

3. *New State Ice Co.* v. *Liebmann*, 285 U.S. 262 (1932), dissenting opinion.
4. *Brown* v. *Board of Education of Topeka*, 347 U.S. 483 (1954).
5. See references to some of the literature in Davis, Foster, Jeffery, and Davis, *Society and the Law* (1962), p. 195, note 6.
6. M. R. Konvitz, "Censorship," *Encyclopedia Britannica* (1962), Vol. 5, pp. 117 ff.
7. See H. M. Hyde, *A History of Pornography* (1964), Ch. 2.
8. Harold D. Lasswell, "Censorship," *Encyclopedia of the Social Sciences* (1935), vol. 3, p. 293.
9. *World Almanac* (1966), p. 142.
10. "Motion Pictures," *Encyclopedia Britannica* (1962), Vol. 15, p. 868.
11. Op. cit. supra, note 9, p. 512.
12. Thomas Buckley, *N. Y. Times*, Oct. 10, 1964.
13. Emma Harrison, *N. Y. Times Magazine*, Nov. 1, 1959.
14. Op. cit. supra, note 9, p. 512.
15. Lewis Nichols, in *N. Y. Times Book Review*, Jan. 10, 1965.
16. *Reader's Digest and Almanac* (1966), p. 352.
17. R. Buckminster Fuller, *Education Automation* (1962), p. 26.
18. Op. cit. supra, note 9, p. 159.
19. U.S. Dept. of Commerce, *Advance Report 1963 Census of Transportation* (Sept. 1964).
20. *Commonwealth* v. *Friede*, 271 Mass. 318, 171 N.E. 472 (1930).
21. *Commonwealth* v. *Isenstadt*, 318 Mass. 543, 62 N.E. 2d 840 (1945).
22. *People* v. *Doubleday & Co.*, 297 N.Y. 687, 77 N.E. 2d (1947); affd. by 4-4 vote, 335 U.S. 848 (1949).
23. *Attorney General* v. *"God's Little Acre,"* 326 Mass. 281, 93 N.E. 2d 819 (1950); information on police raids in cities from American Book Publishers Council.
24. In 1949 Judge Curtis Bok acquitted the defendants in *Commonwealth* v. *Gordon*, 66 D. & C. 101 (Pa., 1949), affd. *sub nom. Commonwealth* v. *Feigenbaum*, 166 Pa. Super. 120, 70 A. 2d 389 (1950).
25. See especially case cited supra, note 22.
26. *Chaplinsky* v. *New Hampshire*, 315 U.S. 568 (1942).
27. *Roth* v. *United States* and *Alberts* v. *California*, 354 U.S. 476 (1957). Justice Harlan concurred in the state case but dissented in the federal case.
28. *Butler* v. *Michigan*, 352 U.S. 380 (1957).
29. It should be noted, however, that the statutes and cases cited had the following dates: Connecticut, 1808, 1821, 1824; Massachusetts, 1712, 1821, 1835, 1836; New Hampshire, 1822, 1843; New Jersey, 1800; Pennsylvania, 1815. These could hardly be thought to have been contemporary with the adoption of the Bill of Rights.
30. *Regina* v. *Hicklin* [1868] LR 3 QB 360. For discussion of this case, see M. R. Konvitz, *Fundamental Liberties of a Free People* (1957), pp. 163 ff.
31. *United States* v. *Kennerley*, 209 Fed. 119 (1913).
32. *United States* v. *Dennett*, 39 F. 2d 564 (1930). See Mary Ware Dennett, *Who's Obscene?* (1930).
33. 18 U.S.C. 1461.
34. 19 U.S.C. 1305.
35. *United States* v. *One Book Called "Ulysses,"* 5 F. Supp. 182 (1933); affd. 72 F. 2d 705 (1934).

36. *Hannegan* v. *"Esquire,"* 327 U.S. 146 (1946). At the Post Office hearing, the publisher had H. L. Mencken, Channing Pollock, Raymond Gram Swing, professors, and many others testify as experts.

37. Zola's *Nana* had sold 3 million copies in soft-bound editions by 1965. *N. Y. Times,* Jan. 10, 1965.

38. The Erskine book sold 8½ million paperback copies by 1965. *N. Y. Times,* Jan. 10, 1965.

39. Case cited supra, note 24.

40. *Commonwealth* v. *Holmes,* 17 Mass. 336 (1821). The earlier case of *Commonwealth* v. *Sharpless,* 2 S. & R. 91 (Pa., 1815), involved a painting. The latter case was cited in the Roth opinion at note 13; but Justice Douglas cited the former case.

41. Hyde, *A History of Pornography,* pp. 164–65.

42. *N. Y. Times Co.* v. *Sullivan,* 376 U.S. 254 (1964); *Garrison* v. *Louisiana,* 85 S. Ct. 209 (1964). See also *Henry* v. *Collins,* 85 S. Ct. 992 (1965); *Rosenblatt* v. *Baer,* 85 S. Ct. 1023 (1965).

43. *United States* v. *Schwimmer,* 279 U.S. 644 (1929).

44. *American Communications Association* v. *Douds,* 339 U.S. 382 (1950).

45. This part of the opinion relied on Lockhart and McClure, "Literature, the Law of Obscenity, and the Constitution," 38 *Minnesota Law Review* (1945), p. 295. See other contributions by these authors: "Censorship of Obscenity: the Developing Constitutional Standards," 45 *Minnesota Law Review* (1960), p. 5; and "Obscenity Censorship: the Core Constitutional Issue—What Is Obscene?" 7 *Utah Law Review* (1961), p. 289.

46. "Obscenity and Censorship," A. C. L. U. pamphlet (1963).

47. For statements that obscene publications cause delinquent and criminal acts, see Hyde, *A History of Pornography,* pp. 21 ff.; cf. Norman St. John-Stevas, *Obscenity and the Law* (1956), pp. 195 ff.; James J. Kilpatrick, *The Smut Peddlers* (1960), pp. 234 ff.; Terrence J. Murphy, *Censorship, Government and Obscenity* (1963), pp. 131 ff.; *Does Pornography Matter?* C. H. Rolph, ed. (1961), Ch. 3; American Book Publishers Council, *Censorship Bulletin,* Vol. 3, No. 1 (Aug. 1958); *Juvenile Delinquency,* Interim Report, Committee on Judiciary, 83d Cong., 2d sess., Senate Report No. 1064 (1954), and 84th Cong., 1st sess. (1955); *Obscene and Pornographic Literature and Juvenile Delinquency,* Interim Report, Subcommittee to Investigate Juvenile Delinquency, Sen., 84th Cong., 2d sess. (1956); Eberhard and Phyllis Kronhausen, *Pornography and the Law* (rev. ed. 1964), pp. 354 ff.; Lockhart and McClure, "Obscenity in the Courts," 20 *Law and Contemporary Problems* (1955), p. 587, and other articles by these authors cited supra, note 45. Statement by N. Y. Academy of Medicine, 39 *Bulletin of New York Academy of Medicine* (1963), p. 545. See J. D. Halloran, *The Effects of Mass Communication* (1964). See also the Kinsey report on sex offenders, according to which there was little or no sexual arousal from pornography—infra note 96; Gebhard, *Sex Offenders* (1965); and report in *N. Y. Times,* July 18, 1965.

48. *Regina* v. *Warburg* [1954] 2 All Eng. 683 (CC); W.L.R. 1138. The charge to the jury is reprinted in entirety at the end of the book by Kauffmann, published 1954 in England, and also in a pamphlet, published by Secker & Warburg. See also St. John-Stevas, *Obscenity and the Law,* pp. 112 ff. The Kauffmann book had been published in the United States in 1952, under the title *The Tightrope,* without any trouble.

49. Lord Campbell's Act, 20 & 21 Vict., c. 83; amended, 33 & 34 Vict., c. 79.

50. *Regina* v. *Hicklin,* cited supra, note 30.
51. Obscene Publications Act, 1959, 7 & 8 Eliz. 2, c. 66. Roy Jenkins, "Obscenity, Censorship, and the Law: the Story of a Bill," *Encounter,* Oct. 1959, p. 62.
52. For this phrase, see John A. T. Robinson, Bishop of Woolwich, *Christian Morals Today* (S. C. M. Press Broadsheet, 1964), p. 8.
53. Leo Hamalian, "The Lady Chatterley Spectacle," *Columbia University Forum,* winter 1960, p. 8.
54. James C. N. Paul and Murray L. Schwartz, *Federal Censorship* (1961), p. 46.
55. Ibid., pp. 55–62.
56. Ibid., p. 60.
57. Op. cit. supra, note 53, p. 12.
58. *Kingsley International Pictures Corp.* v. *Regents of University of State of New York,* 360 U.S. 684 (1959). Concurring opinions were written by Justices Black, Frankfurter, Douglas, Clark, and Harlan.
59. Ibid.
60. Arthur Knight, "Lady Chatterley's Lawyer," *Saturday Review,* July 25, 1959, p. 25.
61. Quoted by Justice Harlan in case cited supra, note 59.
62. *N. Y. Times,* March 19, 1959.
63. Italics in the original.
64. *N. Y. Times,* May 7, 1959, and June 12, 1959.
65. See book review in 71 *Yale Law Journal* (1962), pp. 1351, 1353.
66. *Grove Press* v. *Christenberry,* 175 F. Supp. 488 (1959).
67. *N. Y. Times,* July 28, 1959.
68. *N. Y. Times,* Dec. 3, 1959.
69. Op. cit. supra, note 54, pp. 101–102.
70. *Grove Press* v. *Christenberry,* 276 F. 2d 433 (1960).
71. *N. Y. Times,* March 28, 1960.
72. *N. Y. Times,* June 3, 1960.
73. Op. cit. supra, note 53, p. 13.
74. *The Trial of Lady Chatterley,* C. H. Rolph, ed. (1961), p. 142.
75. Ibid., pp. 194 ff.
76. Ibid., p. 233.
77. Ibid., p. 7.
78. Ibid., p. 249.
79. *N. Y. Times,* Nov. 12, 1960.
80. *Times Literary Supplement,* Nov. 4, 1960.
81. St. John-Stevas, *Obscenity and the Law,* p. 105.
82. Mervyn Levy, *Paintings of D. H. Lawrence* (1964).
83. *Sunshine Book Co.* v. *Summerfield,* 249 F. 2d 114 (1957); reversed, 355 U.S. 372 (1958).
84. A case in which the publishers won a measure of relief is *Summerfield* v. *Sunshine Book Co.,* 221 F. 2d 42 (1954); certiorari denied, 349 U.S. 921 (1955).
85. *Sunshine Book Co.* v. *Summerfield,* 128 F. Supp. 564 (1955). Steven Marcus, "Pisanus Fraxi, Pornographer Royal," *Partisan Review,* winter 1965, p. 105.
86. *One, Inc.* v. *Olesen,* 241 F. 2d 772 (1957), reversed 355 U.S. 371 (1958).
87. Irving Bieber, "Speaking Frankly on a Once Taboo Subject," *N. Y. Times Magazine,* Aug. 23, 1964.

88. Report of the Committee on Homosexual Offences and Prostitution, Sept. 1957, p. 115. See H. Mannheim, "Criminal Law and Penology," in *Law and Opinion in England in the 20th Century*, Morris Ginsberg, ed. (1959), pp. 271 ff.
89. *N. Y. Times*, Aug. 30, 1964.
90. *Perkins* v. *North Carolina*, 234 F. Supp. 333 (1964).
91. See D. C. M. Yardley *The Future of the Law* (1964).
92. Morris Ernst and A. W. Schwartz, *Censorship* (1964), pp. 72–79.
93. In the Matters Concerning Manual Enterprises, Post Office Department Docket No. 1/246, April 28, 1960. Italics supplied.
94. *Manual Enterprises* v. *Day*, 370 U.S. 478 (1962). Justices Frankfurter and White did not participate. The Post Office ruling had been sustained by the lower federal courts—289 F. 2d 455.
95. See Hugh M. Hefner, editorial, "Playboy Philosophy," in *Playboy*, Feb. 1965.
96. See Kinsey, *Sexual Behavior in the Human Male* (1948), Ch. 21; *Sexual Behavior in the Human Female* (1953), Ch. 11.
97. Sec. 484-h, N. Y. Penal Law.
98. Sec. 1141, N. Y. Penal Law.
99. *People* v. *Bookcase, Inc.*, 252 N. Y. S. 2d 433 (1964).
100. *Smith* v. *California*, 361 U.S. 147 (1959).
101. The problem of classification is dealt with in "For Adults Only: the Constitutionality of Governmental Film Censorship by Age Classification," 69 *Yale Law Journal*, p. 141. Lockhart and McClure, "Censorship of Obscenity," 45 *Minnesota Law Review*, pp. 5, 68–88. Gerber, "A Suggested Solution to the Riddle of Obscenity," 112 *University of Pennsylvania Law Review*, pp. 834, 847–52; American Law Institute, *Model Penal Code*, Tentative Draft No. 6, 1957, § 207.10, subd. 2; St. John-Stevas, *Obscenity and the Law*, pp. 212–56. These citations appear in *People* v. *Bookcase*.
102. *Bantam Books* v. *Sullivan*, 372 U.S. 58 (1963). Justice Harlan dissented.
103. Cf. *Kingsley Books* v. *Brown*, 354 U.S. 436 (1957).
104. *Besig* v. *United States*, 208 F. 2d 142 (1953).
105. *N. Y. Times*, April 25, 1961.
106. *N. Y. Times*, June 10 and 15, 1961.
107. *N. Y. Times*, Aug. 11, 1961.
108. *N. Y. Times Book Review*, Jan. 21, 1962.
109. John Ciardi, *Saturday Review*, June 30, 1962.
110. *Zeitlin* v. *Arnebergh*, 31 Cal. Rptr. 800 (1963), and cases cited in note 1 of opinion; *Attorney General* v. *Book Named "Tropic of Cancer,"* 184 N.E. 2d 328 (Mass., 1962); *McCauley* v. *"Tropic of Cancer,"* 121 N.W. 2d 545 (Wis., 1963); *People* v. *Fritch*, 236 N. Y. S. 2d 706 (1963).
111. *N. Y. Times*, Oct. 18, 20, 24, and 28, 1961.
112. *People* v. *Pershina*, No. 16644, Mun. Ct., Cent. Jud. Dist., Marin County, Calif. See D. Bes, "Miller's 'Tropic' On Trial," *Evergreen Review*, No. 23, March–April 1962.
113. See California case cited supra, note 112.
114. Case cited supra, note 112.
115. Ibid.
116. *Grove Press* v. *Gerstein*, 156 So 2d. 537; reversed 372 U.S. 577, 12 L. ed. 2d 1035 (1964).
117. *Jacobellis* v. *Ohio*, 12 L. ed. 2d 793 (1964).

118. A.C.L.U. brief in Jacobellis case before U.S. Supreme Court, p. 51.
119. *Mutual Film Corp.* v. *Ohio Industrial Commission*, 236 U.S. 230 (1915).
120. *Burstyn, Inc.* v. *Wilson*, 343 U.S. 495 (1952).
121. *Superior Films* v. *Department of Education*, 346 U.S. 960 (1953).
122. Case cited supra, note 58.
123. Case cited supra, note 112.
124. *U.S. News & World Report*, Jan. 18, 1965, p. 56.
125. S. J. Res. 116, 86th Cong., 1st sess., introduced July 2, 1959.
126. S. J. Res. 133, 86th Cong., 1st sess., introduced Aug. 17, 1959, by Senator Kefauver for himself and Senators Eastland and Talmadge.
127. *N. Y. Times*, Oct. 25, 1959.
128. *N. Y. Times*, April 2, 1961.
129. Case cited supra, note 24.
130. California case cited supra, note 110. Justice Tobriner's opinion, note 1, referring to *N. Y. Times*, Western ed., April 12, 1963.
131. *N. Y. Times Book Review*, May 5, 1963.
132. April 12, 1963.
133. *The Trial of Lady Chatterley*, C. H. Rolph, ed., p. 20.
134. Cf. Maurice Dolbier's review of *Tropic of Cancer* in *N. Y. Herald Tribune*, June 24, 1961.
135. *Saturday Review*, June 30, 1962, p. 13.
136. Hyde, *A History of Pornography*, pp. 97–98. St. John-Stevas, *Obscenity and the Law*, p. 39.
137. Ibid., p. 99; ibid. The case was *Commonwealth* v. *Holmes*, 17 Mass. 336 (1821). The earlier case of *Commonwealth* v. *Sharpless*, 2 S. & R. 91 (Pa., 1815), was a prosecution for exhibiting an obscene painting. Ernst and Schwartz, *Censorship*, pp. 15–17. But see Hollander, op. cit. infra, note 139, p. 76, footnote 5, in which he refers to the issuance of a warrant for Cleland to appear at the King's Bench, but with no subsequent punitive action.
138. Hyde, *A History of Pornography*, p. 100; M. L. Paul and J. C. N. Schwartz, *Federal Censorship; Obscenity in the Mail* (1961), p. 120.
139. Cf. John Hollander, "The Old Last Act," *Encounter*, Oct. 1963, p. 74.
140. Sec. 22-a of the Code of Criminal Procedure.
141. *Larkin* v. *G. P. Putnam's Sons*, 242 N.Y.S. 2d 746 (Sup. Ct., Special and Term Trial, Aug. 23, 1946, before Arthur G. Klein, Jr.).
142. *N. Y. Times*, Feb. 28, 1964.
143. *Larkin* v. *G. P. Putnam's Sons*, 252 N.Y.S. 2d 71 (1964).
   The Supreme Judicial Court of Massachusetts has held the book to be obscene. The decision was 4 to 3. *Attorney General* v. *A Book Named "John Cleland's Memoirs of a Woman of Pleasure,"* 206 N.E. 2d 403 (1965). This decision was pending on appeal before the U.S. Supreme Court at the end of 1965. The Supreme Court had before it at that time, in addition to the *Fanny Hill* case from Massachusetts, also an appeal of the conviction and sentence of Edward Mishkin in New York for selling sadistic and masochistic literature; and the conviction and sentence of Ralph Ginzburg for mailing issues of his quarterly magazine *Eros*, a newsletter, and a book with the title, *The Housewife's Handbook on Selective Promiscuity*. The oral arguments in these cases were held in December 1965. The Ginzburg case aroused most interest. He was convicted in a federal district court in Philadelphia in 1963 and received a

five-year sentence and a fine of $28,000. The decision was affirmed by the U.S. court of appeals.

In all, twenty-three books were involved in these cases when they reached the Supreme Court. In the course of the oral argument, Chief Justice Warren asked, referring to these books: "Do we have to read all of them to determine if they have social importance? I'm sure this Court does not want to be the final censor to read all the prurient material in the country to determine if it has social value. If the final burden depends on this Court, it looks to me as though we're in trouble." *New York Times,* Dec. 8, 1965. The problem of expedience—whether the Court could possibly carry so heavy a burden—bites into the problem of principle, protection of literature by the First Amendment guarantee. But this is no different from the situation generated by such decisions of the Court as *Mapp* v. *Ohio,* 367 U.S. 643 (1961), and *Gideon* v. *Wainwright,* 372 U.S. 335 (1963), and the Court's decisions in the legislative reapportionment cases, *Baker* v. *Carr,* 369 U.S. 186 (1962), and *Reynolds* v. *Sims,* 377 U.S. 533 (1964). If constitutional issues are involved—and the Court has held that they are involved in censorship cases, regardless whether obscenity is or is not protected by the First Amendment—then the Court must sit as the court of last resort in such cases.

144. *Tralins* v. *Gerstein,* 12 L. ed. 2d 1033 (1964). The division in the Supreme Court was the same as in *Grove Press* v. *Gerstein,* 12 L. ed. 2d 1035 (1964).

145. Hyde, *A History of Pornography,* Appendix, p. 232. This Appendix gives a detailed summary of the case.

146. John Bowen, "Gamesmanship wih Fanny Hill," *N. Y. Times Book Review,* March 15, 1964, p. 4.

147. "The Assumers," *Times Literary Supplement,* Dec. 12, 1963.

148. Op. cit. supra, note 53, pp. 9, 13.
Forum (winter 1960), pp. 9, 13.

149. There was another case against *Fanny Hill* in New York. We dealt with it earlier in this chapter in our discussion of laws that prohibit sales of obscene books to minors. The New York law is cited supra, note 97, and the case in note 99.

150. Terry Southern and Mason Hoffenberg, *Candy,* published by G. P. Putnam's Sons in May 1964. By the end of 1964 it had sold 130,000 copies at $5.00, and early in 1965 Putnam's released over a million copies of the paperback edition at 95 cents. Lancer Books also released a half-million paperback copies at 75 cents.

151. *People* v. *Birch,* 243 N.Y.S. 2d 525 (1963), opinion by Judge J. Irwin Shapiro.

152. *N. Y. Times,* Sept. 10, 1963.

153. *Times Literary Supplement,* Dec. 12, 1963.

154. *Cox* v. *Louisiana* (No. 49), 85 S. Ct. (1965).

155. *Pennekamp* v. *Florida,* 328 U.S. 331 (1946).

156. *Smith* v. *California,* 361 U.S. 147 (1959), concurring opinion.

157. Ibid.

158. *Bantam Books* v. *Sullivan,* 372 U.S. 58 (1963).

159. *Schulz* v. *Pennsylvania Railroad Co.,* 350 U.S. 523 (1956), opinion by Justice Black for the Court.

160. See Justice Black's concurring opinion in *Kingsley International Pictures*

Corp. v. *Regents of University of State of New York,* 360 U.S. 684 (1959). Justice Douglas has not, I think, gone so far as not to read the books or see the movies, but his position is close to that of Justice Black. See his concurring opinion in the same case.

161. See Chief Justice Warren's statement on this in his dissenting opinion in *Jacobellis* v. *Ohio,* 12 L. ed. 2d 793 (1964).

162. *Burnet* v. *Coronado Oil & Gas Co.,* 285 U.S. 393 (1932), dissenting opinion.

163. See supra, note 159.

164. See Chief Justice Warren's dissenting opinion, joined by Justice Clark, in Jacobellis case, cited supra, note 161.

165. Ibid.

166. *West Virginia State Board of Education* v. *Barnette,* 319 U.S. 624 (1943).

167. *Minersville School District* v. *Gobitis,* 310 U.S. 586 (1940).

168. Case cited supra, note 160.

169. *N. Y. Times Co.* v. *Sullivan,* 376 U.S. 254 (1964).

170. *Garrison* v. *Louisiana,* 85 S. Ct. 209 (1964). Cf. *Henry* v. *Collins,* 85 S. Ct. 992 (1965).

171. *Jacobellis* v. *Ohio,* supra, note 161.

172. Justice Brennan's concurring opinion in *Manual Enterprises* v. *Day,* 370 U.S. 478 (1962), relates the historical development of the procedure. See also Paul and Schwartz, *Federal Censorship: Obscenity in the Mail.*

173. U.S. Post Office Department, *Annual Report 1959,* p. 84.

174. U.S. Post Office Department, *Annual Report 1960,* p. 103.

175. U.S. Post Office Department, *Annual Report 1961,* p. 96.

176. *Oakley* v. *United States,* 368 U.S. 888 and 936 (1961).

177. U.S. Post Office Department, *Annual Report 1962,* p. 109.

178. U.S. Post Office Department, *Annual Report 1963,* pp. 104–105; statement of Postmaster General Gronouski, Oct. 23, 1964.

179. For a description of the role of the Judicial Officer and of postal administrative proceedings, see Post Office Department, *Annual Report 1962,* pp. 127–28.

180. U.S. Post Office Department, *Annual Report 1963,* pp. 103–106. The Postmaster General was John A. Gronouski, who succeeded J. Edward Day in 1963; but the new policy was initiated by Day.

181. Ibid., p. 105.

182. Postmaster General Arthur E. Summerfield, Departmental Decision in the Matter of Grove Press and in the Matter of Reader's Subscription, Post Office Department, June 11, 1959.

CHAPTER VI: RACIAL EQUALITY AND DEMOCRATIC GOVERNMENT

1. *Brown* v. *Board of Education,* 347 U.S. 483 (1954); 349 U.S. 294 (1955).

2. *Plessy* v. *Ferguson,* 163 U.S. 537 (1896).

3. M. R. Konvitz, *The Constitution and Civil Rights* (1947); M. R. Konvitz and T. Leskes, *A Century of Civil Rights* (1961); article, "Civil Rights," by M. R. Konvitz, in *International Encyclopedia of Social Sciences.*

4. *Sipuel* v. *University of Oklahoma,* 332 U.S. 631 (1948); *sub. nom. Fisher* v. *University of Oklahoma,* 333 U.S. 147 (1948). Italics supplied.

5. *Sweatt* v. *Painter,* 339 U.S. 629 (1950).

6. This was the second law school for Negroes opened by Texas since 1947. The first school had no independent faculty or library; the teaching was done by four professors from the University of Texas Law School, who were to divide their time between the two schools. The state, realizing that this school could never meet the test of equality, abandoned it for one at the Negro state university, described in the text.
7. Brief for petitioner, *Sweatt* v. *Painter*, U.S. Supreme Court, 52; 26–27, footnotes 29–33.
8. Brief of *amicus curiae* in support of petitioner, *Sweatt* v. *Painter*, U.S. Supreme Court, 22 ff.
9. *McLaurin* v. *Oklahoma State Regents*, 339 U.S. 637 (1950).
10. Memorandum for the United States, as *amici curiae*, in *McLaurin* v. *Oklahoma State Regents*, and *Sweatt* v. *Painter*, filed by Philip B. Perlman, Solicitor General, and Philip Elman, Special Assistant to the Attorney General, in U.S. Supreme Court, 9 ff.
11. *Henderson* v. *United States*, 339 U.S. 816 (1950). Justice Douglas concurred; Justice Clark did not participate.
12. Brief for the United States, *Henderson* v. *United States*, U.S. Supreme Court, 12, 24–25, 29, 33, 34.
13. Ibid., p. 45.
14. Ibid., pp. 65–66.
15. There were, of course, some earlier decisions that might be cited— especially *Missouri ex rel. Gaines* v. *Canada*, 305 U.S. 337 (1938) and *Mitchell* v. *United States*, 313 U.S. 80 (1941); but the cases discussed in the text played a specially important role. See C. H. Pritchett, *Civil Liberties and the Vinson Court* (1954), pp. 129–38.
16. Nine of the states had been Confederate states; the other two states for whom the brief was filed were Kentucky and Oklahoma.
17. See Konvitz and Leskes, op. cit. supra, note 3, pp. 129–30.
18. Ibid., p. 156.
19. See books cited supra, note 3.
20. The list of states is in brief for appellees, *Heart of Atlanta Motel* v. *United States*, filed by U. S. Solicitor General, Appendix C, p. 71. See also map in *U. S. News & World Report*, June 1, 1964, p. 47. In 1965 Utah enacted a civil rights statute—*N. Y. Times*, March 14, 1965; and also Nevada—ibid., April 8, 1965.
21. The eight were: Oklahoma, Nevada, Utah, Arizona, Kentucky, West Virginia, Missouri, and Hawaii.
22. The census of 1960 was used in making the calculations in this section.
23. *Freedom Now* (1964), Alan Westin, ed., Ch. 11 by A. Philip Randolph.
24. Konvitz and Leskes, op. cit. supra, note 3, p. 197.
25. *U. S. News & World Report*, June 1, 1964, p. 47. Konvitz and Leskes, op. cit. supra, note 3, pp. 201–203.
26. Konvitz and Leskes, op. cit. supra, note 3, pp. 59–68, 177–80, 222–24. Herbert Hill, "Twenty Years of State Fair Employment Practice Commissions," 14 *Buffalo Law Review* (1964), p. 22. See Elmer A. Carter, "Policies and Practices of Discrimination Commissions," 304 *The Annals*, March 1956, p. 62.
27. Konvitz and Leskes, op. cit. supra, note 3, pp. 182–83.
28. Ibid., pp. 192–93.
29. Konvitz, *The Constitution and Civil Rights*, p. 64.

30. *To Secure These Rights: Report of the President's Committee on Civil Rights* (1947), p. 114.
31. N.A.A.C.P., *Annual Report,* 1943, p. 3.
32. *To Secure These Rights,* p. 41.
33. Ibid., pp. 41–42. In 1966 the picture still left much to be desired. While Negroes made up 13.4 per cent of all enlisted men in the Army, 10 per cent in the Air Force, and 5.8 per cent in the Navy, only 3.5 per cent were officers in the Army, 1.5 per cent in the Air Force, and 0.3 per cent in the Navy. In the Navy no Negro was a captain and only five held the rank of commander. See report by Eric Pace, *New York Times,* Jan. 3, 1966.
34. Ibid., p. 46.
35. See Leo Bogart, "The Army and Its Negro Soldiers," *The Reporter,* Dec. 30, 1954, p. 8.
36. D. D. Nelson, *Integration of the Negro into U. S. Navy* (1951), pp. 12–13.
37. Spore and Cocklin, "Our Negro Soldiers," *The Reporter,* Jan. 22, 1952, pp. 6–7; Lee Nichols, *Breakthrough on the Color Front* (1954).
38. 13 Fed. Reg. 431 B (1948).
39. See op. cit. supra, note 35, which summarizes the research study conducted for the Army by the Operations Research Office of Johns Hopkins University.
40. Final Report, Military Personnel Stationed and Membership Participation in the National Guard, President's Committee on Equal Opportunity in the Armed Forces, Nov. 1964, p. 20.
41. *N. Y. Times,* Dec. 30, 1964; see also March 9, 1965; March 31, 1965; April 1, 1965
42. Nichols, op. cit. supra, note 37, pp. 223–24.
43. Ibid., p. 97.
44. Quoted in James C. Evans and David A. Leve, Jr., "Integration in the Armed Services," 304 *The Annals,* March 1956, p. 78.
45. When Gambia gained its independence in February 1965, it became the thirty-sixth African colony to become an independent state. Ghana was the first in March 1957.
46. See, for these acts, Konvitz and Leskes, op. cit. supra, note 3, pp. 63, 72–78, 79, 258; 36, 63, 83–89, 123.
47. *N. Y. Times,* Feb. 24 and 26, 1965. The statistics of civil rights martyrs are according to records of the Southern Regional Council, *Wall Street Journal,* May 4, 1965. *Southern Justice: an Indictment,* Special Report of Southern Regional Council, Oct. 18, 1965. By the end of 1965, in only three cases was any punishment imposed: in 1964 a jury in Jacksonville, Fla., sentenced a white man to imprisonment for shooting down a Negro woman; on Dec. 2, 1965, a jury in Anniston, Ala., convicted Hubert D. Strange of second-degree murder in the killing of Willie Brewster; and on Dec. 3, 1965, a jury in a federal district court in Montgomery, Ala., convicted Collie Leroy Wilkins and two others on charges of conspiracy to deprive Mrs. Viola Gregg Liuzzo of her civil rights. In all of the cases the defendants were sentenced to ten years' imprisonment.
   See generally *Southern Justice,* Leon Friedman, ed. (1965); *Law Enforcement, a Report on Equal Protection in the South,* U.S. Commission on Civil Rights (1965); *Hearings,* Vol. II, *Administration of Justice,* held in Jackson, Miss., before U.S. Commission on Civil Rights (1965).
48. Romans 3:8.

CHAPTER VII: THE FIRST AMENDMENT AND
CIVIL RIGHTS DEMONSTRATIONS

1. *Edwards* v. *South Carolina*, 372 U.S. 229 (1963). Justice Clark dissented. Cf. *Cox* v. *Louisiana*, 85 S. Ct. 453. (1965) (Cases Nos. 24 and 49).
2. *Fields* v. *South Carolina*, 375 U.S. 44 (1963), without opinion.
3. *Henry* v. *Rock Hill*, 12 L. ed. 2d 79 (1964). See also *Shuttlesworth* v. *Birmingham*, 86 S. Ct. 211 (1965).
4. Anthony Lewis, *Portrait of a Decade* (1964), p. 94.
5. *Thompson* v. *Louisville*, 362 U.S. 199 (1960).
6. Letter from Louis Lusky to author.
7. After the case was decided, Lusky left Louisville and became a professor at Columbia Law School in New York City. He is a member of the National Committee of the American Civil Liberties Union.

   Actually, Lusky appeared for Thompson in another case ten days before the café incident, when Thompson was arrested while sitting in a bus station; he was charged with vagrancy and loitering. He was fined $20 for loitering and sentenced to thirty days in jail for vagrancy. Lusky appealed the case and obtained a jury trial in another court, which acquitted Thompson. This bus station case was followed by the café case. See op. cit. supra, note 6; also brief of Louis Lusky and Marvin H. Morse for Thompson on petition for writ of certiorari, and Appendix C. Record.
8. *Yick Wo* v. *Hopkins*, 118 U.S. 356 (1886).
9. Forrest W. Lacey, "Vagrancy and Other Crimes of Personal Condition," 66 *Harvard Law Review* (1953), pp. 1203, 1204.
10. *Edelman* v. *California*, 344 U.S. 357 (1953). Justice Douglas concurred in the dissenting opinion of Justice Black. Cf. *Lanzetta* v. *New Jersey*, 306 U.S. 451 (1939). See also David Fellman, *The Constitutional Right of Association* (1963), pp. 77 ff.
11. "The Trial of Iosif Brodsky," *New Leader*, Aug. 31, 1964; George Feifer, "Brodsky: Reactions in Moscow," ibid., Sept. 14, 1964; editorial, ibid., Oct. 12, 1964; S. L. Sheiderman, "Trial in Leningrad," *Congress Bi-Weekly*, Oct. 12, 1964. According to a report in *N. Y. Times*, Nov. 5, 1964, Brodsky was released after serving his sentence from March 1964. His trial apparently had become a *cause célèbre* when a transcript was circulated among Soviet artists and writers, for the trial transcript suggested prejudice against poets and other writers. A copy of the transcript was smuggled out of the Soviet Union and was reprinted in the *New Leader*, as well as in several British periodicals, and it may be that this interest in other countries contributed to his release. But see letter in *New Leader*, Dec. 21, 1964, and news report, *N. Y. Times*, Jan. 10, 1965, that he was not released.
12. *Brown* v. *Board of Education of Topeka*, 349 U.S. 294 (1954).
13. *Browder* v. *Gayle*, 142 F. Supp. 707 (1956); affd. 352 U.S. 903 (1956). For the Montgomery story, see Lewis, op. cit. supra, note 4, Ch. 5.
14. James Peck, *Freedom Ride* (1962), p. 51.
15. N.A.A.C.P., *Report for 1960*, p. 5.
16. Op. cit. supra, note 14, pp. 67–68.
17. Op. cit. supra, note 4, pp. 85–86.
18. Ibid., p. 86.

19. Louis E. Lomax, *The Negro Revolt* (1962, 1963), p. 134.
20. Op. cit. supra, note 4, pp. 86–87.
21. Quoted in ibid., p. 114.
22. Ibid., p. 121.
23. According to the Department of Justice, from May 22, 1963, to Aug. 11, 1963, there were 841 demonstrations in 196 cities in 35 states and the District of Columbia. *N. Y. Times,* Aug. 11, 1963.
24. For discussion of civil rights apart from the free-speech aspects, see M. R. Konvitz, *The Constitution and Civil Rights* (1947); *The Alien and the Asiatic in American Law* (1946); *Civil Rights in Immigration* (1953). M. R. Konvitz and T. Leskes, *A Century of Civil Rights* (1961).
25. *Garner* v. *Louisiana,* 368 U.S. 157 (1961).
26. Quoted in op. cit. supra, note 4, pp. 98–99.
27. Ibid., p. 103.
28. Tuskegee Institute, Alabama, *Race Relations in the South—1963* (1964), p. 29.
29. Claude Sitton, *N. Y. Times,* Aug. 11, 1963.
30. Op. cit. supra, note 14, Ch. 8.
31. *Taylor* v. *Louisiana,* 370 U.S. 154 (1962).
32. *Wright* v. *Georgia,* 373 U.S. 284 (1963).
33. *Cooper* v. *Aaron,* 358 U.S. 1 (1958).
34. Additional reasons offered by the city were: to prevent depreciation of property and to prevent the amalgamation of the races.
35. *Watson* v. *Memphis,* 373 U.S. 526 (1963).
36. *Dawson* v. *Baltimore City,* 220 F. 2d 386; affd. 350 U.S. 877 (1955).
37. The second Brown decision: *Brown* v. *Board of Education,* 349 U.S. 294 (1955).
38. *Terminiello* v. *Chicago,* 337 U.S. 1 (1949).
39. The events are related in Lewis, *Portrait of a Decade,* Ch. 4.
40. Ibid., Ch. 11.
41. *Chaplinsky* v. *New Hampshire,* 315 U.S. 568 (1942).
42. *Cantwell* v. *Connecticut,* 310 U.S. 296 (1940).
43. *Schenck* v. *United States,* 249 U.S. 47 (1919).
44. *Frohwerk* v. *United States,* 249 U.S. 208 (1919).
45. *Abrams* v. *United States,* 250 U.S. 616 (1919).
    For a history of the Clear and Present Danger Doctrine, see M. R. Konvitz, *Fundamental Liberties of a Free People* (1957), Ch. 26.
46. *West Virginia State Board of Education* v. *Burnette,* 319 U.S. 624 (1943), dissenting opinion.
47. *Dennis* v. *United States,* 341 U.S. 494 (1951), concurring opinion.
48. *Garner* v. *Louisiana,* 368 U.S. 157 (1961), concurring opinion.
49. Case cited supra, note 47, concurring opinion. Cf. *Cox* v. *Louisiana,* 85 S. Ct. 453, 476 (1965), in which Justice Goldberg quoted the Holmes example of shouting fire in a theater and causing a panic.
50. *Feiner* v. *New York,* 340 U.S. 315 (1951).
51. Listed in *Guide to Subversive Organizations and Publications,* House Committee on Un-American Activities (1961 ed.), p. 229.
52. *N. Y. Times Co.* v. *Sullivan,* 11 L. ed. 2d 686 (1964).
53. *Herndon* v. *Lowry,* 301 U.S. 242 (1937). See Konvitz, *Fundamental Liberties of a Free People,* pp. 301 ff., esp. note 35, p. 399.
54. *Schenck* v. *United States,* 249 U.S. 47 (1919).
55. Claude Sitton in *N. Y. Times,* March 29, 1964.

56. Ibid.
57. David Caplovitz and C. Rogers, *Swastika 1960* (Anti-Defamation League, 1961).
58. *N. Y. Times*, Nov. 1, 1964. The number forty is a conservative estimate.
59. Joseph Lelyveld, *N. Y. Times*, Sept. 11, 1964.
60. *N. Y. Times*, Sept. 10, 1964.
61. *N. Y. Times*, Sept. 27, 1964.
62. *N. Y. Times*, Dec. 13, 1964.
63. Dallas E. Wood, *Palo Alto Times*, Dec. 14, 1964.
64. Sidney Hook, *The Paradoxes of Freedom* (1962), p. 47.
65. *Memorial and Remonstrance against Religious Assessments*, II *Writings of Madison*, p. 183, quoted in *Engel* v. *Vitale*, 370 U.S. 421 (1962).
66. *Hague* v. *C.I.O.*, 307 U.S. 496 (1939).
67. *Lovell* v. *Griffin*, 303 U.S. 444 (1938); *Niemotko* v. *Maryland*, 340 U.S. 268 (1951); *Kunz* v. *New York*, 340 U.S. 290 (1951); *Rockwell* v. *Morris*, 211 N.Y.S. 2d 25 (1961), affd. 219 N.Y.S. 2d 268 (1961), certiorari denied 368 U.S. 913 (1961); *Morrison* v. *Davis*, 252 F. 2d 102, certiorari denied 356 U.S. 968 (1958); *Edwards* v. *South Carolina*, 372 U. S. 229 (1963).
68. *N. Y. Times*, Dec. 12, 1964.
69. Martin Luther King, Jr., *Stride Toward Freedom* (Ballantine Books ed., 1960), pp. 82–83.
70. See M. R. Konvitz, in *Law and Philosophy, a Symposium*, edited by Sidney Hook (1964).
71. Josephus, *History of the Jewish War*, II, p. 10. *The Quiet Battle*, M. O. Sibley, ed. (1963), p. 111.
72. See Louis Fischer, *Gandhi* (1950), and *The Gandhi Reader*, H. A. Jack, ed. (1956).
73. Philip Taft, *Organized Labor in American History* (1964), p. 525.
74. Ibid. pp. 493–97.
75. Ibid., p. 498.
76. *N.L.R.B.* v. *Fansteel Metallurgical Corp.*, 306 U.S. 240 (1939).
77. See *N.L.R.B.* v. *Jones & Laughlin Steel Corp.*, 301 U.S. 1 (1937).
78. See Konvitz and Leskes, *A Century of Civil Rights; Heart of Atlanta Motel* v. *United States*, 85 L. ed. 2d 348 (1964), Justice Clark's opinion, note 8. See supra, Chapter VI, note 20.
79. In case cited supra, note 77.
80. Samuel Gompers spoke of the Clayton Act of 1914 as "Labor's Magna Carta." Taft, *Organized Labor in American History*, p. 243.
81. *Slaughter-House Cases*, 16 Wall. 36, 21 L. ed. 394 (1873); *Strauder* v. *West Virginia*, 100 U.S. 303 (1880). See M. R. Konvitz, "Use of the Intelligence in Advancement of Civil Rights," in *Aspects of Liberty*, Konvitz and Rossiter, eds. (1958), pp. 79 ff.
82. Paul A. Freund, *The Supreme Court of the United States* (1949), p. 33.
83. *McLaughlin* v. *Florida*, 85 S. Ct. 283 (1964); *Korematsu* v. *United States*, 323 U.S. 214 (1944).
84. *N. Y. Times*, Oct. 8, 1963.
85. *N. Y. Times*, July 30, 1963.
86. *N. Y. Times*, July 11, 1963.
87. *N. Y. Times*, Nov. 1, 1964.
88. Lewis, *Portrait of a Decade*, p. 258.
89. It is difficult to tell from the report on the invasion of the press room in

the building owned by Governor Rockefeller whether the room was for the Governor's private or public use.

90. M. I. Sibley and P. E. Jacob, *Conscription of Conscience* (1952), p. 400.

91. *Peterson* v. *Greenville*, 373 U.S. 244 (1963).

92. On the same day that the Court decided the Peterson case, it also decided *Lombard* v. *Louisiana*, 373 U.S. 267 (1963), in which it held that statements by public officials that segregated service would be continued and that sit-in demonstrations against segregation would not be tolerated had the same effect as the ordinance in the Peterson case. Justice Harlan dissented. Justice Douglas, in a concurring opinion, argued for a broader ground for reversal; viz., that a licensed business must serve the public without racial discrimination—licensing and supervising a business invests it with a public interest and makes it an instrumentality of the state.

On the same day the Court reversed, without opinions, similar convictions in *Gober* v. *Birmingham*, 373 U.S. 374 (1963), and *Avent* v. *North Carolina*, 373 U. S. 374 (1963).

93. Virginia Code of 1950, Sec. 18.1-173, as amended by Virginia Laws of 1960, Ch. 97; quoted in brief on petition for writ of certiorari in *Wood* v. *Virginia*, 374 U.S. 100 (1963).

94. *Bouie* v. *Columbia*, 84 S. Ct. 1963, 12 L. ed. 2d 894 (1964).

95. *Barr* v. *Columbia*, 84 S. Ct. 1734, 12 L. ed. 2d 766 (1964).

96. *Robinson* v. *Florida*, 84 S. Ct. 1693, 12 L. ed. 2d 771 (1964).

97. *Bell* v. *Maryland*, 84 S. Ct. 1814, 12 L. ed. 822 (1964).

98. See Konvitz, *The Constitution and Civil Rights*, and Konvitz and Leskes, *A Century of Civil Rights*, for a full discussion of these cases and the historical background of the Fourteenth Amendment.

99. The opinion cited *Marsh* v. *Alabama*, 326 U.S. 501 (1946); *Shelley* v. *Kraemer*, 334 U.S. 1 (1948); *Terry* v. *Adams*, 345 U.S. 461 (1953); *Barrows* v. *Jackson*, 346 U.S. 249 (1953).

100. *Lombard* v. *Louisiana*, 373 U. S. 267 (1963).

101. The opinion is found in *Bell* v. *Maryland*.

102. See books cited supra, note 98.

103. See note 99 supra.

104. *Southern School News*, Dec. 1964.

105. See "Racial Discrimination in the Southern Federal Courts," *Southern Regional Council* (1965).

106. See tables in *Civil Rights and Civil Liberties Decisions of U.S. Supreme Court for the 1963–64 Term—A Summary and Analysis* (1964), Commission on Law and Social Action of American Jewish Congress.

107. Oliver Wendell Holmes, "The Path of the Law," 10 *Harvard Law Review*, p. 460.

108. Quoted in brief for the United States in the U.S. Supreme Court, p. 17.

109. See Justice Black's "The Bill of Rights," lecture published in 35 *N. Y. U. Law Review* (1960), p. 865, reprinted in Irving Dilliard, *One Man's Stand for Freedom* (1963), p. 32.

110. *Slaughter-House Cases*, 16 Wall. 36, 21 L. ed. 394 (1873).

111. A. N. Whitehead, *Adventures of Ideas* (1933), pp. 21, 22.

112. Isaiah 30:7; 11:1.

113. *Heart of Atlanta Motel* v. *United States*, 85 S. Ct. 348 (1964).

114. Justice Douglas quoted from his concurring opinion in *Edwards* v. *California*, 314 U.S. 177 (1941).

115. See Konvitz, *The Constitution and Civil Rights*, Chs. 2 and 3.

116. *Hamm* v. *Rock Hill* and *Lupper* v. *Arkansas,* 85 S. Ct. 384 (1964).
117. *U. S. News & World Report,* Dec. 28, 1964, p. 40. On December 1, 1965, a federal judge in Jacksonville, Fla., dismissed charges against over four hundred civil rights demonstrators, including Martin Luther King, Jr., and the mother of former Governor Endicott Peabody of Massachusetts. The demonstration included sit-ins, swim-ins, marches, and boycotts. The dismissals were based on the Supreme Court decisions that the Civil Rights Act of 1964 ended prosecution of sit-in cases even when the arrests were made prior to passage of the act. The ruling in these Supreme Court cases, it was held, was not confined to sit-in demonstrations. *New York Times,* Dec. 3, 1965.
118. *N. Y. Times,* Dec. 16, 1964.
119. President Kennedy, in Lewis, *Portrait of a Decade,* p. 192.
120. President Johnson, State of the Union Message, Jan. 8, 1964, in *N. Y. Times,* Jan. 9, 1964.
121. Senate Report No. 872, 88th Cong., 2d Sess., Feb. 10, 1964, p. 16.
122. Benjamin N. Cardozo, *The Nature of the Judicial Process* (1921), p. 46.
123. *McGahey* v. *Virginia,* 135 U.S. 662 (1890).
124. *Hecht Co.* v. *Bowles,* 321 U.S. 321 (1944).
125. See op. cit. supra, note 117.
126. *N. Y. Times,* Nov. 6, 1962.
127. *Cooper* v. *Aaron,* 358 U.S. 1 (1958). Italics supplied.
128. Letter to Madison, Jan. 30, 1787, and letter to W. S. Smith, Nov. 13, 1787.
129. Dissenting opinion in *West Virginia State Board of Education* v. *Barnette,* 319 U.S. 624 (1943).
130. See op. cit. supra, note 106, and reports for other years, especially the cumulative table of votes of Justices for 1957–1962 in the report for the 1961–1962 term of Court, p. 57, where Justice Brennan is given 174 as a total of favorable votes, against 81 for Justice Clark; and 37 unfavorable votes, against 132, respectively.

CHAPTER VIII: "WITH LIBERTY AND JUSTICE FOR ALL"

1. Chinese Exclusion case, 130 U.S. 581 (1889).
2. *Chew Heong* v. *United States,* 112 U.S. 536 (1884).
3. M. R. Konvitz, *The Alien and the Asiatic in American Law* (1946), p. 23.
4. Ibid.
5. Ibid., pp. 80 ff.
6. Ibid., p. 88.
7. Ibid., p. 96.
8. See M. R. Konvitz, *Civil Rights in Immigration* (1953), p. 4; and op. cit. supra, note 3, p. 28.
9. Op. cit. supra, note 3, p. 28.
10. Op. cit. supra, note 8 (Civil Rights), pp. 8–9.
11. Ibid., p. 9.
12. J. Milton Yinger and George E. Simpson, "The Integration of Americans of Mexican, Puerto Rican and Oriental Descent," *Annals,* March 1956, p. 130.
13. Op. cit. supra, note 3, Ch. 11.
14. *N. Y. Times,* Jan. 9, 1964. Italics supplied.

15. *World Almanac* (1965), p. 287.
16. J. N. Hadley, "Demography of American Indians," *Annals,* May 1957, pp. 29–30.
17. See J. T. Conway, "And on Indian Reservations," *Indian Affairs,* Oct. 1964, p. 1. The comparative figures for the United States are from *World Almanac* (1965).
18. 4 Stat. 411 (1830).
19. 24 Stat. 388 (1887).
20. *United States* v. *Kagama,* 118 U.S. 375 (1885).
21. 43 Stat. 253 (1924).
22. Sec. 201.
23. T. H. Haas, "Legal Aspects of Indian Affairs from 1887 to 1957," *Annals,* May 1957, pp. 12, 16.
24. John Collier, "United States Indian Administration as a Laboratory of Ethnic Relations," 12 *Social Research* (1945), pp. 265, 273.
25. 48 Stat. 984 (1934).
26. Report of Commissioner of Indian Affairs, in Annual Report of Secretary of the Interior (1938); reprinted in *The Indian and the White Man,* W. E. Washburn, ed. (1964), pp. 393–94.
27. Oliver La Farge, "Termination of Federal Supervision: Disintegration and the American Indians," *Annals,* May 1957, pp. 41, 42.
28. Resolution is Document 92 in op. cit. supra, note 26, p. 397.
29. For summary of Task Force report, see 1961 Annual Report of Secretary of the Interior, pp. 277–78. See Report to the Secretary of the Interior by Task Force on Indian Affairs, July 10, 1961; the Task Force Report on Alaska Native Affairs, Dec. 28, 1962; also *India Affairs—1964,* Progress Report from Commissioner of Indian Affairs; U. S. Commission on Civil Rights, Book 5, *Justice,* Part VIII (1961).
30. 1962 Annual Report of Secretary of the Interior, p. LX.
31. Ibid., p. LVIX.
32. 1963 Annual Report of Secretary of the Interior, p. 11.
33. Op. cit. supra, note 30, p. lx. Note should be taken of the fact that the Senate Subcommittee on Constitutional Rights of the Senate Committee on the Judiciary conducted extensive hearings on the constitutional rights of the American Indian in 1961, 1962, and 1963. These hearings have been published in four parts, totaling 905 pages. *Constitutional Rights of the American Indian,* Hearings on Senate Res. 260, 87th Cong., and on Senate Res. 58, 88th Cong. (1963, 1964).
34. *Christian Science Monitor,* June 8, 1964.
35. *Indian Affairs,* March 1965, p. 2.
36. Op. cit. supra, note 26, Document 95, p. 407.
37. Text in *N. Y. Times,* April 8, 1965.

CHAPTER IX: AMERICAN POLICY IN INTERNATIONAL
PROTECTION OF HUMAN RIGHTS

1. U.S. Dept. of State, *Bulletin,* Aug. 26, 1963, pp. 322–28, text of letter and of Conventions referred to therein.
2. United Nations, *"United Nations at Work for Human Rights* (1957), p. 6. See *Yearbook on Human Rights,* annually from 1946 on. Egon Schwelt, *Human Rights and the International Community* (1964).

3. S. J. Res. 130, 82d Cong., 2d sess., Feb. 7, 1952.
4. These appear as a document in *American Journal of International Law,* July 1964.
5. Text in *N. Y. Times,* Oct. 29, 1963.
6. *N. Y. Times,* Nov. 21, 1963.
7. *Christian Science Monitor,* Nov. 22, 1963.
8. Richard N. Gardner, "Human Rights and Foreign Policy," *Saturday Review,* Sept. 19, 1964, p. 76.
9. See General S. Rosenne, *International Court of Justice* (1957).
10. A. H. Robertson, *Human Rights in Europe* (1963); Buerganthal, "Domestic Status of the European Convention on Human Rights," 13 *Buffalo Law Review* (1964), p. 354; W. P. Gormley "Procedural Status of the Individual before Supranational Judicial Tribunals," 41 *University of Detroit Law Journal* (1964), pp. 282 and 405. Part I of the Gormley article has extensive documentary and other references; Council release, Jan. 13, 1966.
11. C. W. Jenks, *The Proper Law of International Organizations* (1962).
12. Gormley, op. cit. supra, note 10, p. 327; Council release, Jan. 13, 1966.
13. W. Manger, *Pan America in Crisis: Future of the OAS* (1961); Pan American Union, Inter-American Commission on Human Rights, *Basic Documents* (1963); "Relationship Between Respect for Human Rights and Effective Exercise of Representative Democracy," memorandum by D. W. Sandifer (1962); Pan American Union, *Human Rights in the American States* (1960).
14. *International Agreements of Interest to Non-Governmental Organizations* (1961).

CHAPTER X: THE WORLD OF INTERDEPENDENT IDEALS

1. Revelation 3:20.
2. *The Journals of Ralph Waldo Emerson,* Robert N. Linscott, ed. (1960), p. 106.
3. Josiah Royce, *The Spirit of Modern Philosophy* (1892), p. 275.
4. Ibid., p. 283. Cf. A. N. Whitehead, *Adventures of Ideas* (1933), pp. 21 ff.
5. *N. Y. Times,* Sept. 9, 1964.
6. *N. Y. Times,* March 22, 1965, photograph on p. 1.
7. Edwin Markham, "The Man with the Hoe," 1899.
8. See M. R. Konvitz and T. Leskes, *A Century of Civil Rights* (1961), pp. 5, 21.
9. Op. cit. supra, note 3, p. 283.
10. Exec. Order 10980, Dec. 14, 1961, Appendix A to Report of the Committee on Civil and Political Rights, President's Commission on the Status of Women, 1963.
11. The report of the commission has the title *American Women.*
12. *N. L. R. B.* v. *Jones & Laughlin Steel Corp.,* 301 U.S. 1 (1937).
13. Justice Sutherland in *Adkins* v. *Children's Hospital,* 261 U.S. 525 (1923).
14. Public Law 89-4 (1965); originally S. 3.
15. Message delivered Jan. 8, 1964. Text in *N. Y. Times,* Jan. 9, 1964.
16. Public Law 88-452 (1964); originally S. 2642.
17. C. E. Wingenbach, *The Peace Corps* (rev. 1963).
18. Public Law 304, 79th Cong. See S. K. Bailey, *Congress Makes a Law* (1950).

420 | NOTES

. The Employment Act of 1946 grew out of the report *Assuring Full Employment in a Free Competitive Society,* from the Senate Committee on Banking and Currency, Report 583, 79th Cong., 1st sess., Sept. 22, 1945. See also H. R. 5663 and S. 281, 81st Cong., 1st sess., the "Economic Expansion Act of 1949."

20. Rule 44, Federal Rules of Criminal Procedure.

21. See, for example, *Adamson* v. *California,* 332 U.S. 46 (1947), dissenting opinion of Justice Black, with Justices Douglas, Rutledge, and Murphy concurring with him.

22. *Griffin* v. *Illinois,* 351 U.S. 12 (1956).

23. Leviticus 19:15.

24. *Gideon* v. *Wainwright,* 372 U.S. 335 (1963). See Anthony Lewis, *Gideon's Trumpet* (1964).

25. *Betts* v. *Brady,* 316 U.S. 455 (1942).

26. The so-called Allen report, *Poverty and the Administration of Criminal Justice* (1963).

27. Public Law 88-455 (1964); originally S. 1057.

Index

258, 260, 263, 264, 265, 266, 357,
363, 381
Tydings, Senator Millard E., 121, 192

Udall, Stewart L., 347–48
Ulysses (Joyce), 180–81, 193, 196,
202, 213
Union of Soviet Socialist Republics
(U.S.S.R.): and religious freedom,
362; and world peace, 119; and uni-
versalization, 371; Constitution of,
85; and control of press, 173; "deca-
dent" poetry case, 272–73; forced
labor in, 372; gain in freedom in,
121–22; oppression in, 370, 375
Unions: Communist unions expelled
from C.I.O., 154–55; infiltrated by
Communists, 112, 120. *See also*,
Congress of Industrial Organiza-
tions; Labor; Strikes
Unitarians, 26
United May Day Committee, 153
United Mine Workers, 155
United Nations, xiii, 305, 342, 353–67,
371, 372, 373
United States v. *Macintosh*, 11
United States Military Academy, 20
United States Naval Academy, 20
Universal Roman Inquisition, 173
Universities, 91–95
University of Alabama, 63, 275, 303
University of California, 297, 312,
315
University of Mississippi, 287, 288
University of Oklahoma, 246–47
University of Texas, 247–50
Uphaus, Willard, 74–85

Vatican Council, 292, 374
Vera Foundation, 385
Veterans of the Abraham Lincoln Bri-
gade, 153
Vinson, Chief Justice Frederick M.,
xiv, 14, 118, 122, 136, 245, 247, 250,
254, 264, 265, 288, 294; opinion
quoted, 247–48
Violence, 296–301
Virginia Statute of Religious Liberty,
7, 8, 28
Vista (domestic Peace Corps), 381

Wagner Act. *See* National Labor Relations Act
Waite, Chief Justice Morrison, 6–7, 8
Wallace, Governor George C., 73, 164,
275, 303, 305

Warburg, Fredric. *See Regina* v. *War-
burg*
Warren, Chief Justice Earl, xiv, 41, 43,
60–61, 76, 78, 79, 91, 93, 95, 127,
129, 147, 148, 161, 205, 216, 218,
219, 235, 245, 265, 271, 321, 322,
328, 332, 338, 382; opinions quoted,
92, 93, 235, 277, 281; "Warren
Court," xii, 247, 264
Warren Commission, 133
Washington, Justice Bushrod, 332
Washington, George, 7, 51
Washington Pension Union, 153
Watson v. *Jones*, 4–5, 6, 8
Watson v. *Memphis*, 283, 287
Welch, Robert, 161
Welfare programs. *See* Anti-poverty
programs
Well of Loneliness, The (Hall), 204
*West Virginia State Board of Educa-
tion* v. *Barnette*, 22, 23, 236
White, Justice Byron R., 24, 81, 85,
216, 222, 323, 330, 333, 339
Whitehead, Alfred North, 330–31
Whittaker, Justice Charles E., 85, 99,
195
Wieman v. *Updegraff*, 89–90, 91, 92,
102, 104
Williams, Roger, 375
Wilson, Edmund, 174, 197
Wilson, Major General Winston P.,
262
Wolfenden Report of the Depart-
mental Committee on Homosexual
Offences and Prostitution (Great
Britain), 203
Women: rights of, ix, x, xiii, 353, 355,
366, 372, 375, 377–78; Moslem, 372
Woolsey, Judge John M., 180, 184,
190, 193, 195, 197, 206, 212, 216,
224
Worker, The. See Daily Worker
World Fellowship, 74, 75, 76, 79, 80,
82, 83, 84, 85
"World Strength of the Communist
Party Organizations" (State Depart-
ment Intelligence Report), 109
Wright v. *Georgia*, 280–81, 284

Yates v. *United States*, 124, 126, 127,
128, 130, 147
Yick Wo v. *Hopkins*, 270
Young, Brigham, 6
Young Progressives of America, 293

Zeitlin v. *Arneburgh*, 218
Zimmerman, William, 346
Zorach v. *Clauson*, 20–22, 23, 25

N

A

C

l